SOCIONOMIC CAUSALITY IN POLITICS

HOW SOCIAL MOOD INFLUENCES EVERYTHING FROM ELECTIONS TO GEOPOLITICS

Socionomics — The Science of History
and Social Prediction, Volume 5

Robert R. Prechter, Ed.

Socionomics Institute Press

Socionomic Causality in Politics—How Social Mood Influences Everything from Elections to Geopolitics

Copyright © 2017 Robert R. Prechter

Printed in the United States of America

First Printing, 2017

ISBN: 978-1-946597-05-2
Library of Congress Control Number: 2017914485

Publisher: Socionomics Institute Press
Gainesville, Georgia USA
Address for comments: institute@socionomics.net

The Socionomics Institute
www.socionomics.net

COVER GRAPHICS:
Fireworks: Farnham Brook, © 2016 aewallpaper.xyz.

Bombs: Original image AN-M64 GP Bomb by Mesh-Factory.

City background: Public Domain, Devon S D (Flt Lt), Royal Air Force official photographer. This is photograph CH 15111 from the collections of the Imperial War Museums.

CONTENTS

The Authors

Robert Prechter is President of the Socionomics Institute, the Socionomics Foundation and Elliott Wave International and editor of *The Elliott Wave Theorist*.

Alan Hall, Euan Wilson, Chuck Thompson, Matt Lampert and Ben Hall are researchers at the Socionomics Institute, as was Wayne Parker (deceased).

Peter Kendall is co-editor of *The Elliott Wave Financial Forecast*.

Mark Galasiewski is editor of *The Asian-Pacific Financial Forecast*.

Brian Whitmer is editor of *The European Financial Forecast*.

Dave Allman, Deepak Goel and Gary Grimes contributed while working at Elliott Wave International.

Alastair Macdonald is an entrepreneur, investment consultant and editor of *The Parallax Letter*, a financial market advisory.

FOREWORD

It takes quite an open mind for people to come to grips with socionomic causality, but those who do so will come to view past events with a new clarity. Readers of this book should achieve the counterintuitive perspective that the political actions of human beings—including treaties, tariffs, terrorist attacks, wars, Bretton Woods agreements, Camp David accords, OPEC plans, the EU and all the rest of it—are but momentary expressions of social mood, with no indelible implications. When mood changes, so do human passions, and old political threats and accomplishments just melt away, having no power in and of themselves to make permanent changes in social attitudes and behavior. Sometimes the shift in mood begins about the time the blood or ink is dry on the prior mood trend's main manifestation.

The Socionomics Institute is proud to offer *Socionomic Causality in Politics*, the fifth and final entry in our socionomics book series. Production and layout have been a gargantuan task, which Sally Webb and Angela Hall undertook with grace and dedication. Cari Dobbins and John Watson helped design the book jacket. For coverage of the fun side of social-mood expression, see the fourth book in our series, *Socionomic Studies of Society and Culture*.

Chapter headers include original publication dates and sources: *The Socionomist* (TS), *The Elliott Wave Theorist* (EWT), *The Elliott Wave Financial Forecast* (EWFF), *The European Financial Forecast* (EFF) and *The Asian-Pacific Financial Forecast* (APFF). The material in this volume dates from September 2003 through December 2016. A smattering of early 2017 updates were inserted post-production. Clarifying edits have been made to essays originally published in-house.

Stock market histories are employed in these essays not for the purpose of price forecasting but for elucidating socionomic causality. A few of the charts in this book contain Elliott wave labels in the form of numbers and letters. Wave analysis is incidental to this book's purpose, so we have chosen not to elaborate on it. You can learn about the subject by reading *Elliott Wave Principle* (1978). A few of the Elliott wave labels for U.S. stock indexes have been standardized to current thinking. Some of the incidentally implied market forecasts within the original pieces have been genericized (so that "in the current bear market" might become "in the next bear market") so as to remain accurate with regard to socionomic causality. When a bold market forecast provided the entire basis for a thesis, as in Chapter 50, it remains intact.

In most cases, we use aggregate stock prices as our primary meter of social mood. As explained in previous volumes, social mood fluctuates on its own, and it prompts speculators to revalue overall stock prices up and down while simultaneously inducing other expressions of social mood in the realms of business, culture and politics. As you will see throughout this volume, using the stock market as a benchmark sociometer (so-shee-*om*′-e-ter) allows for useful understanding, and sometimes anticipation, of political trends and actions. Realize that the graphs of social trends plotted alongside those benchmark sociometers are themselves newly identified sociometers, as they all fluctuate in concert with each other as expressions of overall social mood.

—Robert Prechter

Five Tenets of Socionomics

1. Social mood motivates social actions, not the other way around.

2. Social mood is endogenously regulated, not prompted by outside forces.

3. Social mood is constantly fluctuating according to a hierarchical, robust fractal called the Wave Principle. Robust fractals are patterned but quantitatively variable.

4. Social mood is unconscious and unremembered.

5. Waves of social mood arise when humans interact socially. The process appears to be related to the herding impulse.

Applying Socionomics

Socionomics explains shifts in the character of social events. It is not a crystal ball for forecasting specific social or individual actions.

Some social actions—such as buying and selling stocks—express social mood almost instantaneously. Others—such as economic and political actions—lag substantially due to the varying times it takes for people to implement decisions made under the influence of social mood. Leading actions forecast lagging actions.

There is always a mix of positive and negative actions in society, but their quantity and intensity vary with social mood.

Extreme expressions of social mood tend to occur near the end of a positive or negative trend. The breadth and intensity of expressive social actions correspond to the degree of the largest wave that is ending.

Conventional statements of social causality are backwards. For example, leaders and pop stars do not influence social mood; waves of social mood influence which leaders and pop stars society chooses and how their performances are perceived.

Large groups cannot act independently of social-mood impulses, but individuals can learn to act contrarily to impulses arising from social mood.

Part I:

SOCIAL MOOD AND ELECTION OUTCOMES

Chapter 1

A Democrat or Republican in the White House: Is Either Better for Stocks and the Economy?

Matt Lampert

October 31, 2012 / August 31, 2015 (TS)

Does the Party Elected Influence Trends in the Stock Market?

Every U.S. election cycle brings new discussions about which party's presidential candidate will help or hurt the stock market. As the election of 2012 approached, several articles claimed that since 1926 the stock market had gained much more per year on average when the president was a Democrat than when he was a Republican. Does the implication that Democrats are good for the stock market stand scrutiny?

It is true that since 1926 the Dow's average annual rate of return under Democrat presidents has been higher than that under Republican presidents. From 1926 through 2015, the Dow had an average annual gain of 9.77% under Democrat presidents and only 4.57% under Republicans. But it takes judicious data selection to produce this seemingly significant result.

The Republican Party was founded in 1854 and ran its first candidate for president in the election of 1856. It therefore makes sense to analyze the data forward from 1857, the year that the winner of the election of 1856 took office, in order to incorporate the results of every presidential election in which the Democrats and Republicans competed against each other.

We did so and found (see Figure 1) that from 1857 to 2015, there was a 7.08% average annual rate of return in the stock market under presidents who were Democrats, while under Republicans the rate was 5.90%. The difference is not statistically significant.[1] When using all the data, then, we find that the stock market has done about equally well under both parties.

The Democrats still appear to have a narrow lead. Is that lead robust?

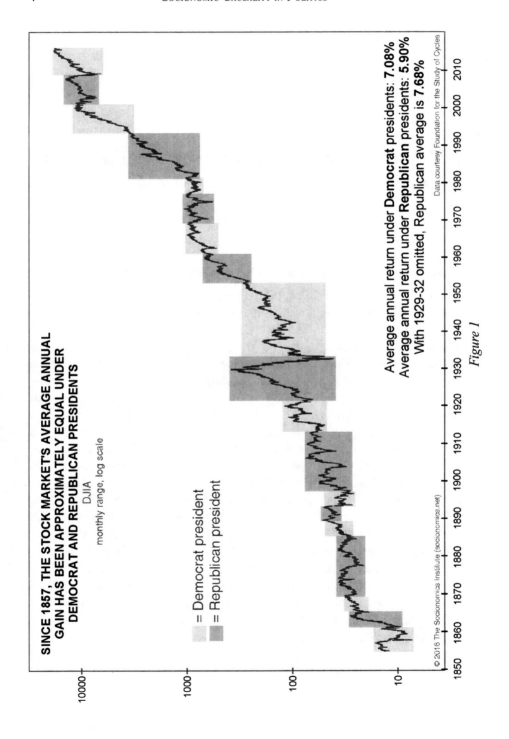

Figure 1

When employing averages, a few extreme values can have a substantial impact on the results. Once you remove them, you get a clearer picture of whether a causal relationship exists. Such is the case here.

From its high in 1929 to its low in 1932, the Dow fell a whopping 89%. The entire drop occurred within a single presidential term. No other presidential term in U.S. history contains anything close to such a move. When we omit the term encompassing 1929-32 from the analysis, the average annual rate of return under Republicans jumps to 7.68%, slightly higher than the 7.08% performance under Democrats.

Thus, all of the advantage in the market's average performance under the Democrats over a period of 159 years is due to a change lasting less than three years, all in a single term when a Republican happened to be president. The Democrats' advantage in the overall data series, then, is not robust.

If we also omit the *next* term, covering 1933-1936, when the stock market rebounded under a Democrat president, the data favor the Republicans even further, by 7.68% vs. 5.52%.

In sum, the market has had nearly the same average annual performance under both parties. Any advantage that one party seems to enjoy over the other is reversed when just a single outlier is omitted, and it is reversed even more when two are omitted.

When it comes to data on any topic, it is important to remember that the conclusions analysts draw may be largely due to the time periods they have chosen to study. When you read qualifiers such as "Since 1926..." or "Over the past 50 years..." ask yourself why the claim utilizes a cut-off point not dictated by the data. In this case, when we look at all the data and consider the effects of outliers, we find that the particular party in control of the White House makes no discernible difference to the stock market's trend.

As discussed in *The Socionomic Theory of Finance* (2016), the idea that politics pushes the stock market around is an intimate aspect of financial theory under the mechanics paradigm of exogenous causality. As with all other presumed exogenous causes (see Part I of that book), it doesn't work. Socionomics offers a better perspective.

Does the Party Elected Influence Trends in Economy?

Here in late 2015, candidates on both sides of the aisle of American politics are gearing up for the 2016 presidential election. We are hearing impassioned arguments from Democrats and Republicans alike about why their party's proposals will be better for the economy. Republicans remind us that GDP grew more per year on average from 2001 through 2008 under a Republican president than it has during 2009-2015 under a Democrat president. Democrats tell us that average annual real GDP growth has been less than 4% for each of the past eleven Republican presidential terms, whereas it has exceeded 4% for six of the past eleven Democrat terms. With more than a century and a half of data available, researchers can select bits of history that shine favorably on one or the other party. But when we study all of the data, we find that implied disparities in economic performance under the two parties evaporate, and the small differences that remain fail to hold up to additional scrutiny.

In a 2013 paper, Professors Alan Blinder and Mark Watson of Princeton University investigated the difference in average annual real GDP growth under Republican and Democrat presidents.[2] They found that since 1947, the economy grew an average of 1.81% more per year when the president was a Democrat. Blinder and Watson also found that the economic performance gap narrowed between the two parties when they extended their study back to 1875.

We wanted to see what would happen if we included all available data in a comparable analysis. We used a data series compiled by Louis Johnston, professor of economics with a chair in public policy at the College of St. Benedict and St. John's University, and Samuel Williamson, professor emeritus of economics at Miami University. These data allowed us to extend the study back to the election of 1856, the first year that Democrats and Republicans competed against each other in presidential politics.[3]

Since 1857, the average annual inflation-adjusted GDP growth rate has been 3.29% with a Republican in the White House and 3.84% with a Democrat in the White House. In nominal terms (without adjusting for inflation), average annual GDP growth has been 5.01% for Republicans and 6.61% for Democrats. In both cases, the Democrats appear to have the lead.

But, again, outlying values can have a substantial impact on averages. To illustrate just how similar the country's average economic performance has been under the two parties, consider what happens when we remove two presidential terms—the one with the highest rate of annual real GDP growth and the one with the lowest—from *each* party's tally.[4] Average annual real GDP growth under Republican presidents becomes 3.53% vs. 3.51% for Democrats, virtually identical values.

These results do not surprise socionomists. Under socionomic theory, it is endogenously regulated social mood—not presidents' policies—that regulate a society's drive to innovate, grow and prosper.[5,6] Even Blinder and Watson concluded that the differences in economic performance under the two parties were largely due to factors that "look a lot more like good luck than good policy."[7]

Socionomic causality, in contrast, produces robust and statistically significant results. Chapter 2 presents our case. For a similar investigation of the purported relevance of the unemployment rate to election outcomes, see Chapter 6.

NOTES AND REFERENCES

[1] To which party President Andrew Johnson belonged is arguable. Johnson was a Democrat for most of his life. During the Civil War, however, Union-sympathetic, pro-war Democrats formed an alliance with the Republicans under the National Union Party. Johnson ran on the National Union ticket as the running mate of Republican President Abraham Lincoln in 1864 and assumed the presidency in April 1865 following Lincoln's assassination. We counted Johnson as a Democrat. If we list him instead as a Republican, we see little effect on the 1857-2015 results. Before adjustment, the results are: Democrats 7.08%, Republicans 5.90%; after adjustment they are 7.19% and 5.87%, respectively.

[2] Blinder, A.S., & Watson, M.W. (2013). "Presidents and the Economy: A Forensic Investigation." Woodrow Wilson School and Department of Economics, Princeton University.

[3] Johnston, L., & Williamson, S.H. (2016). "What Was the US GDP Then?" MeasuringWorth.com.

[4] The Republican presidential term with the highest average annual real GDP growth rate (7.03%) belonged to Rutherford B. Hayes (1877-1880). The lowest (-5.41%) occurred under Herbert Hoover (1929-1932). Franklin Roosevelt presided over the Democrat term with the highest average annual real GDP growth rate (15.41%) during his third term in office (1941-1944). Upon Roosevelt's death in 1945, Harry Truman assumed the Oval Office and presided over the Democrat presidential term with the lowest average annual real GDP growth rate (-2.37%) (1945-1948).

[5] Prechter, R. (2004, September). "Sociometrics: Applying Socionomic Causality to Social Forecasting." *The Elliott Wave Theorist*. Adapted for Chapter 7 of *The Socionomic Theory of Finance* (2016).

[6] Prechter, R., Goel, D., Parker, W.D., & Lampert, M. (2012). "Social Mood, Stock Market Performance, and U.S. Presidential Elections: A Socionomic Perspective on Voting Results." *SAGE Open*. [Chapter 2 in this volume.]

[7] Blinder and Watson, 2013, p. 1.

Chapter 2, a published paper, is designed to lead researchers away from the unproductive approach discussed in Chapter 1. It may be heavy going at times, but it will reward the careful reader by establishing the premise for the rest of the book. Nevertheless, some readers may wish to skip to Chapter 3, which presents our premises and findings in a less formal manner.

Chapter 2

SAGE Open
November 2, 2012

Social Mood, Stock Market Performance, and U.S. Presidential Elections: A Socionomic Perspective on Voting Results[1]

Robert R. Prechter[2], Deepak Goel[2],
Wayne D. Parker[3] and Matthew Lampert[4]

We analyze all U.S. presidential election bids. We find a positive, significant relationship between the incumbent's vote margin and the prior net percentage change in the stock market. This relationship does not extend to the incumbent's party when the incumbent does not run for reelection. We find no significant relationships between the incumbent's vote margin and inflation or unemployment. Gross domestic product (GDP) is a significant predictor of the incumbent's popular vote margin in simple regression but is rendered insignificant when combined with the stock market in multiple regression. Hypotheses of economic voting fail to account for the findings. The results are consistent with socionomic voting theory, which includes the hypotheses that (a) social mood as reflected by the stock market is a more powerful regulator of reelection outcomes than economic variables such as GDP, inflation, and unemployment; and (b) voters unconsciously credit or blame the leader for their mood.

[1] This paper is available online at https://papers.ssrn.com.
[2] Socionomics Institute, Gainesville, GA
[3] Socionomics Foundation, Gainesville, GA; Emory University School of Medicine, Atlanta, GA
[4] University of Cambridge, UK

Introduction

Although many researchers have investigated stock market performance *after* U.S. presidential elections, few studies have investigated the connection between elections and *preceding* stock market performance. When they have, the data were usually limited to the election-year performance of the market and only a subset of elections (Biewald, 2003; Chan & Jordan, 2004; Gleisner, 1992). In this paper, we examine the net percentage change in the stock market in the years preceding all American presidential reelection bids. For this study, "reelection" is an election featuring an incumbent president, whether or not he initially obtained office via an election.

We find a significant positive relationship between the stock market's net percentage change during the 3 years prior to a reelection bid and the incumbent's popular vote-margin percentage. The net percentage change in the stock market for 1-, 2- and 4-year periods preceding the election is each a weaker yet significant predictor of reelection outcomes. Our results are robust to multiple variations in the elements of the testing procedure: measures of the stock market's performance, measures of election outcomes, statistical methods used to gauge the relationship between the two, durations of data, and the presence of additional variables. The relationship does not extend to the incumbent party's candidate when the incumbent does not run. We find that relationships between the incumbent's popular vote-margin percentage and the preceding net percentage change in gross domestic product (GDP), the inflation rate and the unemployment rate are often insignificant and always weaker than those between the incumbent's popular vote margin and net percentage change in the stock market.

Our results contribute to the literature by elucidating the relative value of stock indexes for election forecasting models, challenging economic voting hypotheses, exploring an underlying motivator of financial and political choice, suggesting a strategy for political party officials and candidates, and offering ideas for future research. At the theoretical level, our findings are consistent with Prechter's (1979, 1999, 2003) socionomic theory, which includes the hypotheses that social mood as reflected by the stock market is a powerful regulator of reelection outcomes and that voters unconsciously credit or blame the leader for their mood.

Economic Voting

Many political scientists hypothesize that changes in economic variables cause changes in other social variables such as stock market trends, public mood, and voting results (e.g., Fair, 1996, p. 132). A number of researchers have characterized the relationship between voters and their elected officials in terms of two types of variables: popularity functions, which are primarily economic factors thought to influence voters' views toward their leaders positively or negatively (Lewis-Beck & Paldam, 2000; Mueller, 1970; Nannestad & Paldam, 1994), and reaction functions, which are government policymakers' reactions to their perceived popularity, by which they try to manipulate economic variables to curry voters' favor (Alesina, Roubini, & Cohen, 1997; Brender & Drazen, 2005; Fair, 1978; Kramer, 1971). Many authors have combined vote functions—factors leading to election outcomes—with popularity functions—factors leading to poll results—because almost all of the issues overlap (Chappell, 1990; Nannestad & Paldam, 1994). Political scientists have shown much interest in predicting national election results using economic variables in such functions. The "big three" popularity functions traditionally mentioned in the literature are economic growth, inflation, and unemployment (Norpoth, 1996).

Jones (2002) considered many models developed since 1952 that attempt to predict U.S. elections and concluded that the most effective single predictor of these election outcomes is the state of the election-year economy. Fair (2002) looked for a relationship between a number of different economic factors and the percentage of the popular vote received by the incumbent party's presidential candidates between 1920 and 1996. He found a strong relationship between the election-year GDP growth and the percentage of popular votes received. Biewald (2003), however, repeated Fair's study with an additional 50 years of data and found that election-year GDP growth is only weakly correlated with election results.

Nannestad and Paldam (1994) found that studies relating economic growth to election outcomes yielded inconsistent results, so they discarded GDP as an explanatory variable and instead emphasized inflation and unemployment. Jones (2002) found some evidence for a relationship between the election-year inflation rate and the percentage of popular votes received. Biewald (2003), however, found that with the inclusion of an additional 50 years of data, the inflation rate was no longer related to election results. Chrystal and Peel (1986) found that neither inflation nor unemployment was robustly related to the popularity of the government.

Fair (1978, 1982, 1988) constructed models for predicting the Democratic Party's share of the two-party popular vote based on several factors, including the rate of change in gross national product for two different durations prior to an election, a time trend variable coded according to which party was in power, and whether the election involved an incumbent. One version of this model (Fair, 1988) achieved a strong coefficient of determination (R^2) of 0.89.

To an iteration of Fair's model Gleisner (1992) added the percentage change of the Dow Jones Industrial Average over a 10-month period prior to the election. This addition significantly improved the fit of the model and rendered Fair's time trend variable insignificant. Chan and Jordan (2004) found that the equity market's performance for 10 months prior to an election was a better predictor than GDP growth of incumbents' election results in recent years. The following section explores a possible theoretical explanation for these improved results.

Socionomic Voting

Implicit in much of the economic voting literature is the passive organism model of human action: Humans are seen as essentially reactive. Many of the social sciences have adopted this stimulus-response model of human psychology popularized by behaviorist psychologists such as Watson (1913) and Skinner (1938) in the last century. Although some scholars (Baars, 1986; Gardner, 1987) have since rejected this model as too simplistic or inaccurate, it lives on in many implicit assumptions of other social sciences, including political science.

Specifically, the conceptualization of popularity and reaction functions carries with it three assumptions: (a) that there is a reciprocal causal relationship between the electorate's opinions of its elected leaders (popularity functions) and the economic policy responses of those leaders (reaction functions); (b) that voters react to economic conditions, political events, and manipulation so that various economic and policy inputs have reactive voting outputs; and (c) that voters act consciously and rationally after logically evaluating candidates' political policies and deciding whether these policies have served (under the theory of retrospective voting) or will serve (under the theory of prospective voting) their best interests.

In contrast, socionomic theory offers competing models of mood, human action, and making choices. Prechter (1999) posited that social mood—the aggregate, unconscious levels of optimism and pessimism in a society—emerges spontaneously in self-organizing human social systems, fluctuates according to an internally regulated growth process described by Elliott's (1938) wave model, is impervious to economic and political stimuli, and drives collective human action and nonrational decision making unconsciously in contexts of uncertainty. Presidential elections—the focus of our study—appear to qualify as a context of uncertainty. Delli Carpini and Keeter (1996), Blendon et al. (1997), Paldam and Nannestad (2000), and Aidt (2000) have documented convincingly the typical voter's pervasive ignorance and uncertainty with respect to information about elections. Rahn (2000) found that "public mood" may be an important influence on political decision making, concluding that the degree of uncertainty accounts for the extent to which mood influences political behavior.

Socionomic theory specifically applies to the reelection or rejection of incumbents. Prechter (1989, 1999, 2003) hypothesized that when social mood has been trending toward optimism, voters will be more inclined to desire to keep the incumbent in office; and when social mood has been trending toward pessimism, voters will be more inclined to desire a change from the incumbent. Contrasting sharply with Stimson's (1991) more cognitive "policy mood" concept, Prechter proposed that the policies of the incumbent and his challenger are irrelevant to this dynamic. He surmised that voters unconsciously (and erroneously) credit incumbents for their positive moods and blame incumbents for their negative moods. This explanation appears similar to the responsibility hypothesis (Downs, 1957; Key, 1966), in which voters blame the incumbent for consciously perceived, externally produced, negative economic circumstances. In the socionomic formulation, however, voters blame the incumbent for unconsciously experienced, internally regulated, negative social mood.

Under socionomic theory, policy statements and actions by leaders are powerless to affect the mood of the voters; instead, the mood of the voters has a powerful effect on the policy statements and actions of leaders. Three studies have supported this formulation. Kuklinski and Segura (1995) reviewed literature concerning mood and politics and reported that mood appeared unresponsive to politicians' efforts to influence it. They further argued that Stimson's policy mood concept "might better be viewed as affective: when people become dissatisfied and angry, they come to favor less government or at least a change in the government's current activities" (Kuklinski & Segura, 1995, p. 13). Nofsinger & Kim (2003) found a relationship between the trend of social mood and the subsequent actions of U.S. lawmakers. They reported that Congress tended to tighten investment restrictions after social mood had become more negative, as indicated by a substantial decline in stock prices, and tended to loosen investment restrictions after social mood had become more positive, as indicated by a substantial rise in stock prices. Geer (2006) reported that, rather than negative political ads making voters feel more pessimistic, voters' preexisting attitudes instead affected how candidates chose their advertising. In concert with these suggestive ideas, socionomic theory explicitly proposes that economic and political trends are results, not causes, of social mood, so the direction of predictive power between mood and social events is the opposite of that traditionally assumed.

Socionomic theory affirms the active organism model of human action (Overton & Ennis, 2006; Overton & Reese, 1973) by which humans are innately and spontaneously active in their cognitive, affective and conative processes. Under the socionomic model, voters do not passively wait for politicians' policies and promises to program their responses but rather express social mood spontaneously. Under the hypothesis that changes in social mood unconsciously impel humans to take social actions expressing their moods, socionomic theory proposes that changes in indicators of social mood can be used to anticipate the direction and character of social trends, including those in politics.

Socionomic theory pertains to voting tendencies at the aggregate level. Many individual voters may, to a degree or for a time, consistently cast ballots along party lines, religious lines, single-issue lines, philosophical lines, or some other overriding factor. We suspect that "swing" voters with little or no philosophical anchor are among the ones acting most readily to express social mood in the voting booth. Regardless of departures from socionomic motivation at the individual level, social mood under this theory can powerfully regulate voting outcomes at the aggregate level.

Prechter (1979, 1999; Prechter & Parker, 2007) has argued that, for the present, stock market indexes appear to be the best available indicator of social mood, because investors can act swiftly in this context to express their optimism and pessimism. Recent work in the area of online social sentiment analysis by Bollen, Mao, and Zeng (2011) and Gilbert and Karahalios (2010) provided empirical support for the idea that financial markets are responsive to changes in social sentiment. Because stock market averages register changes in mood and possess an extensive data history, they are uniquely appropriate for the long-term historical analysis that we undertake in this paper.

Riley and Luksetich (1980) saw the stock market as an indicator of social mood. They implied, however, that political parties influence mood by shaping the public's expectations of future business conditions. Socionomic theory, in contrast, proposes that social mood—a hidden, independent variable—simultaneously determines both stock market outcomes and incumbent presidential reelection outcomes. This formulation avoids the error, as we see it, of confusing the indicator with the cause. Santa-Clara and Valkanov (2003) ruminated over whether political variables cause fluctuations in stock returns, or the reverse. According to socionomic theory, neither formulation is correct; rather, social-mood trends regulate stock trends and political trends concurrently.

A popular explanation for why the economy often lags the stock market is that investors accurately anticipate, months in advance, the economic future and then rationally invest on their expectations (Muth, 1961; Sheffrin, 1996). Prechter (2003) challenged this idea on both theoretical and empirical grounds. Socionomic theory proposes instead that macroeconomic indicators, such as rates of economic growth, inflation, and unemployment, respond to social mood to some degree, but they do so far less immediately, as it takes months on average for business people to carry out mood-motivated decisions due to the time requirements of meeting, planning, lending or borrowing, opening or closing facilities, hiring or firing, building or reducing inventory, and so on. In the aggregate, these delayed results show up as increases or decreases in production, expansions or contractions of credit, and increases or decreases in the labor force. Investors, on the other hand, can buy or sell in the stock market almost immediately in response to social mood, so its effects appear there prior to appearing in macroeconomic indicators.

Socionomic theory stands in contrast to expectations theory in postulating that social mood regulates other social variables, including the economy, which is merely another result rather than the cause. We shall offer evidence that the trend of social mood, not the trend of the stock market per se, regulates voting with respect to the reelection or rejection of incumbents.

Socionomic theory (Prechter, 1999) made the following predictions regarding incumbents' reelection attempts:

1. An increasingly positive social mood, indicated by a rising stock market, will positively influence an incumbent's reelection chances.

2. An increasingly negative social mood, indicated by a falling stock-market, will negatively influence an incumbent's reelection chances.

3. Extreme changes in social mood, indicated by extreme changes in the stock market, will tend to motivate more extreme voting preferences for or against the incumbent.

4. [As an immediate] indicator of social mood, the stock market will predict the outcomes of reelection bids better than will [lagging indicators such as] rates of economic growth, inflation, and/or unemployment.

Method and Results

To investigate these formulations, we first examine the relationship between the net change in the stock market and the ensuing popular vote margin—the number of percentage points separating the incumbent from his nearest challenger in the popular vote—for or against incumbent presidents in U.S. elections. The Dow Jones Industrial Average serves to represent the U.S. stock market from 1897 to the present. Prior to 1897, we use the Foundation for the Study of Cycles' data series, which normalizes stock market data from earlier indexes to the Dow to create a longer series (DJIA) that encompasses all U.S. presidential elections from 1789 through 2008. Popular vote margin is a broad measure that is likely to reflect social mood in an election. For purposes of validation, we also consider four other measures of incumbent performance: percentages of total popular vote, percentages of total electoral vote, electoral vote-margin percentages, and overall wins and losses of elections.

Next, we examine the relationship between the stock market and the fates of incumbents in landslide elections. We then relate the stock market to the popular vote margin for an incumbent's political party when the incumbent does not run. A final set of analyses assesses the predictive ability of the "big three" economic indicators—GDP, inflation, and unemployment—when modeled individually and together with the stock market.

Predicting Incumbent Election Results

We first compare the popular vote margin for or against an incumbent president with the stock market's net percentage gain or loss for the 3-year period preceding the election. We operationally define the 3-year period as the span of time from November 1 of the year after the previous election through October 31 of the year of the election under consideration. We select this period because we observe anecdotally that society tends to judge a president by the trends that occur during the bulk of the presidential term, barring much or all of the first year, for which the credit or blame is typically assigned to the predecessor. Our analysis includes all presidential elections in which an incumbent candidate ran, beginning in 1824 when popular vote data were first available. A linear regression analysis yields a large and statistically significant effect, $R^2 = 0.321$, $p = 0.001$. Table 1 displays results for the test described above (see Line 3) as well as further statistical results.

To assess the robustness of the results, we examine a number of variations in model parameters and analytic approaches. As shown in the table,

Table 1. Incumbent Popular Vote Margin and Prior Net Stock Market Movement: Linear Regression and Spearman Rank Correlation

Study period[a]	Prior net stock market movement period[b]	n	B	SE	β	p	R^2	ρ	pρ
1824-2004	Prior 1 year	26	0.281	0.147	0.364	0.034**	0.133	0.264	0.096
1824-2004	Prior 2 years	26	0.144	0.073	0.374	0.030**	0.140	0.314	0.059
1824-2004	*Prior 3 years*	*26*	*0.193*	*0.057*	*0.566*	*0.001*****	*0.321*	*0.592*	*0.001*
1824-2004	Prior 4 years	26	0.132	0.047	0.501	0.005***	0.251	0.431	0.014
1824-1900	Prior 3 years	8	0.200	0.101	0.631	0.047**	0.398	0.905	0.001
1901-2004	Prior 3 years	18	0.188	0.072	0.549	0.009***	0.301	0.494	0.019
1824-1924	Prior 3 years	12	0.163	0.111	0.421	0.087*	0.177	0.629	0.014
1925-2004	Prior 3 years	14	0.210	0.065	0.681	0.004***	0.463	0.569	0.017

Note: n = the number of elections meeting the specified criteria. The above table reports the results of linear regression and Spearman rank correlation analysis. The condition of primary theoretical interest is in **bold**. One-tailed probability values are presented in accordance with the theorized directional hypothesis; *significant at the 0.10 level, **significant at the 0.05 level, and ***significant at the 0.01 level.
[a] Popular vote tallies first became available in 1824; the most recent year in which an incumbent ran for reelection was 2004.
[b] As measured by the Dow Jones Industrial Average and normalized predecessor averages.
The numbers in this table vary slightly from the originally published version due to a correction in the underlying data series. Also, here we report the standard error of the slope instead of the standard error of the estimate.

significant positive predictive relationships continue to emerge when varying the measuring period for the stock market to 1, 2, and 4 years. We also
[divide] the data at two cutoff points: (a) the turn of the 20th century and
(b) the 100-year anniversary of the inception of popular vote tallies, which
also roughly corresponds to the midpoint of the data span. The 3-year results
maintain across these [datasets]. This consistency is compatible with socionomic theory, which proposes that social mood's influence on reelection
results should be comparable despite any changes between the 19th and
20th centuries in terms of campaign strategies, communications technology,
election rules, extent of public participation in the stock market, and so on.
To relax distributional assumptions and lessen the influence of potential
outliers, we also apply the nonparametric Spearman's rank correlation test
to all data conditions, and we obtain similar results, per Table 1.

As a final test of robustness, we repeat the entire analysis, substituting
four other measures of election results in place of popular vote margin. Bi-
variate linear regression models for three of these indicators—percentage of
total popular vote that the incumbent receives, percentage of total electoral
vote that the incumbent receives, and electoral vote margin (the number of
percentage points that separate the incumbent from his nearest challenger

Table 2. Incumbent Reelection Success and Prior Net Stock Market Movement

Study period [a]	Prior net stock market movement period [b]	n	B	SE	p	OR
1824-2004	Prior 1 year	26	0.011	0.025	0.327	1.011
1824-2004	Prior 2 years	26	0.030	0.019	0.058*	1.031
1824-2004	*Prior 3 years*	*26*	*0.074*	*0.036*	*0.022** *	*1.076*
1824-2004	Prior 4 years	26	0.029	0.016	0.031**	1.030
1824-1900	Prior 3 years	8	NA[c]	–	–	–
1901-2004	Prior 3 years	18	0.055	0.037	0.070*	1.056
1824-1924	Prior 3 years	12	0.106	0.064	0.049**	1.111
1925-2004	Prior 3 years	14	0.047	0.037	0.100	1.049

Note: n = the number of elections meeting the specified criteria; OR = odds ratio. The above table reports the results of logistic regression analysis. The condition of primary theoretical interest is in **bold**.
One-tailed probability values are presented in accordance with the theorized directional hypothesis;
*significant at the 0.10 level, **significant at the 0.05 level, and ***significant at the 0.01 level.
[a]The most recent year in which an incumbent ran for reelection was 2004.
[b]As measured by the Dow Jones Industrial Average and normalized predecessor averages.
[c]Unable to interpret results due to small sample size.
The numbers in this table differ from the originally published version. Here, we enter the predictor variable in percentage form rather than decimal form to render the odds ratios amenable to more intuitive
interpretation.

in the electoral vote)—produce similar results to those presented in Table 1. Evaluating the fourth measure, the incumbent's overall success or failure in winning the reelection bid, requires use of logistic regression. Although this dichotomous variable suffers from a reduction in reliable score variance in comparison with the continuously scaled criterion variables considered earlier, positive predictive relationships generally emerge, with a statistically significant ($p = 0.022$) logistic regression coefficient associated with the condition of primary theoretical interest (see Table 2).

To summarize, our results signify that a net gain in the stock market during the 3 years preceding an election is strongly predictive of more votes cast for the incumbent relative to his nearest challenger, and a net stock market decline during that period is strongly predictive of fewer votes cast for the incumbent relative to his nearest challenger. More generally, net stock market changes for 1-, 2-, 3- and 4-year periods preceding Election Day all serve as significant predictors of election outcomes.

Incumbent Wins/Losses in Landslides

Socionomic theory proposes that more extreme changes in social mood tend to motivate more extreme voting preferences for or against the leader. We test this hypothesis with regard to reelection bids by examining the relationship between prior net percentage change in the stock market and incumbent vote margin when both are large.

We look first at landslide victories as measured by electoral vote margins. Records of electoral votes extend farther back in time than popular vote tallies and thus provide more data points to test. To define extreme conditions operationally, we deem an election a landslide victory if the incumbent competed for and won reelection by defeating the nearest competitor with an electoral vote margin of 40% or greater. We deem the election a landslide loss if the incumbent running for reelection trailed the winner by an electoral vote margin of 20% or greater. We define a large positive stock market change as a net gain of 20% or more in the preceding 3-year period, and a large negative stock market change as a net loss of 10% or more. We choose asymmetric percentage thresholds for electoral vote margin and net stock market change, that is, (+40%, −20%) and (+20%, −10%), respectively, to be consistent with the a priori positive biases in both data series: Historically, an incumbent has a better than 50% chance of reelection, and the stock market tends to have a positive trend.

We summarize all historical data meeting these criteria in a contingency table (Table 3). Fisher's exact test indicates a high degree of association between the two variables ($p = 0.009$). Although only 15 elections meet the

Table 3. Large Net Stock Market Movement and Electoral Landslides			
	Direction of prior stock market movement [a]		
Incumbent election result [b]	Large positive	Large negative	Fisher's exact test (p)
In percentage change [c]			
Landslide victory	11 (73.3%)	0 (0%)	
Landslide loss	1 (6.7%)	3 (20%)	0.009***
In lognormal transform [d]			
Landslide victory	9 (75.0%)	0 (0%)	
Landslide loss	0 (0%)	3 (25%)	0.005***

Note: Each data point represents an election result that met the specified criteria. Data are from 1792 to 2004. The most recent year in which an incumbent ran for re-election was 2004; that election did not yield a landslide result.
*significant at the 0.10 level, **significant at the 0.05 level, and ***significant at the 0.01 level.
[a]As measured over a 3-year period by the Dow Jones Industrial Average and normalized predecessor averages.
[b]Landslide victory defined as ≥40% electoral vote margin; landslide loss defined as ≤−20% electoral vote margin.
[c]Large net positive change defined as price rise of ≥20% in prior 3 years; large net negative change defined as price fall of ≥10% in prior 3 years.
[d]Large net positive change defined as log (price) rise of ≥0.2 in prior 3 years; large net negative change defined as log (price) fall of ≥0.1 in prior 3 years.

criteria for analysis, we can have confidence that the observed association is unlikely to have arisen due to chance in view of the exceptional predictive accuracy associated with these data (i.e., a 93% classification rate). Results as good or better would occur less frequently than 1 time in 100 if there is, in fact, no relationship between the variables in the theoretical population.

The strong relationship between landslide elections and stock price movements is robust across a number of variations in the parameter definitions, scaling, and indicators in the model, including the following:

- the computation method used to define net stock market movement (i.e., whether considering percentage changes or lognormal changes);

- the stock market indicator (i.e., whether using the DJIA or an inflation-adjusted DJIA obtained by dividing the DJIA by the Producer Price Index);

- the election result indicator (i.e., whether using electoral vote margin or popular vote margin);

- the electoral thresholds that define an election as a landslide (e.g. +20%, -10%; +50%, -50%);

- the thresholds that define a large net stock market change (e.g. +20%, -10%; +10%, -5%);

- the number of years used to calculate net changes in the stock market (i.e., 1, 2, 3, and 4); and

- various combinations of all of the above.

We illustrate several examples of these comparative analyses below. We find that the predictive success rate when using electoral vote thresholds of (+40%, −20%) and the inflation-adjusted DJIA with stock market thresholds of (+10%, −5%) is 76% (13 out of 17 correct classifications, $p = 0.12$).* Similarly, we find that the predictive success rate when using electoral vote thresholds of (+20%, −10%) and the nominal DJIA with stock market thresholds of (+20%, −10%) to be 94% (15 out of 16, $p = 0.007$). We also test preceding 4-year stock market thresholds in the nominal DJIA of (+0%, −0%), thereby relaxing the requirement that the movements be large, and electoral vote thresholds of (+40%, −20%). We obtain a predictive success rate of 83% (19 out of 23, $p = 0.02$).

With regard to alternative definitions of election results, a large electoral vote advantage can sometimes occur in tandem with only a small popular vote advantage because of the nature of the Electoral College system. Consequently, we analyze popular vote landslides as a further means of testing the relationship under consideration. Because popular vote margins are associated with fewer data points and tend to fall within a tighter percentage range, we use smaller thresholds for popular vote margins (+10%, −5%) and 3-year percentage stock market changes in the nominal DJIA (+10%, −5%).

Even under these conditions, the data produce a predictive success rate of 87% (13 out of 15, $p = 0.01$). In additional analyses, subjecting the popular vote-margin data to the many conditional and definitional variations described above do not diminish this strong relationship. For example, using popular vote-margin thresholds of (+10%, −10%) and 3-year stock market thresholds of (+0%, −0%) in the nominal DJIA, we obtain a predictive success rate of 92% (12 out of 13, $p = 0.01$).

As a final test of robustness, we combine the preceding methodologies and define a landslide election victory as one in which the victor wins by a large margin in either the popular vote (when data are available) or the electoral vote. This is also a somewhat more intuitive definition of what might qualify as a landslide victory. Using the same thresholds as before for electoral vote margin (+40%, −20%), popular vote margin (+10%, −5%), and stock market lognormal change (+0.2, −0.1), we obtain a perfect classification rate (12 out of 12, $p = 0.005$). Again, the results are robust to the many variations we consider. For example, using thresholds of (+50%, −50%) for electoral vote margin, (+20%, −10%) for popular vote margin, and (+0.1, −0.05) for stock market lognormal change results in a 94% predictive success rate (16 out of 17, $p = 0.002$).

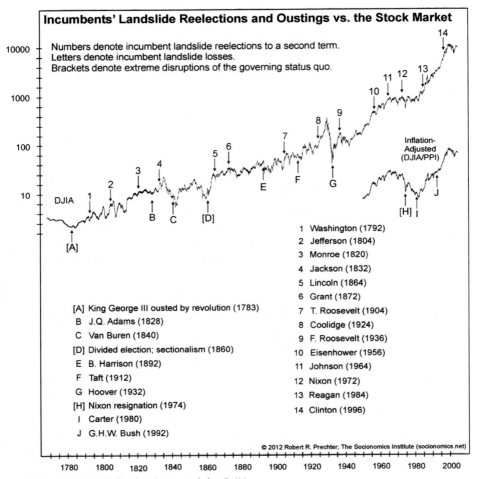

Figure 1. Landslide elections and the DJIA

Note: DJIA = Dow Jones Industrial Average and normalized predecessor averages; DJIA/PPI = DJIA divided by the Producer Price Index. Landslide victory defined as ≥40% electoral vote margin or ≥10% popular vote margin; landslide loss defined as ≤-20% electoral vote margin or ≤-5% popular vote margin. Stock data are from 1760 to 2004. The most recent year in which an incumbent ran for re-election was 2004; that election did not yield a landslide result.

Observing confirmatory findings in response to numerous methodological and analytical variations allows us to conclude with a high degree of confidence that large stock market advances tend to be strongly associated with subsequent landslide victories as opposed to landslide defeats for incumbent candidates in reelection bids. Conversely, large stock market declines tend to be strongly associated with subsequent landslide defeats as opposed to landslide victories for incumbents. The stock market movements and election results shown in Figure 1 illustrate this association visually.

Figure 1 also includes some events that are outside the boundaries of our restrictive statistical tests. We add them to give readers a flavor of the power of extremities in social mood to influence the tenure of leaders. Examples are King George III's ousting as ruler of the American colonies in the late 1700s near the end of a 64-year bear market in English stocks, the regional rejection from ballots of many candidates in 1860 following a 24-year period of lower stock prices, and Richard Nixon's resignation in 1974 during the biggest stock market decline in 32 years.

Predicting Election Results for an Incumbent's Political Party

We next investigate whether the relationship between net stock market change and popular vote margin extends to a president's political party when the president is not running for reelection. As shown in the linear regression results in Table 4, we find no association between the 3-year net percentage change in the nominal DJIA and the popular vote margin for a non-running incumbent's political party. We are inclined to hypothesize that voters project their moods on individual leaders, not parties.

Table 4. Popular Vote Margin for Incumbent's Party and Prior Net Stock Market Movement

Political parties analyzed	n	B	SE	β	p	R^2
Democrats and Republicans	16	0.019	0.095	0.054	0.842	0.003
All parties	20	-0.020	0.080	-0.058	0.807	0.003

Note: n = the number of elections meeting the specified criteria between the years 1824-2008. The above table reports the results of linear regression analysis. The analysis includes only elections in which the incumbent president did not run for another term. Prior net stock market change measured over a 3-year period using the Dow Jones Industrial Average and normalized predecessor averages. Two-tailed probability values are presented due to lack of a theorized directional hypothesis.
Note: Corrected n values precipitated minor amendments to the results in the originally published version of this table. The standard error of the slope is now reported instead of the standard error of the estimate.

Considering Predictors Other Than the Stock Market

Is the stock market a unique predictor of presidential reelection outcomes, or do any of the "big three" economic variables yield stronger results? In this section, we explore the predictive power of GDP, inflation as measured by the Producer Price Index (PPI), and the unemployment rate.

GDP

One might posit that GDP is the determining variable that influences both the stock market and election outcomes, in which case the link we observe between the stock market and election outcomes is spurious. The data do not support this causality, however, for two reasons.

First, in line with the leading indicators literature (Mitchell & Burns, 1938/1961; Moore, 1961), we find stock market movement to be a far better predictor of GDP than GDP is of the stock market. Using data from 1790 to 2008, we observe a simple correlation of 0.35 ($p < 10^{-6}$) between contemporaneous lognormal yearly changes in both the DJIA and GDP. Yet, when lognormal yearly changes in the DJIA are used to predict the subsequent year's lognormal movement in GDP, we observe a significant beta weight of 0.25 ($p < 0.0001$), versus no relationship at all ($\beta = -0.02$, $p = 0.81$) when we use lognormal yearly changes in GDP to predict the subsequent year's lognormal movement in the DJIA. Thus, GDP does not predict stock market movement, but—in accordance with socionomic theory (Prechter, 1999)—the stock market predicts GDP.

Second, we find that GDP exhibits a weaker relationship to incumbents' election outcomes than we observe for the DJIA. We repeat all of the regression analyses for incumbent candidates, applying the same procedures and time intervals described in earlier sections, but use GDP—both nominal and real—as the predictor variable. The resulting regression equations are much weaker in predictive ability than those for the DJIA. For example, substituting the 3-year percentage change in nominal GDP for the DJIA to predict the incumbent's popular vote margin produces weaker relationships across the board, including a reduced linear regression beta weight (0.32 as opposed to 0.57 for the DJIA) and a smaller Spearman's rank correlation (0.30 vs. 0.59). Similar results occur when substituting real GDP as the predictor ($\beta = 0.47$ vs. 0.57, $\rho = 0.49$ vs. 0.59). Although GDP continues to be a statistically significant predictor of reelection outcomes in several of the analyses, the level of significance is weaker than that of the DJIA. When predicting the dichotomous criterion of election win/loss, neither real GDP nor nominal GDP emerges as a significant predictor in logistic regression.

These results lead to the conclusion that GDP alone is not as useful as the stock market alone in predicting reelection outcomes. It is still possible that both GDP and the stock market together predict election results, a scenario we take up shortly.

Inflation and Unemployment

We next apply the analyses described in the above section while using the PPI, a measure of inflation, as the predictor variable in simple regression. Using the 3-year percentage change in the PPI rather than the DJIA to predict an incumbent's popular vote margin results in a sizably worse beta weight (0.15 vs. 0.57 for the DJIA) and Spearman's rho (0.17 vs. 0.59), neither of which is statistically significant. The unemployment rate, with data available from 1940 to the present, fails to register as a significant predictor in the same simple regression analysis. It yields a beta weight of -0.11 and Spearman's rho of -0.18. Neither the PPI nor the unemployment rate is able to predict better than at chance levels with regard to overall election win/loss.

The results are consistent with the negative conclusions reached by Chrystal and Peel (1986) and Biewald (2003), though our study of the unemployment rate may be somewhat affected by loss of power due to small sample size. In sum, these sets of analyses suggest that changes in inflation (as measured by the PPI) and unemployment rates in the 1-, 2-, 3-, and 4-year periods prior to elections have no discernible relationship to presidential reelection outcomes.

Multiple Predictors

All of our analyses up to this point have used single predictors. We now investigate multiple predictors to allow for possible increases in predictive efficacy arising from variable covariations (suppressor effects, variable interactions, etc.). To identify any combinations of indicators that may offer stronger predictive power, we repeat all of the analyses described above using multiple regressions on various sets of predictor variables. We include the set that results from using hierarchical regression to determine the variable entry sequence. We omit the unemployment rate due to an insufficient number of common data points.

In a large number of analyses, the DJIA remains the only significant predictor of election outcomes when combined with nominal GDP, real GDP, and/or the inflation rate. With popular vote margin as the criterion, none of 11 combinations of various independent variables registers as a significant predictor, whereas the DJIA remains a significant predictor in all such combinations. A similar pattern of results arises in conducting nonparametric analyses of these variables. With election win/loss as the criterion, every combination of variables again fails to register as a significant predictor, whereas the DJIA achieves statistical significance in all such combinations.

To address the possibility that our statistically significant results may simply be an outcome of performing a large number of tests, we conduct an omnibus Simes' test for multiple comparisons, where the complete null states that the DJIA is unrelated to election outcomes. Requiring a family-wise error rate of 0.05, and pooling in all the p-values reported in Tables 1 to 3, we find that the complete null stands rejected. Our findings indicate that none of the alternative measures we test are as powerful as the stock market in predicting U.S. presidential reelection outcomes.

Discussion

In summary, we find that the stock market's performance prior to a U.S. presidential election is a significant predictor of an incumbent's reelection success. Our results are robust to variations in the independent variable (nominal returns in the DJIA vs. lognormal returns, and data durations of 1, 2, 3, and 4 years), variations in the dependent variable (popular vote margins, electoral vote margins, and a categorical win/loss measure), statistical methods used, and the presence of intervening variables. Generally, incumbents who preside over a net advance in the stock market tend to obtain a higher vote margin than incumbents who preside over a net decline in the stock market in the 1, 2, 3, and 4 years before the election. Of all the variations we test, the relationship between the 3-year net percentage change in the DJIA and the incumbent's popular vote margin is the strongest and achieves the highest level of significance. Large stock market advances during the final 3 years of incumbent candidates' terms tend to be strongly associated with subsequent landslide victories, as opposed to landslide defeats, for incumbents in their reelection bids. Conversely, large stock market declines during the final 3 years of incumbent candidates' terms tend to be strongly associated with subsequent landslide defeats, as opposed to landslide victories, for incumbents in their reelection bids. The significant relationships between stock market changes and election results do not extend to the incumbent's party during elections that feature no incumbent candidate. This difference suggests that voting behavior changes depending on whether the election includes an incumbent.

We find no significant relationship between the success of reelection bids and prior net percentage change in inflation (as measured by the PPI) or unemployment. GDP-based simple regressions are sometimes significant but always weaker than comparable regressions based on the stock market. The stock market remains a significant predictor of the outcome of incumbents' reelection bids when considered with combinations of the aforementioned macroeconomic variables in multiple regression analyses. The importance of these other variables remains relatively weak or insignificant when examined in combination with the stock market.

As a proposed hidden variable, social mood cannot be tested directly or proven as a voting motivator in these analyses. It is possible that other hidden variables may contribute to or account for our findings. Nevertheless, our results are consistent with the predictions made under the [socionomic] theory that motivated the study while being substantially contrary to economic voting perspectives, a topic we explore next.

Is the Stock Market Per Se a Causal Factor in Reelection Results?

How can we ascertain whether it is more likely changes in social mood—rather than changes in the stock market per se—that influence reelection outcomes? We now consider other economic voting arguments that may account for our findings. For example, from the idea of egotropic voting, one could argue that grateful stockholders—people who made money in the stock market—would credit the incumbent for their financial success and vote accordingly, whereas those losing money in the market would reject the incumbent (see, for example, Chan & Jordan, 2004). Another potential explanation might be a variation on the idea of sociotropic voting, in which presumably "voters are influenced by their subjective views of the national economy even though they are not much swayed by their personal economic standing" (Erikson, 2004, p. 1). Perhaps voters, whether they own stock or not, watch the stock market and vote accordingly for the well-being of society.

The grateful (or ungrateful) stockholder explanation seems untenable given that the data for GDP, PPI, and unemployment fail to support egotropic hypotheses of "grateful economic participants," "grateful savers" or "grateful employees." This problem for such an explanation seems doubly serious given that economic participants, savers and employees have always outnumbered stockholders, usually substantially. We are unaware of any reason why sociotropic voters' basis for judging social well-being should be the stock market averages in lieu of these other variables.

A cursory statistical analysis, moreover, substantially invalidates the grateful stockholder explanation. Data covering more than 100 years show that increased stock ownership within the population does not positively influence the relationship between stock market movement and incumbents' performance in reelection bids. A rigorous test of the grateful stockholder explanation—of gain or loss in stocks per se as a possible lurking variable—is confounded by the lack of compatible data. (Available stock market data, election data, and stock ownership data cover different time periods; historical stock ownership data tend to be sporadic; and election data featuring incumbents are available fewer times than once every 4 years.) We nonetheless devise some simple tests.

Stock ownership was likely negligible across the national population prior to 1900, and indeed we could find no robust data series; stock ownership from 1900 to 1950 ranged from 2.1% to 9.6% for years in which data are available (Cox, 1963); and as of 2005, 50.4% of U.S. households held stock (Investment Company Institute and the Securities Industry Association, 2005). The grateful stockholder explanation would seem to require that the relationship between the stock market and election outcomes should be far stronger after 1900 than it was before 1900, and far stronger after 1950 than it was before 1950. The difference should be enough to reject the null hypothesis that postulates no such difference. To test this idea, we conduct multiple linear regression to predict election outcomes by stock market performance, time period (dichotomous variables of pre-/post-1900 and pre-/post-1950), and the interaction of stock market performance by time period. The interaction effects do not emerge as statistically significant, thus failing to support the grateful/ungrateful stockholder explanation. Furthermore, as we see in Table 1, the association between election outcomes and stock market performance is stronger in the pre-1900 period than the post-1900 period, though both are significant. Thus, we can safely conclude that voter response to stock market gains/losses does not explain our results.

Socionomic theory encounters no such counter indications from the data. Its explanation holds: Voters in the aggregate are not responding to stock market changes, economic changes, inflation rates or the availability of jobs; nor are they voting rationally for social improvement. Rather, they are voting in accordance with trends in social mood. An increasingly positive social mood produces a rising stock market as well as votes for the incumbent, and an increasingly negative social mood produces a falling stock market as well as votes against the incumbent, thus producing the positive relationship we observe. When no candidate in a presidential election is the recognized leader whom voters have unconsciously credited or blamed for their mood, they appear to base their voting decisions substantially on other factors.

Future Research and Practical Implications

Theoretical assumptions can instill "strong prior beliefs on both sides" (Hirshleifer, 2001, p. 1534) of a fundamental question. Bias is especially strong against newer ideas, which in recent years have included the proposal of nonrationality in aggregate human behavior (Burnham, 2005, pp. 41-52). One value of the socionomic hypothesis is that it prompted this investigation of a relationship between certain types of social variables, a tack that previous political researchers' theoretical assumptions seem to have impeded them from considering.

We did not set out to optimize a model for predicting elections but to explore a theoretical point. Nevertheless, we hope our approach will open a new avenue for scholars who build models to predict election outcomes. Instead of assuming that the economy is the primary mover of voting preferences, researchers may wish to begin investigating indicators of social mood as predictors of reelection outcomes and to reinterpret economic data as resulting from voters' moods rather than causing them.

Researchers may also wish to explore some of the nuances that our rigid statistical tests are unable to detect. For example, George H.W. Bush lost his bid for reelection even though the Dow was higher over the three years leading to Election Day. The broader Value Line Geometric Index, however, was down 11% over the 3.1 years prior to Election Day. So, Bush's landslide loss is not incompatible with socionomic theory even though our tests scored it otherwise. Similar subtleties attend other apparent departures from socionomic expectations, but we have assiduously avoided data fitting to capture such results. Also, distinguishing between bull markets and bear market rallies[†] reveals some informative nuances regarding incumbents' popularity and reelection chances. Future researchers may wish to investigate these considerations further. Future political studies might also examine the relationship of social mood to the timing of new dictatorships, the frequency of political apologies, and outbreaks of peace and war. Under a broader umbrella, we propose analyzing social mood as it relates to a wide variety of social activities, from instances of mass celebration or destructive riot to trends in fads, fashions, and popular entertainment.

Our results suggest a practical strategy for political parties: Whenever one of a party's potential candidates is an incumbent who has served during a period of major mood setback as indicated by a large net decline in the stock market—in real or nominal terms—that party may increase its chance of retaining control of the presidency if it chooses to nominate a candidate other than the incumbent. Our findings also may be of practical value to those who wish someday to seek the presidency: A newcomer's chance of success improves when competing against an incumbent who has served during a period of negatively trending social mood. Likewise, an incumbent who has held office during a major negative trend in social mood may wish to consider declining to run for a second term and await more favorable conditions to pursue the presidency again or retire from presidential politics to spend hard-earned political capital on other efforts.

Conclusion

Stock market performance relates significantly and positively to the outcome of U.S. presidents' reelection bids. Hypotheses of economic voting fail to account for our findings. Our results, however, are consistent with Prechter's socionomic theory, specifically that social mood, an internally regulated psychological variable reflected in stock indexes, is more powerful than economic variables in motivating voting behavior whenever a leader faces reelection. Our work supports the inclusion of stock market performance in models that forecast the outcomes of reelection bids of U.S. presidents and, we hope, prompts further literature on socionomic voting.

Acknowledgments

The authors thank John G. Geer (Vanderbilt University), Alan Abramowitz (Emory University), Ludwig Kanzler (McKinsey and Company), Jason King (Baylor College of Medicine), Ming Yuan (Georgia Institute of Technology), Mark Almand (Socionomics Institute) and Gordon Graham for valuable suggestions and encouragement. All errors are the authors'.

Declaration of Conflicting Interests

The authors declared no potential conflicts of interest with respect to the research, authorship, and/or publication of this article.

Funding

The authors reported receipt of the following financial support for the research and/or authorship of this article: Part of this work was performed under the auspices of the Young Scientists Summer Program (YSSP) of the International Institute for Applied Systems Analysis (IIASA), supported by a fellowship from the National Academy of Sciences' U.S. Committee for IIASA, with funds from the National Science Foundation (NSF Award OISE-0738129).

This version of the paper corrects a slight error in an underlying data series, producing among our coefficients and p-values a few instances of very small departures from corresponding numbers reported in the originally published version. These corrections have no bearing on the validity of any calculation method or on the paper's claims and conclusions.—The Authors

* *In the original paper, this line incorrectly read, "(14 out of 17 correct classifications, p = 0.03)."*
† *See Chapter 18.*

————————————

After it was posted on the Social Science Research Network in January 2012, the Institute's elections paper by November had become SSRN's third most-downloaded paper—out of 350,000 on the site—for the preceding 12 months. It was covered that year by *The Washington Post*, *The Los Angeles Times*, *Forbes*, *The Atlantic*, *Barron's*, Yahoo!, The Hill, CNN and NBC, among other media.—Ed.

REFERENCES

Aidt, T.S. (2000). Economic Voting and Information. *Electoral Studies*, *19*, 349-362.

Alesina, A., Roubini, N., & Cohen, G. (1997). *Political Cycles and the Macroeconomy*. Cambridge, MA: Massachusetts Institute of Technology Press.

Baars, B.J. (1986). *The Cognitive Revolution in Psychology*. New York, NY: Guilford.

Biewald, L. (2003). *Changes in U.S. Presidential Election Voting Patterns 1876-2000*. Stanford University, CA. Retrieved from http://www. sociomics.net/archive/ElectionsStanford-Biewald2003.doc

Blendon, R.J., Benson, J.M., Brodie, M., Morin, R., Altman, D.E., Gitterman, D., Brossard, M., & James, M. (1997). Bridging the Gap Between the Public's and Economists' View of the Economy. *Journal of Economic Perspectives*, *11*, 105-118.

Bollen, J., Mao, H., & Zeng, X. (2011). Twitter Mood Predicts the Stock Market. *Journal of Computational Science*, *2*, 1-8.

Brender, A., & Drazen, A. (2005). How Do Budget Deficits and Economic Growth Affect Reelection Prospects? (Working Paper No. 11862). National Bureau of Economic Research. Retrieved from http://www.nber. org/papers/w11862

Burnham, T. (2005). *Mean Markets and Lizard Brains: How to Profit From the New Science of Irrationality*. Hoboken, NJ: John Wiley.

Chan, A., & Jordan, B. (2004). *The Economy, the Market, and Presidential Elections*. Weekly Economic Review: Banc One Investment Advisors.

Chappell, H.W., Jr. (1990). Economic Performance, Voting, and Political Support: A Unified Approach. *Review of Economics and Statistics*, *72*, 313-320.

Chrystal, K.A., & Peel, D.A. (1986). What Can Economics Learn from Political Science, and Vice Versa? *American Economic Review*, *76*, 62-65.

Cox, E.B. (1963). *Trends in the distribution of stock ownership*. Philadelphia, PA: University of Philadelphia Press.

Delli Carpini, M.X., & Keeter, S. (1996). *What Americans Know About Politics and Why It Matters*. New Haven, CT: Yale University Press.

Downs, A. (1957). *An Economic Theory of Democracy*. New York, NY: Harper & Row.

Elliott, R.N. (1938). *The Wave Principle*. In R.R. Prechter Jr. (Ed.), *R.N. Elliott's Masterworks* (pp. 83-150). Gainesville, GA: New Classics Library.

Erikson, R.S. (2004, July). Macro vs. Micro-level Perspectives on Economic Voting: Is the Micro-level Evidence Endogenously Induced? Paper presented at the 2004 Political Methodology Meetings, Stanford University, CA.

Fair, R. (1978). The Effect of Economic Events on Votes for President. *Review of Economics and Statistics*, *60*, 159-173.

Fair, R. (1982). The Effect of Economic Events on Votes for President: 1980 Results. *Review of Economics and Statistics, 64,* 322-325.

Fair, R. (1988). The Effect of Economic Events on Votes for President: 1984 Update. *Political Behavior, 10,* 168-179.

Fair, R. (1996). The Effect of Economic Events on Votes for President: 1992 update. *Political Behavior, 18,* 119-139.

Fair, R. (2002). *Predicting Presidential Elections and Other Things.* Palo Alto, CA: Stanford University Press.

Gardner, H. (1987). *The Mind's New Science: A History of the Cognitive Revolution.* New York, NY: Basic Books.

Geer, J.G. (2006). *In Defense of Negativity: Attack Ads in Presidential Campaigns.* Chicago, IL: University of Chicago Press.

Gilbert, E., & Karahalios, K. (2010, May). Widespread Worry and the Stock Market. Paper presented at the Fourth International AAAI Conference on Weblogs and Social Media, Washington, DC.

Gleisner, R.F. (1992). Economic Determinants of Presidential Elections: The Fair Model. *Political Behavior, 14,* 383-394.

Hirshleifer, D. (2001). Investor Psychology and Asset Pricing. *Journal of Finance, 56,* 1533-1597.

Investment Company Institute and the Securities Industry Association. (2005). Equity Ownership in America, 2005. Washington, DC.

Jones, R. (2002). *Who Will Be in the White House? Predicting Presidential Elections.* New York, NY: Longman.

Key, V.O., Jr. (1966). *The Responsible Electorate.* New York, NY: Vintage.

Kramer, G.H. (1971). Short term Fluctuations in U.S. Voting Behavior, 1896-1964. *American Political Science Review, 65,* 131-143.

Kuklinski, J.H., & Segura, G. M. (1995). Endogeneity, Exogeneity, Time, and Space in Political Representation: A Review Article. *Legislative Studies Quarterly, 20,* 3-21.

Lewis-Beck, M.S., & Paldam, M. (2000). Economic Voting: An Introduction. *Electoral Studies, 19,* 113-121.

Mitchell, W. C., & Burns, A. F. (1961). Statistical Indicators of Cyclical Revivals. In G.H. Moore (Ed.), *Business Cycle Indicators (Vol.1,* pp. 184-260). Princeton, NJ: Princeton University Press. (Original work published 1938.)

Moore, G.H. (Ed.) (1961). Leading and Confirming Indicators of General Business. *Business cycle indicators (Vol. 1,* pp. 45-109). Princeton, NJ: Princeton University Press.

Mueller, J.E. (1970). Presidential Popularity from Truman to Johnson. *American Political Science Review, 64,* 18-34.

Muth, J.F. (1961). Rational Expectations and the Theory of Price Movements. *Econometrica, 29,* 315-335.

Nannestad, P., & Paldam, M. (1994). The VP-function: A Survey of the Literature on Vote and Popularity Functions After 25 Years. *Public Choice*, *79*, 213-245.

Nofsinger, J., & Kim, K. (2003). Protecting Investors (Not). In R.R. Prechter Jr. (Ed.), *Pioneering Studies in Socionomics* (pp. 221-225). Gainesville, GA: New Classics Library.

Norpoth, H. (1996). Presidents and the Prospective Voter. *Journal of Politics*, *58*, 776-792.

Overton, W.F., & Ennis, M.D. (2006). Cognitive-developmental and Behavior-analytic Theories: Evolving Into Complementarity. *Human Development*, *49*, 143-172.

Overton, W.F., & Reese, H.W. (1973). Models of Development: Methodological Implications. In J.R. Nesselroade & H.W. Reese (Eds.), *Life-span Developmental Psychology* (pp. 65-86). New York, NY: Academic Press.

Paldam, M., & Nannestad, P. (2000). What Do Voters Know About the Economy? A Study of Danish Data, 1990-2003. *Electoral Studies*, *19*, 363-391.

Prechter, R.R., Jr. (1979). What's Going On? In R.R. Prechter Jr. (Ed.), *Pioneering Studies in Socionomics* (p. 1). Gainesville, GA: New Classics Library.

Prechter, R.R., Jr. (1989). *A Turn in the Tidal Wave*. Gainesville, GA: New Classics Library.

Prechter, R.R., Jr. (1999). *The Wave Principle of Human Social Behavior and the New Science of Socionomics*. Gainesville, GA: New Classics Library.

Prechter, R.R., Jr. (Ed.). (2003). *Pioneering Studies in Socionomics*. Gainesville, GA: New Classics Library.

Prechter, R.R., Jr., & Parker, W.D. (2007). The Financial/Economic Dichotomy in Social Behavioral Dynamics: The Socionomic Perspective. *Journal of Behavioral Finance*, *8*, 84-110.

Rahn, W.M. (2000). Affect as Information: The Role of Public Mood in Political Reasoning. In A. Lupia, M.D. McCubbins, & S.L. Popkin (Eds.), *Elements of Reason: Cognition, Choice, and the Bounds of Rationality* (pp. 130-150). New York, NY: Cambridge University Press.

Riley, W.B., Jr., & Luksetich, W.A. (1980). The Market Prefers Republicans: Myth or Reality. *Journal of Financial and Quantitative Analysis*, *15*, 541-560.

Santa-Clara, P., & Valkanov, R.I. (2003). The Presidential Puzzle: Political Cycles and the Stock Market. *Journal of Finance*, *58*, 1841-1872.

Sheffrin, S.M. (1996). *Rational Expectations* (2nd ed.). Cambridge, UK: Cambridge University Press.

Skinner, B.F. (1938). *The Behavior of Organisms*. New York, NY: Appleton-Century.

Stimson, J. (1991). *Public Opinion in America: Moods, Cycles, and Swings*. Boulder, CO: Westview Press.

Watson, J.B. (1913). Psychology as the Behaviorist Views It. *Psychological Review*, *20*, 158-177.

Chapter 3

Testing Social Mood as a Hidden Causal Variable

Robert R. Prechter

(Adapted from a presentation to the second annual Socionomics Summit,
Atlanta, Georgia, April 14, 2012)

Introduction

When I first cast a vote many years ago, I cast it according to a political philosophy. Every single vote I've cast since then has been according to that same philosophy. And I'm very proud to say that no person I've voted for has ever won political office. So, I can't be blamed for any politician's or government's behavior.

Plenty of people have a political philosophy, and they vote accordingly. Some people are one-issue voters who don't care what other policies a candidate proposes. Many people are party loyalists. I think this is a less rational position, along the lines of "My team has all good guys; the other team has all bad guys." Democrats and Republicans will judge the same policies as being well-meaning when proposed by their team and of evil intent when proposed by the other. The policies of Barack Obama and G.W. Bush have been nearly identical in every major area,[1] yet passions run high in preference for one president over the other. And, finally, there are a few people who on philosophical grounds refuse to vote at all.

The types of people I mention here rarely sway elections, because they vote consistently. But swing voters do determine election outcomes. Based on the history of U.S. presidential voting-ratio extremes—when landslides occur—it seems that in the past two centuries some 20 to 30% of the eligible population has comprised swing voters. According to news reports, some voters make up their minds as late as the last minute. Socionomics is uniquely suited to propose a reason for their ultimate, aggregated decisions.

My colleagues and I wanted to investigate the question of *why* voting outcomes occur as they do and to see if socionomic theory could suggest a useful line of inquiry and even anticipate voting results. We started with the essential socionomic hypothesis. The conventional view, stated or assumed in many economic and political studies, is that social actions motivate social mood. The socionomic hypothesis is precisely the opposite: that social mood motivates social actions.

Our political starting point came from a list of statements that I have often shown to demonstrate the difference between conventional thinking and socionomic thinking. The standard view of political leaders would be something like "talented leaders make the population happy," whereas the socionomic view is "a happy population makes leaders appear talented"; in other words, unconscious social mood determines how people judge the efficacy and value of their leader. That's a very different view of causality.

Most people in political science seek to find out whether or not A causes B. For example, they might ask, "Do voting results influence economic change?" For example, "Is the Democratic Party better for the economy than the Republican Party?" Sometimes statistical results appear to be significant, but when you take the data back further [see Chapter 1], they're not. Other researchers investigate the converse question, whether B causes A. Plenty of studies have asked, "Does economic change influence voting results?" There are different sub-theories about why a change in the economy might change voting. Under the idea of egotropic voting, people are voting to promote their own well being, whereas under the idea of sociotropic voting, people vote according to what's best for society. Some researchers postulate that politicians can affect election outcomes by taking actions that affect voters' views, opinions and moods. None of these hypotheses has proven reliable.

Among election studies, many of the investigations into whether A causes B or B causes A do not produce useful results. Socionomists, on the other hand, postulate something quite different. We still allow that A might cause B, or B might cause A, but we have a third way of looking at things, which is that C—a third variable—can cause related changes in both A and B. In other words, there's an anterior common cause: waves of social mood.

The difficulty in trying to show that C is operative is that social mood is a hidden variable. We can't hook up electrodes to 300 million people to measure their mood changes directly. We can judge their moods only by their actions. This makes the job of showing causality extremely difficult. It took a lot of thought to figure out how we could demonstrate whether socionomic causality affects election outcomes.

Does the Stock Market Predict Election Results?

The following three postulations under socionomic theory led us to our first study question:

(1) The stock market is an immediate register of changes in social mood.

(2) As social mood becomes more positive, the stock market will rise, and vice versa.

(3) Voters will judge current leaders based on changes in social mood during the leader's tenure.

If these statements are true, the trend of the stock market should predict whether leaders will be retained or ousted. So, our first study question was: "Does the stock market predict reelection outcomes?"

Anecdotally, we had noticed that political commentators tend to give a new president a break during the first year in office. If the economy is in bad shape, they tend to agree, "That's the predecessor's legacy." If the economy is in good shape, the ousted party will insist, "*We* are the reason that things are still good this year." But a president almost always gets credit or blame for the last three years of a first term. So, our expectation was that the stock market's performance in the three years leading up to an election would best determine whether an incumbent would win a second bid.

Yet we didn't want to test only what we thought was true. Our theory should have validity across all time frames. So, we tested election outcomes and stock trends not only for the three years before each election but also for one year, two years, and four years before each election.

We also wanted to make sure our results would be robust with respect to election-outcome indicators. So, we tested multiple measures. We tested popular vote margin, popular vote percentage, electoral vote margin, and electoral vote percentage. We also considered simple win/loss as well as landslides vs. large stock market moves. We wanted to see if there was a correlation between the sizes of the market's gain or loss and the incumbent's gain or loss. We measured landslides by popular vote, by electoral vote, and either/or. For further robustness, we tested multiple landslide thresholds and multiple stock-movement thresholds, just to make sure we didn't luck into the one that gave us the best result. We tested percentage changes and log-normal changes. And—I think this is very important—*we tested all available data.* Many studies go back fewer than a hundred years. We haven't run across an elections study that incorporated the entire 200-plus-year history of stock market prices and voting results, both of which are available. Choosing the amount of data to test can introduce bias toward a desired result. Using all the data protected us against inadvertent data-mining.

Another way we made sure that our test was robust is that we didn't use only nominal stock prices; we also divided them by the PPI to adjust for inflation. We wanted to see if both types of measures were valid, or at least figure out which one was. We didn't want to ascribe social-mood causality to our result if the stock market had risen simply because of inflation.

The final thing we did to ensure a robust result was to use many different types of statistical tests: linear regression, linear rank regression, logistic regression and Fisher's exact test, as applied by co-author Deepak Goel. We pursued this very broad and deep coverage because we wanted to make sure that we were reporting real results. You can imagine why our study took a number of years to do.

Table 1 shows one of our tables: "Incumbent's Popular Vote Margin vs. Prior Net Stock Market Movement." As you can see, we discovered that stock-market movement in all four durations—one, two, three, and four years prior to the election—has been an extremely good predictor of how an incumbent would fare when running for reelection. As we suspected, the three-year period was the best. As you can see in the second-to-last column, its p value is .001. That's a statistically significant number. It means that had we put random data through our tests, they would have given us a result this good or better only one time in a thousand.

Table 1. Incumbent Popular Vote Margin and Prior Net Stock Market Movement

Study Period[a]	Prior Net Stock Market Movement Period[b]	N	B	SE	β	p	R^2
1824 – 2004	Prior 1 yr	26	0.281	0.147	0.364	0.034**	0.133
1824 – 2004	Prior 2 yrs	26	0.144	0.073	0.374	0.030**	0.140
1824 – 2004	**Prior 3 yrs**	**26**	**0.193**	**0.057**	**0.566**	**0.001***	**0.321**
1824 – 2004	Prior 4 yrs	26	0.132	0.047	0.501	0.005***	0.251

Note. The above table reports the results of linear regression analysis. The condition of primary theoretical interest is in **bold** font. N = the number of elections meeting the specified criteria. One-tailed probability values are presented in accordance with the theorized directional hypothesis; asterisks indicate statistically significant values: *significant at the 0.10 level, **significant at the 0.05 level and ***significant at the 0.01 level.

[a] Popular vote tallies first became available in 1824; the most recent year in which an incumbent ran for re-election was 2004.

[b] As measured by the Dow Jones Industrial Average and normalized predecessor averages (DJIA).

The Socionomics Institute

Table 1

You can examine our thesis visually in Figure 1, which has been updated to add the outcome of 2012. For a description of our statistical parameters for landslides, please see Chapter 2. Generally speaking, the numbers above the graph indicate times that a president won a second term in a landslide, and the letters below the graph indicate times when the leader was ousted in a landslide. Those in brackets represent extreme disruptions to the governing status quo. There are a few exceptions along the way; it's not a perfect result. But the tendency is clear, and the correlation is strong and highly significant. As far as we know, it's a better predictor than any other study has uncovered. And we never polled a single voter.

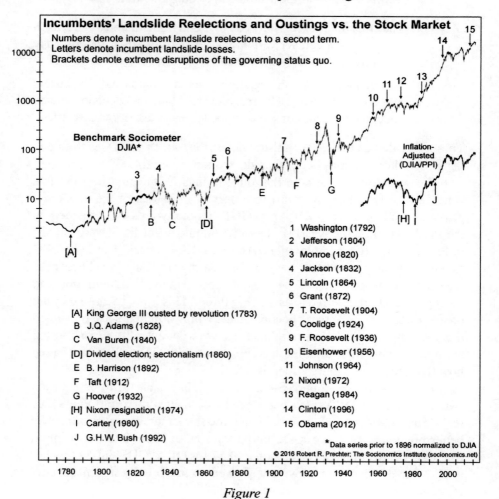

Figure 1

Our first conclusion from this study, then, was that the stock market predicts elections extremely well, confirming our first hypothesis.

Yet our result could simply lead to yet another paper saying, "Here's another correlation you can use when creating your election-prediction model." That's not what we were after. To go beyond merely enhancing a component model, we had to go further. We needed to ask another question.

How Does the Stock Market Compare to Economic Variables as an Election Predictor?

The hypotheses behind the second study question are:

(1)   The stock market registers social mood immediately. The reason is that people can act very quickly to express their moods; they just have to press a button or call a broker.

(2)   The economy lags in registering social mood, and it registers mood less precisely. The reason is that business decisions made under the influence of social mood typically take months to effect.

These ideas led us to the second study question, which is: "Does the stock market predict elections better than do economic variables?"

We wanted to make sure that our findings here would be robust as well. So, we tested changes in four different measures of the economy: gross domestic product (GDP); real GDP, in other words GDP divided by the Producer Price Index (PPI); the inflation rate according to the change in PPI; and finally, unemployment. All these data go back to at least 1902 except for unemployment, for which the data start in 1940. We chose these measures because in several political science papers, GDP, inflation and unemployment are referred to as the "big three." This is not because they are proven effective motivators of people in the voting booth; it's just presumed that they should be. To ensure robustness, we went even further and tested all of these economic variables in combination with the stock market to see how that procedure would affect the result.

Here is what we found: Stock prices going back to the late 1700s (which we labeled DJIA) are a better predictor of election results than GDP, real GDP, PPI or unemployment. In fact, the stock market is a *dramatically* better predictor. As you can see in the top row of Table 2 under "Simple Regression," we found a correlation of 0.57 for DJIA. GDP did pretty well at 0.32, but PPI and unemployment showed no statistically significant correlation at all.

The second row, under "Multiple Regression" and "Hierarchical Regression," shows a highly significant result for DJIA, whereas GDP, PPI and unemployment were all useless.

Our studies of landslides, summarized in the third row, produced the same type of result. We found a very good *p* value for DJIA going all the way back to 1796.

GDP had some stand-alone predictability, but in testing it in combination with DJIA, its significance disappeared. In other words, when we added GDP to DJIA, it did not improve the ability to predict reelection outcomes. The stock market, on the other hand, remained a significant predictor when tested in combination with each economic variable, and it remained the *only* significant predictor when combined with all the economic variables. So, DJIA remained significant in all the ways we tested it.

As you might be thinking, this is a highly counter-intuitive result. After all, political scientists call these economic variables the "big three," right? And political analysts tell us, "It's the economy, stupid." But we showed that economic variables have had little to no value in predicting election outcomes, especially relative to stocks. Our conclusion for the second part of our study, then, confirmed another socionomic hypothesis: The stock market predicts elections *better* than do economic variables.

DJIA is better than GDP, PPI and Unemployment for predicting election results				
The Socionomics Institute	**Mood**	**Economic Variables**		
	DJIA	**GDP**	**PPI**	**Unemployment**
Simple Regression (many variations, tests)	β = 0.57 (★ ★ ★)	β = 0.32	β = 0.15	β = -0.11
Multiple Regressions, Hierarchical Regression	**(highly significant)**	(not significant)	(not significant)	(not significant)
Landslide victory/loss (+ variations)	*p* = 0.009 (★ ★ ★)	N/A	N/A	N/A

Table 2

We knew that our study was not yet sufficient to show anything about socionomic causality. So, the next question was: "*Why* is the stock market a good predictor of election outcomes?" Is it really due to social mood? Maybe there's another reason. Maybe people are voting rationally according to how much money they made or lost in the stock market. In other words: People made money in their portfolios, so they liked the president, and they wanted him to stay in office. Or, they lost money, so they didn't like him, and they wanted to kick him out. Most people would impulsively consider that conclusion reasonable. Do you? If that's the case, then we're just showing a conventional result: A causes B.

Socionomic Causality or the Same Old Rational Response?

To counter that notion, we first noted that the preceding portion of our study presents a *logical problem* with the rational-response formulation that voters might be responding to gains or losses in their stock portfolios, because, if you believe that's what they are doing, you would have to ask yourself the following questions:

Why are they responding less to the state of the economy?

Why are they not responding to changes in the value of their savings?

Why are they not responding to changes in unemployment?

A lot of voters have jobs, a lot of voters have savings, and a lot of voters participate in the economy. Far fewer people over the past 200 years have owned stocks. Yet voters up and down the economic spectrum don't seem to care about economic variables nearly as much as they seem to care about the stock market. Under stimulus-and-rational-response theory, that doesn't make much sense.

We're getting closer, then, to our goal. We can at least say that the idea that people are reacting to the stock market is a very slippery claim, because voters are not responding to economic variables, which should mean far more to them.

At this point, rational-response theorists can still say, "All you've shown is that voters care more about their portfolios than about their jobs. A still causes B. You haven't convinced us at all that social mood is involved."

All right, then. Think hard: *Can you conceive of a way to disprove the idea that A is still causing B, that voters' reactions to their rising or falling portfolios are creating these election results?*

Testing the Supposed Portfolio Effect

Here's what we did: We asked a third study question: Is there a "portfolio effect"? Are voters responding to gains and losses in their stock portfolios? We reasoned: *If so*, this "portfolio effect" would have to be stronger during times when more voters own stock. If voters owned stock, they could respond to changes in the value of their portfolios; if they didn't, they couldn't. If nobody owned stock, there could be no portfolio effect; and if everyone owned stock, then any such effect would be strong. If you hypothesize a stimulus and a response, you cannot escape the conclusion that the response would disappear if the stimulus did.

With 200 years' worth of data available, we could test for a portfolio effect. In the 19th century, most Americans were *farmers*. People didn't have stock portfolios, and they weren't watching CNBC. Even in the first half of the 20th century, very few people owned stock. Only recently have stock portfolios become an important part of Americans' lives.

We divided our entire test period into times when people owned more stock and less stock to see if doing so had an effect on the predictability of elections. To assure robustness, we divided the data twice.

First we split the 20th century into halves. For most of the time from 1900 to 1950, only 2 to 4% of households owned stock, although for a brief time near the stock market peak in the 1920s it was briefly about 10%. From 1950 to 2000, about 5% to 50% of households owned stock, a huge difference. Guess what. There was almost no difference between the predictability of the stock market in the first half of the 20th century and its predictability in the second half.

Then we split the entire test period in half, essentially pitting the 19th century against the 20th. For the 1800s, statistics on stock ownership mostly round to zero. The upper end of the range is estimated at 2%, a very low number. In the 20th century, as I have already noted, it was between 2% and 50%. Again, we found virtually no difference in our test results between those two periods. In fact, the stock market predicted elections slightly better in the 1800s—when hardly anyone owned stock—than it did in the 1900s. As Table 3 shows, the correlation coefficient for the portion of the 19th century for which popular vote data are available is 0.63, and for the 20th century it is 0.55.

To put it mildly, these results pose an empirical problem for the A-causes-B explanation. To put it more emphatically, we think we have demonstrated that the A-causes-B explanation is false. Voters cannot possibly be reacting to stock market gains and losses. A is not causing B.

Table 3. Incumbent Popular Vote Margin and Prior Net Stock Market Movement

Study Period[a]	Prior Net Stock Market Movement Period[b]	N	B	SE	β	p	R^2
1824 – 1900	Prior 3 yrs	8	0.101	0.631	**0.665**	0.047**	0.398
1901 – 2004	Prior 3 yrs	18	0.188	0.072	**0.549**	0.009***	0.301

Note. The above table reports the results of linear regression analysis. N = the number of elections meeting the specified criteria. One-tailed probability values are presented in accordance with the theorized directional hypothesis; asterisks indicate statistically significant values: *significant at the 0.10 level, **significant at the 0.05 level and ***significant at the 0.01 level.

[a] Popular vote tallies first became available in 1824; the most recent year in which an incumbent ran for re-election was 2004.

[b] As measured by the Dow Jones Industrial Average and normalized predecessor averages (DJIA). *The Socionomics Institute*

Table 3

We may therefore come to this conclusion: *The socionomic explanation holds.* Voters in the aggregate are not *responding*, rationally or otherwise, to economic changes, inflation rates, the availability of jobs, *or to the stock market.* Our results are consistent with the hypothesis that, in the aggregate, investors in the stock market and voters in the voting booth are both making decisions in accordance with trends in a single hidden variable, social mood. In other words, C is causing both A *and* B.

Might There Be a Different Hidden Variable?

We are aware of the potential objection that there could be a different hidden variable, one we haven't considered, that is making the stock market go up and down and causing elections results to coincide with its movements. But we can't think of one that a sensible person would suggest.

We did try, though: Climate change is a popular topic. Maybe the climate is making the stock market move and also making people vote a certain way. Or maybe it's planetary alignments. Some people think they affect human behavior. But in such cases, it seems that changes in social mood would still have to be an intermediate step. What about smart vs. stupid politicians? Perhaps smart politicians know how to force the stock market up *and* engineer a reelection, while the stupid ones blunder into pushing stocks downward and getting thrown out in a landslide. Unfortunately, this idea doesn't quite work, because of presidents such as Richard Nixon. He would have to have been brilliant in forcing the stock market up into his reelection in 1972 but then an idiot when he pushed it back down and got thrown out of office. So far, we have been unable to come up with a realistic, alternative hidden variable that someone could offer to explain our results.

Finally, consider that *we designed this study to test socionomic theory*. The results both confirmed our expectations and neutered a conventional, A-causes-B explanation.

Do Voters Credit or Blame Parties for Their Mood?

We also tested all the times when an incumbent was not running for reelection. Our question was: Do people blame or reward the *party* that has been in power if the sitting president is not running? We found that the stock market does not predict election outcomes when the incumbent president is not in the race. This lack of correlation makes sense in light of our long-standing socionomic statement, "A happy population makes *leaders* appear talented." Apparently, an election is a referendum on the leader, and if the same person is not running, that dynamic is absent.

We suspect that reelection outcomes are greatly determined by a primitive area of the brain. An unconscious human-to-human connection, we posit, trumps voters' conscious connection to abstract political views, especially among the swing voters who decide elections. If the leader is running, the brain has a referent for unconsciously applying mood change as a basis for judgment. If the leader is not running, then the feelings arising from social mood changes have no political referent.

Practical Application

We think this study is useful for practical application. Do you want to go down in history as one of the best presidents ever? Try to get elected at an extreme in negative social mood—as evidenced by a major bottom in the stock market—and let the voters credit you for their ensuing change toward positive mood. It won't matter what your politics are. You can be socialistic, like Franklin Roosevelt, or you can be more of a free marketer, like Ronald Reagan. Both candidates gained office at nadirs in social mood and benefitted from the change toward positive mood that followed—as indicated by a rising stock market—and their stellar reputations have maintained ever since within their respective parties [see Chapter 17]. If you obtain office as social mood swings from negative to positive, the voters, and history, will love you. Or, suppose you are a first-term president, and the stock market is moving strongly downward heading into the reelection year, indicating a negative trend in social mood. In that case, you should step aside and let your party put up another candidate. There are several ways Machiavellian politicians could take advantage of this information. Thankfully, we doubt many will.

NOTES AND REFERENCES

[1] Both presidents sponsored sweeping new entitlements for medical services; both promoted uniform testing in education; both pushed for adopting a national identification card; both increased domestic spying; both ostracized related whistleblowers; both prosecuted the Drug War, Obama overriding state laws to do it; both leaped into wars in the Middle East, to which Obama added secret attacks by drones; both supported trillion-dollar bailouts of investment banks; neither closed the prison at Guantanamo Bay; and both operated secret courts under FISA—to name a few shared policies. Yet many voters supported the actions of only one of these two presidents, and condemned those of the other, depending on whether he was on the good or bad guys' team.

Chapter 4

The Dow, NYSE Composite and Intrade All Reflect Obama's Reelection Odds Accurately

Alan Hall

July 30, 2012 (TS)

Pollsters and pundits use a wide variety of indicators to predict the outcomes of U.S. presidential elections. They cite unemployment, GDP, the inflation rate, gas prices, surveys, the Hispanic vote, Electoral College simulations, gubernatorial races, inflation, the Chinese economy, European debt, opinions on gay marriage, the "Lichtman/DeCell formula" and even the divinations of Mexico's Grand Warlock, "Brujo Mayor."

Figure 1 plots three other election indicators. The top line is the Dow Jones Industrial Average, and the middle line is the broader NYSE Composite index. Because these indexes fluctuate in accordance with the aggregate optimism and pessimism of investors, they serve as indicators of social mood. The lower line plots real-money bets at Intrade.com on whether Barack Obama will be reelected President in 2012. Though the available history of Intrade data is brief, the similarity among these graphs fits the hypothesis that one motivator is behind them all. We believe that motivator is social mood.

Personal, political, ideological and sociological factors play roles in determining leaders' popularity, but socionomic causality often plays the lead role. Socionomics suggests that an optimistic society tends to propel the Dow Jones Industrial Average higher and revere its leader. A pessimistic society tends to bid down the DJIA and be disappointed in its leader. Intrade bettors participate in this dynamic. Chapter 16 of *The Wave Principle of Human Social Behavior* (1999) explained,

> The social psychology that accompanies a bull or bear market is the main determinant not only of how voters select a president but also of how they perceive his performance. Correlation with the stock market…suggests that social mood is by far the main determinant of presidential popularity.

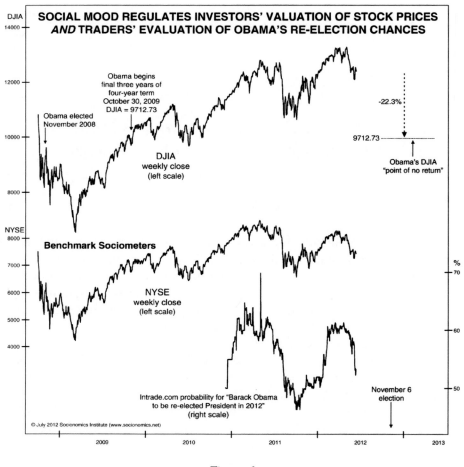

Figure 1

Voters then rationalize their unconsciously motivated decisions to keep or reject the incumbent. The economy fluctuates substantially in accordance with social mood, too, but it does so with a lag, making it less useful as a sociometer.

Our elections study set out to determine whether the socionomic model explains U.S. Presidential reelection outcomes. It did not seek to create an elections prediction model. Others may nevertheless wish to do so using the study's findings as a starting point.

Chapter 5

Who Will Win the November Election?

Robert R. Prechter

September 12, 2012 (EWT)

On September 7, a conservative columnist cited the weak unemployment numbers asked, "Given the state of the economy, by any historical standard, Barack Obama should be 15 points behind Mitt Romney. Why is he tied?" The answer is that presidential popularity is not due to "the economy, stupid"; it's due to social mood.

No specific election outcome is ever assured, but we can say that social mood has become much more positive during Mr. Obama's tenure as President, elevating his chances for reelection. All four of the stock-market durations used in our tests—currently dating from November 1, 2008, 2009, 2010 and 2011—are positive in both nominal and PPI-adjusted terms. Given the net inflation during this time, the PPI-adjusted measures are less positive. Through the close of September 12, 2012, the in-progress 4, 3, 2 and 1-year gains in the Dow are 43%, 36%, 20% and 14%. Those in the Dow/PPI are 29%, 25%, 14% and 15%. So, the in-progress, 3-year-period gains are 36% and 25%, respectively, both positive. Even though the economy remains weak, the three-year trend toward more positive social mood should have made voters less inclined to express bad feelings toward the leader. Reflecting this expectation, polls consistently show President Obama scoring high on the "likeability" scale despite widespread misgivings about his economic policies.

Chapter 6

The 2012 Presidential Election

Robert R. Prechter

November 16, 2012 (EWT)

Socionomics did a good job of calling the 2012 election. Our study showed that a positive trend in social mood over the final three years of a President's term helps his reelection chances, and a negative trend hurts them. We measure the change in social mood by the net change in the stock market.

The DJIA gained 34.8% from the close of Friday, October 30, 2009 through Wednesday, October 31, 2012. The PPI-adjusted Dow gained 24.1%. The market even tacked on another 0.5% to these measures in the four days going into Election Day. This large net gain in stock prices reflected a strong shift toward more positive social mood during the key years of President Obama's first term.

Stock market gains of this magnitude have often led to landslide victories for the incumbent as measured by popular vote, Electoral College vote, or both. Our study examined electoral landslide victories for incumbents at varying degrees of vote-tally spread: 50%, 40% and 20%. Landslide wins above each of these amounts were significantly linked to strong pre-election stock market rises.

Although the popular-vote spread in the latest election was narrow, Obama's 332 electoral votes represented 61.7% of the total, and Romney's 206 electoral votes represented 38.3% of the total. The electoral-vote spread was 23.4 percentage points, enough to qualify as a moderate landslide. Several news outlets used that term even before Florida confirmed its vote tally for Obama. In the end, Obama won ten of the eleven closely contested "swing" states. As far as we know, ours is the only academic study to suggest that the outcome would be a big win for Obama.

Does Polling Really Predict?

Polling is like asking someone what he's going to have for lunch today. He says, "A chicken sandwich." So pollsters "predict" he will have a chicken sandwich. Then they take a bow when they're right. How much "forecasting" is really going on?

Asking people what they are going to do right up to Election Day is nearly the same thing as counting votes. No wonder the results are reasonably accurate much of the time.

Even so, sometimes the person changes his mind and has a tuna sandwich, so the polling approach is far from foolproof. At times, it is shocking to see how inaccurate polls can be. Since the socionomic approach predicts reelections well without asking anyone how he plans to vote, it probably means we have figured out something important.

Consider, moreover, the cost/benefit ratio. Pollsters—both independent and partisan—spend tens of millions of dollars attempting to predict the outcome of elections by asking prospective voters for whom they will vote. Some of the resulting forecasts are right on; others are wrong. Isn't it better to have a way of predicting incumbents' reelection outcomes at least as well without having to ask a single person about his or her voting plans and without spending a dime?

Our study shows that when an incumbent is running, all you need for a reasonably accurate forecast is knowledge of socionomic causality and three minutes with a calculator. This year, very few of the number-crunchers anticipated the mild electoral-vote landslide for the incumbent. From what we have read, *New York Times* blogger Nate Silver and Emory University's Drew Linzer were the main exceptions. Yet our study did it, too. At no cost. Without polling a soul. This result shows the power of socionomic theory.

Did the Unemployment Rate Matter?

Our study also found that the unemployment rate has been irrelevant to reelection outcomes. In the 2012 election, this irrelevance applied once again.

Many pundits said that the unemployment rate would matter more than anything else to the outcome of the 2012 election. Up until the election, certain data miners generated much media ink by repeating a definitive-sounding statement: "Since 1940, no president presiding over an unemployment rate above 7.2% has won reelection." Their statement is accurate, but it nevertheless furthers a lie. Notice the sneaky caveats: "Since 1940" and "above 7.2%." Why did they choose that date and that percent?

Table 1 shows a record of U.S. presidents who ran for reelection at times when the unemployment rate was 7% or higher, and the results:

Year	President	Unemployment rate	Reelection Result
1936	F. Roosevelt	16.6%	won
1940	F. Roosevelt	14.5%	won
1976	Gerald Ford	7.5%	lost
1980	Jimmy Carter	7.8%	lost
1984	Ronald Reagan	7.2%	won
1992	George H.W. Bush	7.3%	lost

Table 1

So, prior to the 2012 election, the win/loss tally from 1936 was exactly equal: 3 wins, 3 losses. All six winners and losers, moreover, won or lost in landslides, so there was no hint from the data that a high unemployment rate has any effect on whatsoever the fate of incumbents.

No statistician would conclude that there is any one-sided significance in these numbers. So, how did the data-fitters make their widely reported claim accurate? They began by saying, "*Since* 1940." As you can see, by eliminating 1936 and 1940, they got rid of two winners. Then they added a careful cutoff: "*above 7.2%.*" That's how they got rid of the third winner (Reagan), whose rate was—you guessed it—exactly 7.2%. They kept the next *loser* (G.H.W. Bush), whose rate was 7.3%, just a tick higher. Their claim was accurate, but the implication was fraudulent. Obviously, it was deliberately so.

Given the outcome of the latest election, we can add one more line (temporarily using the unemployment figure from October):

2012	Barack Obama	7.9%	won

Do you think we'll soon see a claim that high unemployment is *good* for an incumbent? Let's hope not. After all, when we add the 1932 election to the above list, the score is still tied: 4 to 4.

1932	Herbert Hoover	24%	lost

Using the eight above-listed unemployment figures, the average unemployment rate for the four times the incumbent won is 11.6%, and for the four times the incumbent lost it is 11.7%. You can hardly get results more even than that.

Based on unemployment figures back to 1890 (courtesy of a Duke University posting) and the outcomes of past presidential elections, it seems safe to say that the reelection record for presidents in office with a 7%-or-higher unemployment rate is exactly tied (at 4 to 4) going back at least to 1889, a span of 123 years.

The primary lesson here (once again) is that exogenous-cause arguments don't work, so their proponents have to torture data to make them appear as if they do. Our publications have drawn this lesson several times, using various data series. Yet our work will never change most minds, because the mechanics paradigm and its exogenous-cause model of social change are people's commonsensical default, despite being dead wrong.

Hints That Voters' Mood Swung the Election

An editorialist wrote, "Incumbent presidents are tough to beat, but Barack Obama was about as vulnerable as they come. The economy is stagnant; his signature legislative achievement is unpopular; his party weathered sharp losses in the midterm elections." (AJC, 11/8) In other words, Obama was vulnerable on the basis of political *facts*. Such facts led George Will, Larry Kudlow, Dick Morris, Michael Barone and Newt Gingrich to predict electoral-college vote counts for Romney ranging from 300 to 330. In fact, it was Obama who got 332 electoral votes. Romney was vulnerable on the basis of facts, too. But swing voters don't bother with facts. They vote according to their *feelings*, and social mood influences those feelings in the aggregate.

Is that what happened this time? Let's review some anecdotal evidence. AP reported, "Gone are the days when President Barack Obama was seen as a youthful, messianic figure capable of magically curing the world's woes. *But he remains widely popular....*" (AP, 11/8) Focus on the key words in this next assessment: "According to exit polls conducted Tuesday, about 53 percent of voters *felt* Obama was more *in touch* with people like them than Romney was." (Gainesville *Times*, 11/8) Socionomics explains the source of such blather: It's a rationalization from voters who have credited the political leader with their experience of more positive mood during his tenure.

Europe has been so enamored of Obama that "Even Tom McGrath, president of Republicans Abroad France, conceded: 'It's clear that if they could vote, Europe would vote 80 percent for Obama.'" (AP, 11/8.) It's not just Europe, either:

> A BBC survey during the run-up to the election found remarkable support for an Obama second term. More than 21,000 people in

21 countries were questioned in July, August and September, with residents in all but one country backing Obama. Only Pakistan where Obama's heavy reliance on drone strikes has been unpopular, preferred Romney. (*ibid.*)

In other words, Obama's penchant for strafing and bombing civilians with drone planes could turn only the populace of one country against him, namely the one that he repeatedly attacked. That's the power of this incumbent's political Teflon, courtesy of a less negative global social mood in 2012 than in 2009.

Here is an interesting twist that I would not have anticipated: As theorized in our paper, voters unconsciously—based on their mood—tend to credit or blame a first-term President for economic trends during the final three years of his term. So, it is natural that voters have credited President Obama for improvements in the economy since 2009. Yet they have gone so far as to refrain from *also* pinning the recovery's weakness on him. According to an Associated Press-GfK poll conducted in August,

While Republicans have pushed to cast the sputtering economy as Obama's fault, Americans place their blame elsewhere. Fifty-one percent say George W. Bush deserves "almost all" or "a lot but not all" of the blame, while 31 percent said the same of Obama. (*Politico*, 8/25)

This seeming anomaly actually fits socionomic theory well. Positive social mood has caused voters to feel good about Obama, which in turn has prompted them to rationalize who is at fault for the slow-growing economy. Rationalization requires at least a flimsy basis in reality, and they have one: The economy was contracting severely as Bush left office and began expanding five months after Obama took over. It seems that their good feelings about Obama prompted them to deem Bush at fault for what could be perceived as the lingering effects of the former downtrend. The same thing probably happened in 1936. Even though the unemployment rate was 16% that year, voters no doubt blamed Roosevelt's predecessor, Hoover, for the lingering effects of the Great Depression, justifying their retention of the sitting President in a landslide vote. One could well argue that Obama, not the president who had been *retired* for nearly four years, was to blame for the slowest U.S. recovery on record. But objectivity doesn't matter much in this context. Many voters easily rationalize decisions based unconsciously on social mood.

Chapter 7

A Striking Lesson in the
Socionomic Causality of Political Trends

Robert Prechter

November 12, 2008 (EWT)

It's November 2008, and the U.S. has just held a presidential election, won by Barack Obama over Mitt Romney, following two terms by George W. Bush. Read this report carefully and fill in the blanks:

> Voters chose _____ to help navigate the country through the global financial meltdown, handing long-serving _____ an election defeat. The 47-year-old leader of the _____ party ousted _____'s _____ party after _____ years in office. _____ has promised a more ____-leaning government than _____'s, which for almost a decade made _____ a key policy issue. In a country where the environment is a mainstream political issue, _____ has vowed to _____ a gas-emission trading scheme. The economy fell into recession early this year, and the worldwide downturn is the most immediate problem. "Today, voters have spoken, and they have voted for change," _____ told supporters at a packed victory celebration. The global financial crisis means that the road ahead may well be a rocky one," _____ said. "Tomorrow, the hard work begins."

Now turn the page.

If you are an American, you know what words go in those blanks. Here is what you would expect to read:

> Voters chose <u>a liberal man of the people</u> to help navigate the country through the global financial meltdown, handing long-serving <u>right-wing President George W. Bush</u> an election defeat. The 47-year-old leader of the <u>Democratic</u> Party ousted <u>Bush</u>'s <u>Republican</u> party after <u>eight</u> years in office. <u>Obama</u> has promised a more <u>left</u>-leaning government than <u>Bush</u>'s, which for almost a decade made <u>war in Iraq</u> a key policy issue. In a country where the environment is a mainstream political issue, <u>Obama</u> has vowed to <u>initiate</u> a gas-emission trading scheme. The economy fell into recession early this year, and the worldwide downturn is the most immediate problem. "Today, voters have spoken, and they have voted for change," <u>Obama</u> told supporters at a packed victory celebration. The global financial crisis means that the road ahead may well be a rocky one," <u>Obama</u> said. "Tomorrow, the hard work begins."

Now turn the page to read the original article.

November 9, 2008 - WELLINGTON, New Zealand (AP)

New Zealanders chose a <u>wealthy, conservative</u> former financier Saturday to help navigate the country through the global financial meltdown, <u>handing long-serving left-wing Prime Minister Helen Clark a crushing election defeat</u>. John Key, the 47-year-old leader of the <u>conservative National Party</u>, swept easily to power in this South Pacific country of 4.1 million people, <u>ousting Clark's Labour party after nine years in office</u>. <u>New Zealand's farming-export-dependent economy</u> fell into recession early this year, and Key said the worldwide downturn is the most immediate problem for the country. "Today, <u>New Zealand</u> has spoken; in their hundreds of thousands, they have voted for change," <u>Key</u> told supporters at a packed victory celebration in the country's largest city, Auckland. "The global financial crisis means that the road ahead may well be a rocky one," <u>Key</u> said. "Tomorrow, the hard work begins."

Before being elected to parliament in 2002, <u>multimillionaire Key was a currency trader at Merrill Lynch</u>, working in the U.S. and Singapore. Key has promised a more <u>right</u>-leaning government than Clark's, which for almost a decade made <u>global warming</u> a key policy issue. In a country where the environment is a mainstream political issue, Key has vowed to <u>wind back</u> Clark's greenhouse-gas-emission trading scheme to <u>protect businesses from financial losses, and to reduce red tape he says entangle important dam projects</u>.

<u>Clark</u>...blamed a "time-for-a-change factor, and that took us out with the tide" for the election loss. "So with that it's over and out from me. Thank you <u>New Zealand</u> for the privilege of having been your <u>prime minister</u> for the last nine years. Kia ora Tatou," she said, reciting a farewell in the indigenous Maori language.

Does this not make socionomic causality crystal clear? For 20 years, I have argued as follows:

> When social mood waxes positive, as reflected by persistently rising stock prices, voters desire to retain the leader who symbolizes their upbeat feelings and who they presume helped cause the conditions attending them. When the social mood becomes more negative, as reflected by persistently falling stock prices, voters decide to throw out the incumbent who symbolizes their downbeat feelings and who they presume helped cause the conditions attending them. *The political policies of the incumbent and his challenger are irrelevant to this dynamic.* The key is a desire for change *per se*, not any particular type of change. The standard presumption has no explanation for reconciling the relationship between these phenomena.
>
> —*The Elliott Wave Theorist*, November 1999,
> reprinted in *Pioneering Studies of Socionomics*

(For charts and further commentary backing up this case, please see *The Wave Principle of Human Social Behavior*, pp. 273-281 and *Pioneering Studies in Socionomics*, pp. 57-58.)

Here we have two elections, concluded within five days of each other, in which voters *ousted* leaders of the right and left, respectively, and *elected* new leaders of the left and right, respectively. Cheering attendees at each victory party claimed to be celebrating new ideas—liberal ones in America and conservative ones in New Zealand—but all of it is a charade. First of all, the ideas are not new but as old as politics. Second, and more important, the new leaders' ideas, and in America even the challenger's racial heritage, were irrelevant. The only thing that mattered to the primitive portions of voters' brains in the aggregate was an overwhelming impulse to *change the leader*.

The newly elected leaders are within months of the same age. But otherwise they are remarkable for their differences. One new leader is anti-wealthy; the other is a millionaire financier. One leader pledges to initiate global-warming legislation; the other vows to reverse it. One leader is a liberal, the other a conservative. Amusingly, despite completely different ideas on political economics, both men claim to have been elected to fix the economy! And the people cheer and cheer.

The only thing that both elected candidates got right is that "People voted for change." The change *from* what and *to* what, however, did not matter to voters in the aggregate. This is how humanity shifts its political experience from freedom to socialism, from nationalism to internationalism, from religiousness to secularism, from meddling in other countries to leaving them alone. They unconsciously lurch from one leader to another, regardless of their policies. Each time, the solutions to whatever crises exist sound plausible to voters.

Election results stem from socionomic causes, but wins for specific political agendas are the result of chaotic forces and therefore little more than the luck of the draw. Sometimes the ideas are good, but usually they are bad. According to Paul MacLean (see *The Wave Principle of Human Social Behavior*, p. 281), herding and leader selection derive from the same primitive areas of the brain. Socionomics harnesses this knowledge. So can you.

Chapter 8

European Stock Markets Predicted European Elections

Alan Hall

July 30, 2012 (TS)

In January 2012, the Socionomics Institute posted its study of a strong statistical connection between incumbent U.S. presidents' winning/losing reelection bids and the U.S. stock market's prior net percentage change. Its paper, "Social Mood, Stock Market Performance and U.S. Presidential Elections: A Socionomic Perspective on Voting Results," has generated considerable media interest and is among the Social Science Research Network's ten most downloaded papers of the past twelve months. [Four months later, it reached the top three—Ed.]

Now the Institute is examining what swept heads of state from power in the latest elections all across Europe. We decided to compare recent European election results to each country's prior stock market performance.

There is no way to assess each country's experience using precisely the same methodology as the one employed in our U.S. study. Europe's various electoral systems differ in important ways from the United States' and from each other's. For example, some EU countries have both prime ministers and presidents; some leaders are elected and some appointed; and term lengths vary. For such reasons, it is difficult to formulate an apples-to-apples comparison in Europe.

Nevertheless, the evidence is compelling that voters in European countries, like those in the U.S., unconsciously credit or blame the national leader for their changes in mood, as reflected in the aggregate by each country's stock market. In other words, when the trend in mood is negative, they tend to vote their leader out of office; and when it is positive, they tend to vote for their leader to stay. This relationship appears to hold regardless of factors that most political analysts believe to be important.

How Each Country Fared in 2012

The authors of the U.S. study—Prechter, Goel, Parker and Lampert—found that stock market performance, especially during the three years prior to an election, was significantly predictive of a reelection's outcome. The authors surmised that voters tend to give the incumbents a pass for the first year of their first four-year term in office.

In the present review, we apply the same logic. That is, we compare the result of each recent election to that country's stock market performance over the term of that leader's office minus the first year. We do so in fifteen European countries that underwent elections. The bottom line is that, of the fifteen elections, fourteen outcomes unequivocally support the socionomic hypothesis, and the one remaining is compatible with it.

© July 2012 Socionomics Institute (www.socionomics.net)

Of 15 elections in Europe, 14 (shown in dark gray) conform to the socionomic hypothesis.

Elections That Conformed to Socionomic Expectations

1. UNITED KINGDOM

Sociometer: (FTSE): <u>Down</u> 14.25%.
Result: Prime Minister Gordon Brown <u>resigned</u>.

In mid-2008, during the initial third of the FTSE's plunge, members of Parliament began calling for Prime Minister Gordon Brown's resignation. He finally resigned in 2010 after two more years of stock market decline. *The Daily Mail* wrote, "Mr. Brown...has presided over Labour's worst defeat at the polls in decades.... He leaves with his record for economic 'prudence' in complete tatters." (May 12, 2010)

2. IRELAND

Sociometer: (ISEQ): <u>Down</u> 54.46%.
Result: Taoiseach Brian Cowen <u>resigned</u>.

Cowen's approval had plummeted to 8% in 2010, making him "the least popular incumbent politician in the history of Irish opinion polling," according to the news website www.thejournal.ie. *The Irish Independent* called Cowen the "worst Taoiseach in the history of the State." (December 8, 2010)

3. PORTUGAL

Sociometer: (BVLX): <u>Down</u> 23.12%.
Result: The Socialist government of Jose Socrates was <u>voted out</u>, and Socrates <u>resigned</u> from office.

4. GREECE

Sociometer: (ASE): <u>Down</u> 71.77%.
Result: Prime Minister George Papandreou <u>resigned</u>.

In addition, observers were stunned when the neo-nazi Golden Dawn Party [see Chapter 45] won 18 of Greece's 300 Parliamentary seats.

5. SPAIN

Sociometer: (IBEX): <u>Down</u> 11.67%.
Result: Prime Minister Jose Luis Rodriquez Zapatero called for early elections, <u>resigned</u> and said he would not run again.

The Telegraph reported, "Spain's ruling socialist party were reeling from an unprecedented battering in local elections Sunday as voters punished Prime Minister Jose Luis Rodriquez Zapatero for his handling of the economic crisis." (May 23, 2011)

6. ITALY

Sociometer: (FTSE MIB): Down 31.04%.
Result: Prime Minister Silvio Berlusconi, who was appointed to his second term on May 8, 2008, resigned to jeers on 16 November 2011.

  Prior to Berlusconi's resignation, Reuters covered the elections: "'What happened in Milan, Naples, Trieste, Cagliari, Novara and other centers resembles a revolution,' the somber business daily *Il Sole 24 Ore* said in the aftermath." (May 31, 2011)

7. FRANCE

Sociometer: (CAC 40): Down 37.27%.
Result: Voters ousted incumbent President Nicolas Sarkozy on May 6, 2012.

  The Financial Times detailed the French public's "hatred" of Sarkozy and noted that Sarkozy's defeat was a historic landmark. "Only one other president of the fifth republic—Valéry Giscard d'Estaing—has tried and failed to be reelected for a second term," the paper said. (April 19, 2012)

8. NETHERLANDS

Sociometer: (AEX): Down 0.38%.
Result: Prime Minister Mark Rutte resigned on April 23, 2012.

  The Economist wrote, "The results may point to a long-term polarisation of politics in the Netherlands, a country once renowned for its consensual model of decision-making." (March 4, 2011)

9. FINLAND

Sociometer: (HEX25): Down 2.76%.
Result: The government was reconfigured in the April 17, 2011 elections.

  The BBC reported, "Tampere University political analyst Ilkka Ruostet-saari told AFP news agency the election outcome was astonishing. 'The True Finns' [nationalist party] victory, surpassing every poll and every expectation of a drop on election day...plus the total collapse of the Centre—the whole thing is historic,' he said." (April 18, 2011)

10. DENMARK

Sociometer: (KAX): Down 15.38%.
Result: Prime Minister Lars Lokke Rasmussen resigned.

Denmark elected its first woman prime minister, Helle Thorning-Schmidt, on 15 September, 2011. The BBC reported, "Denmark's centre-left has won the country's general election, ending nearly a decade in opposition. ...Incumbent Lars Lokke Rasmussen has admitted defeat." (September 16, 2011)

11. LATVIA

Sociometer: (RIGSE): Down: 14.24%.
Result: Election results were mixed.

Andris Bērziņš defeated incumbent President Valdis Zatlers in a parliamentary vote on July 8, 2011. Yet Bērziņš re-appointed Prime Minister Valdis Dombrovskis on September 17, 2011. *The New York Times* wrote, "A pro-Russian party has gained the most votes in a snap parliamentary election in Latvia, with economic worries and anger over perceived government malfeasance trumping the anti-Russian sentiments." (September 18, 2011)

12. RUSSIA

Sociometer: (RTSI$): Up 219%.
Result: Incumbents prevailed.

After the Russian index soared upward on March 2, 2008, Dmitry Medvedev was elected President and Vladimir Putin was elected Prime Minister. They switched places on March 4, 2012, in a dual reelection of incumbents.

13. POLAND

Sociometer: (WIG): Up 13.47%.
Result: Prime Minister Donald Tusk won a second consecutive term in parliamentary elections on October 9, 2011.

Tusk and his party were the first government to be reelected since the fall of communism in Poland in 1989.

14. ESTONIA

Sociometer: (TALSE): Up 15.34%.
Result: The President re-nominated Prime Minister Andrus Ansip, the head of government, to his third term on April 6, 2011.

Only One Election Less Clearly Conformed to Socionomic Expectations

1. SWEDEN

Sociometer: (OMX): <u>Down</u> 6.8%.
Result: Voters <u>reelected</u> Prime Minister John Fredrik Reinfeldt.

The September 2010 general election in Sweden was the first one in almost a century that resulted in the reelection of a full-term center-right government. The minor net trend toward negative social mood nevertheless had some impact on voters. First, Reinfeldt failed to secure a majority. Second, as *The New York Times* reported under the headline, "Political Earthquake Shakes Up Sweden," "Elections on Sunday gave an anti-immigration party its first parliamentary seats and deprived the governing coalition of its majority, plunging the country into rare political instability." (September 20, 2010) Political instability in which no one receives a majority is a classic negative-mood outcome. In Sweden it was also a "rare" one.

Conclusion

We find that social mood is a more powerful determinant of European election outcomes than party loyalty, a candidate's charisma, or even right or left-wing ideology. The negative social mood this spring led to the dual ousting of Prime Minister Gordon Brown, a British Labour Party *liberal*, and President Nicholas Sarkozy, a French fiscal *conservative*. Similar results occurred across the board. [To see how social mood has affected the makeup of the European Parliament, see Chapter 46.]

These outcomes are in impressive conformity with socionomic theory. We doubt any other hypothesis of causality could match it for predictive success.

Chapter 9

Parliamentary Elections in Singapore

Mark Galasiewski

May 6, 2011 (APFF)

The fact that Singapore's constitution does not specify when elections must be held has helped the ruling People's Action Party (PAP) retain power since the nation gained political independence from Malaysia in 1959.

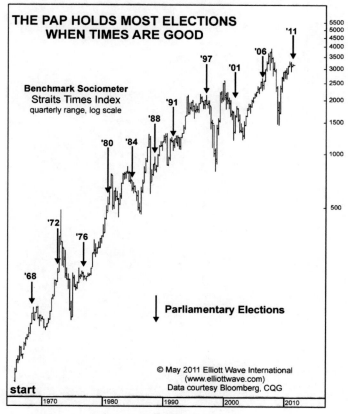

Figure 1

By convention, Singapore's leaders hold elections every several years, but the ability to choose their timing allows the PAP to conduct them during periods of rising stock prices and good economic performance, when social mood is trending positively, making voters more likely to retain incumbent leaders. Figure 1 shows that the PAP has held 10 of the 11 parliamentary elections after the Straits Times Index has rallied strongly. (In a lone exception, the 2001 election took place only five weeks after that year's low in stock prices). With the index now having more than doubled over the past two years, and with a parliamentary election historically overdue, it should come as no surprise that in late April PAP decided to hold elections on May 7.

Singapore's administrators have a reputation for managing the city-state's affairs well. It seems that the ruling party manages its politics just as shrewdly.

Chapter 10

Prime Ministerial Elections in Japan

Mark Galasiewski

September 2, 2011 (APFF)

Japan's parliament this week elected its sixth prime minister in five years. While conventional analysts cite the outgoing PM's supposed policy failures and dismal public opinion ratings as reasons for the change, socionomics offers a better reason at a glance. Figure 1 shows that from 1950

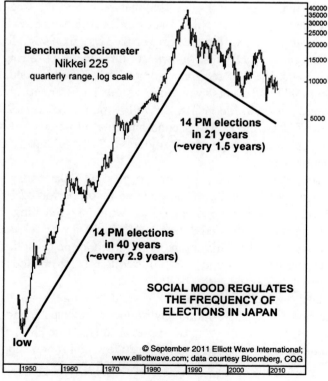

Figure 1

through 1989, when positive mood in Japan prompted a bull market in stocks, prime ministerial elections came up once every 2.9 years. Since then, as negative mood has prompted a bear market in stocks, elections have come around every 1.5 years, almost twice as often.

The more frequent ousters during this trend toward negative social mood are no coincidence. The same mood trends that cause stock prices to rise and fall also determine whether society tends to demand continuity or a change in its leadership.

From Centrism to Fracture

A shift in election frequency is not the only change that occurred after 1989. A tectonic shift simultaneously occurred in Japan's party politics.

Almost all PMs since the end of the Pacific War have been members of the Liberal Democratic Party (LDP), which was formed when the two dominant conservative parties—the Liberal Party and the Democratic Party—joined together in 1955. The mood of cooperation that attends positive mood trends unified the party at that time.

The negative mood trend since 1989 has seen the LDP fragment. The initial split occurred after the Nikkei stock index collapsed 63% from 1989 to 1992. A large faction within the party broke away in 1993 to form a new party, resulting in the LDP losing power for three years to a string of coalition governments. The LDP recovered somewhat as mood trended positively during 2003-2007 and voters awarded it with its largest majority since the positive mood period of the 1980s. But following the Nikkei's 2007-2009 decline, voters dealt the LDP a second and final blow when they gave a center-left opposition party—the Democratic Party of Japan (DPJ)—an outright majority by a landslide.

Following the opposition's victory, former PM Nakasone, whose term of office spanned the middle of the positive mood period of 1974-1989, called the event a "national opening on par with the wrenching social and political changes that followed defeat in the [Pacific] war." (*The New York Times*, January 30, 2010) This comment fits socionomic causality, because the negative mood that wrought the LDP's collapse also created the largest decline in stock prices since the 1940s.

The DPJ—which promised "hope" and "change"—has since also suffered during the negative-mood environment. In fact, the party has just chosen its third prime minister in two years. The Japanese PM's office door will continue to revolve speedily until positive social mood supports both a new bull market and a more stable political climate.

Chapter 11

Negative Mood in Australia Prompts
Ruling Party Turnover

Mark Galasiewski

October 4, 2013 / October 2, 2015 / July 1, 2016 (APFF)

Long term trends toward positive social mood, as indicated by lengthy bull markets in stocks, tend to coincide with continuity of political leadership—even political dynasties—whereas negative trends tend to accompany more frequent changes of leadership [see Chapter 10]. That relationship is especially true in parliamentary systems, because the timing of their elections is flexible, not fixed as in the U.S. presidential system.

When a society's mood is trending positively, its stock market booms, its economy performs well, and its voters are content to extend a presiding leader's time in office. But, during times of negative mood, the stock market falls, the economy slows or contracts, and parliaments sometimes call early or even immediate elections in response to pressures from constituents brought on by negative social mood, resulting in higher leadership turnover. Consider these examples:

- Japan changed its Prime Minister 14 times during the 40-year trend toward positive social mood from 1949 to 1989 (on average, every 2.9 years). Japan changed its PM 15 times during the 23-year trend toward negative social mood from 1990 to 2012 (on average, every 1.5 years), twice as often.

- Australia changed its Prime Minister five times in the nine years of negatively trending mood between 1966 and 1974 (on average, every 1.8 years). Australia changed its Prime Minister only four times in the 33 years of positively trending mood from 1975 to 2007 (on average, every 8.3 years). Australia has already changed its PM four times in the six years since the 2007 high to the present (on average, every 1.5 years). Changes during negative mood trends have occurred five times as often.

Social mood clearly regulates the frequency of elections in Australia; positive mood lowers it, and negative mood raises it.

Next let's investigate how one of the longest periods of negative social mood in Australia's history has reversed the fortunes of the Australian Labor Party since an interim high point for the party in early 2010 (see Figure 1).

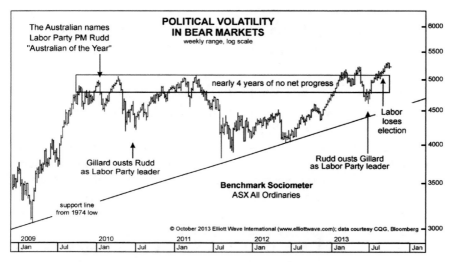

Figure 1

In January 2010, with the All Ordinaries having risen nearly a year from their 2009 low, Australia's national newspaper, *The Australian*, named Labor Party Prime Minister Kevin Rudd "Australian of the Year"—an honor equivalent to *Time* Magazine's "Person of the Year." We called the award a sell signal for Australian stocks. The All Ords would make no net progress for the next three and a half years.

Five months later, just prior to the 2010 Federal Elections, with both the All Ords and Rudd's popularity plunging, Deputy PM Julia Gillard conspired with other Labor party leaders to install herself as Prime Minister in place of Rudd. We interpreted that event as a sign of extremely negative social mood and used it to forecast a significant intermediate-term low in the Aussie stock market. The All Ords bottomed two trading days later and rallied 20% over the next several months.

The Labor Party under Gillard managed to cling to power after the 2010 elections, but only as a minority government. As Australian stocks moved net sideways for three more years, Gillard's tenuous support eroded even further. When negative mood prompted stocks to plunge to their June

2013 lows, Rudd got his revenge by successfully challenging Gillard for the party's leadership. Two days later we wrote in APFF, "Rudd's overthrow of Gillard should mark another significant low in Australian social mood and stocks." From the day of Gillard's ousting, stocks rallied 10% going into September's federal elections.

But the more important factor for Australian politics overall was that Australia's stock market had made almost no net progress for nearly four years at the time of the 2013 federal elections. We wrote that month,

> Ralph Nelson Elliott observed that sideways markets can wear participants down just as much as declining markets can. So, with the All Ords only now emerging from a multiyear sideways move, social mood in Australia remains quite negative. And that explains why the incumbent Labor Party's prospects look increasingly bleak with just a week to go before the nation holds its general elections.

Sure enough, the opposition coalition trumped the incumbent Labor Party handily. Social mood leading into the 2013 elections was so negative after years of stagnation that voters simply wanted regime change.

October 2015: Negative Social Mood Mauls Another Prime Minister

After 18 months of relative stability, the ASX has fallen hard, and the anti-incumbency trend in Australian politics has claimed another victim. In mid-September, Malcolm Turnbull successfully challenged Tony Abbott

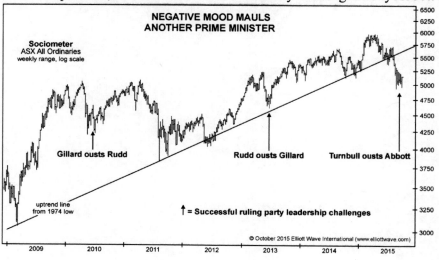

Figure 2

for leadership of the ruling Liberal Party, thereby turning over the prime minister's chair for the fifth time in eight years. As Figure 2 shows, three of those five turnovers have occurred because of ambushes from within each prime minister's own party. These ambushes have been a particularly good indicator of negative extremes in social mood. In light of the precedents of 2010 and 2013, this most recent turnover should be intermediate-term bullish for the ASX All Ordinaries.

July 1, 2016: As Yet, No Significant Change in Mood

The social conditions that have hindered progress in the stock market have also made incumbency a political liability for several years now, and the current juncture is no different. Australia has had five prime ministers in six years, and, ahead of the federal elections scheduled for July 2, 2016, polls point to another tightly contested race. No matter which parties form the government after the election, Australian politics are likely to remain fractious until a new positive mood gives rise to both a bull market in stocks and a more middle-of-the-road political consensus.

Chapter 12

Socionomic Causality in Brazilian Elections

Peter Kendall

September 26, 2003 (EWFF)

In preparation for a recent lecture tour of Brazil, Santa Fe Institute scholar John Casti asked if our team at Elliott Wave International could use Brazil's recent history to create a chart that would illustrate how social mood shapes social events. We dove in, and with the help of some of Casti's Brazilian colleagues we brought to light a socionomic profile in which economic and political developments in Brazil have shifted almost perfectly in concert with the country's benchmark sociometer, the Bovespa.

The only missing element was any evidence that 2000—when the Bovespa topped—was a peak time for positive social actions. Based on the headlines and the recollections of Brazilians, the best of times was definitely 1997. In that year, Brazil received its first long-term syndicated loan since the Latin American debt crisis of 1982, the constitution was changed to allow free market crusader Henrique Cardoso a second term as president, and a host of pro-market edicts made Brazil "one of the most attractive emerging markets." Was the seemingly premature conflagration of positive news an exception to socionomic causality?

No, it wasn't. We realized that the discrepancy was due to the fact that the higher Bovespa in 2000 was due to rapidly inflating reals, the Brazilian currency. By simply shifting to a far less inflated, dollar-based Bovespa, the events of 1997 took their rightful place as manifestations of peak positive mood occurring right at the top of Brazil's 1990s bull market. Using this more accurate sociometer, Figure 1 tells the story of a classic socionomic cycle from the impeachment of Brazilian president Fernando Collor near the stock market bottom of late 1992 to Brazil's coming of age in 1997 to the ousting of the ruling free-market party at the October 2002 stock market low.

At that bottom, an angry Brazilian populace elected Lula DaSilva, the first leftist candidate to gain the presidency in Brazil's history. In a telling nod to the ensuing trend toward more positive social mood, however, DaSilva

Figure 1

has done little to disrupt earlier free market reforms. In recent weeks, as the inflation-adjusted Bovespa has charged to a new high for the rebound, DaSilva compatibly shifted his actions. His administration has enacted pension reforms and deficit reduction schemes that will reputedly restore investor confidence. At this month's global trade talks, DaSilva even turned the tables on the G7 countries in demanding the elimination of their agricultural subsidies, a far cry from the leftist stances that earned him his reputation.

Chapter 13

Social and Political Troubles in Brazil

Chuck Thompson and Alan Hall

April 29, 2016 (TS)

A five-year trend toward negative social mood is wreaking political, financial and social havoc on Brazil, which is scheduled to host the Summer Olympic Games in August. There has been a rout in the stock market, the worst recession in a generation, scandals, presidential impeachment and even an epidemic. All these developments have resulted from a long trend toward negative social mood.

As we noted last year, the nation's president, Dilma Rousseff, has become a "textbook study of the political and economic consequences of negative mood on formerly adored public figures."[1] As *The Wave Principle of Human Social Behavior* explained, social mood is—among other factors [see Chapter 4]—the "main determinant" of presidential popularity:

> What a leader does is mostly acausal with respect to the public's opinion of him. There are two reasons for this fact. First, his actions, despite their endless analysis in the press, do little to affect his popularity. Second, his popularity is dependent upon a social mood over which he can exercise no countertrend influence.[2]

Rousseff was elected, with 56% of the vote,[3] to her first four-year term as Brazil's president in October 2010, just days before a major top in the Sao Paulo Stock Exchange (see Figure 1). Consumer confidence likewise was elevated (see Figure 2). Unemployment that year fell to a record low of 6.7%, and the country's economy recorded its fastest growth since 1985.[4] All of these events were products of a strongly positive social mood.

Since then, a trend toward negative mood has reversed all these conditions. The Sao Paulo Stock Exchange has trended lower and is now down 27%. Consumer confidence has plummeted, and unemployment averaged 8.5% last year[5] as the country lost 1.5 million jobs.[6] Brazil is in the midst

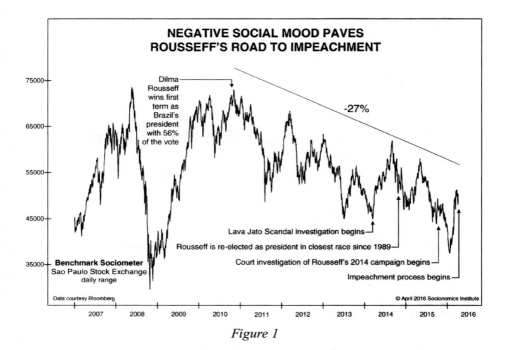

Figure 1

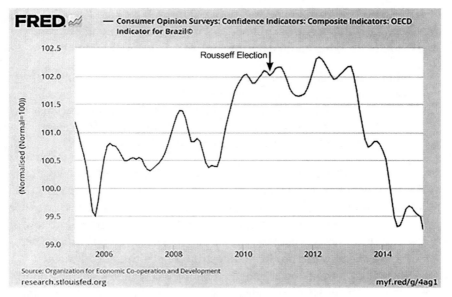

Figure 2

of its longest economic downturn since the 1930s.[7] Its economy shrank 3.8% in 2015 and is expected to shrink 3.5% this year.[8]

While Rousseff defied the odds in 2014 to win reelection, it was the country's closest race since 1989,[9] and her popularity during a second term has plummeted. In February 2015, her approval rating crashed to 23%.[10] Last month, only 10% of survey respondents rated the government as good or very good.[11] Anti-government protesters took to the streets on multiple occasions last year, and in March 2016, an estimated 3 million Brazilians participated in the biggest-ever protests calling for Rousseff's removal.[12]

Negative social mood is a "natural chemical for ripening scandals, and the taste for them," observed Peter Kendall in the February 1997 issue of *The Elliott Wave Theorist.*[13] In October, Brazil's highest electoral court began investigating allegations that Rousseff financed her 2014 campaign with donations from companies involved in a corruption scandal. If the court finds her guilty, it could demand new elections or even name Aecio Neves, the runner-up, as the winner.[14]

In addition, a committee in Brazil's lower house has investigated Rousseff on charges of using state banks to fill a budget shortfall—a procedure prohibited by the country's fiscal responsibility law. The committee recommended impeachment, and at a time when Rousseff needed the support of her political allies most, her governing coalition in the lower house fell apart. In March, the Democratic Movement Party dropped out of the coalition.[15] This month, two smaller parties dropped out.[16]

On April 17, a majority of lower house members voted to impeach Rousseff. If the Senate accepts the impeachment case, Rousseff would step down temporarily until her fate is decided.[17] The normal procedure would be for Vice President Michel Temer to assume the presidency, but a judge in Brazil's Supreme Federal Court ruled that the legislature must also begin impeachment proceedings against Temer, who faces the same budget-fixing charges as Rousseff.[18]

Rousseff and Temer are not the only casualties of the trend toward negative mood in Brazil. The country is also in the midst of a massive scandal known as Operação Lava Jato (Operation Car Wash), which involves allegations that construction companies obtained lucrative contracts by paying large kickbacks to politicians and to executives of Petrobras, Brazil's state-owned oil company.[19] *The New Yorker* reported,

> Every day seems to bring news of another high official under investigation, another corrupt arrangement uncovered, another grant of immunity in exchange for information…. There are now almost

two-dozen separate investigations under way under the broad rubric
of the Lava Jato scandal.[20]

Investigations have resulted in the jailing of almost 40 politicians,
business people and black-market money dealers. Prosecutors are also investigating the leaders of both chambers of Brazil's legislature and Brazil's
former president, Luiz Inacio Lula da Silva (known as "Lula"), who allegedly accepted a vacation home from a Brazilian construction company that
received generous contracts from Petrobras. Rousseff attempted to appoint
Lula as her chief of staff, which would have partially shielded him from
prosecution, but a judge suspended the appointment.

Negative mood and a bear market in oil have put the squeeze on Petrobras, too. On March 21, the company reported a quarterly loss of $10.2
billion, its largest ever.[21]

The country's public health situation is in turmoil. In the inaugural
issues of *The Socionomist* in May and June 2009 [see Chapter 52 of *Socionomic Studies of Society and Culture*, 2017], Alan Hall explored the
relationship between negative social mood and epidemic disease across a
200-year history. He warned of a "looming season of susceptibility" and
identified mosquito-borne diseases as a threat on the horizon.[22] He focused
on Brazil in the December 2015 issue, noting that the country's negative
mood is "fostering unsanitary conditions, which pose health threats." These
threats include the mosquito-borne Zika virus, which could infect as many
as four million people in the Americas, according to the World Health Organization.[23] Another team of researchers claimed that about 2.17 billion
people around the world live in areas that are suitable for transmission of
the virus, and one of them is Brazil.[24]

Disease is but one concern as the Olympics approach. Brazil's Olympics budget was cut by $500 million in January, raising doubts about the
country's ability to complete the construction of venues before the Summer
Games open in August. The acting governor of Rio de Janeiro said of the
area's finances, "This is the worst situation I've seen in my political career.
I've never seen anything like it."[25] On March 31, the country's sports minister, George Hilton, resigned.

Demand for tickets has been low, and half the seats remain unsold.
Ricardo Leyser, the country's new sports minister, said the government
might end up buying tickets and distributing them to public schools.[26] Even
if the government manages to fill the venues with schoolchildren, the dark
cloud of negative social mood and its effects are lingering over the event.

NOTES AND REFERENCES

[1] Thompson, C. (2015, September). Global Mood Gets Darker. *The Socionomist.*

[2] Prechter, R. (1999). *The Wave Principle of Human Social Behavior* (p. 273). Gainesville, GA: New Classics Library.

[3] Brazil Elects Dilma Rousseff as First Female President. (2010, November 1). *BBC News.*

[4] Besta, S. (2011, January 27). Brazil Unemployment Drops to Record Low in 2010. *International Business Times.*

[5] Biller, D. (2016, March 15). Brazil's Unemployment Jumps in 2015, Adding to Rousseff's Woes. *Bloomberg.*

[6] Romero, S. (2016, April 3). Insider's Account of How Graft Fed Brazil's Political Crisis. *The New York Times.*

[7] Hume, T. (2016, March 31). Brazil in Crisis: Five Reasons President Dilma Rousseff Should Be Worried. *CNN World.*

[8] Gillespie, P. (2016, March 31). Brazil: Economic Collapse Worse Than Feared. *CNN Money.*

[9] Why Dilma Rousseff won. (2014, October 27).

[10] Rousseff Approval Rating Plummets After Mass Brazil Protest. (2015, March 18). *Newsmax.*

[11] Rousseff Approval Near Lows as Impeachment Vote Looms in Brazil. (2016, March 30). *Newsmax.*

[12] Flynn, D., & Soto, A. (2016, March 14). Record Brazil Protests Put Rousseff's Future in Doubt. Reuters.

[13] Kendall, P. (1997, February). Cultural trends: Politics and the Positive Social Mood. *The Elliott Wave Theorist.*

[14] Galvao, A. (2015, October 6). Rousseff Worries Grow as Brazil Court Opens Case on Campaign. *Bloomberg.*

[15] Garcia-Navarro, L. (2016, March 29). Brazil's President in Further Danger of Being Ousted. NPR.

[16] Brazil's Dilma Rousseff Loses Another Coalition Partner. (2016, April 14). *Al Jazeera.*

[17] Jacobs, A. (2016, April 17). Brazil's Lower House of Congress Votes for Impeachment of Dilma Rousseff. *The New York Times.*

[18] Jelmayer, R., & Lewis, J.T. (2016, April 5). Brazil Judge: Start Impeachment Process Against Vice President. *The Wall Street Journal.*

[19] See endnote 6.

[20] Lemann, N. (2016, March 30). The Collapse of Dilma Rousseff, the Richard Nixon of Brazil. *The New Yorker.*

[21] Reuters. (2016, March 22). Petrobras Posts Record Loss as Oil Price Slump Forces Writedowns. *CNBC*.

[22] Hall, A. (2009, June). A Socionomic View of Epidemic Disease. Part II: Stress, Physiology, Threats and Strategies. *The Socionomist*.

[23] Miles, T., & Nebehay, S. (2016, January 28). WHO Says Zika Virus Spreads Explosively, 4M Cases Forecast. *AOL News*.

[24] Fox, M. (2016, April 19). New Map Finds 2 Billion People at Risk of Zika Virus. *NBC News*.

[25] Durden, T. (2016, March 31). Olympics in Doubt as Brazil Sports Minister Quits, Rio Governor Says "This is the worst situation I've ever seen." *Zero Hedge*.

[26] Wattles, J. (2016, April 4). Tickets to the 2016 Olympics Aren't Selling, and Brazil is Scrambling to Boost Demand. *CNN Money*.

Chapter 14

Social Mood and the Fortunes
of Four Politicos

Alan Hall

July 17, 2013 (TS)

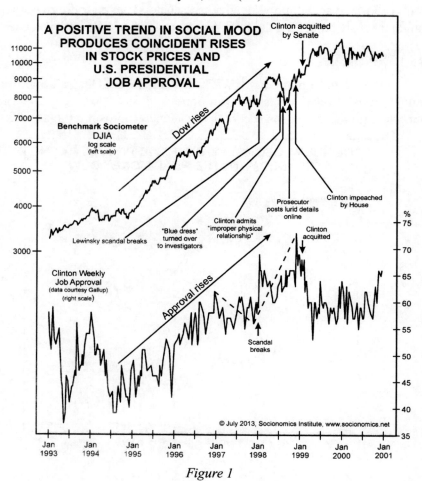

Figure 1

Positive Social Mood Coated Bill Clinton in Teflon

Figure 1 shows that the upward trend in President Bill Clinton's job approval ratings accompanied the positive trend in social mood during his presidency as indicated by a strongly rising stock market. Clinton's approval peaked in December 1998, between positive extremes in two important sociometers: the April 1998 peak in the Value Line Composite index (not shown) and the January 2000 peak in the Dow.

Note that some of the most serious events in the Monica Lewinsky sex scandal followed setbacks in the DJIA, one of which was the largest downturn of Clinton's presidency. As the Dow recovered, so did Clinton's approval ratings. Then, despite a $70-million prosecution of perjury and obstruction of justice charges against Clinton, the Senate acquitted the President as positive social mood heightened senators' desire to forgive while simultaneously propelling the stock market to a historically high valuation.

Bush and Obama

Figures 2 and 3 plot George W. Bush's and Barack Obama's approval ratings, respectively, versus the Dow Jones Industrial Average valued in ounces of gold. As you can see, both presidents' approval ratings trended

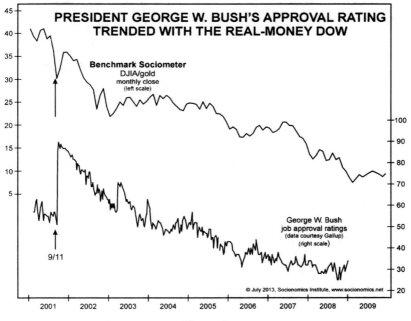

Figure 2

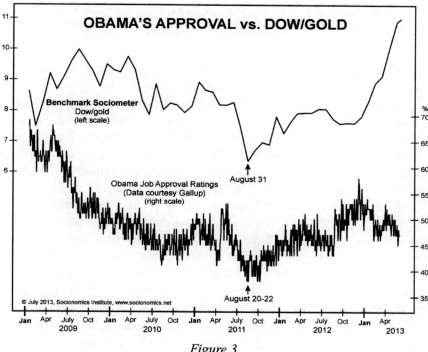

Figure 3

similarly to the Dow/gold ratio. This sociometer hit a low in August 2011 along with Obama's approval ratings, and both measures have trended mostly upward since.

Presidential approval ratings generally tend to trend lower during a President's term of office.[1] We surmise that the more a president's popularity bucks this inherent drift, as happened with FDR and Clinton, the more likely it is that a strongly positive social mood trend is under way. Social mood, as recorded by the stock market, should continue to regulate Obama's approval ratings throughout the remainder of his second term.

Mark Sanford: Political Phoenix

Former two-term South Carolina Governor Mark Sanford's fall from grace in 2009 led many pundits to conclude his political career was over. But on May 7, 2013 he won a seat in the U.S. Congress. The next day, flabbergasted, *The Washington Post* asked,

> The central question we and everyone else is asking the day after is how the hell did he pull it off? How did a governor who left office

in 2010 dogged by his admission of an extramarital affair who then faced trespassing charges from his ex-wife during the campaign wind up winning?[2]

Socionomics answers that question simply and concisely: Sanford, a former incumbent, rode to his comeback victory upon a strongly positive social mood trend. That trend also disadvantaged his non-incumbent opponent.

Sanford's career has tracked social mood for a decade, as depicted in Figure 4. He got his start by unseating an incumbent made vulnerable by a negative social mood extreme in 2002. He was reelected in 2006 during a strongly positive mood trend. Following the largest collapse in our benchmark sociometer since 1932, scandal rocked his career.

As social mood has trended toward the positive over the past three years, his Teflon returned. The protection was so strong that Sanford, a Republican in a conservative state, survived even the glowing endorsement of Larry Flynt, publisher of the pornographic *Hustler* magazine. Flynt wrote, "[Governor Sanford's] open embrace of his mistress in the name of love, breaking his sacred marriage vows, was an act of bravery that has drawn my support."

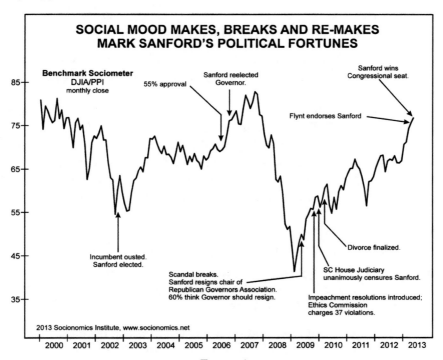

Figure 4

In its post-election analysis, *The Washington Post* tried to answer its own question ("How the hell did he pull it off?") with standard exogenous-cause analysis. The newspaper wrote that Sanford won because: (1) he ran in a Republican district; (2) he was the better candidate; (3) he worked hard; and (4) his campaign team was outstanding. But such elements become plausible causes only after the fact. The *Post* marveled, "Mark Sanford's victory…puts an exclamation point on one of the most remarkable comebacks in political history." One should also marvel at its underlying cause: an accommodating social mood.

Marion Barry, "Mayor For Life"

Figure 5 charts Marion Barry's tumultuous political career. As an upstart challenger, he ousted an incumbent and was elected mayor of

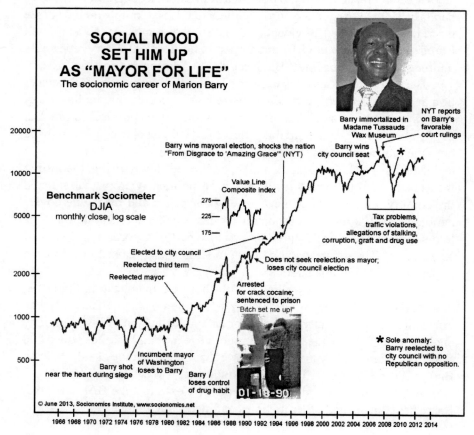

Figure 5

Washington D.C. in 1978, near the end of the negative mood period of 1966-1982. He was reelected as an incumbent three more times, each during a positive trend in social mood. He also won seats on the city council three times, two of which were during positive mood trends. One, anomalously, was during the negative mood trend of 2008, but in that election Barry garnered the fewest votes of any contest in his career, winning only because he faced no Republican opposition.

Barry's travails during times of negative social mood are equally instructive. In 1977, he survived a gunshot wound near the heart when radicals seized a government building. The event made him a hero and set up his initial mayoral victory the next year.

Since then, setbacks in Barry's career as an incumbent have corresponded with setbacks in our benchmark sociometer. In 1987, the year the stock market crashed, Barry, by his own admission, lost control of his drug habit. In 1990, during a deep drop in the Value Line Composite index (see insert in Figure 5), the FBI videotaped him smoking crack at the Vista Hotel. Lured there by a former girlfriend turned FBI informant, Barry repeatedly muttered his infamous line, "Bitch set me up," during his arrest.[3]

Barry served six months in prison before deciding not to seek reelection as mayor. After a short, sharp stock market correction, he lost a city council election. As a result, most people wrote off his political future. But as social mood edged toward the positive in 1992, he clawed his way back onto the city council.

Then in 1994, as the stock market continued slowly rising, the former incumbent won a fourth term as mayor, a political victory that stunned the country and dominated newspaper front pages and magazine covers nationwide. "We moved a mountain of despair that was in our way," he told supporters at a "wild and noisy victory party," according to *The New York Times*.[4] The greatest stock mania in U.S. history kicked into an even higher gear two months later.

On July 18, 2007, just three months before a major top in the DJIA, *The Washington Post* reported, "Washington's new Madame Tussauds wax museum is giving the city's Mayor for Life an extension of his seemingly endless reign."[5] To decide whom to immortalize in wax, Tussauds polled 600 Washingtonians and found, "People were laughing, but they said, 'Marion Barry, Marion Barry.' … It was overwhelming. It was a landslide."

As social mood trended toward a positive extreme, the *Post* wrote that Barry beat out several other notable candidates, including:

Cal Ripken, Al Gore, Denzel Washington, Carl Bernstein, Halle Berry, Martin Sheen, Marilyn Monroe, Nancy Reagan and Oprah Winfrey for the honor.... Barry will be joining 49 others, including American forefathers—Washington, Jefferson and Lincoln—plus Bill and Hillary Clinton, both George Bushes, John and Jackie Kennedy, Ronald Reagan and other political names; civil rights leaders Martin Luther King Jr., Rosa Parks and Malcolm X; and such media hotshots as Bob Woodward and Katie Couric. "I'll be among the greats of the world," Barry said.

In August 2007, *The New York Times* wrote, "A pair of courthouse victories this summer—an acquittal on a drunken driving charge and a favorable ruling in connection with a tax-evasion case—has only added to an air of invincibility."[6]

When social mood is trending negatively, nearly all incumbent leaders lose popularity. When the trend in mood is positive, almost nothing can shake their elevated images.

NOTES AND REFERENCES

[1] Wikipedia, "United States Presidential Approval Rating," graphs.

[2] Cillizza, C., & Sullivan, S. (2013, May 8). How Mark Sanford Won. *The Washington Post.*

[3] Thompson, T., & Walsh, E. (1990, June 29). Jurors View Videotape of Barry Drug Arrest. *The Washington Post.*

[4] Janofsky, M. (1994, September 14). The 1994 Campaign: The Comeback Man in the News; From Disgrace to 'Amazing Grace': Marion Shepilov Barry Jr. *The New York Times.*

[5] Johnson, D., & Roberts, R. (2007, July 18). Washington's Mayor for Life to be Truly Immortalized—In Wax. *The Washington Post.*

[6] Sabar, A. (2007, August 8). Marion Barry to be in Wax Museum. *The New York Times.*

Chapter 15

In France, Sarkozy's Approval
Ratings Track the CAC 40

Alan Hall

May 30, 2008 (EFF)

Elliott Wave International has often demonstrated that the popularity of political leaders correlates with stock market trends. When social mood trends positively, a generally confident and happy populace bids up stock prices and judges its leaders favorably; in times of negative mood, it's the opposite. France's leader has been subject to the same dynamic.

Nicolas Sarkozy was elected president of France in 2006 as the CAC 40 was rising. At that time, he enjoyed the highest approval ratings since François Mitterrand's in 1990 and was even heralded as the new Napoleon.

Sarkozy's fortunes reversed when the downturn in stocks signaled a negative social mood. That change brought opposition to his policies and proposals, disgust with his overexposed private life, defeat for his political party in municipal elections and a disparaging nickname: "President Bling Bling."

Figure 1 offers another illustration of the fact that no matter how adroit a politician may be, he is nearly always at the mercy of social mood. Sarkozy could not have avoided all the damage to his popularity, but perhaps if he had known to keep track of his country's benchmark sociometer, he could have tempered it. Whatever the objective merit of his ambitious efforts to rein in social entitlements, expand the 35-hour work-week and increase the eligibility age for the full state pension, he was swimming for nearly a year against a subjective, judgmental tide.

Sarkozy's approval rating fell by 13 points in January 2008 during the CAC 40's steepest plunge since 2003. On February 7, *The Economist* wrote, "Nearly nine months into his presidency, a majority (55%) of the French have 'a negative opinion' of him...." Only Jacques Chirac's 9-month popularity plunge—which ended in February 1996 along with nearly five years of languishing prices in the CAC 40—matches Sarkozy's. On May 1, *The Economist* declared that Sarkozy's presidency has resembled a "play in three strangely disconnected acts. In Act One, he was electrifying.... In Act Two...he was mortifying.... In Act Three...he is dissatisfying." In that one description, you can discern the effects of social mood in wave 5 up, wave A down, and then wave C down, in which Sarkozy's approval ratings fell "lower than any recorded in the first 12 months of a presidency during the 50-year-old Fifth Republic."

A 28% drop in the CAC 40 yielded a 43% drop in Sarkozy's approval rating, from 65% in July 2007 to 37% in April 2008. The rebound from the CAC 40's March bottom has coincided with a small lift, but his popularity remains near its previous low, an indication that negative social mood continues to hold sway.

The waves of social mood that generate bull and bear markets in stocks also buffet the images of leaders. Elected officials unwittingly agree to ride these waves when they run for office. If they were to recognize them for what they are, they would have a better chance of navigating the swells and troughs.

Chapter 16

France's President Ousted in Runoff

Alan Hall

May 7, 2012 (TS)

Nicholas Sarkozy's May 6 loss to socialist candidate Francois Hollande made him the first one-term French president since 1981, near the end of a 16-year period of negative social mood.

"Wait!" you protest, "Is this the same Sarkozy whom *The Economist* cited as 'France's Chance' just a few years ago and showed him dressed as Napoleon on a rearing horse? *What happened?*"

Social mood happened. Figure 1 shows that in the five years since Sarkozy was elected in 2007, France's benchmark sociometer, the CAC 40 index, shed nearly 50% of its value. Our recent study of U.S. elections

Figure 1

[Chapter 2] proposed that voters choose whether to oust or re-elect an incumbent president "in accordance with trends in social mood." We explained further, "An increasingly positive social mood produces a rising stock market as well as votes for the incumbent, and an increasingly negative social mood produces a falling stock market as well as votes against the incumbent."

Since Sarkozy took office, the CAC has lost 49% of its value. This strongly negative trend in French social mood spelled Waterloo for France's modern Bonaparte.

Chapter 17

One Way To Become a
Revered Historical Figure

Robert R. Prechter

August 13, 2004 (EWT)

A good way to get one's portrait on the face of U.S. coins and notes is to become President near the start of a big bull market in stock prices. The most revered American politicians held office early in positive social mood periods, when the national feeling of triumph over adversity was the strongest. George Washington (featured on the $1 dollar bill and quarter), Abraham Lincoln ($5 dollar bill and penny) and Franklin Roosevelt (dime) are among the most honored presidents because their images are forever linked to major shifts from negative to positive social mood, as indicated by major shifts in the stock market's trend from down to up.

The latest example of the benefit that resonates from being the leader when positive mood takes hold of a society is the reaction to Ronald Reagan's death in June 2004. In terms of the nominal Dow, he took office at an upturn of Cycle degree, but in Dow/gold terms, it was an upturn of Supercycle degree, occurring at the beginning of wave (b), as shown in Figure 1.

Eulogists say that Reagan single-handedly "won the Cold War" and "transformed our nation's psyche with his optimism and positive vision." Figure 1 shows that the nation's psyche—all on its own—had its most dramatic reversal ever the year he was elected. The shift toward more positive social mood is a big reason why so many people love him. Nearly two decades ago, the January 1987 issue of *The Elliott Wave Theorist* used socionomic causality to predict, "President Reagan will eventually exit as the most loved president in U.S. history." That may not turn out to be precisely correct, but it's close, as these newspaper clippings attest:

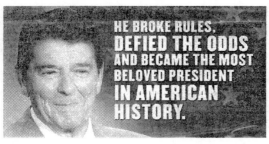

But even *The New York Times*, the media's most anti-conservative bastion, said Monday: "After more than a decade of political mean-spiritedness, we have to admit that [Reagan's] collegiality and good manners are beginning to look pretty attractive. He will almost certainly be ranked among the most important presidents of the 20th century, forever linked with the triumph over communism abroad and the restoration of faith in free markets at home."

–AJC, June 9, 2004

Mourners certainly agreed with those assessments. In a week-long ritual, long lines of people waited hours for the privilege of viewing President Reagan's coffin. "He was probably the most human of any president we've ever had," said a Hollywood celebrity. Republicans to this day envoke his name to curry favor.

Reagan was a fine president, but the drive to put his likeness on the $10 bill was primarily a testament to the power of the turn toward positive social mood that took place while he was in office. Chances are that Reagan won't be remembered for arriving at the right moment in the progress of the waves of social mood, but that is an important element of his treasured place in history, as it was for Washington, Lincoln and Roosevelt.

Figure 1

Chapter 18

A Reelection Nuance:
Bull Markets vs. Bear Market Rallies

Robert R. Prechter

September 12, 2012 (EWT)

A Nuance: Bull Market Advances vs. Bear Market Rallies

The Elliott wave model offers the best context in which to understand social mood. We excluded discussions of nuances within the model in our elections paper [Chapter 2], but they can be significant. Under the Wave Principle, stock market advances can be part of a larger rising wave or part of a corrective (down or sideways) wave. When prices rally within a bear market, as they did in 1842-1852, 1966-1968, 1970-1973 and 2002-2007, the social mood trend is not full-on positive but mixed, reflecting opposing trends at adjacent degrees.

Sitting U.S. Presidents during those years (see Figure 1) did not enjoy the same degree of admiration and success that presidents presiding over bull markets did. Presidents John Tyler (1841-1845), James Polk (1845-1849), Millard Fillmore (1850-1853) and Lyndon Johnson (1964-1969) served during rising B waves within larger corrective formations, and they did not go on to serve additional terms. Tyler was expelled from his own party and was disinvited to run again; Polk declined to run; Fillmore's party fell apart, and he was not nominated; Johnson was so unpopular, and ill, that he did not seek reelection. On the other hand, Richard Nixon, who served during an advance (wave D) within a bear market that took the form of a triangle, was reelected in a landslide. The anomaly did not maintain, however, as he was hounded from office less than two years after his reelection triumph. G.W. Bush won reelection in 2004. Unfortunately for him, it was during a bear market rally. By the end of his second term, he was the least popular president in over half a century. All of these conditions are compatible with the Elliott wave model in that despite the rising stock market the larger-degree trend in social mood was toward the negative.

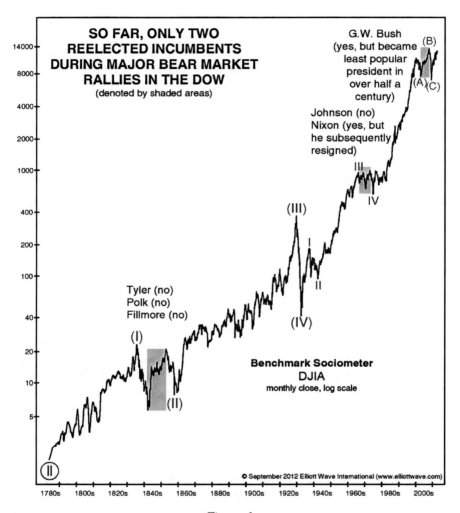

Figure 1

Chapter 19

My Basal Ganglia Made Me Do It!

Alan Hall

February 26, 2016 (TS)

With another U.S. Presidential election rapidly approaching, it's worth exploring how people actually choose their leaders. It appears that one part of the brain trumps (pun intended) another part in regulating voting choices.

In Chapter 8 of *The Wave Principle of Human Social Behavior*, Robert Prechter discussed the work of Paul MacLean, former head of the Laboratory for Brain Evolution at the National Institute of Mental Health, who proposed that

> the primitive brain stem, called the basal ganglia…controls brain functions that are often termed instinctive: the desire for security, *the reaction to fear*, the desire to acquire, the desire for pleasure, fighting, fleeing, territorialism, migration, hoarding, grooming, choosing a mate, breeding, the establishment of social hierarchy and *the selection of leaders*.

On January 4, *The Washington Post* published this photo, taken at a Donald Trump rally the night before. The photo's subject expresses strong emotion, but which emotion? The *Post* wrote, "you might at first glance think she is horrified to see Trump… But, you'd be wrong. [She] was, in fact, ecstatic to catch an up-close-and-personal glimpse of The Donald…."[1]

This Is Your Brain on Politics: Woman is emotional about a close encounter with Donald Trump. (Image courtesy of Reuters/Brian Snyder, photographer.)

Leader selection is an impulsive, non-rationally regulated attempt to achieve security and safety or to express bravado. Voters in the aggregate do not objectively and rationally consider and weigh all the pros and cons of each candidate. The impulsivity of their decision-making is apparent in the rationales that voters construct to justify their unconscious decisions. Bill Clinton won the presidency in 1992 amidst a negative social mood trend and an economic recession in which voters had "a bleak picture of the American economy, with more than two-thirds describing it as 'not so good' or 'poor....'" The electorate's hunger for change was so strong that it didn't matter that "Nearly half of the voters said Mr. Clinton was lying about his draft record and his activities during the Vietnam War. In the end...nearly half of those who said they were military veterans voted for him anyway."[2] Some voters said they preferred George W. Bush in 2004 because they would rather have a beer with him than with his opponent.[3] Pew Research found that some people voted for Barack Obama in 2008 because he promised "hope and change, [and] they felt Obama has the right judgment to make a good president [and] is in touch with people like them...."[4] Today, many on the right who supported George W. Bush now support Donald Trump,[5] who harshly criticized Bush in a recent debate. It didn't matter.

Leader selection takes place under conditions of uncertainty, which make people prone to pre-rational herding. The most electable politicians are those who most adeptly appeal to the mood—not the rationality—of the populace.

NOTES AND REFERENCES

[1] Cillizza, C. (2016, January 5). The Only Donald Trump Photo You Need to See Today. *The Washington Post.*

[2] Schmalz, J. (1992, November 4). The 1992 Election: The Nation's Voters; Clinton Carves a Wide Path Deep Into Reagan Country. *The New York Times.*

[3] Benedetto, R. (2004, September 17). Who's More Likeable, Bush or Kerry? *USA Today.*

[4] Inside Obama's Sweeping Victory. (2008, November 5). Pew Research Center.

[5] Wright, C. (2016, February 18). Donald Trump Was Right to Hit Bush on 9/11 and Iraq. *Brietbart.*

Chapter 20

Who Will Win in November?
Don't Ask GDP, Inflation,
Unemployment—or the Stock Market

Matt Lampert

July 29, 2016 (TS)

Democrats and Republicans have their presidential nominees, and election prognostications continue. To get an edge in forecasting, handicappers look at a variety of measures, including economic growth, inflation, unemployment and even the stock market. This year, none of those variables will help them to call a winner. Our elections study of four years ago [Chapter 2] explained why.

That study found a strong, statistically significant relationship between the percentage change in the stock market in the years leading up to presidential elections and how incumbents fared in their re-election bids. We also found that GDP was significantly related to incumbents' fates in some of our tests, but its significance disappeared when we used GDP jointly with the stock market to account for election results. In other words, everything GDP explained, the stock market explained, too, and then some.

These results make sense only in light of socionomic theory, which posits that unconscious social mood drives trends in the stock market, GDP and voters' appraisals of leaders. Since people can express their moods faster in the stock market than in behavior that later results in GDP growth, the stock market is a more sensitive sociometer and, thus, a superior indicator for predicting elections. This insight proved valuable in the 2012 presidential race. U.S. stocks gained nearly 35% in the three years leading up to the election, and the incumbent achieved a decisive win.

The stock market's power as an election forecasting indicator disappeared, however, when we looked at elections that lacked an incumbent candidate. In such cases, the preceding three-year percentage change in the stock market had no statistically significant, predictive relationship with the incumbent party's results.

We wanted to see if the same would be true for the other variables we studied in the 2012 paper. As Table 1 shows, none of them were significantly related to the incumbent party's popular vote margin in elections that involved no incumbent candidate. We didn't look just at recent history, either. We carried the analysis all the way back to 1824, the first year for which we have reliable national-level popular vote data as well as GDP and PPI data. (High-quality, national-level unemployment data are available only from 1940, so our analysis in that regard begins then.)

Financial and Macroeconomic Variables
Have No Significant Relationship to the Incumbent Party's Popular Vote Margin
in U.S. Presidential Elections That Lack an Incumbent Candidate

Variable (3-Year % Change)	Correlation with Incumbent Party's Popular Vote Margin	Two-tailed p-value (<0.10 is statistically significant)	% of Vote Margin Accounted for
Nominal Dow Jones Industrial Average	-0.058	0.807	0.3%
PPI-Adjusted Dow Jones Industrial Average	0.013	0.956	0%
Producer Price Index (PPI)	-0.16	0.501	2.6%
Nominal Gross Domestic Product (GDP)	-0.358	0.121	12.8%
Real GDP	-0.241	0.306	5.8%
Unemployment	0.14	0.792	2%

Notes:
Elections data are from Dave Leip's Atlas of U.S. Presidential Elections: http://uselectionatlas.org/RESULTS/
Study period is 1824-2015 for all variables except for unemployment, for which data are only available beginning in 1940.
We exclude the election of 1824 because all candidates were members of the same party.
In cases where the incumbent party is unclear, we designate the party that won the previous presidential election as the incumbent.

Table 1

To show just how hopeless it is to use financial and macroeconomic variables to forecast presidential elections that lack an incumbent candidate, consider the strongest indicator in Table 1: nominal GDP. It accounts for just under 13% of the incumbent party's popular vote margin. It might seem intuitively logical that voters would consider long-term economic trends when evaluating whether to return a party to the White House. But that idea is unequivocally wrong. Why? Because if you look at the correlation between nominal GDP and the incumbent party's popular vote margin, you'll see that it's negative. That's right: The two variables have an inverse relationship; the more GDP grows, the worse the incumbent party tends to do in the popular vote, and vice versa. Since it would be difficult to come up with a logical explanation for this result, and since the relationship falls short of being statistically significant, we can safely conclude that these election results are simply unrelated to GDP.

When an incumbent is running, GDP is a good predictor of presidential election results and the stock market is an outstanding predictor of presidential election results. But neither indicator is any good when there's no incumbent running. As we said in the paper, "We are inclined to hypothesize that voters project their moods on individual leaders, not parties. …When no candidate in a presidential election is the recognized leader whom voters have unconsciously credited or blamed for their mood, they appear to base their voting decisions substantially on other factors."

Chapter 21

Reflections on
the 2016 Election

Matt Lampert
November 29, 2016 (TS)

"Shocking," "surprising" and "unthinkable" were among the words pundits used to describe the election of Donald Trump to the presidency on November 8. Yet throughout this year, *The Socionomist* has detailed how social mood opened the door for a candidate such as Trump.

Our January issue[1] revealed how an underlying negative mood trend planted the seeds for the crop of unconventional, status-quo-bucking Primary candidates, including Trump, Bernie Sanders and Ted Cruz. The February issue [Chapter 19] explored how the primitive portions of our brains unconsciously lead us to make political decisions based on mood instead of logic and reason. Robert Folsom's article, "Why Trump? Why Now?—The Violent Death of Political Correctness," in the March issue linked Trump's rise to a

The President-Elect: Donald Trump addresses the 2016 Republican National Convention in July.

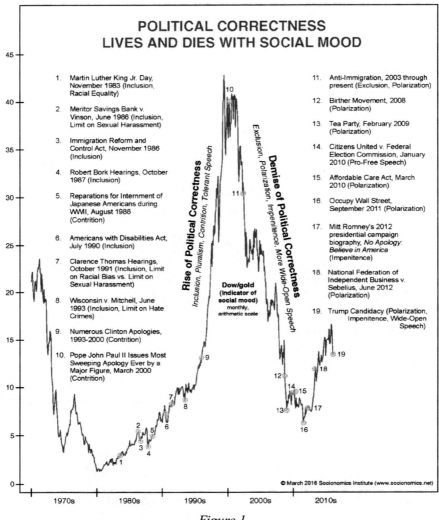

Figure 1

17-year negative-to-mixed mood trend as recorded by the Dow/gold ratio (see Figure 1), illustrating that Trump was succeeding not in spite of his politically incorrect rhetoric but largely because of it. Folsom also showed that Trump's success is not an anomaly in American politics but is in fact consistent with the appeal of candidates who made political inroads when social mood turned negative. The July issue[2] investigated other important political manifestations of the long term trend toward negative mood, including an increase in polarization and feelings of anger and distrust toward the political opposition. Most recently, the October issue[3] forecast a threat to the two-party establishment from outsider candidates and third parties.

Yet unlike the pollsters, we never called a winner. In the August[4] [Chapter 20] and September[5] issues, we reminded readers of our 2012 study [Chapter 2], which found that although the stock market is an excellent indicator for whether an incumbent seeking reelection will retain the White House, it is unhelpful for forecasting which party will win in contests that feature no incumbent candidate. Nor in this case could we find another socionomic basis for identifying a likely winner. In line with our neutral stance, the election was extremely close, as Trump won the electoral vote but lost the popular vote.

In our elections webinar in October, we investigated popular methodologies that purported to use the stock market effectively to forecast elections featuring non-incumbent candidates. We found [see Chapter 6] that they fail to hold up to historical scrutiny, regardless of their apparent efficacy or lack thereof in calling any particular election.

We did, however, use the trend of social mood to understand the backdrop of this year's political theatre. That context was helpful for understanding why all of the establishment presidential candidates ultimately failed, why the two major-party candidates had record-high unfavorable ratings, and why so many Americans had grown disgusted with the political status quo.

Libertarian Gary Johnson garnered the most votes for a third party candidate since Ross Perot,[6] but we were surprised that third party candidates were unable to make a bigger splash. I found myself wondering aloud during Elliott Wave International's Post-Election Analyst Roundtable whether Trump was actually one of the most successful third-party candidates in American history. Of course, as the Republican Party's nominee, he does not fit the literal definition of a third party candidate. But if we think more loosely about a third party candidate as an outsider who takes on the establishments of both major parties, then Trump certainly qualifies. He first challenged and defeated the Republican establishment during the primaries and then beat the Democrat establishment in the general election.

In a twist of irony, Trump now holds the mantle of the incumbent. The very mood that gave him the opening to become president could sink his chances to stay in the White House. If he wants to last the full four years in office and win another term, he should hope for positive mood. Political outsiders with even more radical agendas should hope for negative mood, which will help them the most.

NOTES AND REFERENCES

[1] Hall, A. (2016, January). Radicals Ride Again: Negative Mood is Fueling Extreme Politics. *The Socionomist.*

[2] Hall, A. (2016, July). Negative Social Mood Has Increased Political Polarization on Both Sides of the Pond. *The Socionomist.*

[3] Thompson, C. (2016, October). Third Parties Make a Splash in 2016 Election Waters. *The Socionomist.*

[4] Lampert, M. (2016, August). Who Will Win in November? Don't Ask the Stock Market—or GDP, Inflation and Unemployment. *The Socionomist.*

[5] Socionomics Institute staff. (2016, September). Mailbag. *The Socionomist.*

[6] Walker, J. (2016, November 9). Where the Third-party Candidates Were Strongest. Reason.com.

Chapter 22

Socionomics Foundation Proposal to the
American National Election Survey (ANES)
Excerpted from materials dated June 16, 2006-January 31, 2007

Election Hypotheses and Political Polling

Wayne D. Parker

Project Description

In September 2006, the principal investigators for the American National Election Survey (ANES) announced that the Socionomics Foundation was one of 30 research organizations nationwide that had won a competition to submit the best proposals for new questions for the Pilot Study for the next national survey. The Pilot Study will evaluate questions that have not been included on previous ANES surveys but which could prove valuable to researchers in the future. The selection criteria for the winning proposals included factors such as novelty of idea, theoretical foundation, empirical support, breadth of relevance and generalizability.

Our proposal focused on questions about social mood. The questions aimed to determine respondents' levels of optimism and pessimism regarding their own personal futures and the future of U.S. society as a whole.

Most social-science forecasting methods simply extrapolate present trends into the future. Socionomics meets an important need in offering a new approach to predicting social trends by analyzing the structure of social mood, which fluctuates in a patterned fractal form that allows probabilistic prediction of societal trend changes.

We have written a working paper concerning the outcomes of future U.S. presidential elections (Prechter, Goel and Parker, 2002-2006) [see final version in Chapter 2]. Our goal with our proposal for ANES is to collect data regarding social mood to use in our research in that area. Our thesis is that an increasingly positive social mood will result in more votes for an incumbent president, and that an increasingly negative social mood will result in more votes against an incumbent. In the most recent election, that of 2004, our method projected a win for the incumbent U.S. president, George W. Bush [and later a win for Obama in 2012].

Our findings suggest that waves of social mood regulate reelection probabilities even in the face of contradictory predictions suggested by the logical relationship between a politician's promises and the conscious opinions of the voting public, as collected in self-report measures such as polls of voters' political policy preferences. A rational set of ideas about policies may predict what voters say, but measures of social mood better predict what voters will do, as they unconsciously act upon their moods.

Background Information

Socionomics challenges the rational-choice model of human behavior that underlies much of the current theory in the social sciences. Mechanistic theories are failing to yield accurate predictions in fields such as economics, sociology, political science and social psychology. In contrast to mechanistic theories, socionomic theory considers aggregate human behavior to be more like complex biological phenomena than like the operation of a machine or computer. We are in the initial stages of researching the implications of these differences for applications in all the major social sciences.

Statement of Proposed Research Topic

Here are the questions from our proposal to ANES:

When you think about your own personal future, are you generally (extremely/somewhat) optimistic, (extremely/somewhat) pessimistic or neither?

And when you think about the future of the United States as a whole, are you generally (extremely/somewhat) optimistic, (extremely/somewhat) pessimistic or neither?

Theoretical Overview

In order to explain our choices, we need a quick theoretical overview of our goals for using these survey items in our group's research. The literature regarding theories of emotion and theories about how emotional responses affect political behavior is complex and voluminous (Diener & Emmons, 1984; Watson & Tellegen, 1985; Frijda, 1988; Marcus, 1988; Cacioppo &

Berntson, 1994; Damasio, A., 1994; Barrett & Russell, 1998). We will not attempt to review here all the nuances of valence models (unidimensional) vs. circumplex (two-dimensional) theories of emotion, whether the dimensions are valence and activation/intensity, or mastery and threat (Marcus, 1988) or some other theoretical framework. The overall theoretical framework is what matters, and almost all of these studies and models are concerned with conscious perceptions of information and of emotional responses rather than with what we call social mood.

Unfortunately, some theorists have created considerable confusion in the literature by using "emotion" and "mood" as synonyms. It is important to understand the difference between endogenous *mood*, as conceptualized in socionomic theory, and *emotions*. Mood, as we use the term, is an endogenous, global activation state with expectational, evaluative and affective components but no specific external referent, while emotions are affective reactions to exogenous stimuli (Wright, Sloman & Beaudoin, 1996). Mood can lead to emotions when an external referent allows mood to manifest in conscious feelings. Though our research group's main interest is in unconscious social mood, we think that the mood-related measures of conscious affect on a self-report instrument such as the 2006 ANES Pilot Study can also offer valuable data for our purposes.

Social psychologists have found that implicit or unconscious social cognition is measurable. We believe that unconscious mood is measurable, also. We believe that the neural substrate of unconscious social mood and that of emotional reactions will be found to be different. We posit that paralimbic structures mediate unconscious mood, while cortical structures are more involved in the mediation of conscious emotional reactions.

It is also important, in a political context, to distinguish between our definition of affective "mood" and the more cognitive or attitudinal definition of "mood" used by Stimson (1991), by which he means "policy sentiment." There is certainly nothing wrong with different academic disciplines assigning different meanings to the same term, whether the discipline is political science, psychology or socionomics. It is confusing, however, if these meanings are not clearly specified, especially given that the term may mean two different things in the same context.

News Events: Exogenous Shocks vs. Endogenous Mood Trends

We propose to utilize the causal inferences made possible by the panel-study design to examine the relative causal influence on voting behavior of social mood vs. news events.

The effect of news on election outcomes has been a central focus in the political science literature for many years. Gronke and Newman (2003) mentioned this focus as representative of a "third wave" of popularity function research in electoral studies during the period since the late 1980s. Most of this literature may be grouped into two main hypotheses:

(1) Cognitive hypothesis—This camp of theorists, exemplified by Popkin (1991) and Lupia, McCubbins and Popkin (2000), proposes that the main effect of news is to influence election outcomes by means of cognitive persuasion of the electorate to the main platform points of one or another of the presidential candidates. The assumption implicit in this hypothesis is that of rational choice theory, i.e. that voters cognitively evaluate the proposals of various candidates and logically sort out which candidate's platform would maximize their own utility.

(2) Affective hypothesis—This camp, exemplified by Marcus, Neuman and MacKuen (2000) and Rahn (2000, 2004), suggests that, rather than cognitive influences, the emotional impact of news on voters is the primary means by which the news affects voting behavior. While the mechanism is different (news effects here are said to be mediated by affective rather than cognitive reactions to the news), the general assumption is still the same: that voters respond to the news and that their behavior is governed by utility maximization. In this case, however, the utility that voters are attempting to maximize is a feeling payoff ("Which candidate will make me feel the best?") rather than a financial payoff ("Which candidate will most likely increase my income?") or an issue payoff ("Which candidate will best support my core values regarding the environment, war in Iraq?" etc.).

In contrast to these traditional political theories, the new science of socionomics (Prechter, 1999, 2003) offers entirely different hypotheses about the effect of news events on human social behavior, including presidential elections. Socionomic theory posits that endogenous social mood, rather than exogenous social conditions (whether news events or other external factors), is the primary cause of aggregate behavior related to decision-making under uncertainty. According to socionomic theory, an evolutionarily derived unconscious impulse to herd in uncertain situations, including seeking leadership to insure that one's survival needs will be met, is operative in voting behavior in presidential elections, and the character of this herding behavior is determined by the nature of the wave-form of social mood at the time of the election. Specifically, voters tend to retain incumbent presidents during waves of positive social mood and reject them during waves of negative social mood (Prechter, 2003, p. 57 [and Chapter 2]).

Socionomic theory (Prechter, 1999, 2003) posits that rather than functioning as exogenous shocks, news events are merely *results* of the endogenous herding process in self-organizing, unconscious social mood trends. The socionomic hypothesis about voting therefore differs from both the "cognitive hypothesis" and the "affective hypothesis" of traditional political science researchers in rejecting the assumption of rational choice and utility-maximization as prime determinants of voting behavior. Our proposed study of the impact of news of economic conditions on voting behavior attempts to provide empirical evidence for or against our thesis that endogenous mood is the more important cause of voting behavior.

Project Goals

Given our theoretical approach to mood, we can use a number of existing items from the 2004 survey in conjunction with our proposed "social mood" items. The items that interest us relate to our proposed questions in connection with socionomics. The first and last of the basic principles of socionomic theory are the ones most relevant to our present purposes: We want to examine both the *uncertainty* of voters in the political context of presidential elections and the *character of their social actions* in the context of voting.

A key theoretical principle that underscores our research into aggregate social behavior is that changes in unconscious social mood lead to changes in social actions and events. We have found that the best measures of unconscious social mood are various indices of the U.S. stock market because they instantly register the degree of optimism or pessimism the society holds about its future. In the current study, we wish to explore the measures of *conscious* feelings represented by our questions for the ANES Pilot Study. With insights gained from studying the relationship between how conscious feelings vs. unconscious social mood serve as predictors of voting behavior, we can refine our theoretical model and better predict political trend changes.

Other goals of this project include:

(1) Examining correlations between optimism/pessimism concerning one's personal future and optimism/pessimism concerning the nation's future relative to a variety of items in the Pilot Study. This will enable us to compare the dynamics of "egotropic" voting with those of "sociotropic" voting (Nannestad and Paldam, 1994).

(2) Examining whether respondents are active participants in the stock market. Given that socionomics uses the major stock market indices as its benchmark sociometer, or primary indicator of social mood, we want to find out whether current stock market participation affects the relationship we hypothesize between mood, recent stock market performance and election or rejection of incumbent presidents. If the relationships we hypothesize do not hold for voters who are not stockholders, this finding would weaken the theoretical basis for using the stock market as a general sociometer. Conversely, if these relationships hold whether or not voters are stockholders, this finding would add support for the theoretical basis for using the stock market as a general sociometer.

(3) Examining whether respondents are self-described liberals or conservatives. We would hypothesize that the relationships we predict relative to social mood would hold regardless of how liberal or conservative the voter is. Analyzing the responses to this item will allow us to test this hypothesis.

(4) Examining answers to questions such as "Generally speaking, would you say that you personally *care a good deal* who wins the presidential election this fall, or that you *don't care very much* who wins?" This item allows us to analyze the general level of affective activation relative to social mood, which may help us differentiate the relationships we find among the items. For instance, the predictive value of social mood may (or may not) hold only among voters who are highly activated ("*care a good deal*").

(5) Examining whether respondents are in favor of the use of military force. Socionomics finds a positive correlation between negative social mood and aggressiveness toward outsiders.

(6) Examining respondents' degree of uncertainty regarding for whom to vote, what the salient issues are in the election, etc. Socionomic theory suggests that uncertainty is a prerequisite for herding; thus, the patterns of political behavior predicted by socionomic theory may hold only among voters with a certain degree of uncertainty, and we wish to test this hypothesis.

Methods

We plan to analyze the above-suggested relationships using various statistical tests. Based on the exact nature of the data, these tests will be one or more of the following: Fisher's exact test, correlation matrices, F-statistics, chi-square test and t-test.

Staff

Principal Investigator

Wayne D. Parker, Ph.D., will have primary responsibility for the research and liaison between the Socionomics Foundation and Stanford University.

Research Staff

Deepak Goel, M.A., will assist with statistical analysis.
Robert Prechter will serve as consultant for theoretical analysis.

Note: Dr. Parker was unable to continue this line of research due to health issues.

REFERENCES

Barrett, Lisa F., and James A. Russell (1998). Independence and Bipolarity in the Structure of Current Affect. *Journal of Personality and Social Psychology*, 74(4), pp. 967-984.

Cacioppo, J.T., and G.G. Berntson (1994). Relationship Between Attitudes and Evaluative Space: A Critical Review, With Emphasis on the Separability of Positive and Negative Substrates. *Psychological Bulletin*, 115, pp. 401-423.

Damasio, A. (1994). *Descartes' Error: Emotion, Reason and the Human Brain*. New York: Grosset/Putnam Books.

Diener, Ed, and Robert A. Emmons (1984). The Independence of Positive and Negative Affect. *Journal of Personality and Social Psychology*, 47, pp. 1105-1117.

Doherty, R. William (1997). The Emotional Contagion Scale: A Measure of Individual Differences. *Journal of Nonverbal Behavior*, 21(2), p. 131.

Elliott, R.N., *The Wave Principle* (1938) and *Nature's Law* (1946), reprinted in Prechter, 1993.

Frost, Alfred John, and Robert R. Prechter, Jr. (1978/1998). *Elliott Wave Principle—Key to Market Behavior*. Gainesville, GA: New Classics Library.

Frijda, N.H. (1988). *The Emotions*. Cambridge, UK: Cambridge University Press.

Greenwald, Anthony G., Debbie E. McGhee, and Jordan L.K. Schwartz. (1998). Measuring Individual Differences in Implicit Cognition: The Implicit Association Test. *Journal of Personality and Social Psychology*, 74(6), pp. 1464-1480.

Gronke, Paul, and Brian Newman. (Dec. 2003). FDR to Clinton, Mueller to ?: A Field Essay on Presidential Approval. *Political Research Quarterly*, 56(4), pp. 501-512.

Lupia, Arthur, Mathew D. McCubbins, and Samuel L. Popkin, Eds. (2000). *Elements of Reason: Cognition, Choice, and the Bounds of Rationality*. Cambridge, UK: Cambridge University Press.

Marcus, George E. (Sep. 1988). The Structure of Emotional Response: 1984 Presidential Candidates. *American Political Science Review*, 82(3), pp. 737-761.

Marcus, George E., W. Russell Neuman, and Michael B. MacKuen. (2000). *Affective Intelligence and Political Judgment*. Chicago: University of Chicago Press.

Nannestad, Peter, and Martin Paldam. (June 1994) The VP-function: A Survey of the Literature on Vote and Popularity Functions After 25 Years. *Public Choice*, 79(3-4), pp. 213-245.

Popkin, Samuel L. (1991). *The Reasoning Voter: Communication and Persuasion in Presidential Campaigns*. Chicago: University of Chicago Press.

Prechter, Robert R. (1999). *The Wave Principle of Human Social Behavior and the New Science of Socionomics*. Gainesville, GA: New Classics Library.

Prechter, Robert R. (2001). Unconscious Herding Behavior as the Psychological Basis of Financial Market Trends and Patterns, *Journal of Psychology and Financial Markets* [now *Journal of Behavioral Finance*], 2(3), pp. 120-125.

Prechter, Robert R., Ed. (2003). *Pioneering Studies in Socionomics*. Gainesville, GA: New Classics Library.

Prechter, Robert R., Deepak Goel, and Wayne D. Parker. (2006). We Know How You'll Vote Next November: Social Mood, Financial Markets and Presidential Election Outcomes. Working paper, Socionomics Foundation, Gainesville, GA.

Rahn, Wendy M. (2000). Affect as Information: The Role of Public Mood in Political Reasoning. In Lupia et al., (2000), pp. 130-150.

Rahn, Wendy M. (2004). Feeling, Thinking, Being, Doing: Public Mood, American National Identity, and Civic Participation. Paper presented at the Annual Meeting of the Midwest Political Science Association, Chicago, April 17, 2004.

Stimson, James (1991). *Public Opinion in America: Moods, Cycles, and Swings*. Boulder, Colorado: Westview Press.

Watson, David, and Auke Tellegen (1985). Toward a Consensual Structure of Mood. *Psychological Bulletin*, 98, pp. 219-235.

Whyte, Jacqueline C. (1989). *Cycles of Time: Charting the Mood Swings of America*. South Hamilton, Massachusetts: Manifest Press.

Wright, I.P., Sloman, A., & Beaudoin, L.P. (1996). Towards a Design-based Analysis of Emotional Episodes. *Philosophy, Psychiatry and Psychology*, 3(2), pp. 101-137.

Part II:

FUNDAMENTAL OBSERVATIONS OF POLITICAL CAUSALITY

Chapter 23

Women in Politics

Mark Galasiewski

April 10, 2007 (EWT)

In *Popular Culture and the Stock Market* (1985), Prechter wrote, "'Feminism' gains power during [stock market] corrections, as it did in the 1850s...around World War I...and again in the 1970s...." *The Elliott Wave Theorist* has since noted that political power among females also waxes in periods of negative social mood. A notable example of this phenomenon is Margaret Thatcher's election to the post of prime minister of the United Kingdom in 1979, late in the negative mood period of the 1970s.

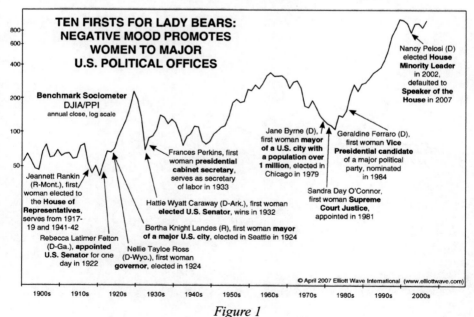

Figure 1

Figure 1 supports our case. It shows that the first woman to hold each major U.S. political office made her breakthrough near the end of a major bear market in stocks, when negative social mood was near an extreme. Most recently, Nancy Pelosi's victory came just one month after the stock market bottom in 2002, when the Democratic Party elected her to the post of House Minority Leader. (This position defaulted to Speaker of the House of Representatives when the Democrats gained a majority in Congress in January 2007, making Pelosi the highest-ranking woman office-holder in U.S. history.)

Since some of the examples in Figure 1 follow war periods, it might be tempting to assume that during wartime women expand their authority in men's absence. But the examples from 1932-1933 and 2002 negate this hypothesis.

A more likely explanation for the record of successes depicted in Figure 1 is that women benefit from the general call for change that attends periods of negative social mood. Since men are traditionally both the source and the symbols of power during booms, their authority is frequently stripped in the retrenchments that follow. In their place arise non-traditional leaders, a group that has historically included women.

Chapter 24

Voters in 2012 Produce Multiple Socionomic Milestones

Chuck Thompson

November 30, 2012 (TS)

The presiden-
tial election captured
most of the head-
lines in the U.S. this
month, yet there were
multiple watershed
results in local vot-
ing, too. Empowered
women, marijuana
legalization [see
Chapter 72], gay
marriage referenda
and rising polariza-
tion all tell the story
of a nation whose

Source: The Boston Globe

Unprecedented Achievements: Democrat Elizabeth Warren will
be among a record 20 women serving in the U.S. Senate. She
will also be the first female senator in Massachusetts' history.

mood has turned increasingly negative, as indicated by the downtrends in
the Dow/gold ratio and real estate prices, as depicted in Figure 1.

Women in Politics

Following the DJIA's plunge of 2007-2009, deep bear markets in Dow/
gold and real estate carried on until recent months, indicating a residual negative mood as the 2012 election approached. Accordingly, female politicians
have been gaining ground. This January, there will be a record 20 women

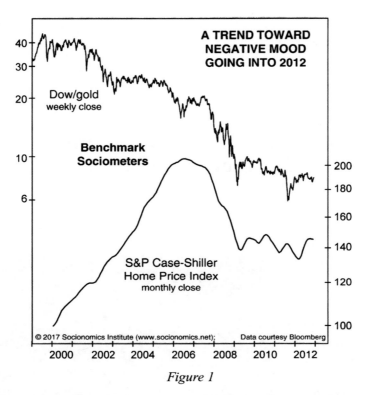

Figure 1

among the 100 members of the U.S. Senate. Among them will be Elizabeth Warren, the first female senator from Massachusetts, and Mazie Hirono, the first one from Hawaii. Hirono also is the U.S.'s first Buddhist senator.

Same-Sex Marriage

As Robert Prechter pointed out in 1999, a cultural mark of negative mood trends is the "acceptance of alternative sexual lifestyles."[1] Accordingly, Barack Obama was the first presidential candidate to publicly announce support for same-sex marriage, and votes this year on same-sex marriage ended in victory for gay-rights activists in four states. Maine and Washington now allow same-sex marriage, voters in Maryland upheld an existing statute that allows same-sex marriage, and Minnesota voters rejected a law that would have banned same-sex marriage. *Time* magazine reported,

> By winning at the polls in these four states, gay rights supporters
> ended an unbroken losing streak that had dated to 1998, when Ha-
> waii voters overwhelmingly voted to amend their constitution to let

lawmakers ban gay marriage. State legislatures, notably New York's last year, have legalized gay marriage, but never before had voters endorsed the idea at the ballot box.[2]

In addition, Wisconsin voters elected the nation's first openly lesbian senator, Democrat Tammy Baldwin.

Increasing Polarization

Prechter elaborated on this trend in the November 2012 *Theorist*: "Since 2000, when a new bear market started, the electorate has become more polarized." That shift has shown up in gender comparisons. The Hill says the 20-point gender-vote gap—President Obama's 12-point advantage with women and Mitt Romney's 8-point advantage with men—is the "largest since Gallup began tracking the metric in 1952."[3] The Huffington Post says that exit polls show that Obama won 71% of the Hispanic vote, 93% of the black vote and 73% of the Asian vote. Challenger Mitt Romney received 59% of the white vote.[4]

Socionomists see history and the social future as results of continuously fluctuating waves, not disparate, mechanistic incidents. Such incidents do not shape social attitudes. Rather, when mood changes, so do attitudes, which in turn lead to incidents. As we research what the future will bring, we hope more colleagues will see how deep, detailed and accurate socionomic insights can be compared to those derived from long-practiced methods based on the old paradigm of mechanics.

NOTES AND REFERENCES

[1] Prechter, R. (1999). *The Wave Principle of Human Social Behavior*.

[2] Lindenberger, M. (2012, November 12). America's Coming Out Election; How Gay Issues Became Mainstream. *Time*.

[3] Easley, J. (2012, November 9). Gallup: 2012 Election Had the Largest Gender Gap in Recorded History. The Hill.

[4] Mosbergen, D. (2012, November 9). Black, Latino Obama Vote Provokes Emergence of 'Pernicious Narrative' Among Conservative Pundits: report. The Huffington Post.

Chapter 25

Fibonacci Regulates the Occurrence of Landmark Political-Equality Events

Dave Allman

June 9, 2008 (EWT)

Everyone recognizes the historical significance of the current U.S. election: A man of partially African-American heritage is the presumptive presidential nominee of the Democratic Party, and a woman received (though by a disputed calculation) the largest popular vote for any presidential candidate in primary-voting history. These historic events piqued our interest.

The Wave Principle of Human Social Behavior linked socionomically motivated events to the Fibonacci sequence, suggesting a line of inquiry. Some quick research turned up the following data concerning some of the most important measures ever adopted in the U.S. with respect to the social recognition of equal political status for various groups of people:

—The thirteen original colonies of the U.S. were declared independent of Great Britain in 1776, courtesy of the Declaration of Independence—**233** years before the next president will be inaugurated in <u>2009</u>.

—Slavery was officially abolished and prohibited in 1865, courtesy of the 13th Amendment to the U.S. Constitution—**144** years before the next president will be inaugurated in <u>2009</u>.

—Women won the voting privilege in 1920, courtesy of the 19th Amendment to the U.S. Constitution—**89** years before the next president will be inaugurated in <u>2009</u>.

—Brown vs. Board of Education, the most important Supreme Court decision outlawing school segregation, occurred in 1954, **55** years before the next president will be inaugurated in <u>2009</u>.

As the Fibonacci durations have gotten shorter, the historical significance of each major instance of rights recognition has diminished proportionately.

All of the events cited here relate to social recognition legitimizing the equal political status of some portion of the population. In 1776, representatives of the colonies declared a claim to self-determination, a status equal to that of the British government; in 1865, African-Americans won their right to live freely, equating their status with the rest of the population; in 1920, women won the voting privilege, equating their political status with that of men; and in 1954, African-Americans were granted (at least in principle) equal access to tax-funded schools. Electing either a woman or an African-American to the presidency would be a social recognition of their equal status as national leaders. If either Obama or Clinton takes office in 2009, it will fall right into the set of Fibonacci durations depicted in Figure 1.

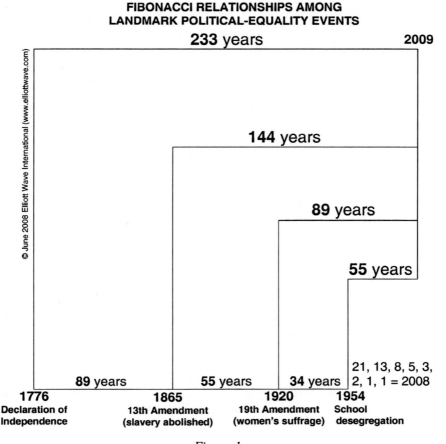

**FIBONACCI RELATIONSHIPS AMONG
LANDMARK POLITICAL-EQUALITY EVENTS**

Figure 1

As you can also see at the bottom of that graphic, the durations *between* each of these events produce a series of three consecutive, declining Fibonacci numbers. This series seems to have ended in 1954, without more events of this kind in 1975, 1988, etc. But perhaps we should point out that continuing this series down to the final "1" in the sequence naturally brings us to 2008, the year of this historic primary as well as the coming election.

It is perhaps of some note that American society gave the vote to African-American men (1870) before giving it to women (1920) and that Congress ratified the 13th and 15th amendments more quickly than it did the 19th amendment. These precedents suggest that the U.S. is more likely to choose an African-American male president before it does a female president.

Along those lines, if the general election is close and Mississippi is the deciding state, the country likely will vote in John McCain. Mississippi was the last state to ratify two of these crucial amendments—the 19th in 1984 and the 13th in 1995.

One might argue that the Civil Rights Act of 1964 is an equally important event that does not fall along this continuum, thus challenging the pattern. But this legislation is not like the other events. The instances noted above conferred and extended equal political rights or privileges. The Civil Rights Act, in contrast, took away property rights (as well as rights related to assembly) and granted unequal privileges to specified groups. (Whether one thinks this law is good or bad is not at issue here.)

One might also argue that the 15th amendment, which gave African-Americans the right to vote and was ratified in 1870, should be viewed as the proper companion to the 19th amendment. If Obama doesn't win the upcoming election, then perhaps he would become president at the next opportunity, in 2013 (1870 + 143). But the best overall Fibonacci web clearly targets 2008-2009. [In a most fitting result, Obama won both elections.—Ed.]

We extrapolated this series backwards from 1776 to see if any other important historical events turned up, but we didn't find anything notable.

Given the lengths of these durations and their common termination in 2008-2009, we suspect that these years may mark the end of a major spiral of political equalization dating from 1776. Given this perspective, we would predict that ensuing events along these lines might trend in the other direction.

Chapter 26

Initial Waves of Negative Mood
Tend Not to Produce Major Wars

Alan Hall

March 8, 2012 (TS)

Negative trends in social mood, as indicated by bear markets in stocks, unfold in down-up-down (A-B-C) Elliott wave patterns, although triangles feature two additional waves, D and E. Within such patterns, the first and second downtrends (waves A and C) tend to produce qualitatively different types of social actions.

Within major periods of negative social mood, *second* declines in the stock market tend to coincide with major wars. That is not the case with first declines, when wars are typically absent or comparatively mild. In Chapter 16 of *The Wave Principle of Human Social Behavior* (1999), Robert Prechter hypothesized why this is the case:

> Apparently society handles the first retrenchment in social mood, no matter how severe. "A" waves surprise optimistic people, who are unprepared and unwilling to wage war. It is the second drop that makes a sufficient number of increasingly stressed people angry enough to attack others militarily.

As you can see in Figure 1, *none* of the initial declines illustrated produced major wars.

First declines, however, still bring plenty of risks. The initial declines of 1720-1723, 1835-1842 and 1930-1932, which kicked off the largest-degree negative mood trends of the past three centuries, all began with intense deflation. The initial decline of 2000-2003 featured the 9/11 attacks and led to the relatively mild Iraq War. The initial wave down in the next period of negative social mood should likewise spark deflation and conflict, although not global war.

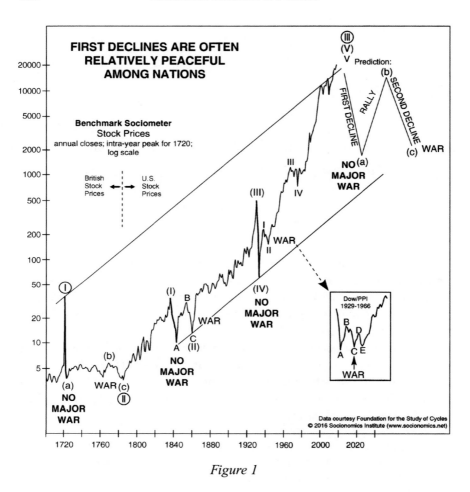

Figure 1

Elliott Wave International believes the stock market's next major down-trend will be wave (a) within a larger-degree bear market. If this outlook is correct, World War III is unlikely to commence until after the second decline begins, decades in the future, as illustrated at the top right of Figure 1 [with prices updated through 2016].

Chapter 27

A Survey of U.S. Secessionism

Alan Hall

February 16, 2010 (TS)

Figure 1 relates the Dow/PPI to the timing of wars involving Americans. The width of each rectangle indicates the duration of the war. The height of each rectangle indicates the percentage of the American population killed and wounded in the war.

Negative mood trends foster social anger in proportion to their degree. The three largest-degree trends toward negative social mood—wave (II), and waves (II) and (IV) within wave (III)—generated the three deadliest wars for Americans: the Revolutionary War, the Civil War and World War

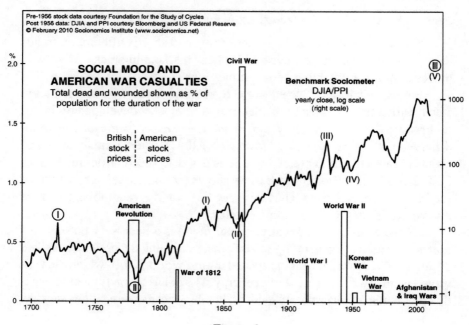

Figure 1

II. Compatibly with the explanation offered in Chapter 16 of *The Wave Principle of Human Social Behavior* [see also Chapter 26 of this book], the five wars with the largest death tolls occurred within or just after the second decline of each associated bear market.

The Vietnam War had the sixth-largest number of casualties and was the result of a negative mood trend that produced the bear market of 1966-1974 in the DJIA [see Figure 1 in Chapter 26]. That war, however, started earlier than usual in terms of socionomic causality, its most intense phases occurring throughout the Dow's waves A, B and C in 1966-1970.

The most lethal among these wars was the Civil War. The preceding bear market lasted 24 years—from 1835 to 1859— and included two periods of intense deflation. The process allowed ample time for deep anger to develop. After the second decline, people's anger needed expression, and because no external common enemy provided a suitable target, society expressed its rage internally.

Secessionism springs from the negative-mood impulse among people to separate and polarize. To examine such behavior in light of social mood, we studied the United States, which has stock price data for its entire history *and* endured one of history's deadliest civil wars. This report includes the first-ever index of U.S. secessionism and places it in a socionomic context.

Secessionism and Civil War vs. External War

Secessionist sentiment increases during and shortly after major trends toward negative mood as indicated by bear markets in stocks. Civil war, however, erupts only under certain conditions.

Figure 2 evaluates 234 years of U.S. secessionist activity as it relates to stock market trends. Most of the data come from a list developed by James L. Erwin for *Declarations of Independence: Encyclopedia of American Autonomous and Secessionist Movements* (2007). The 85 movements and events in these tallies expressed a serious desire to secede from the U.S. or from a U.S. state. The thin black line shows the individual yearly total of scored secessionist events. The thick grey line is a five-year moving average that we call our U.S. Secessionism Index.

As the chart shows, negative social mood is a necessary but not sufficient condition for generating secessionist sentiment. Secessionism spiked during the Civil War but was dampened during World War II, which the U.S. waged against a common external enemy. The polarization typical of negative mood periods was clearly evident, but Americans were all on one side.

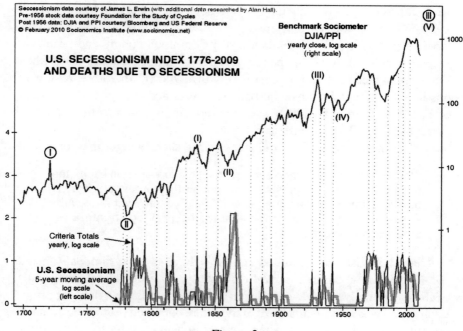

Figure 2

Internal or External War?

Whether belligerents express their anger within a country or against external foes appears to be due to specific chains of events within the chaos of social interaction. One factor—the availability of an external common enemy—seems to be the main determinant of whether conflict breaks out internally or externally. The existence of a common enemy can undercut rebellious impulses. Absent an external foe, a drawn-out trend toward more negative social mood directs anger and division inward, leading to increasingly secessionist expressions and eventually, if conditions are right, civil war.

Examples from the past and present show this dynamic in action. War with Carthage redirected ancient Rome's internal conflict for many years. Once Rome defeated its enemy, civil war intensified and the empire began its famous decline. The Spanish-American War of 1898 provided a common enemy that helped Americans heal the residual bitterness between North and South. The 1919 Anglo-Afghan War united long-adversarial Pashtun tribes against the British. The intensity of the Chinese Civil War waned when Japan expanded its incursion from northern China into Manchuria in 1931. When the Russian Empire experienced economic and military collapse during World War I, Finland lost its common enemy and promptly erupted in civil war in 1918. The prolonged intra-political enmity eased when Finns again faced a common enemy in World War II. In 2009, previously hostile Pakistani and Afghan Taliban factions united to oppose the buildup of 17,000 U.S. troops. Taliban groups are again bonding as they face the current surge of 30,000 American troops.

Thomas Hobbes in *Leviathan* recognized such changes in orientation:

When there is no common enemy, [men] make war upon each other for their particular interests.... For though they obtain a victory by their unanimous endeavor against a foreign enemy, yet afterwards, when...they have no common enemy [they] fall again into a war amongst themselves.

Psychologists have studied similar behavior, most famously in the 1954 Robbers Cave Experiment. In that study, researchers sent two groups of eleven twelve-year-old boys of similar backgrounds to an outdoor camp. Each group was initially unaware of the other, but when they made contact, hostilities quickly followed. Then the researchers introduced "super-ordinate" goals, problems that can be solved only through cooperation. This modification reduced hostilities significantly more than other strategies, including increased contact and communication.

Politicians and government propagandists are well aware that the portrayal of a common enemy can rouse emotional solidarity and group identity, which in turn redirect internal dissent and discord. Alexander De Conde's *History of American Foreign Policy* reported that William Seward, Abraham Lincoln's Secretary of State, advocated "a policy of hostility or war" against several European nations to "win back the loyalty of the seceded states and avoid civil war." But Lincoln famously urged "one war at a time" and refused to initiate or respond to foreign provocations during the war.

The Trend Toward Negative Social Mood Beginning in 2000 Has Fueled Secessionist Sentiment

The negative mood trend that began in 2000 has produced the largest one-decade loss in U.S. stock-market history (Figure 3). It also caused secessionist activity to increase.

The media have reported on Vermont's first slate of secessionist candidates since the Civil War and Texas Governor Rick Perry's veiled threats

Returns for the S&P 500 by Decade

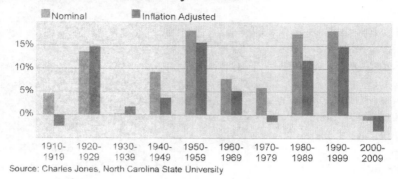

Source: Charles Jones, North Carolina State University

Figure 3

to urge Texas to leave the Union. Daniel Miller, the head of the Texas Nationalist Movement, says Texas would be better off as a separate country:

> We currently have one of the strongest economies in the world. We've got everything we need to be not just a viable nation, but a thriving, prosperous nation, except for one thing—independence from the United States.
>
> —*Star-Telegram*, September 19, 2009

Fox News issued this report on May 26, 2009:

> At least 35 states have introduced legislation this year asserting their power under the Tenth Amendment to regulate all matters not specifically delegated to the federal government by the Constitution.

Seven states among these 35 have passed sovereignty resolutions, and the so-called "Tenther" movement is growing:

> Tentherism...in a nutshell, proclaims that New Deal-era reformers led an unlawful coup against the "True Constitution," exploiting Depression-born desperation to expand the federal government's powers beyond recognition.
>
> —*The New York Times*, September 29, 2009

Nullification by states is a legal theory nearly as old as the Constitution. It asserts that any state has the right to nullify any federal law it finds unconstitutional. Over a dozen states plan to reject any proposed national health care plan. The "Bring the Guard Home" campaign is pushing legislation in 25 states that would empower governors to recall their National Guard units from foreign wars.

Montana has exempted itself from federal gun control laws via the Firearms Freedom Act, a Tenth Amendment challenge to the powers of Congress under the commerce clause. The federal government  filed suit in Montana to stop the move. Meanwhile, Tennessee passed virtually identical legislation and more than a dozen other states have introduced it.

Maine resisted the Bush Administration's Real ID Act, a law that would require states to issue federally regulated biometric identification cards. Some 20 other states did likewise, forcing the federal government to push its deadline to 2011. Thirteen states now have medical marijuana laws that directly oppose federal laws. (See *The Socionomist*, July 2009 [Chapter 70].)

South Carolina had advocated secession for years before it became the first state to secede from the Union in 1861. On February 2, [2010,] the same state's legislators introduced a bill that would make silver and gold coins legal tender in the state. H.4501 reads,

> The South Carolina General Assembly finds and declares that the State is experiencing an economic crisis of severe magnitude caused in large part by the unconstitutional substitution of Federal Reserve Notes for silver and gold coin as legal tender in this State. The General Assembly also finds and declares that immediate exercise of the power of the State of South Carolina reserved under Article I, Section 10, Paragraph 1 of the United States Constitution and by the Tenth Amendment, is necessary to protect the safety, health and welfare of the people of this State, by guaranteeing to them a constitutional and economically sound monetary system.

The bill lists specific methods for calculating the value of gold and silver coins and stipulates, "The State shall denominate all public accounts, and record the value of all public assets and liabilities, in standard silver dollars." This bill aims a warning shot across the bow of the Federal Reserve System.

A battle looms in Utah, where the federal government owns more than 60% of the land. Legislators introduced a bill in the Utah House on

February 11 aimed at empowering the state to use eminent domain to take federal lands. One Utah legislator said he thinks their timing is right: "Ten years ago we were not quite as fed up as we are now. To me it is much more likely that we can accomplish this in the current environment." (*Deseret News*, February 10, 2010) His reference to "ten years ago" denotes Q1 2000, pinpointing the peaks in the Dow/PPI and the S&P/PPI, when hardly anyone was "fed up" about anything.

Some academics are participating in the rising secessionist trend. An Emory University professor, whose secessionist ideas attracted little interest in the 1990s, founded the Abbeville Institute in 2003, at a major bottom in global stock prices. The institute now comprises 64 associated scholars from various colleges and disciplines. It is, for the first time, advertising its annual conference in Charleston, SC. The topics: secession and nullification.

Overt Secessionism Will Provoke Federal Opposition

Governments always fight to hold their strategic assets, such as, for example, the state of Texas. With a GDP of nearly $2 billion, Texas produces 13% of U.S. GDP. It ranks second in GDP among U.S. states and would rank twelfth among nations. It leads most other states in mineral development, agriculture, technology and other sectors.

There seems no question that the federal government would suppress an overt attempt at secession by any state. Later activity could well move from the courts to the streets and maybe even to battlefields.

Secessionists Sentiment in the EU

A secessionist mindset has become evident in Europe ever since the Euro Stoxx 50 index [see Figure 1 in Chapter 46] topped in 2000. A strategist at Société Générale, a leading French bank, claimed on February 12 that Europe's single currency faces an "inevitable break-up" followed by "the ultimate denouement: the break-up of the eurozone."

Today's separatist psychology in Europe has drifted far from the unity movement of a decade ago at the peak of positive social mood. The Wave Principle implies that this new trend toward division will eventually reach an extremity opposite that of the peak impulse to merge that brought the Eurozone together.

Looking Ahead

The upcoming wave Ⓘ bear market should last for decades, as did its wave Ⓘ predecessor in the 1700s. As social mood becomes more negative, anger will need expression. The appearance of an external enemy would bring cohesion and dampen secessionist feeling, but without it, a surge in secessionism is virtually inevitable.

Secessionist sentiment and activity should increase when wave (a) downward [see Figure 1 in Chapter 26] unfolds, but not to a level that could bring civil war. In later years, during wave (c), expressions of secessionism are more likely to succeed, unless external war curtails them.

Those who prepare for change can help themselves and others. As the pattern develops, we will adjust and apply our observations to gauge whether coming wars will be internal or external and offer our socionomic perspective regarding their destructive potential.

Chapter 28

Even in an Environment of Positive Conditions, Negative Social Mood Can Lead to War— Case in Point: the American Revolution

Euan Wilson

August 2013 (TS)

U.S. history courses teach that the American Revolution (1775-1783) was inevitable: The British Empire was relentless in taxing and subjugating of its fledging colonies. Rebellion came only after the Navigation Act, the Molasses Act, the Sugar Act, the Stamp Act, the Quartering Acts and finally the Townshend Acts. Each act spurred colonial anger, which led to more parliamentary crackdowns and further repressive acts. These activities hurt the American economy, causing further distress.

When positioned in such a way, it seems perfectly clear why the colonists rebelled. But if we look deeper at the circumstances in the years leading up to the Revolution, it negates the case that these acts were causal.

Background

Britain had just come through the Enlightenment, also known as the Age of Reason, which spawned such noted pragmatic political philosophers as John Locke, Adam Smith and David Hume. They influenced leaders William Pitt and George Grenville, capable prime ministers who were strongly disinclined to be so reckless as to drive away one of their choicest colonial prizes.

Across the pond, American colonists in the 18th century enjoyed what is believed to be the highest standard of living in the world—higher even than that of their counterparts in the British Isles.[1] American Revolution expert Jack P. Greene, author of *Pursuits of Happiness: The Social Development of Early Modern British Colonies and the Formation of American Culture*, reported on the situation:

McCucsker and Menard estimate that the gross national product multiplied about twenty-five times between 1650 and 1770, increasing at an annual average rate of 2.7 percent for British America as a whole and 3.2 percent for British North America. This increase, they posit, may have represented a real annual per capita growth rate of 0.6 percent [in the American colonies], which was twice that of Britain and was "sufficient to double income" over that period.

By the time of the American Revolution, this vigorous economic growth had produced a standard of living that may have been "the highest achieved for the great bulk of the free population in any country up to that time." In her massive study of the wealth of the continental colonies, Alice Hanson Jones has found that for the continental colonies as a whole in 1774, average per capita wealth— composed of land, slaves, livestock, nonagricultural productive goods, and consumer goods—was 60.20 pounds.

Let's put that number into perspective: In 2010 money, 60.20 pounds comes to 87,800 pounds ($137,846) on average for every man, woman and child. This is an incredible degree of wealth for a population to be enjoying. By comparison, the net worth per person in the U.S. in 2010, 236 years later, was moderately higher at $182,000, although the average is not only "pulled up by a small group of the very wealthy"[2] but also puffed up by historically overpriced stocks, bonds and real estate, whereas the cited figure for colonial times came 54 years into a 64-year bear market in British stocks.

Why would a people who are living better than anyone else in the world rebel against their government? We propose that social mood is the real reason the colonists broke away from Britain.

As in all times, citizens of the day never realized they were under the influence of unconscious social mood. So, they rationalized their feelings of anger and rebellion.

To develop our case further, let's first look at why the British passed their tax acts in the first place.

Taxing the Colonies

Figure 1 shows that the American Revolution came after a decline in British stock prices that lasted 64 years. In 1720, British stocks suffered the notorious crash following the South Sea Bubble, the peak of which is marked wave ①. Following a lackluster recovery, stocks declined from 1755 to about 1762, to their lowest level since the crash. The resumption of the negative trend in social mood spawned the Seven Years War, known in the colonies as the French and Indian War, which pitted the British colonies against an alliance of French and Native American warriors in what is now the American Midwest. The British sent money, troops and supplies. Basically, they did everything a mother country normally would do to defend a territory from foreign aggressors. The war spread to theatres

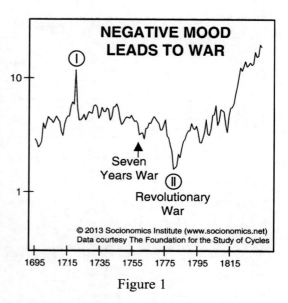

Figure 1

in Europe, India, West Africa and the Philippines. Eventually, the British won the Hydra-headed conflict.

Wars are not cheap, and the British government incurred a substantial debt. Britain's pre-war debt was £74 million, and by the end of the war, it had doubled to £150 million. That's roughly £236 billion ($370 billion) in today's money.[3]

The British did not require the colonists to pay the full amount. In fact, of the £200,000 it cost annually to defend the colonies, Parliament expected the colonies to provide only £78,000,[4] or just over half a million pounds total for the full Seven Years War. That is a paltry percentage of Britain's expenditures on the war.

Taxes were so low in the American colonies that colonists paid as little as one-fiftieth of what British subjects in the homeland paid. Yet shortly after the stock market low in 1762, negative mood drove colonists to begin protesting Parliament's tax acts.

Mood then turned positive, fueling a bear-market rally in stock prices. During this period, the British Parliament repealed most of its tax acts. By 1770, it drove an already-low colonial tax rate almost to zero. The table below demonstrates that all the tax acts the American colonists later objected to were repealed before 1770 during the time social mood was trending more positively. This trend toward positive mood had the British parliament feeling good enough to concede to colonial demands for lower taxes. After mood resumed its negative trend, however, the conciliatory posture ceased.

Act	Passed	Repealed
Navigation Act	1651	1764
Molasses Act	1733	1764
Sugar Act	1764	1766
Stamp Act	1765	1766
Quartering Acts	1765	1767
Townshend Acts	1767	1770 (except Tea Tax)

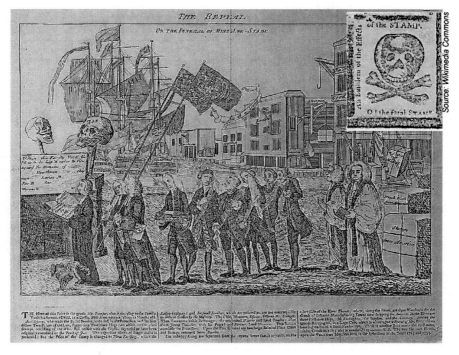

Zero Tolerance: The colonists' attitude toward England's various tax acts is reflected in the advertisements and political cartoons of the day. The cartoon above used a funeral procession to depict the death of the Stamp Act, which required that items such as legal documents, newspapers and magazines be printed on stamped paper that was produced in England. The man carrying the coffin is George Grenville, England's prime minister at the time and originator of the act. The inset (upper right) is a newspaper ad that predicted the Stamp Act would result in the death of journalism.

The Final Decline from 1768 through 1785 Brings on War

After 1770, only one provision within the Townshend Acts remained: the Tea Act. It was designed to aid the British East India Company, which was a major source of income and trade for Britain but was now in financial straits. The Tea Act shifted the taxes on tea from the East India Company to consumers, allowed the company to bypass the British Isles when distributing its tea and further enabled the company to sell tea already housed in Britain without paying further taxes. These changes substantially lowered costs for the company.[5] Parliament believed these cost breaks and incentives would enable the company to sell higher quality tea to colonists and others at lower prices while simultaneously reducing American smuggling.

But social mood had begun trending negatively in 1768, and the trend accelerated after the peak in 1775 (see Figure 1). Accordingly, Americans branded the Tea Act negatively, calling it an attack on colonial trade and an attempt to control the colonies through taxation. They staged the Boston Tea Party and tortured tax collectors with tar and feathers. Shortly thereafter, the American Revolution began.

The able Doctor, or America swallowing the Bitter Draught.

Source: Wikimedia Commons

Feeling Violated: This cartoon, which was circulated throughout the 13 colonies, used the rape of a woman (symbolizing America) to depict the injustices of the Intolerable Acts, which followed the Townshend Acts.

Primary Cause: Events or Mood?

To review: American colonists had the highest standard of living in the world. Their government rushed to their defense in the French and Indian War. Colonists paid a fraction of the taxes that British Isle citizens paid. And colonists had the promise of higher-quality, less-expensive tea. The British government had responded to American protests, negotiated with American leaders and repealed many unpopular Parliamentary Acts. These events and conditions hardly justified all-out rebellion.

Had the period been one of positively trending social mood, sociologists would be citing such conciliatory actions as engendering loyalty. But a negative mood trend has the opposite influence: It inspires people to cast events and conditions in a negative light. Anger erupts whether it is justified or not.

Once the colonial rebellion began, the British gave in to their own negative mood and sent one army after another with orders to destroy the revolutionary armies and restore British rule through martial law. The war drove apart friends, families and countrymen. Like any war, it had its share of atrocities and brutal engagements.

In times of positive social mood, society focuses on positives and tries to avoid war. In times of negative social mood, society focuses on negatives and invites war. In the case of the American Revolution, both sides took actions expressing the rage that had been brought on not by adverse actions but by a prolonged trend toward negative social mood.

NOTES AND REFERENCES

[1] Greene, J. (1988). *Pursuits of Happiness: The Social Development of Early Modern British Colonies and the Formation of American Culture.* (p. 137). Chapel Hill, NC: The University of North Carolina Press.

[2] Whitehouse, Mark. (September 18, 2010). Americans' Net Worth Falls Along With Stocks. *The Wall Street Journal.*

[3] Souter, G. (2006). *The Founding of the United States.* (1st ed.). New York, NY: Presidio Press.

[4] Miller, J. (1943). *Origins of the American Revolution.* (1st ed.). Palo Alto, CA: Stanford University Press.

[5] Unger, H. (2000). *John Hancock: Merchant King and American Patriot.* (1st ed.). Hoboken, NJ: Wiley.

Chapter 29

Parting of Peaceful Ways:
A Socionomic Review of Civil War

Euan Wilson

January 20, 2010 (TS)

Few events devastate society as does a civil war, when participants treat their neighbors in ways they would consider atrocious in any other context. Modern peacekeeping efforts have done little to slow the human appetite for this brand of conflict. In fact, the rates of emergence for new civil wars have remained constant in bear markets for the past 150 years. Since World War II, over 25 million people have died as a result of civil wars.

The Process of War

In *The Wave Principle of Human Social Behavior*, Prechter explained that negative social mood leads to "a collective increase in discord, exclusion...restriction...hostility...feelings of heterogeneity with others, and feelings of opposition toward others." He also observed that the degree of a war's destruction reflects the degree of the preceding or concurrent negative trend in social mood, as measured by the depth and duration of declines in stock prices.

We propose that in especially sizeable bear markets, such as those labeled in Figure 1, civil wars are just as likely to erupt as external wars. Note that two of the conflicts in the chart were civil wars: English colonists fought mother England in the Revolutionary War, and Northerners fought Southerners in the American Civil War.

Looking at other civil conflicts, we encounter a data problem. While we have more than 300 years of data on the British and U.S. stock markets, data for other areas and times are typically unavailable. Thus we have to rely on less precise sociometers, such as records of economic activity, for our analysis.

As shown in *The Wave Principle of Human Social Behavior*, 1999

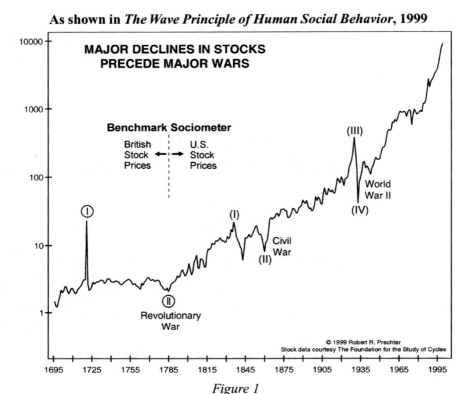

Figure 1

The U.S.: Two Violent Steps Down

Conventional historians hold that slavery, tariffs, fears about the balance of new slave and free states in the West and states' rights issues drove the founding of the Confederacy. Historians are quick to refute any issue as the sole cause. Socionomics has its own story to tell, which is that negative social mood exacerbated political frictions beyond the reach of compromise and into a basis for violence.

Prechter's 1999 book (p. 266) [see also Chapter 26] observed that the deadliest wars tend to come during and after the second of two big declines within a bear market in stocks. The first decline of the bear market of the mid-1800s took place from 1835 to 1842. The second decline, from 1852 to 1859 (see Figure 2), led to war.

A positive social mood extreme occurred in 1835, a time when Southerners defeated their countrymen's nascent secessionist efforts. "No

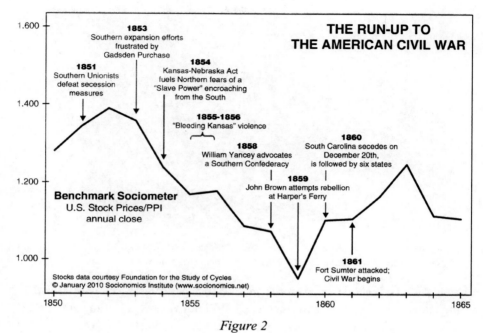

1853
Southern expansion efforts
frustrated by
Gadsden Purchase

**THE RUN-UP TO
THE AMERICAN CIVIL WAR**

1851
Southern Unionists
defeat secession
measures

1854
Kansas-Nebraska Act
fuels Northern fears of a
"Slave Power" encroaching
from the South

1855-1856
"Bleeding Kansas" violence

1858
William Yancey advocates
a Southern Confederacy

1860
South Carolina secedes on
December 20th,
is followed by six states

1859
John Brown attempts rebellion
at Harper's Ferry

Benchmark Sociometer
U.S. Stock Prices/PPI
annual close

Stocks data courtesy Foundation for the Study of Cycles
© January 2010 Socionomics Institute (www.socionomics.net)

1861
Fort Sumter attacked;
Civil War begins

Figure 2

government," wrote a newspaper contributor named Old Hickory, "could
be supposed to contain a provision for, or to sanction as a right, its own
destruction."

When the trend toward negative mood resumed, however, calls for
secession grew louder. The Gadsden Purchase (1853), a territorial expansion
that was to benefit Southern railroad interests, was smaller than expected,
prompting Southerners to howl anew.

The trend toward more negative social mood stirred new anger over
old disagreements on issues such as slavery. The Kansas-Nebraska Act of
1854, which created the territories of Kansas and Nebraska, allowed settlers
to decide the slavery issue in their territories for themselves. The act was
extremely unpopular among Northerners, who saw it as forcing slavery on
new territories. A year later, the conflict over slavery led to violence, and
"Bleeding Kansas" began.

Bleeding Kansas was a border conflict between free-territory Kansas
and pro-slavery Missouri. Casualties were light because it was early in the
negative mood trend, but the polarization of opinion and the open conflict
presaged the war to come.

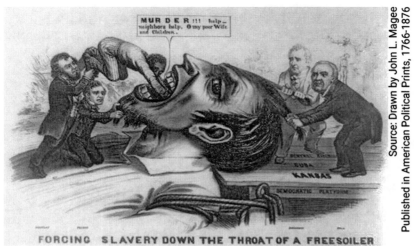

Source: Drawn by John L. Magee

Published in American Political Prints, 1766-1876

FORCING SLAVERY DOWN THE THROAT OF A FREESOILER
This political cartoon appeared in 1854, during the second decline in stock prices

As social mood turned more negative during the years following Bleeding Kansas, secessionist calls increased. William Yancey, a leading advocate of slavery and southern states' rights, made this suggestion in 1858:

> No National Party can save us; no Sectional Party can do it. But if we could do as our fathers did, organize Committees of Safety all over the cotton states (and it is only in them that we can hope of any effective movement) we shall fire the Southern heart—instruct the Southern mind—give courage to each other, and at the proper moment, by one organized, concerted action, we can precipitate the cotton states into a revolution.[1]

The phrases "no party can save us" and "give courage to each other… by one organized, concerted action" display no room for the compromises typically sought during periods of positive social mood. Such antipathy mixed with resolve is a classic expression of negative social mood.

Negative social mood, along with the bear market in stocks, reached the end of its Elliott wave form in 1859. A year later, following Abraham Lincoln's election as the 16th president of the Union, South Carolina seceded. More states followed. The newly elected president voiced the sentiment sweeping the northern side of the divide. In his 1861 inaugural address, Lincoln asserted that the United States shall "hold, occupy, and possess the property and places belonging to the government." The population clearly understood him to mean federal assets in the Confederacy. After five tense months, the first shots of the war rang out on April 12, 1861, during an intra-year setback in the stock market. The next four years were the bloodiest in U.S. history; some 600,000 Americans lost their lives, and another 400,000 were wounded before the violence finally came to an end in 1865.

Economic Contraction Is a Lagging Sociometer

Chapter 16 of Prechter's 1999 book identified economic expansion and contraction as a lagging sociometer. It takes longer for social mood changes to show up in inventory reductions, debt retirement, hiring and layoffs, etc., than in stock prices. To confirm the link, we obtained historical data on U.S. GDP per capita in 2005 dollars and then compared a graph of those figures to major highs and lows in the Dow Jones Industrial Average. Figure 3 shows that extremes in GDP per capita reliably follow peaks and troughs in the stock market by zero to twelve months.

Based on this record, we can use GDP per capita as a sociometer, albeit typically a lagging one. This measure is a useful substitute when we have no stock data with which to work, as is the case for the next two studies.

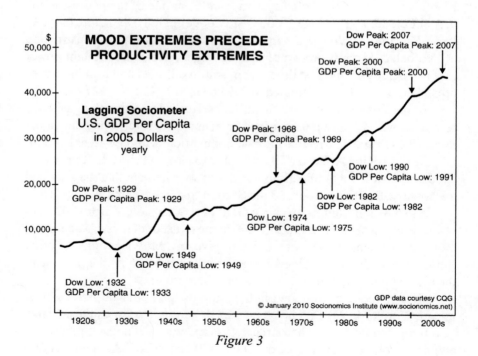

Figure 3

Spain: Violent Decline, Violent War

We have shown that most wars begin after a second decline within a major bear market in stocks and that most such wars are presaged by a milder conflict during or after a first decline. The Spanish Civil War followed this pattern.

In the 1920s, Spain was prosperous but troubled. The Spanish happily tolerated a mild military dictatorship but could not muster enough will to settle social problems such as unemployment and political unrest over Spain's colonial war with native tribes in Morocco. King Alfonso XIII enjoyed broad public support, even when in 1923 he practically invited the Spanish military to overthrow parliament. The coup's leader, General Miguel Primo de Rivera, claimed legitimacy for, and announced the good intentions of, the coup: "Our aim is to open a brief parenthesis in the constitutional life of Spain and to re-establish it as soon as the country offers us men uncontaminated with the vices of political organization." Primo de Rivera's regime benefitted from a positive social mood trend throughout the 1920s.

The Spanish economy thrived during the seven years of Primo de Rivera's regime. Spain's road system went from one of the poorest to the best in Europe. The positive-mood desire for dominion over nature (see *The Wave Principle of Human Social Behavior*, p. 228) drove the construction of hydroelectric dams on two of Spain's largest rivers and brought power to rural regions for the first time. Spain's railroad, steel and iron industries prospered. Foreign trade jumped 300% between 1923 and 1927.

At the close of the decade, Spain's mood turned negative along with the rest of the world's. The public turned on Primo de Rivera, demanding elections. Even Primo de Rivera's military compatriots withdrew their support.

In 1930, King Alfonso XIII attempted to replace Primo de Rivera with another dictator, but public disapproval was so vehement that the king fled the country. Elections produced the Second Spanish Republic in 1931.

As shown in Figure 4, Spain's GDP per capita slowed from 1929 onward, reaching an interim low in 1933. In the midst of that year's depressed mood, parliamentary elections failed to give any party a simple majority. Sitting president Niceto Alcalá Zamora did not even invite the party with the highest plurality vote totals to form a government.

GDP per capita continued falling, and the parliamentary crisis burst into civil discord. Hostility between the left and right grew as the socialist government violently crushed strikes, riots and revolts. Partisans reportedly attempted 543 assassinations, of which 330 succeeded. As many as 160 religious buildings were torched.

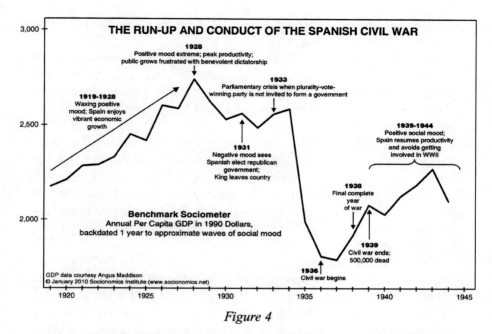

Figure 4

Spain finally succumbed to a brutal civil war between left and right political forces in 1936, the very year of the low in Spain's economy. The war lasted three years and claimed as many as 500,000 lives. Supposedly civilized Europe saw factions from both sides massacre massive numbers of civilians. Historians estimate that as many as 55,000 civilians were executed in Republican-held territories, while as many as 200,000 non-combatants were executed by Francisco Franco's right-leaning nationalists, the ultimate victors.

Spain's parochial war fully expressed its deeply negative social mood. Exhausted, it opted out of World War II. It was a bloody silver lining.

China: Huge Nation, Huge Conflict

As with the U.S. and Spain, China experienced its own two-step march toward negative social mood in the 1930s and 1940s. But with millions more people involved in the conflict, far more lives were lost.

A global trend toward negative social mood and the resulting down-turn in economic activity led to the collapse of China's imperial dynasty in 1911. In the aftermath, warlord-led bands terrorized the countryside into the early 1920s. Chiang Kai-Shek's army of the central government collared rural warlords and worked to restore order. China's social mood during the

1920s became increasingly more positive, producing a respite in conflict, but outlaw factions remained active.

In 1928, at the peak in positive social mood, Chiang led an attempt to unify the country. That same year he captured China's capital, Beijing. A relatively positive mood helped rally the Chinese people to him, and in 1929 most international powers recognized his government as the sole ruler of China.

As social mood turned toward the negative thereafter (see Figure 5), Chiang invaded areas controlled by Mao Zedong's Communist Party of China (CPC). Fighting continued for four years. Chiang garnered some early successes but no lasting control. Japan invaded Manchuria from the east in 1931, and Chiang let them possess it. He remained steadfast, focused on a motto of his civil war, saying, "First internal pacification, then external resistance."

Chiang's fifth campaign to destroy the CPC army in 1933-1934 ended in embarrassment. Chiang's enemies somehow slipped past his mercenaries and embarked on their famous Long March. The retreat was brutal, lasting 370 days and covering 8,000 miles. It cost the CPC army nearly 90% of its men. But as the trend in social mood continued toward the negative, Chiang lost the support of the people while Mao gained it. Mao described the March:

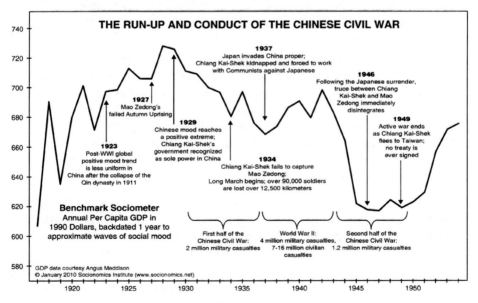

Figure 5

The Long March is a manifesto. It has proclaimed to the world that the Red Army is an army of heroes, while the imperialists and their running dogs, Chiang Kai-shek and his like, are impotent. It has proclaimed their utter failure to encircle, pursue, obstruct and intercept us. The Long March is also a propaganda force. It has announced to some 200 million people in eleven provinces that the road of the Red Army is their only road to liberation.

His words are not much different from those of Yancey, the southern secessionist, at a similar point in the social mood trend: uncompromising, contemptuous of his opponent, singularly convinced of his destiny, and resolved to win at any cost.

An interim extreme in China's negative social mood in 1937 coincided with Japanese troops' emergence from Manchuria to invade China's heartland. The invasion put the civil war between Mao and Chiang on hiatus but only after Manchurian Nationalists kidnapped Chiang and forced him to negotiate a compromise with the CPC against the Japanese. The truce produced little by way of coordinated effort between the two factions.

The next few years saw brutal fighting and a high death toll, but social mood in China still hadn't reached its ultimate negative extreme. After the U.S. secured the surrender of Japan in 1945, Mao and Chiang resumed fighting almost immediately. The global negative mood that had precipitated World War II persisted through 1949 by several measures, including the Dow/PPI. During those four years, the carnage in China continued. Active hostilities finally ended in 1949, when Chiang fled to Taiwan. In the end, the two-decade-long shift toward negative social mood cost as many as 23 million Chinese lives. Millions more followed at the hands of the brutal communist government that assumed power at the end of the civil conflict.

Three Charts, One Theme

Each of the civil wars discussed here shares a common trait: two consecutive waves of negative social mood. In the first one, the U.S. had Bleeding Kansas; Spain had the parliamentary crisis and unofficial exile of their king; and China had the first half of its civil war. In each case, much worse was to come during or shortly after the second trend toward more negative social mood. The second downward wave in the U.S. cost 600,000 lives. For Spain the cost was 500,000 lives. China felt the effects of its second negative mood period for nearly 30 years, ultimately costing the country more than 20 million lives.

Breaking Up Can Be Easy To Do

National breakups, even during times of negative social mood, do not always require violence. Several political unions have peacefully dissolved. Each modern example that we investigated has occurred in a sideways trend in the stock market, indicating a mild trend toward negative mood. In such environments, malaise did not shatter societies. The attitude was not, "Everything you believe is wrong, and we'll kill you to prove it," but instead, "What we are doing isn't working. We respectfully request a divorce."

Examples of this rare development include the Norwegian secession from Sweden in 1905, which established the first truly independent Norway in 500 years; Singapore's split from the U.K. in 1963 and then from Malaysia in 1965; the U.S.'s 1977 agreement to turn over the Panama Canal Zone to Panama at century's end; and the Czech/Slovak split in 1993. Singapore and Norway's respective secessions came when the two areas were without stock indexes, but Britain influenced the two territories heavily, and British markets were stuck in sideways patterns at the time of both splits. The U.S.-Panama agreement took place in the midst of a 16-year sideways trend in nominal U.S. stock prices from 1966 to 1982 [see Figure 1 in Chapter 70]. The Czechoslovakian split had a proxy stock market by which to measure local social mood. Let's take a closer look.

The Czechoslovakian Split

The Velvet Revolution of 1990, itself peaceful, ended both the Soviet domination and the communist rule of Czechoslovakia. Just three years later, the Czechs and Slovaks dissolved their 80-year-old union. The second parting came after six years of a sideways trend in European stock prices, as depicted in Figure 6.

The split was remarkably smooth and quick. Negotiations began in July 1992, and by December the respective leaders had agreed to dissolve the union. Their accord split assets based on population. Both sides agreed almost immediately to the newly drawn border. Citizens of the Czech Republic and Slovakia can still cross the border without a passport and work in either country without a permit. Both countries honor any treaties signed during the time of Czechoslovakia. An unwritten rule makes it customary for the elected presidents to pay their first and last official "foreign" visits of their term to their counterpart. Neither state claimed the former Czechoslovakia's status as a member of the United Nations; the UN therefore admitted the two new countries separately.

Figure 6

The former alliance did choose to break apart, thereby indicating a level of frustration and disunity between the two sets of participants. But they showed a remarkable willingness to cooperate and move on. Such a compromise would have been extremely difficult to achieve amidst a condition of strongly negative social mood.

Summary

The lesson is clear: Ill feelings generated by negative social mood during the initial decline in a major bear market in stocks are not to be ignored. In most cases, they are harbingers of worse to come during the second decline. Human nature has not changed with the advent of the 21st century. Any society experiencing a two-part major corrective wave is at risk of deep unrest during the initial wave down and war during and shortly after the second. When bear markets are mild, peaceful splits are possible.

NOTES AND REFERENCES

[1] William L. Yancey, in a public letter to James S. Slaughter, as published in *The New York Times* on May 9, 1860.

Chapter 30

Social Mood Has Regulated the
Success of the Tea Party

Alan Hall

June 6 / October 20, 2011 (TS)

A decade ago, the September 2001 issue of *The Elliott Wave Theorist* said,

> The coming trend of negative social psychology will be character-
> ized primarily by polarization between and among various perceived
> groups.... Such a sentiment change typically brings conflict in
> many forms, and evidence of it will be visible in all types of social
> organizations. Political manifestations will include protectionism in
> trade matters, a polarized and vocal electorate, separatist movements,
> xenophobia, citizen-government clashes, and the dissolution of old
> alliances and parties and the emergence of radical new ones.[1]

The Tea Party movement arose in the negative mood climate around
the March 2009 low in the stock market and continued throughout 2010.
The Tea Party had great appeal when people were angry and fearful.

The two-year trend toward positive social mood since 2009 has doubled
the Dow Jones Industrial Average and slackened society's overall level of
fear and anger. Accordingly, CNN and Pew Research Center polls[2] indicate
that the Tea Party movement has lost popularity, as have its spokesmen [see
Chapter 6 of *Socionomic Studies of Society
and Culture*]. It's as if people reviewed the
Tea Party's anti-big-government aims and
thought, "Things are getting back to normal; maybe we don't need drastic reform
after all."

DONT TREAD ON ME

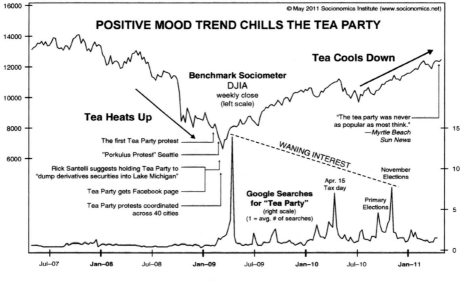

Figure 1

Figure 1 plots the DJIA in the top line and Google searches for "Tea Party" in the bottom line. The first sharp spike in searches closely followed the negative extreme in social mood in March 2009. That is when the Tea Party began nationwide protests and adopted the Gadsden Flag—originally an emblem of colonial America's angry revolt against British rule—as its symbol. Subsequent spikes in Google searches occurred on tax and election days, when news reference volume (not shown) peaked. But in general, as social mood continued toward the positive in late 2010, interest in the Tea Party, as reflected by Google searches, waned.

Dale Robertson, a Tea Party activist and self-proclaimed founder of the movement, exemplified the angry mood in February 2009 by displaying a highly polarizing sign. The Tea Party mainstream has distanced itself from Robertson. Robertson himself now presents a far more diplomatic face in a recent video interview

Vitriolic Past: The self-proclaimed founder of TeaParty.org carried a controversial sign at the February 27, 2009 Tea Party in Houston. The word at the top of the sign is "Congress."

posted at teaparty.org. The Tea Party's proponents in Congress have also tempered their vitriol as the social-mood environment has become more positive. ABC News reported on April 20, 2011, "They swept into power on a wave of popular enthusiasm less than a year ago, but it's not so easy being a Tea Party Congressman these days."[3] One freshman Tea Party House Representative says, "I desperately want to vote 'no'" on raising the debt ceiling, but "I also desperately don't want [the economy] to crash."[1]

Figure 2 graphs the rising Dow versus the declining Tea Party popularity, plotted as the ratio of favorable/unfavorable responses in two polls.

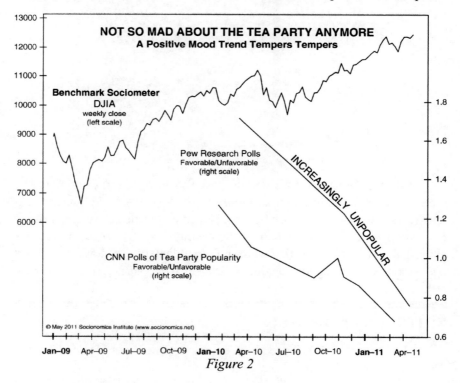

Figure 2

Socionomically speaking, the very decisions to start such polls was an indication of a peak in Tea Party popularity. Two years of increasingly positive social mood led to the highest-ever levels of unfavorable views of the Tea Party movement.[3] With sentiment similar to Alice's in this cartoon,[4] political commentator Nate Silver recently wrote, "If the Tea Party ain't over yet, the point in time at which it was an electoral asset for Republicans soon may be."[5]

Joshua Green, editor of *Atlantic* magazine, wrote on May 12 that the Tea Party

> appears to have reached the limit of its influence in Washington. [It] is looking like a spent force…. Glenn Beck is waning. Sarah Palin's presidential hopes are passing into rapid eclipse. Even Representative Michele Bachmann of Minnesota—founder of the congressional Tea Party caucus…has begun cautiously backing away.[6]

"It's the stupidest tea party I ever was at in all my life," said Alice.

William Temple, chairman of the Tea Party Founding Fathers, recently complained in *The Washington Post*, "Instead of a fighter for U.S. taxpayers, [Republican House Speaker] Boehner has been a surrenderist."[7] Socionomics explains this change: Increasingly positive social mood has altered the political forces that were so favorable to the Tea Party two years ago. If mood turns negative again, the Tea Party or a variant of it will likely return.

NOTES AND REFERENCES

[1] Prechter, R. (2001, September). Forecasting the Tenor of Social Events. *The Elliott Wave Theorist.*

[2] CNN poll: Unfavorable View of Tea Party on the Rise (2011, March 30). CNN.com.

[3] Falcone, M. & Walter, A. (2011, April 20). No Cup of Tea: GOP Freshman Under Pressure on Debt Plans. ABC News.

[4] Stupidest Tea Party. About.com political humor.

[5] Silver, Nate. (March 30, 2011). Poll Shows More Americans Have Unfavorable Views of Tea Party. *The New York Times.*

[6] Green, Joshua, (2011, May 12). The Tea Party is Losing Steam. *The Atlantic.*

[7] Milbank, D. (2011, May 9). Muskets in Hand, Tea Party Blasts House Republicans. *The Washington Post.*

Chapter 31

One month after the London riots occurred (see Chapter 32), protests broke out in the U.S. It was for the same reason: a trend toward negative social mood, as indicated by a falling stock market.—Ed.

The Occupy Wall Street Protests

Robert Prechter and Alan Hall

October 21, 2011 (EWT) / October 20, 2011 (TS)

Many commentators are writing articles about what the Occupy Wall Street protests "mean." But *Conquer the Crash* (2002) predicted that the negative social mood behind the bear market would also lead to class conflict. To us, this news *fulfills our analysis*; it is not something *to be analyzed.* Here is how that book put it:

> The main social influence of [negative mood] is to cause society to polarize in countless ways. That polarity shows up in every imaginable context—social, religious, political, racial, corporate and by class.... It is probably a product of the anger [that negative mood fosters], because each social unit seems invariably to find reasons to be angry with and to attack its opposing unit.

Religious conflict had erupted on 9/11. *Political* conflict was evident in the Tea Party movement. *Racial* conflict manifests currently in the global anti-immigrant movement. Recent protests express primarily *class* conflict.

Do you think the Occupy Wall Street movement is rational? Some commentators say that the protesters are quite reasonably upset that there is an income disparity and that monied interests influence the government. But the income disparity has been extreme for twenty years, and people with money and influence have always bought government representatives. Why protest now?

Socionomics can answer that question. In the U.S., there were hardly any large-scale protests during the 1990s, when the trend of social mood was toward the positive. The same thing was true up to 2007, when sociometers such as stock prices, real estate prices and total dollar-denominated debt were near all-time highs. All these conditions were results of a historically elevated social mood.

In 2009, after stocks had fallen hard for 2½ years, however, the Tea Party formed and protests suddenly broke out. Was the Tea Party movement motivated primarily by rational thought? No. For more than 70 years, many people have believed that government over-spends and that Americans are over-taxed. Why did people wait until 2009 to take to the streets over it? They got mad, thanks to the rapid trend toward negative social mood of 2007-2009. Anger is one of the emotions that negative social mood un-consciously predisposes people to experience and express. To justify it, rational thought is not predominant; rationaliza-tion is. Demonstrating this causality, the Tea

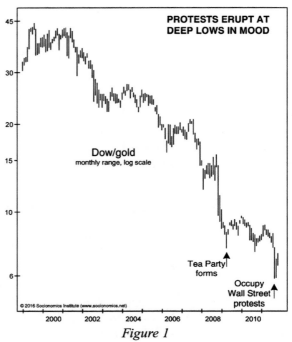

Figure 1

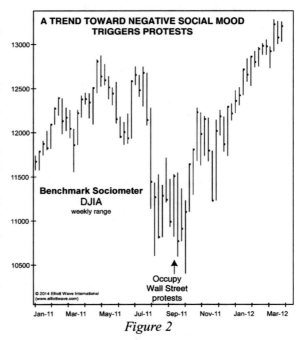

Figure 2

Party got started at the very bottom in the DJIA [as shown in Figure 1 in Chapter 30] and at an interim low after a prolonged decline in Dow/gold (refer to Figure 1).

Positive social mood then supported a rise in the stock market from March 2009 through April 2011, and the Tea Party's energy waned. But by September, a new excuse to protest emerged after social mood—as evidenced once again by plunging stock prices (see Figure 2)—had turned negative enough, for long enough (see Figure 1), that people once again needed an outlet for anger.

Sociologists cast about when trying to explain why the world's young adults have suddenly taken to the streets:

> You're looking at a generation of 20- and 30-year-olds who are used to self-organizing. They believe life can be more participatory, more decentralized, less dependent on the traditional models of organiza-tion....[1]

But this generation is *not* inherently different. Like previous genera-tions, it comprises *Homo sapiens*, who have fundamentally the same brains as their predecessors. The protestors are simply expressing negative social mood.

MSNBC reported on Occupy Wall Street's utter lack of focus:

> It's messy. It's disorganized. At times, the message is all but incoher-ent. All of which makes Occupy Wall Street, the loosely organized protest in lower Manhattan...a lot like the rest of the current American political discourse.[2]

ABC News also described the protests' lack of definition:

> These protesters have adopted that same decentralized structure.... One of the beautiful things about [Occupy Wall Street] is that it is a movement defining itself as it "becomes."[3]

All these media interviews suggest that the protestors' mental state is: "I'm just mad, but if you press me I'll come up with a reason." The reasons don't matter. A socionomist's blog post at FifthWaveFinancialAnalysis.com captures Occupy Wall Street's true impetus:

> People think these protestors are being rational. They aren't; they are just finding something to protest because of the predominately negative social mood. If the trend were up, all the inequity on Wall Street would be like water off a duck's back. Indeed that was the case up until the May 2 top.[4]

The photo at right offers a flash of socionomic clarity in the form of a succinct and honest placard.

Both the left and right sides of the political spectrum have expressed anger in recent years, indicating an emotion ultimately experienced society-wide. According to media reports, the Tea Party on the right wants less government spending, lower taxes and fewer regulations; and the Occupy Wall Street protesters on the left want more jobs, more student loans, more environmental regulations and more money from the rich. Both groups are angry because, they say, they aren't getting what they want. The *stated reasons* for upset, however, vary as much as people do, and in many cases they are the polar opposite of other people's reasons. There is only one true reason: negative social mood.

NOTES AND REFERENCES

[1] Kulish, N. (2011, September 28). 'Voting is Worthless'? Global Protests Share Contempt for Democracy. MSNBC.com.

[2] Schoen, J.W. (2011, September 27). Familiar Refrain: Wall Street Protest Lacks Leaders, Clear Message. MSNBC.com.

[3] Krieg, G.J. (2011, October 5). Occupy Wall Street Protests: Police Make Numerous Arrests. ABC News.

[4] State of the markets (2011, October 7). Fifth Wave Financial Analysis.

Chapter 32

Twitter Study Shows an Increase in Negative Mood Leading Up to the London Riots of 2011

Chuck Thompson

October 2, 2012 (TS)

On April 29, 2011, Londoners were joyfully tweeting about the royal wedding and swooning over the details of Kate Middleton's wedding dress. Social mood was so benign that the newlyweds left church in an open air coach, seemingly carried along by the ebullient crowd of Londoners all around them.

Four months later, over August 6-9, 2011, riots erupted in London. The violence was so severe that it forced the cancellation of five professional football (soccer) games and closed down commuter trains, public buses and even some underground tube stations. Five people died.

As firefighters hosed down London's rubble in the aftermath of the riots, many Brits blamed Twitter, where rioters had reported the locations of unguarded stores easy to loot and instructions for making a Molotov Cocktail. What *really* caused the dramatic shift in public behavior?

A Study of Tweets

Thomas Lansdall-Welfare and other researchers at the University of Bristol's Intelligent Systems Laboratory examined 484 million tweets in the United Kingdom from July 2009 to January 2012 and published their findings in a paper titled "Effects of the Recession on Public Mood in the UK."[1]

The researchers investigated a pair of one-time events: the announcement of major UK budget cuts on October 20, 2010, and the August 2011 riots in London and other UK cities. They chose these events based on the severity of sentiment surrounding them, which they calculated by "counting the frequency of emotion-related words in each [tweet] published on a given day." The researchers selected words commonly associated with four key human emotions. Their lists include 146 anger words, 92 fear words, 224 joy words and 115 sadness words. The researchers then compared the mean of the emotional intensity expressed 50 days before and after each day in the time period, ultimately identifying the days that were followed by the greatest rate of change for the next 50 days compared to the previous 50 days.

Figure 1 is reproduced from the researchers' study. The thick grey line tracks the rate of change in expressions of anger, and the thin black line tracks expressions of fear. Vertical lines indicate the dates of the budget cuts and the riots. When the thick and thin lines are above zero, they reflect the rates of rises in the 50-day means of anger and fear, respectively. Peaks represent the days of fastest ascent. When the lines are below zero, they reflect the rates of declines in anger and fear. Troughs reflect days on which those declines were the fastest.

The fact that fear and anger have trended so closely together supports Prechter's proposed list of mood-related emotional polarities offered in Chapter 14 of *The Wave Principle of Human Social Behavior* (1999). The list shows that when negative mood increases, society moves from forbearance to anger, from confidence to fear, and from concord to discord.[2]

The researchers pointed out that the budget cuts announced on October 20, 2010 had received extensive media coverage and came as no surprise to the population. The public had been expecting cuts since June of that

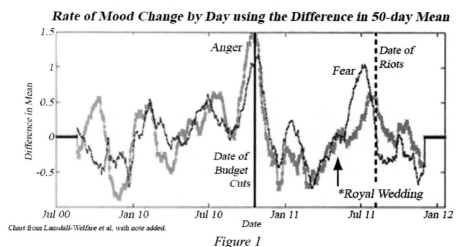

Rate of Mood Change by Day using the Difference in 50-day Mean

Chart from Lansdall-Welfare et al, with note added.

Figure 1

year, when the government announced details of a spending review. But the researchers nevertheless contended that Twitter content indicated that the announcement had a dramatic effect on emotions in the UK.

The researchers also observed a temporary decline in ill feelings in early May 2011, which they hypothesized could be a result of the royal wedding between Prince William and Kate Middleton. The event occurred on April 29, a day of celebration in which bells rang in central London. We have marked the date of the wedding on Figure 1. Lansdall-Welfare cautioned, "The involvement of social scientists would be crucial in determining causes and analyzing *reactions to events* [emphasis added] in a more thorough manner."

A Socionomic Look at the Researchers' Findings

The researchers' goal was to "see if the effects of social events can be seen in the contents of Twitter, and to speculate if some of them could even be predicted." As you can see from such statements as well as the very title of the paper, mechanical causality underlies their premises.

In the case of the UK riots, however, they found something intriguing: a "build up of anger and fear in Twitter content, beginning in early spring 2011, until just before the riots happened." The increase in tweeters' use of negative words *before* the violent event runs

Hot Pursuit: Mounted police officers chase rioters amid the flames in Tottenham, where the riots began.

counter to the conventional idea that events drive changes in social mood. The authors wrote, "we have seen signals preceding the riots that could possibly be used as indicators. For this conclusion to be reached in more certain ways, we need more data, but we observe that *a steady increase in anger* was observed in the weeks *preceding* the riots." (emphasis added) Socionomic theory explains this finding.

Budget Cuts and Austerity Programs Do Not Cause Riots

As noted earlier, the researchers determined that the announcement of budget cuts had an effect on emotions (they used the term "mood") in the United Kingdom after the event. They reported a "large peak in the mean difference of fear and anger" (Figure 1) in conjunction with the cuts. The cuts were the deepest in 60 years and included an average 19% reduction in spending by government departments, sharp reductions in welfare benefits, an increase in the retirement age and the elimination of hundreds of thousands of public sector jobs.[3] One might have expected riots to ensue. But Figure 2 shows upward movement at that time in two sociometers: the FTSE 100, an index of companies on the London Stock Exchange, and the Euro Stoxx 50, an index of European blue chips, both of which indicated a positive trend in social mood.

The difference helps illustrate two important socionomic points. First, *emotions* can be triggered by either social mood or social events. Events such as holidays, for example, tend to inspire emotional tweets. In the case at hand, the budget-cutting event precipitated an outpouring of negative emotion, which the Twitter study captured. Second, the cuts *triggered no riots* like the ones that erupted less than a year later, because social mood in the UK in October 2010, as reflected by the stock indexes shown in Figure 2, was not negative enough to motivate social unrest.

Consider the case of Greece in February 2012, when rioters set fire to more than 40 buildings. The riots occurred around the time that Greece's parliament voted to approve an unpopular austerity package, which included a 22% cut in the minimum wage and the loss of 150,000 government jobs. But Greece's riots occurred *before*, not after, the austerity vote took place. So, the vote could not have been the cause of the riots. Figure 3 suggests a better reason for the riots: extremely negative social mood, as indicated by a steep fall in Greece's stock index. That social mood—not events—motivates decisions to riot or not is exactly what we found in our study of three New York City blackouts, reprinted in Chapter 12 of *Pioneering Studies in Socionomics*.

The Root Cause of Riots in London and Elsewhere

Expressions of negative social mood tend to erupt during a sideways or downward trend in stock prices. As Figure 2 shows, the FTSE 100 turned sharply downward just before the UK riots. That is why Lansdall-Welfare and his team found a "build up of anger and fear" in July-August, *leading up to* the event, as shown in Figure 1.

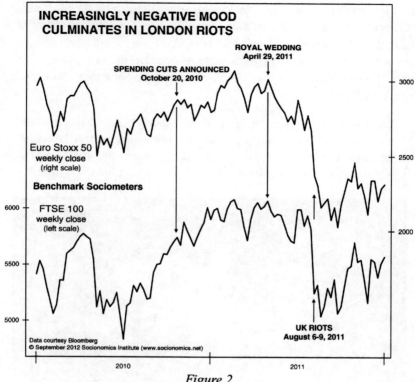

Figure 2

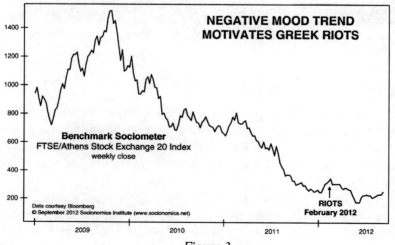

Figure 3

There was a corresponding downturn in the Euro Stoxx 50. This shift in European social mood explains why riots and vandalism broke out not only in the UK but also in Sweden and Germany, one week later. Those riots were obviously not due to British budget cuts, or, in fact, any exogenous cause. Prechter discussed these outbreaks in the September 2011 issue of *The Elliott Wave Theorist*:

> Articles on Sweden say, "It was not immediately clear what provoked the unrest...." The cause is definitely not immediately clear, because the cause is not immediate. The primary cause is the trend toward negative social mood, which had been developing for some time.

Season of Fire: The Association of British Insurers estimated damage from the riots at £200 million ($325 million).

"Triggers" are Not to Blame

Prechter noted that people often point to a "'trigger' for mob action—a police beating, an assassination, etc.—but usually the cited event is itself an expression of negative social mood that just happened to precede the event in question." [See fuller discussion in Chapter 23 of *The Socionomic Theory of Finance.*]

In the case of the UK riots, the supposed trigger event was the August 4 killing of a suspect by police, who were investigating crime in a minority community. The victim, 29-year-old Mark Duggan, was riding in a taxi in Tottenham, when he was stopped and fatally shot. On August 6, some 200 to 300 people, including friends of Duggan and his family, gathered outside the Tottenham police station for what began as a peaceful protest. Three hours later, following an argument between a protester and a police officer, protesters threw bottles at police vehicles and set two of them on fire. The unrest grew into three days of rioting in which participants threw petrol bombs at officers and police cars, torched buildings, looted shops and even broke into private homes. Riots occurred in 22 of 32 London boroughs and in dozens of cities outside London, including Manchester, Liverpool and Nottingham. "They were black and white, rich and poor, old and young," *The Telegraph* said of the participants.[4] In the September 2011 issue of *The European Financial Forecast*, editor Brian Whitmer pointed out that the worst offenders included a "law student, a ballerina, a lifeguard, a Baptist mentor, an organic chef, a schoolteacher's assistant—and the daughter of a millionaire London businessman"—not your typical hooligans.

A minor, focused protest over the shooting of Mark Duggan was only the first event in a nationwide expression of negative social mood. It was not a chain of individually caused events; it was a *social* event. The leading decline in financial markets, coupled with the leading increase in the use of anger and fear words on Twitter, fit the socionomic explanation.

Methodology

We commend Lansdall-Welfare et al. for their contribution to the growing volume of research on public mood and hope their efforts will inspire others to study this fascinating and critical subject. We believe that socionomics can help to guide and to expand the value of such investigations.

For example, the researchers used a 100-day moving window (50 days on either side) to detect abrupt changes in emotion before and after the particular day of an important social event. By this method's very construction, it is clear that the researchers began with the assumption that events cause changes in social mood. That assumption nearly wipes out the forecasting value of the data. It also negates its practical value. In crisis situations, planners cannot wait fifty days to compile a forecast, and they cannot wait for a violent event to tell them that there might be a violent event. Because socionomists constantly monitor stock market trends as meters of social mood, they can detect changes in mood well ahead of events. Socionomics can also help analysts anticipate the types of events social mood might motivate as well as the public's likely positive or negative interpretation of those events. Tweets could be a helpful addition to this early warning system.

Socionomists can help planners distinguish between mood and emotion and to gauge the effect that the former may have on the latter. Negative mood spurs negative emotions and actions. Sometimes an action will stir an emotion apart from mood. If a negative event were to prompt negative emotions at a time when social mood is trending positively, there is less potential for social unrest—as was the case in London when the spending cuts were announced in October 2010. But if a negative event were to prompt negative emotions at a time when social mood is trending negatively, the likelihood of social unrest is far greater—as was the case when Mark Duggan was killed in August 2011.

Socionomically informed authorities observing a declining stock market in the months leading up to the UK riots would have been aware that social mood was trending negatively and could have prepared for social unrest. The lack of such knowledge is an impediment to action. As London's *Sunday Telegraph* reported, "the decision which finally stopped the trouble in London—to deploy 16,000 police officers on the streets—was not made until 9 a.m. on Tuesday [August 9]...61 hours after the violence first started.... Even on Tuesday...the looters were still ahead of the law. The violence simply moved to Manchester, Liverpool, Nottingham and dozens of other towns."[5] Individuals as well should be cognizant of mood trends, because actions expressing social mood affect all of us personally.

NOTES AND REFERENCES

[1] Lansdall-Welfare, T., Lampos, V., & Cristianini, N. Effects of the Recession on Public Mood in the UK.

[2] Prechter, R. (1999). *The Wave Principle of Human Social Behavior* (pp. 228-229). Gainesville, Georgia: New Classics Library.

[3] Lyall, S., & Cowell, A. (2010, October 20). Britain Plans Deepest Cuts to Spending in 60 Years. *The New York Times.*

[4] Gilligan, A. (2011, August 14). UK Riots: A Festival of Broken Glass. *The Telegraph.*

[5] Gilligan, A. (2011, August 14). UK Riots: A Festival of Broken Glass. *The Telegraph.*

Chapter 33

Study Finds Swearing on Twitter Increased Before the Iranian Protests

Euan Wilson

February 28, 2013 (TS)

Last year, the RAND Corporation released a report[1] describing a relationship between Iran's Green Revolution and the content of local messages on Twitter. In "Using Social Media to Gauge Iranian Public Opinion and Mood After the 2009 Election," the authors used "Linguistic Inquiry and Wordcount" (LIWC, pronounced "Luke") to examine language used in Iranian tweets. They looked at emotion-laden words: swear words, anxiety words and happiness words. The authors then charted each of these expressions and compared them with major events in Iran in the months following the June 2009 election. Their fascinating finding: "Surprisingly, [Iranian] people's use of swear words on Twitter tracked more closely than any other indicator did with events and protests on the ground, and *it did the best job of forecasting when protests would occur*"[2] (emphasis added).

We compared the authors' swear-words graph to the Iranian stock market. As we expected (see Figure 1), the two indexes track each other quite closely. The reason, in our view, is that they are both manifestations of changes in social mood.

On July 30, 2009, the Iranian government announced plans to crack down on mourners protesting the violent death of a protestor. Despite the government's action, incidences of swearing continued to decline through the immediate period. Why? Because Iranian social mood, as illustrated by Iran's stock market, was trending positively. A similar situation occurred around October 7. A huge *decline* in swearing occurred despite an unprecedented crackdown on protests. Again, throughout that period, Iranian social mood was in a positive trend.

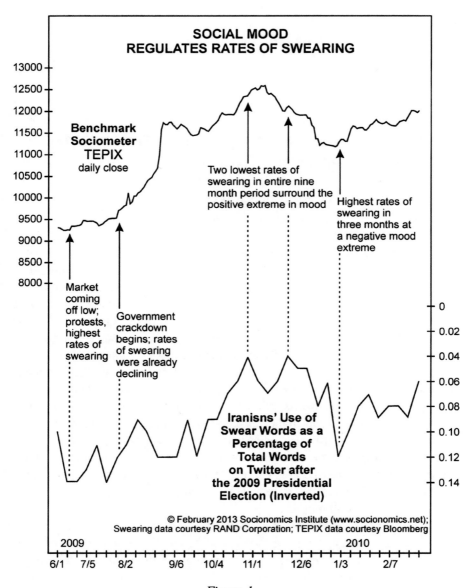

Figure 1

Over the weeks of October 18-24 and November 15-21, 2009, rates of swearing hit their lows. These two periods came on either side of the highest point in Iranian stock prices for the entire nine-month span. As of late February 2010, as shown at the end of the chart, swearing was again on the decline, while our benchmark sociometer was simultaneously reaching its most positive point in over three months.

Finally, consider the peaks in swearing. All of them occurred at lows in the stock market, indicating that social mood was predominantly negative at those times.

Why are these trends coincident? Socionomic theory posits that increasingly negative social mood impels feelings of fear, anger, sadness and frustration. Swearing expresses such feelings. Doing so alleviates the uncomfortable emotions produced by negative, unconscious social mood. When social mood is positive, sunnier emotions reduce the impulse to swear.

NOTES AND REFERENCES

[1] Elson, Sara Beth, Douglas Yeung, Parisa Roshan, S.R. Bohandy and Alireza Nader (2012). "Using Social Media to Gauge Iranian Public Opinion and Mood After the 2009 Election." RAND Corporation.

[2] RAND Corporation (n.d.). "Can Social Media Help Analyze Public Opinion? A Case Study of Iranian Public Opinion After the 2009 Election." RAND Corporation Research Brief.

Chapter 34

Gallup's Measure of Public Sentiment May Be Another Indicator of Social Mood

Chuck Thompson

January 31, 2013 (TS)

A recent Gallup survey known as the "Negative Experience Index" supports the socionomic case that a society's mood can be used to forecast significant social events such as revolutions, political changes and future productivity as measured by GDP. The findings are significant because, as Gallup CEO Jim Clifton—a speaker at our 2013 Social Mood Conference—said, "Virtually all world leaders and heads of states and cities are focused on the wrong things. They are looking through the rearview mirror at GDP in an attempt to see the road ahead. Consequently, they are managing their countries and cities after the fact."[1]

The Survey

Gallup's 2011 World Poll surveyed adults in 148 countries. Researchers queried respondents on a number of questions to assess their "wellbeing," a measure of their emotional state. Researchers then quantified the levels of "anger, stress, worry, sadness, and physical pain" in the responses to create a Negative Experience Index (NEI).

The Index data came from telephone and face-to-face interviews with at least 1,000 adults in each of the 148 nations Gallup surveyed. Survey respondents were asked to consider the previous day and to rank how their wellbeing was on that particular day. The survey uncovered several notable facts:

1. Major Natural Events Do Not Impact a Country's Mood

Gallup's NEI provides two dramatic examples of this observation:

Haiti suffered a calamitous 7.0-magnitude earthquake on January 12, 2010, in which 300,000 people were killed, one million were made homeless and huge swaths of the country's infrastructure were leveled. Yet, Gallup says, Haiti's Negative Experience Index score *did not change* from December 2008 to June 2010.

On March 11, 2011, Japan experienced a 9.0-magnitude earthquake off its coast that triggered a massive tsunami and tens of thousands of deaths. Multiple nuclear accidents forced hundreds of thousands of people to leave their homes. Despite this tragedy, Japan's score on the Negative Experience Index in 2011 was the same as its score in 2010.

Source: GlobalPost

No Change in Mood: A young woman in the Japanese Coastal city of Ishinomaki surveys the devastation wreaked by the 2011 earthquake and tsunami. Japan's score on Gallup's Negative Experience was the same after the dual event as it was before.

2. A Country's Mood Paints a More Accurate Picture of its Stability Than Does GDP

In 2010, according to the International Monetary Fund, Lebanon's GDP growth was 7.5% and Egypt's was 5.1%. Their average was twice, three times and 40% higher than GDP growth in the U.S., the UK and Japan, respectively. Despite their relatively high GDP growth, Lebanon and Egypt were touched in 2011 by the Arab Spring revolution and its protests, sectarian violence and government collapses. Gallup's NEI painted a more accurate picture than did GDP of Egypt's and Lebanon's high risk of instability. The index listed both countries in the quartile of nations with the highest Negative Experience Index scores, with Egypt coming in at number five.

3. A Country's Emotional State Can Forecast Significant Social Events

Gallup noted that in both Egypt and Bahrain, "negative emotions were running high well before the unrest" that shook both nations in 2011. "I think it was a surprise to a lot of us [when Bahrain made this list]," Gallup's Jon Clifton said, "particularly because at the time their GDP per capita was so high compared to the rest of the world." The Arab Spring protests in Egypt escalated on January 25, 2011, and on February 11 former President Hosni Mubarak resigned. During that 18-day period, about 900 people were killed and more than 6,000 were injured. Bahrain's Arab Spring protests resulted in about 30 deaths.

Socionomic Implications

The poll's findings align with socionomic causality in a number of ways:

First, natural events don't change social mood; rather, social mood governs the way people react to events. Sociologists might have expected earthquakes in Haiti and Japan to produce significant changes in either nation's mood, but socionomists never would have, and they didn't. Major events *can* create a short-term change in a country's emotional condition, but such changes are temporary, and any event-caused change in a country's emotional condition will soon return to a state that reflects the country's mood.

Second, socionomic theory recognizes that social mood is endogenously regulated, not exogenously driven. Socionomists would not have expected Egypt's and Lebanon's favorable GDP levels to trump their societies' negative mood and erase their penchant for protests and violence, and they didn't.

Third, Gallup found that negative emotions were running high in Egypt and Bahrain well *before* the unrest that shook those nations occurred. As Prechter noted in Chapter 14 of *The Wave Principle of Human Social Behavior* (1999), when positively trending mood gives way to negatively trending mood, concord gives way to discord, alignment is displaced by opposition, and convergence is reversed to polarization. These transitions were obvious in Egypt and Bahrain as negative mood built to a crescendo, prompting hundreds of thousands of protesters to take to the streets.

Accounting for an Anomaly

One of Gallup's polls ran starkly contrary to socionomic causality. Gallup's highest NEI belonged to Iraq, a country whose stock market at the time had risen substantially. We have not delved into possible sociological reasons for this disparity, but social mood's unconscious nature makes us quite certain that a country's stock market trends will reflect social mood better than records of people's verbal responses to questions. People express social mood non-rationally and impulsively, not necessarily in a setting in which they are asked to be thoughtful. Designing the question so as to inquire only about one's feelings on a single particular day, moreover, opens the door quite widely to recollections of emotions attached to specific events rather than to mood.

What Socionomics Offers World Leaders

For the most part, Gallup's findings undermine the typical assumption that events cause changes in public mood. In the cases covered here, mood trends *preceded* compatibly toned events. Gallup's polls also support the formulation derived from socionomics that social mood determines how people will feel about events, both social and natural.

Gallup CEO Jim Clifton wrote, "Almost no one knows or understands this: [changes in] gross national wellbeing (GNW) occur *before* [changes in] GDP in cities and countries. GNW, or the lack of it, occurs *before* revolutions and before significant political change."[1] This is a concise expression of the chronology behind socionomic causality.

NOTES AND REFERENCES

[1] Clifton, J. (2013, January 14). Why World Leaders Must Track Gross National Wellbeing. *Gallup Business Journal*.

Chapter 35

An Elliott Wave in Nuclear-War Fears

Alan Hall

November 28, 2014 (TS)

Concern about nuclear weapons involves contexts of uncertainty and substantial emotion, suggesting that it may be amenable to Elliott wave analysis. Figure 1 plots the relative occurrence of the term "nuclear weapon" in Google Books' corpus of word data from 5.2 million English-language books. The chart seems to reflect public interest, concern and awareness regarding nuclear weapons.

Peaks in the chart coincide with related events. The bombings of Hiroshima and Nagasaki preceded the peak of wave 1. The Cuban Missile Crisis of October 1962 and Stanley Kubrick's black comedy, *Dr. Strangelove or: How I Learned to Stop Worrying and Love the Bomb*, released 15 months later, rang in the peak of wave 3. The peak of wave 5 came soon after what Israeli historian Dmitry Adamsky called "the moment of maximum danger of the late Cold War,"[1] namely Able Archer 83, a U.S. war game that simulated military escalation and a nuclear attack on the USSR. Amid tension between these two powers in September 1983, a Soviet fighter jet

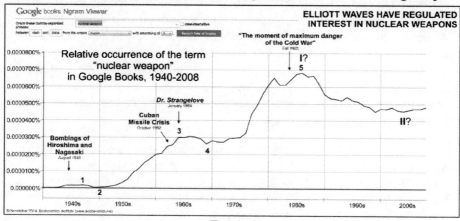

Figure 1

shot down Korean Air Lines Flight 007, killing all aboard, including a U.S. Congressman. Newly declassified documents reveal "how the world's rival superpowers found themselves blindly edging toward the brink of nuclear war through suspicion, belligerent posturing and blind miscalculation" in 1983,[2] at the most dangerous extreme in a long deterioration in U.S.-Soviet relations. Books and movies take a couple of years to write and publish, so the peaks for Google's data in 1947, 1964 and 1985 perfectly reflect the implied pinnacles of nuclear war fears in 1945, 1962 and 1983.

It is tempting to link the wave 5 peak in Figure 1 to the 16-year extreme in negative social mood of 1982 (as recorded in the Dow/PPI, not shown) that immediately preceded it, and the decline since then to the trend toward positive mood that has followed. But the rise of authors' interest in nuclear weapons over a decade and a half from the early 1950s to the mid-1960s ran perfectly contrarily to the trend of the stock market. The graph in Figure 1, then, is not a societal sociometer [see Chapter 7 of *The Socionomic Theory of Finance*] but a specialized one that moves at least somewhat independently of overall social mood. [For more on independent Elliott waves in certain social activities, see Chapter 80 of *Socionomic Studies of Society and Culture*.] One possibility is that the positive trend in social mood that ran simultaneously in Russia in the 1950s and 1960s [see Chapter 36] emboldened the USSR and thereby stoked nuclear-war fears, which would have been more of a sociological effect than a direct expression of social mood. The clear Elliott wave in Figure 1 is nevertheless highly suggestive of socionomic causality in the overall ebb and flow of people's interest in nuclear weapons.

The five-wave advance to a high in 1985 resolved into a subsequent period of nearly 30 years of fewer mentions of "nuclear weapon," indicating a time of relative complacency regarding this threat. Nobel Peace Prize nominee Dr. Helen Caldicott described nuclear complacency as "psychic numbing," and added, "We are lemmings. We are all into manic denial."[3] Although concern over nuclear war could someday fall to zero, the Elliott waves depicted in Figure 1 allow that today's nuclear complacency may eventually give way to another wave of nuclear concern, as represented by the "I?" and "II?" labels on the graph.

NOTES AND REFERENCES

[1] Gray, S. (2014, November 7). Noam Chomsky on Russia: "The Worst-case Scenario, Of Course, Would Be a Nuclear War." *Salon.*

[2] Birch, D. (2013, May 28). The U.S.S.R. and U.S. Came Closer to Nuclear War Than We Thought. *The Atlantic.*

[3] Sieff, M. (2014, October 13). Nuclear War Could Be Near, According to a Nobel Laureate. *Global Research.*

Chapter 36

Social Mood Regulates Perceptions
of Political Normality

Alan Hall

April 28, 2010 (TS) / April 2016 (Summit speech)

A society's definition of what is socially, politically and morally "normal" constantly changes. Different social mood trends and conditions create dramatically different perceptions of normalcy, even within the same country. Positive mood trends produce increasing confidence and consensus; negative mood trends produce fear, anger, polarization, discord and challenges to the status quo.

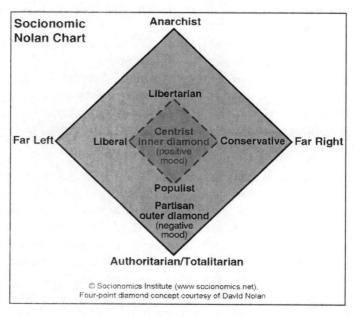

Figure 1

Introducing the Socionomic Nolan Chart

Social polarization is not limited to the one-dimensional political spectrum of left versus right. It includes the more clearly opposing views favoring liberty versus authoritarianism.

Figure 1 is our adaptation of the Nolan Chart, a simple diagram that depicts these complex political dynamics. David Nolan[1] posited that left-wing liberalism advocates personal freedom, right-wing conservatism advocates economic freedom, libertarians advocate both, and authoritarians neither. We added the inner diamond to Nolan's picture to distinguish between the relative consensus of political opinion that occurs during a positive mood trend and the greater polarization of views that occurs during a negative mood trend.

Figure 2 portrays how a society's perception of what is "normal" shifts over time. Their depictions are as follows:

1. *Positive mood extreme*: A consensus, typically centrist view dominates politics.
2. *Negative mood trend begins*: Polarization increases. People abandon the consensus view.
3. *Negative mood trend*: Society desires separation, opposition and the destruction of the status quo. The consensus on what is normal dissolves.
4. *Negative mood extreme*: Coalitions form, and one prevails. Society's new normal gels nearer one of the corners.
5. *Positive mood trend begins*: Polarization decreases. Partisans begin to reduce opposition and to embrace compromise.
6. *Positive mood trend*: Society desires unity, cooperation and a peaceful status quo. Optimism and willingness to compromise prevail. A consensus forms on political normalcy.

A large-degree reversal in social mood can accomplish a shift in political views in a relatively short time. The rapid change toward negative social mood globally in 1929-1932 set up a dramatic, worldwide shift in consensus views of normalcy. It polarized societies and diffused consensus, throwing "normal" into flux. New diamonds depicting "normal" coalesced further from the center. In the U.S., a new normal—lower and further to the left—gelled in the 1930s, when U.S. citizens displayed unusual compliance with reduced economic freedom via new government agencies and record-high tax rates.

As social mood trended toward the positive from 1949 until the late 1960s, a middle-of-the-road consensus in the U.S. held for 50 years, with

SOCIETY'S PERCEPTION OF "NORMAL" CHANGES CONSTANTLY

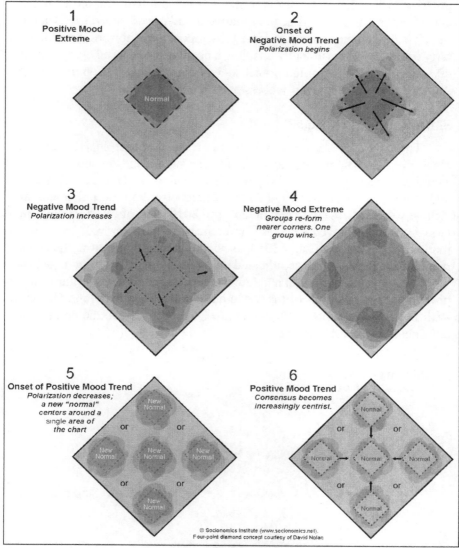

Figure 2

moderate Republicans Eisenhower, Nixon and G.H.W. Bush and moderate Democrats Kennedy and Clinton reflecting centrist political views.

Positive mood generates consensus even in societies that are very near a Nolan extreme. For instance, within the global negative-mood period of 1929-1949, the initial decline in 1929-1932 caused Soviet society to polarize as Russian leader Joseph Stalin effected a hard-left shift toward authoritarianism. By the time the negative mood period ended in 1949, the Soviet centrist diamond had become fully repositioned toward the authoritarian pole. From this unlikely position, a positive mood trend over the next 20 years calmed and unified Soviet society enough that it supported itself economically and achieved success in its space program.

Shifts in What's "Normal"

The Elliott wave model incorporates the fact that social mood is always in flux. Major changes in mood usher in changes in social norms. Trends toward negative social mood tend to lead to calls for more freedom and more authoritarianism, and authoritarians offer both far leftist and far rightist solutions. As recounted in the April 2010 issue of *The Socionomist*, Google Trends showed that news references to "new normal" increased markedly between 2007 and 2010, as sociometers ranging from the stock market to real estate prices indicated an intensely negative trend in social mood. As a result, both right and left-wingers staged protests. Figure 3 approximates the positions of the moderately radical Tea Party and Occupy Wall Street movements of 2009 and 2011, respectively, in the context of our Socionomic Nolan Chart.

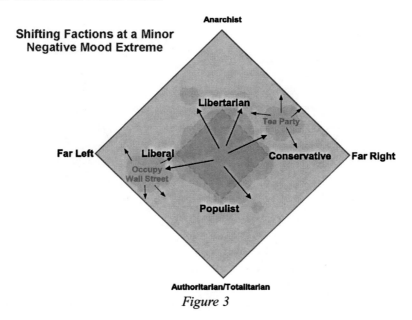

Figure 3

Societies tend to look far different after major-degree trends toward negative mood than they did before them. Where they end up is far less predictable.

NOTES AND REFERENCES

[1] Nolan, David. "Classifying and Analyzing Political-Economic Systems." *The Individualist*, International Society for Individual Liberty, January 1971.

Part III:

SOCIAL MOOD AND AUTHORITARIANISM

Chapter 37

The New Global Bull Market in Socialism

Alan Hall

October 31, 2008 (EFF)

Here in 2008, socialism is suddenly a hot topic. In Japan, young people are joining the Japanese Communist Party in "droves." In Russia, there is renewed reverence for Stalin. Latin American leftists are "gloating over Comrade Bush's Bailout," which one paper described as "the biggest socialist act since the New Deal." In the U.S. presidential campaign, John McCain has seized upon Barack Obama's comment about "spreading the wealth" as reminiscent of Europe's socialist policies.

The timing of this change is no accident. We observe that socialism tends to become popular during the bear markets that follow financial manias. Free-market ideas that typically accompany the boom period are challenged after the reversal. Also, when social mood turns strongly negative, the character of social desire changes from desire for power over nature to desire for power over people. This new desire eventually restricts free markets and individual liberty. The U.S. bailouts are just one instance of rejecting free-market principles.

The *Elliott Wave Theorist* Special Report of 1989 explained political shifts away from individual liberty:

> In a formalization of the negative mood within a bear market, one or more of the new parties is likely to represent ideals inimical to individual liberty (such as socialist, racist, fascist or fundamentalist). In some cases, such as in Russia in the 'teens, Germany in the 'thirties, China in the late 'forties, Cambodia in the 'seventies, and Iran in the late 'seventies, such parties have achieved power.

Figure 1 shows a brief history of socialism plotted against a sociometer comprising three centuries of British equity prices. The data show four financial manias, each one followed by a stronger expression of socialism appearing near the low points within waves (a), (c) and (e).

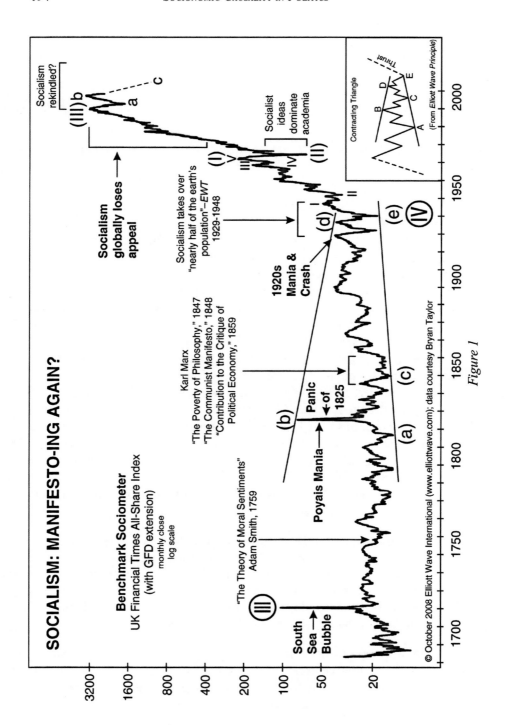

Figure 1

Wave (a)

Adam Smith was a political economist and moral philosopher regarded as the father of modern economics. In 1759, after observing society's despair in the aftermath of the South Sea Bubble, Smith wrote "The Theory of Moral Sentiments," which contains the first mention of his famous "invisible hand" metaphor. Read in context, that passage describes the apparent benefits to society of people behaving in their own interests. But it also contains ideas that Karl Marx and others used a century later to expand socialistic ideology:

> The rich...*divide with the poor the produce of all their improvements.* They are led by an invisible hand to make nearly the same distribution of the necessaries of life, which would have been made, *had the earth been divided into equal portions among all its inhabitants....* (Emphasis added)

Wave (c)

In 1843 in Paris, Marx studied the ideas of Hegel, Smith, Engels and others while he lived through the economic contraction that followed the Panic of 1825 and observed the suffering of the working class. Between 1847 and 1867, he wrote several books that formed the ideological foundation for socialists to take over Russia in 1917.

Wave (e)

The 1920s boom featured capitalistic sentiments such as "What's good for General Motors is good for America." The 1929 crash led globally to the Great Depression. From 1929 to 1949, socialism took over "nearly half of the earth's population, in Germany, Italy, Eastern Europe and China" (*The Elliott Wave Theorist*, September 2001). In the grip of negative social mood, socialist utopian ideas morphed into Joseph Stalin's Great Purges, leaving some 30 million Russians dead, and Adolf Hitler's holocaust. This period marked both the end of wave Ⓘ and the zenith of the past century's rush to embrace socialism.

Recent Shifts

When the Soviet Union collapsed in 1991 during a global trend toward positive social mood, socialism was seen as a failure. Today, in the midst of a financial crisis, capitalism is being cited as a failure. While the main result of negative mood is to produce a desire for political change no matter in what manner [see Chapter 7], society's general tendency is to favor individual liberty in positive-mood periods and collectivism in negative-mood periods.

Chapter 38

Negative Social Mood
Furthers Authoritarianism

Alan Hall

April 28, 2010 / May 21, 2010 (TS)

Mention authoritarianism and most people imagine its ultimate incarnation—a dictator wielding top-down control. The socionomic perspective, however, paints a fuller picture.

Authoritarianism begins with a trend toward negative social mood, which in turn spawns a desire among some people to submit to authority and among others to coerce their fellows to submit. At the same time, still others, befitting the polarizing, negative-mood climate, battle *against* authoritarianism.

Fear's Role in Authoritarian Submission

Negatively trending social mood generates increasing fear within society. As society becomes more fearful, many individuals yearn for the safety and order promised by strong, controlling leaders. In such environments, autocrats can rise to power via popular demand or coups d'état.

As Prechter's 1999 book (pp. 149, 174) related, the survival-oriented portions of the brain respond strongly to fear. Fear overwhelms rational thought, alters individuals' perceptions and causes people to bond with in-groups and become hostile toward out-groups. The desire to belong to in-groups becomes more intense during a negative mood trend.

"Authoritarianism and Economic Threat: Implications for Political Behavior," by Edward J. Rickert, bolstered this case. He found that when people feel threatened and vulnerable, they are more likely to submit to authority, and they become less tolerant of and more aggressive toward outside groups and dissenters. As explained on pages 227-233 of *The Wave Principle of Human Social Behavior* (1999), these are classic behaviors during periods of negative social mood.

Bob Altemeyer, author of *The Authoritarian Specter,* noted that some individuals are more likely than others to welcome authoritarianism. He writes in his online book, *The Authoritarians,*

> Authoritarian followers...are in general, more afraid than most people are.... A person's fear of a dangerous world predicts various kinds of authoritarian aggression better than any other unpleasant feeling.... We do have to fear fear itself.... Fear can increase submission as well as aggression.[1]

Altemeyer found that predisposed followers of authoritarians are willing to behave aggressively on behalf of authorities, especially when they believe the authorities will sanction punitive action against some out-group. He noted that predisposed followers are prone to

> sloppy reasoning, highly compartmentalized beliefs, double standards, hypocrisy, self-blindness, a profound ethnocentrism, and... dogmatism that makes it unlikely anyone could ever change their minds with evidence or logic. These seven deadly shortfalls of authoritarian thinking eminently qualify them to follow a would-be dictator.[2]

Herding's Role in Authoritarian Submission

The famous 1961 Milgram experiment showed that an individual's propensity to herd influences his or her willingness to submit to authority. Milgram assigned participants three roles. An authority figure—the experimenter—led the team. He directed the teacher, an unwitting subject, to dole out tasks and punishment (electric shocks) to a third person—the learner—who was an actor pretending to attempt the tasks and to suffer shocks when he failed. Milgram recorded the subject teacher's responses to the experimenter's orders and found that 62% of participants inflicted the strongest possible shock.

In one scenario, two planted teachers sat with the subject. When the planted teachers disobeyed the experimenter and refused to continue increasing the punishment, 90% of the subjects joined their peers and disobeyed the experimenter. But when the two planted teachers submissively continued shocking the learner, 92% of the subjects delivered the top voltage. The experiment shows, then, that at least 90% of people will follow their peers either in submitting to the pressure of an authority or in rebelling against it.

Social Mood's Role in Authoritarian Herding

Negative mood increases the impulse to join an authoritarian herd. A recent French TV documentary/experiment called "The Game of Death" tested the ease with which contestants will become torturers, apparently shocking a man—actually, an actor—to death as the audience cheered.

[Eighty one] percent of the participants obeyed the sadistic orders of the television presenter.... One contestant interviewed afterwards said she went along with the torture despite knowing that her own grandparents were Jews who had been persecuted by the Nazis.[3]

This show's fifteen participants displayed a higher degree of authoritarian submission than those in the Milgram experiment, which had been conducted during a time of extremely positive social mood as indicated by substantial new all-time highs in stock indexes. "Game of Death," on the other hand, was conducted on the heels of the most negative global social mood since the 1940s. That's probably why the percentage of participants delivering a supposed deathblow is one-third larger. The show's producer said, "[Future] television can—without possible opposition—organize the death of a person as entertainment, and 8 out of 10 people will submit to that." (Time.com, March 17, 2010)

The Authoritarian Progression

The progression from social fear to authoritarianism during negative-mood periods unfolds roughly in the following fashion: A general fear of the future causes people to coalesce into groups with polarized views both on the type of authoritarianism needed and on authoritarianism per se vs. anti-authoritarianism. These groups avoid messages that contradict their opinions. Cass R. Sunstein, in a 2001 essay in *The Boston Review*, noted the growing power of consumers to "filter" what information they read or see. He writes, "insulation from alternate views breeds increasing extremism." Socionomists, as usual, flip the causality to propose that increasing extremism breeds a desire to insulate oneself from alternate views. Aspiring authoritarian and anti-authoritarian leaders alike use exclusionary propaganda to leverage this tendency. Leaders encourage their groups to see other groups as threats; actions escalate in a quid pro quo. As society's calm consensus morphs into fearful discord, authoritarianism gains footholds. The majority of people see each authoritarian step as merely temporary, necessary inconveniences—small freedoms traded for promises of safety. As fear increases, society makes ever-larger concessions. If a negative trend in social mood is strong enough, blatantly authoritarian leaders emerge and promise security. They attract strident support as well as energetic opposition.

Two Centuries of Authoritarianism

Long term data on the U.S. stock market, with British data preceding it, have proved to be a fairly good global sociometer. Figure 1 shows that over the past 300 years major negative mood trends have led to most of the notable eruptions of authoritarianism. There are incidents of authoritarianism during positive mood trends, but they are fewer and smaller. Let's review the history.

Wave ⅠⅠ of 64 years' duration, from 1720 to 1784, supported increasing authoritarianism in Great Britain. The liberty-oriented American Revolution was a polar response.

Historians call the 1850s—the time of the second decline within wave (II)—the Authoritarian Decade in Great Britain, Austria and Prussia. In *Europe Reshaped 1848-1878*, J.A.S. Grenville wrote, "The decade of the 1850s presents an extraordinary contrast to the turmoil of the 'hungry forties'.... The state was paternalist and authoritarian."[4]

The authoritarian impulse was not limited to those countries. In the United States in the early 1860s, President Lincoln suspended the writ of habeas corpus, which allows appeal against imprisonment, and dismissed the states' understanding that they could secede peacefully from the Union. In France, Napoleon III revived and extended Napoleon I's authoritarian nationalism. His police-state tactics—involving spies, arrests, political trials and restrictions on freedom of speech, assembly and the press—"provided the old ruling classes of Europe with a new model in politics." (*A History of Western Society*, McKay, Hill, Buckler)

Later, wave IV of (III) brought the initial rise of the authoritarian left via the Bolsheviks in the 1917 Russian Revolution. To a lesser degree, it also brought authoritarianism to the United States. Sociologist Robert Nisbet wrote,

The West's first real experience with totalitarianism—political absolutism extended into every possible area of culture and society, education, religion, industry, the arts, local community and family included, with a kind of terror always waiting in the wings—came with the American war state under [President Woodrow] Wilson.[5]

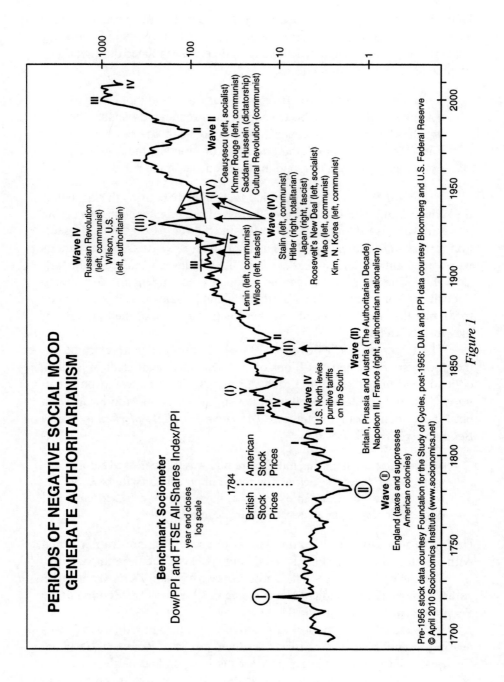

Figure 1

During this time, the American Protective League—a quarter-million-strong association of volunteer vigilantes authorized by the U.S. attorney general—spied on, assaulted, detained and otherwise violated the civil rights of citizens. They were joined by:

A mammoth web of patriotic organizations enlisting thousands of volunteer spies…. The Liberty League, the American Defense Society, the Home Defense League, the National Security League, the Anti-Yellow Dog League…the Boy Spies of America, the American Anti-Anarchy Association, and the Sedition Slammers.[6]

In *Liberal Fascism*, Jonah Goldberg detailed that during the late teens, the Wilson Administration censored, harassed and threatened the American press. In Abrams v. United States (1919), the Supreme Court upheld a sedition verdict and a sentence of 20 years in prison for five Russian immigrants who tossed anti-American leaflets from the windows of buildings in New York City. The government also imprisoned U.S. citizens for verbalizing opposition. For example, "In Waterbury, Conn., a salesman was sentenced to six months in jail for remarking that Lenin was 'one of the brainiest' of the world's leaders."[7]

The larger wave (IV) from 1929 to 1949 brought more extreme authoritarianism elsewhere. Millions of Russians died as a result of Stalin's collectivization of agriculture and his Purges. Fascists seized power in Italy, Germany and Japan. Authoritarianism increased in America as well, but less so than in other countries. *The Wave Principle of Human Social Behavior* (p. 284) observed,

One manifestation of [the] mood extremity was the increased enrollment in and disruptive activity by the Communist Party in the U.S. In contrast to the German experience, however, the most extreme political forces never achieved political control….[8]

During this period, the Franklin Delano Roosevelt administration flirted with dictatorship, redistributed wealth and "packed" the Supreme Court.

Wave (IV) also launched the careers of two of history's most notorious authoritarians: Kim Il Sung of North Korea in 1948 and Mao Zedong of the People's Republic of China in 1949.

In 1965, as a long period of positively trending mood (wave I) was nearing an end, Nicolae Ceaușescu assumed power in Romania. Early on, Ceaușescu enjoyed popular support for his independent nationalism and challenges to Soviet dominance. But as the negative mood of wave II from

1966 to 1982 progressed, Ceauşescu became a totalitarian. He expanded government control into many areas of Romanian life, devastating the country's economy. Like the Kims of North Korea, he controlled the media to create an idealized and heroic public image of himself.

Mao's violent Cultural Revolution (1966-1976) also came during wave II. It killed an estimated 30 million people. In 1975, with wave II still under way, Pol Pot of Cambodia led the Khmer Rouge to power. He imposed agrarian collectivism, civilian relocations, slave labor and executions. His genocides killed as many as 2.5 million Cambodians.

In Iran, the shah's increasingly despotic reign ended with the even more authoritarian Islamic Revolution in January 1979. A few months later, Saddam Hussein used security forces to assume control of the government in nearby Iraq and quickly suppressed all political opposition. In 1980—as wave II was grinding to its end—Saddam invaded Iran. The eight-year conflict, the deadliest war of wave II, ended in a stalemate, with estimates of up to 1 million dead.

As global social mood trended positively in the 1980s and 1990s during wave III, authoritarians' activity waned. In 1989-1991, even the Soviet Union gave up its iron fist.

Resurging Authoritarianism in Wave IV

Liberal democracies, in which governments more or less adhere to constitutional protections of individual rights, have risen in concert with the Dow Jones Industrial Average since the early 1800s. After a long trend toward positive social mood, liberty's popularity hit a peak in 1989-1999, when the Soviet Union collapsed and political scientist Francis Fukuyama proclaimed "the universalization of Western liberal democracy as the final form of human government."[9]

As a decade-long, global negative mood trend began in 2000, authoritarianism once again waxed along with it. The February 2010 issue of *The Elliott Wave Financial Forecast* (EWFF) observed,

> According to Freedom House, 2009 was "marked by intensified repression against human defenders and activists in 40 countries." It was the fourth straight year of increased repression, "the longest stretch of civil rights setbacks" in 40 years.[10]

Freedom House's Arch Puddington wrote "Civil Society Under Threat," published in the spring 2009 issue of the *Harvard International Review*. It begins with this warning:

After several decades of consistent progress, the state of global freedom has entered a period of stagnation and possibly even de- cline.... Among the principal targets of the new authoritarianism is civil society. The result has been a notable reversal for freedom of association throughout much of the world.[11]

Both Russia and China have histories of extreme authoritarianism, and both countries are now attempting to recast democracy as a blend of free markets and authoritarian politics. British historian Timothy Garton Ash called authoritarian capitalism "the biggest potential ideological competitor to liberal democratic capitalism since the end of communism." A June 2009 *Foreign Policy Magazine* article, "Authoritarianism's New Wave," described the countries' impressive new global-media tactics:

Today's authoritarian regimes are undermining democracy in updated, sophisticated, and lavishly funded ways.... The Kremlin has launched Russia Today, a multimillion-dollar television venture.... Beijing has reportedly set aside at least $6 billion for these media expansion efforts.[12]

Wave IV prompted many liberal democracies to become increasingly authoritarian. In October 2001, President George W. Bush signed the USA Patriot Act, giving law enforcement officials unprecedented access to Ameri- cans' telephone and electronic communications. The Bush administration has been widely criticized for suspending habeas corpus and employing torture in off-shore prisons such as Guan- tanamo Bay and Abu Ghraib.

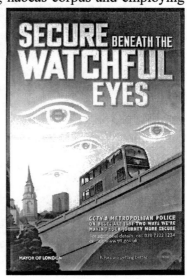

The Adam Smith Institute reported that the UK, a nation with less than 1% of the world's population, possesses one quarter of the world's security cameras. In February [2010], Britain introduced a new law—Section 76 of the Counter-Terrorism Act 2008—that can send those who pho- tograph police to jail for 10 years.

A graphic example of Britain's na- scent authoritarianism, reminiscent of Orwell's *1984*, is this poster, which first appeared throughout London in October 2002, the month of a multi-year low in U.S. stock indexes. It advises citizens to feel secure under surveillance. In a more recent example, the popular British radio show TalkSport broadcast a government anti-terrorism advertisement—available on YouTube—encouraging citizens to be suspicious of neighbors who keep to themselves, close their curtains or use cash instead of credit cards. The ad ominously counsels, "If you suspect it, report it."

Authoritarian tragedies have begun this way. Robert Gellately, author of *The Gestapo and German Society: Enforcing Racial Policy 1933-45*, read a collection of 19,000 Gestapo files that Nazi officers were unable to burn before the Allies arrived and reported,

> I had found a shocking fact. It wasn't the secret police who were doing this wide-scale surveillance and hiding on every street corner. It was the ordinary German people who were informing on their neighbors ...business partners turning in associates to gain full ownership; jealous boyfriends informing on rival suitors; neighbors betraying entire families who chronically left shared bathrooms unclean or who occupied desirable apartments.[13]

A Princeton University Internet expert wrote, "The inconvenient truth is that authoritarianism is adapting to the Internet age" ("St. Louis Today," March 4, 2010). In addition to providing governments a cheap online channel for distributing propaganda, the Internet makes it easier for them to spy on their own citizens. Here are just a few examples:

In February, U.S. President Barack Obama extended three provisions of the Patriot Act, allowing the government "to obtain roving wiretaps over multiple communication devices, seize suspects' records without their knowledge...and conduct surveillance of someone deemed suspicious." (*Christian Science Monitor*, March 1, 2010) The Obama administration also recently unveiled a new computer intrusion detection system called Einstein 3 to guard against cyber attacks.

Also in February, the French National Assembly passed a bill to "allow unprecedented control over the Internet...a new level of censorship and surveillance." (*Der Spiegel,* February 17, 2010) The bill creates "one of the toughest censorship regimes of any robust democracy in the Western hemisphere." (*Ars Technica*, February 17, 2010) Google Inc. noted, "The number of countries that censor the Internet has grown from a handful eight years ago to more than 40 today."

The European Union is considering expansive new control measures, too:

Civil rights groups are worried about a new EU proposal that would enhance a "dangerously authoritarian" European surveillance and security system that will include ID card register, Internet surveillance systems, satellite surveillance, automated exit-entry border systems operated by machines reading biometrics and risk profiling systems.[14]

The Council of the European Union's February 15, 2010 Draft Internal Security Strategy reflects the fearful mood and the desire to control:

The Union must create a safe environment in which people in Europe feel protected. Furthermore, the necessary mechanisms must be put in place to maintain high security levels, not only within EU territory,

source unknown

Street Signs in Barcelona, Spain: Even when the reality of rising authoritarianism stares society in the face, many people tend to laugh *it off as situational or historical irony.*

but also as far as possible when citizens travel to third countries or find themselves in virtual environments such as the Internet.[15]

On March 4, Republican Senator John McCain and Democrat Senator Joe Lieberman introduced a bipartisan yet little-noticed U.S. Senate bill titled the "Enemy Belligerent Interrogation, Detention, and Prosecution Act of 2010." It reads,

> An individual who is suspected of being an unprivileged enemy belligerent shall not...be provided the statement required by Miranda v. Arizona or otherwise be informed of any rights that the individual may or may not have to counsel or to remain silent.... An individual, including a citizen of the United States, determined to be an unprivileged enemy belligerent...may be detained without criminal charges and without trial for the duration of hostilities....

This legislation would explicitly deny citizens the three core legal rights of the American judicial system: the right to a Miranda warning ("You have the right to remain silent..."); the right to legal counsel; and the writ of habeas corpus, the right of the imprisoned to a trial that dates to the Magna Carta in 1215 and is enshrined in the U.S. Constitution.

The Road Ahead

Years hence, someone will say something to the effect that it is impossible to know you are in an authoritarian trend when you are in one. We disagree. Socionomics provides a map of where society has been and where it is likely to go. Future large-degree positive mood trends will weaken authoritarian regimes and foster general respect for individual freedom, whereas future large-degree negative mood trends will produce increasingly authoritarian impulses and eventually lead to the appearance of severe authoritarian regimes around the globe. Map in hand, you can watch for signs along the way and seek the safest path.

NOTES AND REFERENCES

[1,2] Altemeyer, R. (1996). *The Authoritarians*. Self published and on-line: http://home.cc.umanitoba.ca/~altemey/, 55. See also: Altemeyer, R. (1996). *The Authoritarian Specter*. Cambridge, MA: Harvard University Press.

[3] Parry, R. (2010, March 16). Contestants Turn Torturers in French TV Experiment. *AFP*.

[4] Grenville, J.A.S. (1976). *Europe Reshaped 1848-1878*. Malden, MA, USA: Blackwell Publishers. 124.

[5] Nisbet, R. (2000). *The Twilight of Authority*. Indianapolis: Liberty Fund Inc.

[6] Hagedorn, A. (2007). *Savage Peace: Hope and Fear in America, 1919*. New York: Simon & Schuster.

[7] Cohen, S. (1963, June 21). Books: The Reds Who Were Not There. *Time*.

[8] Prechter, R. (1999). *The Wave Principle of Human Social Behavior and The New Science of Socionomics*. Gainesville, GA: New Classics Library, 284.

[9] Fukuyama, Francis. "The Universalization of Western Liberal Democracy as the Final Form of Human Government," in *The End of History and the Last Man*. Reissue edition, March 1, 2006, Free Press.

[10] Kendall, P. and Hochberg, S. (2010, February). *The Elliott Wave Financial Forecast*. 10.

[11] Puddington, A. (2009). Civil Society Under Threat: Bureaucratic Strategies of the New Authoritarians. *Harvard International Review*, 31(1).

[12] Windsor J, Gedmin, J. and Liu, L. Authoritarianism's New Wave. (2009, June 3). *Foreign Policy*.

[13] Gellately, R. (1990). *The Gestapo and German Society: Enforcing Racial Policy 1933-45*. New York: Oxford University Press.

[14] *European Digital Rights*, 7(12).

[15] The Council of the European Union. (2010, February 23). *Draft Internal Security Strategy for the European Union: "Towards a European Security Model."* Brussels, Belgium.

Chapter 39

Democracy Under Attack

Alan Hall

October 20, 2011 (TS)

A Growing Appetite: A protester on Wall Street displays his predisposition.

So forceful was the mood shift from 2000 through 2009 that democracy, a form of government most recently idealized during the two-century uptrend in stock prices dating from 1784, has come under widespread attack from within democracies.

In the United States, Peter Orzsag, the former director of President Obama's Office of Management and Budget, wrote an article titled "Too Much of a Good Thing: Why We Need Less Democracy." Orszag said U.S. "political polarization was growing worse—harming Washington's ability to do the basic, necessary work of governing." Beverly Purdue, the governor of North Carolina, called for suspending elections for two years so that Congress can "get over the partisan bickering and focus on fixing things."[1]

Russia is about to re-elect Vladimir Putin in a "mockery of democracy," said the *Economist*.[2] *The Washington Post* lamented waxing authoritarianism in "Russia, once almost a democracy."[3]

Citizens, too, are increasingly questioning whether representational democracy works. "'Voting is worthless'? Global protests share contempt for democracy," reads a September 28, MSNBC headline. The article cites a common theme in the recent street demonstrations, boycotts and strikes in New York, London, Spain, Greece, India and Israel: "wariness, even contempt, toward traditional politicians *and the democratic political process they preside over.*"[4] (emphasis added)

"We're the first generation to say that voting is worthless," said a young Spanish woman. A young Indian woman said, "We elect the people's representatives so they can solve our problems, [but] that is not actually happening. Corruption is ruling our country." A young Israeli man said, "the political system has abandoned its citizens."

One woman, who told *USA Today* she walked 200 miles to protest in Washington, said, "We are the 99 percent. We don't have a government that represents us. That is the message."[5]

Decreasing Democracy

Socionomists have long anticipated that a trend toward negative social mood would precipitate a decline in the number of democracies. Figure 1 updates the original chart from the June 1992 issue of *The Elliott Wave Theorist*, which made these observations:

> The numbers [Francis Fukuyama] presents showing the rise of liberal democracy merely track the trend of the stock market, i.e. of positive social mood, from its Grand Supercycle degree low in 1784 to its current all-time high. In fact, the two "corrections" of the trend roughly coincided with bear phases in stocks.... As the worldwide decline in fortunes takes hold, the number of liberal democracies will shrink.[6]

Under a September 2011 headline, "The compass fails," *The Economist* noted,

> Freedom House, a New York-based body that monitors a range of political and civil rights, reported that 2010 saw a net decline in liberty across the world for the fifth year in a row, the longest continual decline in four decades of record-keeping.... Western governments have become shy about spreading the idea that certain human rights, enshrined in United Nations conventions, are universal.[7]

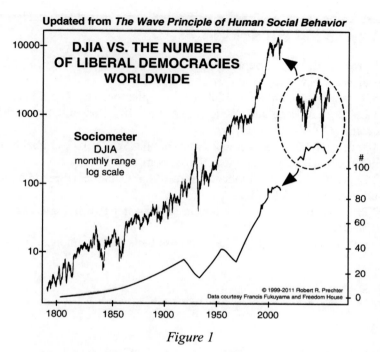

Figure 1

A five-year period of decline in liberty and democracy seems small on a chart showing two centuries of a rising trend, yet it is *"the longest continual decline in four decades."* Governments across the world are stepping up authoritarian repression—becoming less democratic—as their citizens begin to distrust democracy. As we have documented and predicted in previous issues, society is both rebelling against and submitting to a wide variety of new regulations, bans, security requirements and privacy intrusions. Liberal democracy will surely become a far less widespread political structure in the next major-degree trend toward negative social mood.

NOTES AND REFERENCES

[1] Wolf, Z.B. (2011, September 28). Too Much Democracy? A Modest Proposal From N.C. Gov Bev Perdue. ABC News.

[2] Russia's Humiliator-in-chief (2011, September 26). *The Economist*.

[3] Lally, K., & Englund, W. (2011, August 18). Russia, Once Almost a Democracy. *The Washington Post*.

[4] Kulish, N. (2011, September 28). 'Voting is Worthless'? Global Protests Share Contempt for Democracy. MSNBC.com.

[5] Leger, D.L. (2011, October 7). Protesting 'Occupiers' Spread Message Beyond Wall Street. *USA Today*.

[6] Prechter, R. (1992, June). Sentiment/Investor Psychology. *The Elliott Wave Theorist*.

[7] (2011, September 17). The Compass Fails. *The Economist*.

Chapter 40

Fluctuations in Paternalism in Washington

Alan Hall

January 31, 2012 (TS)

Ancient Greek philosophers presented the state as a larger model of the family, implying that citizens are the children who have needs and leaders are the parents who know best how to meet them. Ever since, the rules of many monarchs, aristocrats and dictators have been characterized by paternalism, which appears to be increasing in America.

Our May 2010 study [see Chapter 38], predicted times when society would be receptive of that image: "Negatively trending social mood generates increasing fear. As society becomes more fearful, many individuals yearn for the safety and order promised by strong, controlling leaders." In accordance with this observation, *The Palm Beach Post* recently reported that the U.S. Federal Emergency Management Agency (FEMA) has recently been referring to the U.S. government as the "federal family."[1]

Figure 1 plots two leading sociometers and two lagging sociometers against the yearly number of references to "federal family" on FEMA's website. We inverted the graphs of "federal family," food stamp participation and the percentage of people living below the poverty line to highlight their correlation with the Dow/gold ratio and the Consumer Confidence Index. (We show the "federal family" graph on log scale, as FEMA's use of the term increased over 1000% during the first eight months of 2011.)

FEMA's use of the phrase "federal family" surged during the negative trend in social mood of 2000-2003. Uses then fell to near zero as social mood turned positive from 2003-2007. This dramatic change was not due to FEMA taking a low profile; on the contrary, its activities and visibility soared during the August 2005 Hurricane Katrina disaster. "Federal family" usage then surged again as society's mood became increasingly negative after 2007, in concert with plunges in U.S. stock prices, real estate and consumer confidence, and spikes in food stamps and the poverty rate.

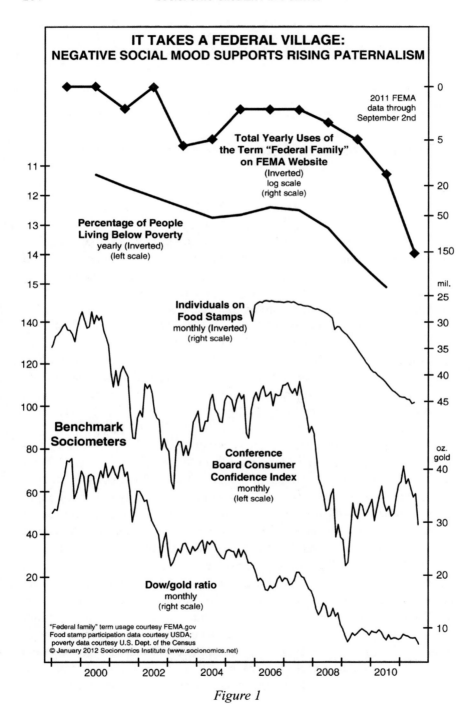

Figure 1

During the Great Depression, President Franklin Roosevelt employed a similarly paternalistic tone in his famous Fireside Chats. On April 14, 1938, he said,

> This recession has not returned us to the disasters and suffering of the beginning of 1933. Your money in the bank is safe; farmers are no longer in deep distress and have greater purchasing power; dangers of security speculation have been minimized; national income is almost 50% higher than it was in 1932; and government has an established and accepted responsibility for relief…. I know that many of you have lost your jobs or have seen your friends or members of your families lose their jobs…I conceive the first duty of government is to protect the economic welfare of all the people in all sections and in all groups…. I am constantly thinking of all our people—unemployed and employed alike—of their human problems of food and clothing and homes and education and health and old age. You and I agree that security is our greatest need. I am determined to do all in my power to help you attain that security.

Today, according to FEMA's website:

- "President Obama has asked that we continue to lean forward as a team…a team that includes our cities, states and the *federal family…*."

- "We're part of Department of Homeland Security, we're part of the *Federal family*, we're part of a partnership…."

- "On behalf of the entire *federal family*, our hearts go out to those who lost their loved ones…."

- "The *federal family* is dedicated to staying for as long as it takes to help them recover…."

Paternalism as Authoritarianism

In his August 2004 article, "Statist Quo Bias," Daniel B. Klein included the definition of *paternalism* from *The Blackwell Encyclopaedia of Political Thought*: "In modern use, the term usually refers to those laws and public policies *which restrict the freedom* of persons in order that their interests may be better served" (italics added by Klein).[2]

If social mood becomes more positive, expect FEMA's use of paternalistic phrases to abate. If social mood continues to trend toward the negative, government paternalism will increase.

NOTES AND REFERENCES

[1] Bennett, G. (2011, September 1). FEMA's Use of Term 'Federal Family' for Government Expands Under Obama. *The Palm Beach Post*.

[2] Klein, D.B. (2004). Statist Quo Bias. Economic Journal Watch, 1(2), 260-271.

Chapter 41

Tyrannical Behavior Toward Ireland in the Mid-1800s

Alan Hall

March 17, 2014 (TS)

For many expressions of social mood, the duration of a trend seems to be as important as its extent in influencing collective behavior. In long-lasting negative mood trends, a society tends to display increasing pessimism and fear about the future, which build toward a pervasive extreme.

Expressions of authoritarianism generally increase with the amount of time society undergoes a large-degree trend toward negative social mood, and they intensify during smaller-degree downtrends within it. In this study, we will look at a historical example of these manifestations.

Britain underwent a 128-year trend toward negative social mood as reflected in the bear market in the Financial Times All-Share Index from 1720, at the peak of the South Sea Bubble, to 1849 [see Figure 1 in Chapter 37]. Britain's long history of authoritarianism toward the Irish tended to intensify during declining waves within this large-degree trend toward negative mood.

During the second declining wave, which followed the Poyais mania and began with the Panic of 1825, English society attempted numerous ineffective schemes to fix economic problems and deal with an expanding underclass. These efforts included draconian trade restrictions that worsened the plight of the impoverished Irish over 13 decades. Figure 1 provides a list of events in the culminating years of this period.

Over the quarter-century decline in stock prices, Britain endured the closure of some sixty banks including six major London banks, widespread bankruptcies, credit contraction, high unemployment, and increasingly overcrowded and unsanitary conditions in London. The crisis reached its extreme at the October 1849 low in the FTSE All-Share Index, which also coincided with the deadliest of London's four cholera epidemics [see

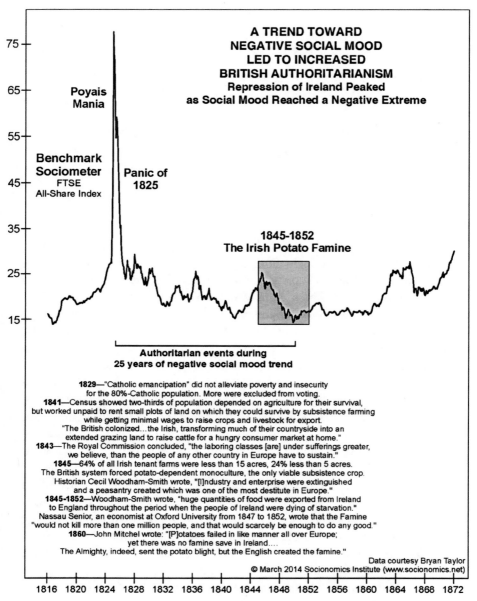

Figure 1

Chapter 52 in *Socionomic Studies of Society and Culture*]. As if cholera weren't enough trouble, the Irish Potato Famine killed an estimated one to two million people—up to 25% of the population of Ireland. More than a million Irish emigrated.

Britain's repression of Ireland increased throughout the 1825-1849 period of increasingly negative social mood. Irish Catholics, who made up over 80% of the Irish population, lived as impoverished tenant farmers growing food for English and Anglo-Irish landlords, who exported most of the food. In his 1962 book, *The Great Hunger: Ireland 1845-1849*, British historian Cecil Woodham-Smith wrote, "Ireland was on the verge of starvation, her population rapidly decreasing, three-quarters of her labourers unemployed, housing conditions appalling and the standard of living unbelievably low."[1] John Mitchel, a leader in the Young Ireland Movement, wrote in 1860,

> I have called it an artificial famine: that is to say, it was a famine which desolated a rich and fertile island that produced every year abundance and superabundance to sustain all her people and many more. The English...ascribe it entirely to the blight on potatoes. But potatoes failed in like manner all over Europe; yet there was no famine save in Ireland. The British account of the matter, then, is first, a fraud; second, a blasphemy. The Almighty, indeed, sent the potato blight, but the English created the famine.[2]

Many scholars agree with Cecil Woodham-Smith, who wrote of "the indisputable fact that huge quantities of food were exported from Ireland to England throughout the period when the people of Ireland were dying of starvation." Ireland's Great Hunger Museum relates the findings of Christine Kinealy, author of the 1994 book, *This Great Calamity: The Irish Famine, 1845-1852*:

> Almost 4,000 vessels carried food from Ireland to the ports of Bristol, Glasgow, Liverpool and London during 1847, when 400,000 Irish men, women and children died of starvation and related diseases. The food was shipped under military guard from the most famine-stricken parts of Ireland.... The most shocking export figures concern butter.... In the first nine months of 1847...822,681 gallons of butter [were] exported to England from Ireland....[3]

Numerous recorded comments reflect the British government's authoritarian attitude toward the Irish during this time. Lord Clarendon, the Lord Lieutenant of Ireland, begged the British government for famine relief in 1849: "I do not think there is another legislature in Europe that would disregard such suffering as now exists in the west of Ireland, or coldly persist in a policy of extermination." Dennis Clark, an Irish-American historian, claimed that the famine was "the culmination of generations of neglect, misrule and repression. It was an epic of English colonial cruelty and inadequacy."[4] In a speech on March 23, 1846, former British Prime Minister Earl Grey laid the blame for the disaster squarely on the British government:

> My Lords, it is only by its government that such evils could have been produced: The mere fact that Ireland is in so deplorable and wretched a condition saves whole volumes of argument, and is of itself a complete and irrefutable proof of the misgovernment to which she has been subjected.... We have a military occupation of Ireland, but that in no other sense could it be said to be governed: that it was occupied by troops, not governed like England.[5]

Others saw the disaster as a boon. Nassau Senior, an Oxford professor of economics from 1847 to 1852 who advised the British government in economic and social policy, wrote that the famine "would not kill more than one million people, and that would scarcely be enough to do any good."[6] Other Britons calculated "how far English

Ireland's Holocaust Mural, "An Gorta Mór" Resentment toward authoritarian Britain lingers today.

colonization and English policy might be most effectively carried out by Irish starvation"[7] and described the famine as "a direct stroke of an all-wise and all-merciful providence."[8] Reflective of the broader sentiment in Britain, an editorial in *The Economist* magazine of January 1847 took a hard line toward the Irish poor, opining, "the people, rapidly increasing, have been reduced, *by acts for which they are chiefly to blame*, to a sole reliance on the precarious crop of potatoes."[9] For many historians, these and other such comments exemplified the British contempt for the Irish. Negative social mood allowed such sentiments to flourish.

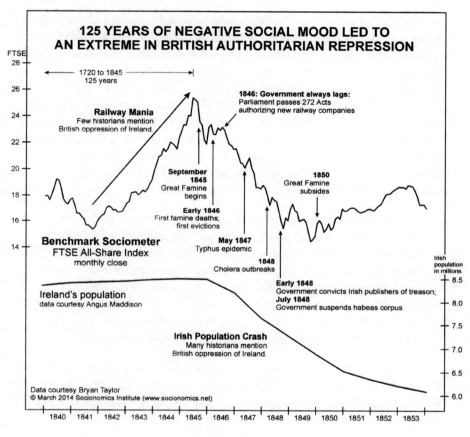

Figure 2

Figure 2 zooms in on the famine period. The lower graph shows the grim reduction in Ireland's population that accompanied the negative mood trend. *Elliott Wave Principle* describes C waves in such trends as "devastating in their destruction," and as wave (c) within the 129-year trend [see Figure 1 of Chapter 37], this one was certainly so. In addition to disease outbreaks, negative social mood in 1845-1849 brought a harsh extreme in Britain's repression of Irish citizens' rights, which included Irish newspaper publishers convicted of treason, the suspension of habeas corpus to allow imprisonment of Irish people without trial, and forced evictions of starving tenant farmers. According to Helen Litton in *The Irish Famine: An Illustrated History*,[10] British landlords evicted tenants in droves during 1847. Police did not begin counting evictions until 1849. By 1854, they had recorded almost 250,000. Starving people crowded into soup kitchens, food depots and workhouses, ideal conditions for spreading infectious diseases such as typhus and typhoid. Cholera arrived in Ireland in 1849, intensifying the misery. In 1846, as Irish society grew weaker and more susceptible to disease, fever may have taken as many lives as hunger.

A century and a half later, in 2012, *The Economist* reviewed Tim Pat Coogan's book, *The Famine Plot: England's Role in Ireland's Greatest Tragedy*. The article described the anti-Irish xenophobia of the time, but as Henry Farrell, a professor at George Washington University, noted, it failed to mention its own hardline editorial of 1847. Nevertheless, its exposé of other, more egregious editorials is enlightening:

> Trevelyan and other architects of the famine response had a direct hand in filling the newspapers with the "oft-repeated theme that the famine was the result of a flaw in the Irish character." And *Punch*, a satirical magazine, regularly portrayed "'Paddy' as a simian in a tailcoat and a derby, engaged in plotting murder, battening on the labor of the English workingman, and generally living a life of indolent treason," explains Mr. Coogan. The result of such dehumanizing propaganda was to make unreasonable policy seem more reasonable and just.[11]

Britain's authoritarian history toward the Irish is yet another example of trends toward negative social mood first impelling societies to devalue their stocks, and later to devalue their fellow human beings.

NOTES AND REFERENCES

[1] Woodham-Smith, C. (1991). *The Great Hunger: Ireland 1845-1849.* London, England: Penguin Books.

[2] Gallagher, T. (1987). *Paddy's Lament, Ireland 1846-1847: Prelude to Hatred.* Boston, MA: Houghton Mifflin Harcourt.

[3] Exports in famine times. Ireland's Great Hunger Museum.

[4] Uris, J., & Uris, L. (2003). *Ireland: Terrible Beauty.* New York, NY: Bantam Books.

[5] Coogan, T.P. (2013). *The Famine Plot: England's Role in Ireland's Greatest Tragedy.* Basingstroke, United Kingdom: Palgrave Macmillan.

[6] Gallagher, T. (1987). *Paddy's Lament, Ireland 1846-1847: Prelude to Hatred.* Boston, MA: Houghton Mifflin Harcourt.

[7] Donnelly, J.S. Jr. (1995). Mass Eviction and the Irish Famine: The Clearance Revisited. In Cathal Póitéir (Ed.), *The Great Irish Famine.* Cork, Ireland: Mercier Press.

[8] Trevelyan, C.E. (1848). *The Irish Crisis.* London, England: Longman, Brown, Green & Longmans.

[9] The Economist and the Irish Famine. (2012, December 13). Out of the Crooked Timber of Humanity, No Straight Thing Was Ever Made.

[10] Litton, H. (1994). *The Irish Famine: An Illustrated History.* Dublin, Ireland: Wolfhound Press.

[11] Opening Old Wounds. (2012, December 12). *The Economist.*

Chapter 42

Extreme Parties Thrive
After Financial Crises

Chuck Thompson
May 27, 2016 (TS)

In a recent study, a team of German economists led by Manuel Funke of the Free University of Berlin analyzed the political changes that occurred in the wake of financial crises and associated recessions over the past 144 years. The researchers used a data set encompassing 827 parliamentary elections in 20 countries from 1870 to 2014.[1]

Funke and his colleagues found substantial increases in political polarization in the aftermath of financial crises, as evidenced by weaker government majorities, stronger opposition parties, greater fractionalization of parliaments, greater incidents of government instability and an increased likelihood of executive turnover. The researchers also found that street protests tended to rise and that voters were more inclined to support parties with "nationalistic or xenophobic tendencies." They said that the degree of social unrest is "very volatile and can double from one decade to another."

Socionomic theory posits that the trends toward negative social mood produce financial crises and recessions while also impelling anger, polarization, exclusionism, protests, the ousting of incumbents and the rise of radical politics—right in line with the conclusions of Funke and his colleagues.

In the wake of the global financial malaise of 2007-2012, Alan Hall reported on European voting results in the elections of 2012 [see Chapter 8], and last year Brian Whitmer reported on the shift in parliamentary representation in the EU [see Chapter 46]. Funke's research confirmed that after the financial crisis of 2008, two-party systems in the Eurozone that were "stable for decades" were "swept away." New political forces entered parliaments and gained ground, as others disappeared. They noted that in the aftermath of the financial crisis, "far-right and right-wing populist parties more than doubled their vote share in many advanced economies, including France, the UK, Sweden, Finland, the Netherlands, Portugal and Japan." They reported similar outcomes in the 1920s and 1930s.

The researchers made two observations that we have a mind to challenge. They said, "on average, the far left did not profit equally from episodes of financial instability." They sampled 16 European countries, plus Australia, Canada, Japan and the U.S. They also stated that the political consequences of financial crises began to fade about five years after the onset of the crises: "While some political after-effects of financial crises are measurable for a decade, the good news from our regressions is that the political upheaval in the wake of financial crises is mostly temporary."

As our team at the Socionomics Institute discussed Funke's findings, we noted two strong exceptions to the above claims. First, in Russia and China, negative mood drove left-wing revolutions in 1917 and 1949, respectively, and extreme parties assumed power and remained in charge for generations. Second, far-right leaders in Europe held power for periods of time that one would hesitate to call "temporary." Examples are Hitler in Germany, Mussolini in Italy, Salazar in Portugal and Franco in Spain. We wondered if restricting data for statistical reasons had led to an incomplete picture.

We asked Funke via email about these cases, and he graciously offered the following response: "We did not include China or Russia as, with respect to measuring election outcomes, the democratic history of these countries is simply too poor/short." He expressed disappointment with the lack of sufficient data for these countries, as they are "among the largest economies" in the world. Funke explained that he and his colleagues "disqualified single-party elections where no opposition was allowed (no other party contested)." This very condition began in 1929 in Italy, 1933 in Germany and 1934 in Portugal. He further noted that Spain, Austria and Greece did not have any elections under one-party rule, so their study excluded the years of dictatorship for these countries as well. Funke added, "I suppose/ hope that Hitler, Mussolini, Salazar and Franco would have been removed from power earlier (via elections) had they not changed the political system from a democracy into a dictatorship." We note, however, that the extreme depth of the negative mood trend allowed these leaders to do just that. If negative mood takes root throughout much of society and reaches extreme proportions, leaders can sometimes jettison democracy and build political structures that eliminate threats to their power. In these situations, society, or a body representing it, often undertakes collective action to enact sweeping new policies, which then become entrenched despite any trend toward positive mood that follows. In some cases, as Prechter observed in *Popular Culture and the Stock Market* (1985), mood extremes allow the imposition of structural rigidity on a society. Because it takes time to mobilize machinery and play out the consequences of the actions taken at a mood extreme, the effects of institutionalization may continue to be felt for a long time. Russia in 1917 and China in 1949 are prime examples.

During the past several years, we have been thrilled to see studies that validate aspects of socionomic theory, usually by researchers who are unaware of socionomics. We applaud Funke and his colleagues for their important work. Their findings highlight social mood's influence on a wide range of social behavior.

NOTES AND REFERENCES

[1] Funke, M., Schularick, M., & Trebesch, C. (2015, October). Going to Extremes: Politics After Financial Crises, 1870-2014. CEPR Discussion Paper No. DP10884. Available at SSRN: http://ssrn.com/abstract=2676590.

Part IV:

EUROPE

Chapter 43

A Socionomic Study of the European Union

Brian Whitmer

December 16, 2009 (TS)

History shows that major trends toward negative social mood—as indicated by large bear markets in stocks—foreshadow political conflict. The same political relationships that were rock-solid when mood was positive dissolve when it's negative. Cross-border agreements that formerly were seen as beneficial are seen as burdensome. Old grudges revive, new gripes arise, and regions that even recently got along with each other descend into trade disputes, financial disagreements, territorial contention, and, if the negative mood trend is large enough, armed conflict.

Trends in political change mirror patterns in the stock market, which reflect naturally occurring waves of social mood. The early history of the United States offers an excellent case in point. In 1835, a 24-year bear market began in U.S. stock prices. The downturn reflected a trend toward negative mood that eventually led to the outbreak of civil war. The young nation's experience left an indelible mark that testifies to the societal impact that major wave of negative social mood can have.

We have been predicting that an equally perilous period is coming to the European Union. The continent's own trend toward negative mood began in 2000 and has years to go before it is complete. We see substantial socionomic parallels between early America and modern Europe. As in 1859-1861 in the U.S., discord erupted in Europe around the March 2009 nadir in stock prices. The expected large size and duration of this period of negative mood in Europe [see Figure 1 in Chapter 46] should eventually produce the greatest threat to European peace and solidarity since World War II.

Social Mood Regulates the Drive for Unity

The September 1992 issue of *The Elliott Wave Theorist* described the psychological link between political associations and the stock market:

> At a peak [in mood], it's all 'we'; everyone is a potential friend. At a bottom it's all 'they'; everyone is a potential enemy. When times are good, tolerance is greater and boundaries weaker. When times are bad, intolerance for differences grows, and people build walls and fences to shut out those perceived to be different. Ultimately, persecution and war result.

The ebb and flow of the EU's fortunes have unmistakably exhibited either the "we" or "they" sentiment implied by the stock market's main trend. Figure 1 plots significant EU milestones against the DJ Euro Stoxx 50 Index. Without exception, waves of positive social mood have produced expressions of unity, whereas extremes in negative mood have generated Euro-skepticism and setbacks. The unification movement's dependence on trends toward positive social mood extends back to its earliest days.

Post-War Europe

Positive social mood trends dominated the continent's early years following World War II, and European unity strengthened along with them. The treaties of Paris and Rome created two economic communities that became the basis for later EU legislation. Member countries signed both agreements in the 1950s as social mood became more positive. More cooperation occurred during the 1960s. When positive mood reached its peak, the 1965 Merger Treaty combined Europe's three economic communities into one institutional structure.

In the 1970s, during a negative trend in social mood, the movement toward European integration came to a standstill. Mainstream economists have used standard causality—the notion that events govern mood—to explain the setback. Former Director General of the European Central Bank Hanspeter Scheller said, "Integration...lost momentum under the pressure of divergent policy responses to the economic shocks of the period."[1] Socionomically speaking, Scheller has it exactly backwards. Divergent policy responses (an event) did not cause European integration to lose momentum. Rather, a lack of desire to integrate (the mood imperative) caused policy responses to diverge. The "economic shocks" were a result of negative mood as well, not a cause.

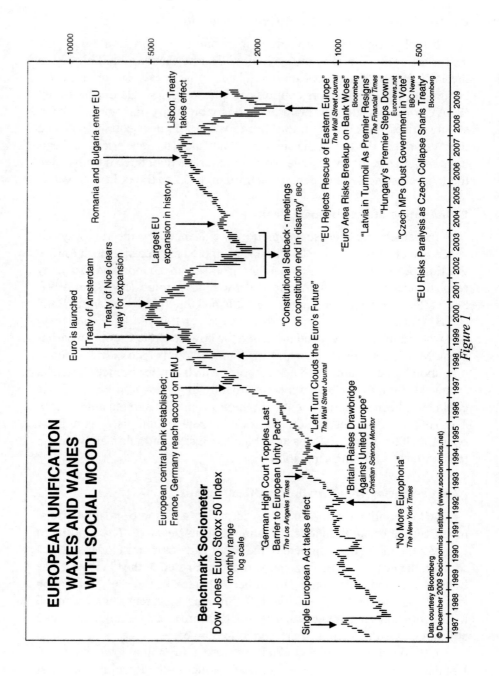

Figure 1

Positive Mood Reignites European Fellowship

It took a big new positive trend in social mood to rekindle Europe's desire for political and monetary union. The momentum built slowly in the early 1980s, then picked up steam later in the decade (where Figure 1 begins). In 1987, the Delors commission enacted the Single European Act (SEA), which was the first major revision to the Treaty of Rome. The SEA set objectives for a common European market. Member countries signed the Act right at the top of the substantial advance in stock prices, indicating a major extreme in positive social mood. Less than three months later, the 1987 crash erased more than one third of the Euro Stoxx Index's value.

Culmination at the Ultimate Peak

Extremely elevated social mood, as evidenced by the runaway advance in stock prices of the late 1990s, prompted the decisive push toward the European Union that exists today. Bellwethers France and Germany reached accord on an Economic and Monetary Union (EMU) in 1997. Soon afterward, member countries established the European Central Bank (ECB). The ECB launched the euro in November 1998. In 1999, the Treaty of Amsterdam took effect and increased the powers of the European parliament. March 2000 marked an all-time high in the Euro Stoxx Index. Some nine months later came the Nice summit, which former French President Jacques Chirac extolled as a meeting that "will go down in history."[2] He could have been speaking about both the stock market and the union itself. The Treaty of Nice marked the climax of European optimism, as it threw open the doors to the EU's eastern-bloc expansion and, ultimately, set up the continent's coming separation.

Negative Social Mood Divides Political Unions

All the political progress achieved during a period of positive social mood can be brutally undone when mood turns negative. The top line of Figure 2 tracks the development of the American union from independence through the period of negative mood that culminated in the Civil War. The bottom line (updated through December 2016) tracks Europe's unification trends from the end of World War II through its current negative-mood trend, which has not yet ended. The timelines are clearly similar, but more striking still is the form of social mood in both cases.

Observe that both potential unions were in turmoil at lows of equivalent degree in stock prices. Two massive conflicts—the Revolutionary War

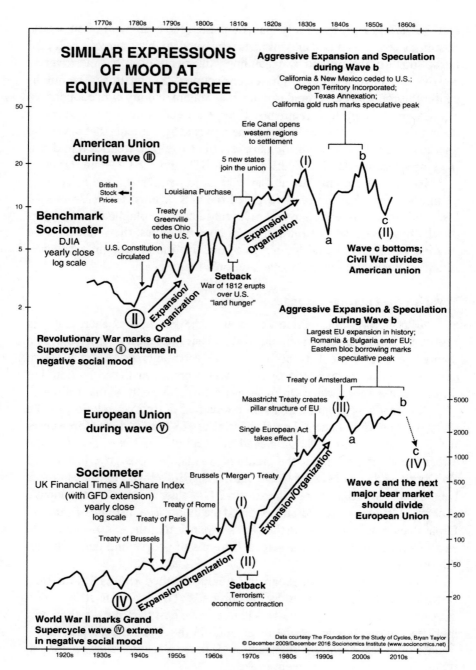

Figure 2

and World War II, respectively—accompanied the bottoms. In both cases, hostilities waned as mood and markets recovered, and both unions reflected the optimism of the uptrend by expanding. Nineteenth-century America grew westward as governments purchased or occupied new territory. Twentieth-century Europe developed and expanded its sphere of unity with cooperative treaties and economic agreements. Europe's trend toward positive mood during the 1940s, '50s and '60s included myriad agreements that paved the way to today's EU. This period parallels the early land treaties that drove the United States westward during the late 18th and early 19th centuries.

The analogy continues in that each union suffered a major setback along the way. The War of 1812 pitted the U.S. against Great Britain for a second time, and terrorism and political instability plagued Europe during the negative mood of the 1970s. In both instances, the setbacks were relatively short-lived, and the return of positive mood brought a renewed round of expansion that led to each union's major peak.

Feverish Speculation Presages a Plunge

Note the a-b-c correction depicted at the far right of each graph in Figure 2. Both depictions display the classic three-wave structure of a countertrend movement. In both cases, the most aggressive steps toward expansion did not occur at the top of the waves preceding the corrections but during the b-wave advance within an a-b-c corrective pattern that followed.

America's westward expansion intensified during wave b despite the country's ongoing financial hardship after the 1837 panic. In the three years from 1845 to 1848, the U.S. annexed the Republic of Texas, acquired the Oregon territory and signed the Treaty of Guadalupe Hidalgo, which ceded California and New Mexico to the union. The EU's b-wave expansion has been equally broad. Its big push came in 2004, when despite the continent's economic difficulties ten countries joined the union. The Institute of Cultural Diplomacy reports that—like the U.S.'s expansion of the 1840s—the 2004 expansion of the EU was the largest in terms of people and landmass but the smallest in terms of GDP.

Both b-wave orgies of expansion quickly reached zeniths. In America, fortune seekers migrated west by the hundreds of thousands to strike it rich in gold mining. In Europe, western banks drove east to strike it rich in new markets. Both eras marked the fever pitch in the "speculators' paradise"[3] of a rising b-wave. Only a tiny fraction of those chasing riches prospered, while the majority simply went broke.

We know what happened after Cycle wave c in America: It ended in 1859, and the Civil War erupted in April 1861. If the analogy holds up, the European continent will soon reach a similar crossroads.

2016 Update

Figure 2 has been updated to reflect the FTSE All-Share's continuing advance in wave b. The socionomic implication that wave c will gravely threaten the European project remains the same.

NOTES AND REFERENCES

[1] Scheller, Hanspeter K. *The European Central Bank: History, Role and Functions*. European Central Bank, 2004.

[2] *The Economist*, December 14, 2000.

[3] Frost, A.J. and Robert R. Prechter, *Elliott Wave Principle*, New Classics Library, Gainesville, Georgia, 1978/2014, p. 81.

Chapter 44

Using Socionomics to Make Specific Forecasts—Case in Point: The European Union

Chuck Thompson

January 31, 2012 (TS)

Socionomics is a tool for understanding the "tendency of the social system,"[1] not a crystal ball for predicting specific events. Nevertheless, we at the Socionomics Institute have made some specific forecasts using socionomics.

One recent example is the fracturing of the European Union, which Prechter and Kendall first anticipated in 1998—four years before the first euros even exited the printing press. A full breakup hasn't happened yet, but the drumbeat for dissolution has gotten louder.

When is it appropriate to use socionomics to make a specific forecast, and what principles should you follow?

In this article, we'll use our anti-intuitive forecasts for the disunion of Europe—issued even as the union itself was being established—to demonstrate socionomic principles in action.

Staying Off the EU Bandwagon

The most helpful socionomic forecasts are the ones that no other method can make.

In 1989, when the Berlin Wall came down, German chancellor Helmut Kohl and French president François Mitterrand saw an opportunity for European integration. Calls for a united Europe had been stirring for decades as worldwide social mood continued in a positive trend during the second half of the 20th century. A few weeks after the euro entered circulation on January 1, 2002, Rodrigo Rato, chairman of the European Union's Council of Finance Ministers, proclaimed, "I don't think Europe has ever enjoyed such good economic conditions."[2] Robert Mundell, who won the Nobel Prize for economics in 1999, said that in his judgment there was not a single country in the world that would lose from the advent of the euro.[3] In addition, Mundell and C. Fred Bergsten, director of the Peterson Institute for International Economics, both predicted that the euro would challenge the dollar for global supremacy.[4] The following year, when leaders of ten countries signed treaties to join the European Union, French president Jacques Chirac said, "A wonderful dream is coming true."[5] And when EU leaders signed their first constitutional treaty in 2004, the union's president, Jan Peter Balkenende, announced, "Today, Europe enters a new era."[6] Expressions of optimism and assured success revealed a consensus opinion held at the highest levels of intellectual, political and economic authority.

Against this ebullient backdrop, Elliott Wave International's analysts stood virtually alone in their assertion that the creation of the euro and the union "represented merely an optimistic extreme [implied] by decades of rising stock prices" and, as such, were "doomed to fail."[7] EWI's commentaries to this effect number in the dozens. Here is a sampling:

> By May 3, most of the countries in Western Europe were expected formally to join Germany in actions that would "irrevocably bind their currencies together." (*New York Times*, 4/28/98) Since joiners will not be allowed to leave, this is a rather strong expression of inclusionism, as well as a setup for future conflict.[8]
> —*The Elliott Wave Theorist*, May 1998

> The consummation of the European Union follow[ed] 1500 years of repeated conflict in the region. [T]he concurrent wonderful atmosphere of international peace and cooperation are consistent with my Elliott wave case that an uptrend of Grand Supercycle degree is ending.[9] [That year marked the all-time highs to date in the Euro Stoxx index (see Figure 1 in Chapter 46), U.S. stocks valued in terms of gold (see Figure 1 in Chapter 77) and the inflation-adjusted World Stock Index (see Figure 1 in Chapter 77).—Ed.]
> —Chapter 16, *The Wave Principle of Human Social Behavior*, 1999

> After a half century of reconciliation and cooperation…Europe is suddenly battling xenophobic and racist demons. …During the bear market, the independent nations of Europe will rediscover their borders and rekindle the animosities that kept them apart for centuries.[10]
> —*The Elliott Wave Financial Forecast*, May 2005

> [M]uch of what's come together in Europe will come apart in coming years.[11]
> —*SocioTimes*, December 2006

Germany and Russia in the 1930s and early 1940s are examples of the extreme forms these impulses [to shut others out] can ultimately take in extended bear market periods. The EU expresses the opposite, inclusionary force, one that has apparently run its course.[12]
—SocioTimes, October 2007

Unlike many mainstream forecasters, Elliott Wave International remained staunchly skeptical of the grand experiments that were hatched near the top of the Grand Supercycle-degree bull market. Chief on that list was the culmination of a political and monetary union among countries that, just a short time before, were openly warring with each other.[13]
—The European Financial Forecast, April 2009

In 1835, a Supercycle-degree correction began in U.S. stock prices. The downturn reflected a trend toward negative mood that eventually led to the outbreak of civil war. ...We predict that an equally perilous period is coming to the European Union soon. The continent's own Supercycle-degree correction began in 2000 and has years to go before it is complete.[14]
—The Socionomist, December 2009

With the aid of the Wave Principle and the insight it provides into the nature of bear markets, the euro's eventual dissolution can only be viewed as virtually unavoidable.[15]
—The Elliott Wave Financial Forecast, March 2010

The European Union was supposed to unite Europe by providing a common currency and a lender of last resort, the European Central Bank. ...When there is a lender of last resort, everyone is encouraged to act imprudently until the credit system fails. ...Within the next few years, after every authoritarian trick is exhausted, the supposed infinite powers of central banks to inflate and of their governments to spend are going to melt like ice cream in the sun.[16]
—The Elliott Wave Theorist, July 2011

Recently, the effects of the most recent trend toward negative social mood—unanticipated elsewhere—have become manifest. Sovereign debt crises have plagued Ireland, Portugal, Spain, Italy and Greece. Agencies have cut bond ratings across Europe. Economists doubt that the European Financial Stability Facility, one of three EU bailout funds, is large enough to "assure markets that Italy and Spain are protected."[17] Europe's central banks are considering what to do should countries leave the Eurozone. New studies reveal that investors in Greece, Portugal and Italy are increasingly converting deposits into Swiss francs, setting up trusts as far away as Singapore and buying real estate outside the Eurozone.[18] In last year's elections in Finland, the True Finns, an anti-establishment, anti-euro party, increased their voting strength from 4% to 20% in Finland's parliament.

Granted, the European Union has held together thus far. But now, 14 years after Prechter and Kendall's initial forecast, dissolution is being treated as a viable topic in the mainstream press, and intra-European tensions are taken as logical and given.

This shift was predictable a decade ago when the union was established with nearly universal fanfare, but only if you based your expectations on socionomics rather than then-current sentiment and events.

Looking Far Ahead with Socionomics

How did socionomics enable such a clear, specific forecast of trouble in the face of so much ebullience? Let's take a look at some of the principles that came into play.

1. Social Mood Is Unconscious, Powerful and Reflected throughout Society

Social mood—which underlies social actions—is unconscious.[19] To recognize how mood is affecting current events, you must train yourself to step outside of it, see it, and judge it objectively. This means staying unmoved by mood-impelled arguments posited by economists, politicians, analysts, friends and the media. Doing so takes practice and fortitude.

2. Social Mood Determines Events, Not Vice Versa

Increasingly negative social mood, not any particular event or set of events, ultimately accounts for the worsening economic scenario in Europe. As Brian Whitmer stated in the November 2011 issue of *The European Financial Forecast*,

> The fact is, the euro neither united Europe in the late 1990s, nor is it dividing Europe today. Again, the euro was the result, not the cause, of a dominant mood trend that operated silently behind the scenes. Knowing it's there and understanding how it works will keep you dozens of steps ahead of the crowd.[20]

In a recent interview with Kate Welling (goo.gl/35N3S), Prechter explained the causality:

> Let me show the chasm of difference between my way of thinking—with socionomics—and the way most futurists and economists approach things. When the European Union was being formed people said, "What does it *mean*?" They speculated there would be more cooperation and trade, more power centered in Europe, and so on. They thought the EU was a new *cause*, so they were trying to figure out the *results*. Under socionomics, the formation of the EU wasn't a cause; it was a result. At the peak of the greatest optimism of all time, these countries, which had been fighting each other off and on for a thousand years, decided to come together. That's a *result* of extremely positive social mood. And *at the time*, in 1999 and 2000, we said *this union is going to fail* because it's coalescing at one of the greatest positive-mood extremes of all time; there's no way it's going to be able to survive a major downturn in social mood. And look: Just a dozen years later, it's already starting to break apart. Unions that are formed at major social-mood bottoms, such as the United States at the end of the 1700s, tend to hold together very well. But I think by the time the global bear market is over, the European Union won't exist.

3. Extreme Events Presage Imminent Reversals

Non-socionomists miss reversals because they don't recognize the influence of social mood, which creates the very emotions and events upon which they are basing their judgments. The conventional forecaster's approach is, "As today is, so shall tomorrow be, only a little more or a little less." In contrast, socionomists work from the position that "extremes in social psychology prepare the socionomist for coming changes."[21] When social mood is extreme, it "implies nearness of a trend change in the opposite direction."[22]

Socionomists do not advocate simple contrarianism. Often, a trend will remain in effect for some time. Probabilistically predictable Elliott wave patterns and their associated mood-event *extremes* are keys to predicting dramatic reversals in social trends.

4. Mood Polarities Describe Social Climate Extremes

In *The Wave Principle of Human Social Behavior*, Prechter listed 35 pairs of polar emotional tendencies that society tends to express to a degree commensurate with the extremity of positive or negative social mood. Referencing these polarities helps a socionomist envision the broad climate within which it is possible to posit specific events and outcomes. For example, one set of polarities evident in the development of the European Union is inclusion/exclusion (#23). Prechter wrote,

> A waxing positive social mood accompanies increased inclusionary tendencies in every aspect of society, including the cultural, moral, religious, racial, sexual, economic, national, regional, social, financial and political. A waxing negative mood accompanies increased exclusionary tendencies in every aspect of society. With that realization, you can predict increasing cooperation and acts of brotherhood in all those areas in bull markets and the opposite in bear markets.[23]

From 1999 to 2007, at the pinnacle of the decades-long trend toward positive social mood, "euro-phoria hit peak pitch," and the EU rushed to *include* more and more nations.[24] This push for inclusion occurred "despite concerns about the financial stability of prospective entrants."[25] When social mood trend turned decisively negative in 2008, the impulse to *exclude* set in. In March 2010, Hochberg and Kendall noted some specific animosities that were being rekindled in Europe:

> In Greece, for instance, strikes are escalating and growing more violent while an "overwhelming majority of Germans are hostile to the idea of bailing out Greece." The crisis "revived old resentments and stereotypes between Greeks and Germans," says the latest Reuters dispatch from Athens. "Now Greeks are starting to get outraged at German outrage." As we go to press, Athens riots are intensifying and Greece's deputy prime minister attacked Germany over its Nazi past.[26]

Recently, *The Washington Times* noted that German taxpayers are "fed up with having to constantly bail out suicidal spendthrift policies in irresponsible countries."[27]

Another polarity in play within the European Union is concord/discord. Some European leaders are striving to increase the size of the European Financial Stability Facility. But *The Wall Street Journal* reported,

> Discussions to increase the lending capacity of the European Financial Stability Facility...have yielded no real progress as major differences persist among member governments, said a European diplomat.[28] (emphasis added)

A negative-mood expression on the convergence/polarization scale is also coming into play as EU nations begin to "rediscover their borders" and "rekindle the animosities that kept them apart for centuries," as Kendall predicted way back in 2005. In August [2011], Hans-Olaf Henkel, former president of the Federation of German Industries and an early supporter of a unified European currency, wrote an article in *The Financial Times* calling for Austria, Holland, Germany and Finland to break away from the EU and launch their own currency. A senior EU official reported that Germany and France have been exploring the idea of a smaller Eurozone.[29] In October, *The New York Times* declared that nationalism is now "degrading the collective responsibility and shared sovereignty" that previously defined the EU.[30]

5. Leaders Cannot Affect Social Mood

Most forecasters make the mistake of assuming that powerful leaders have the ability to control the waves of mood in society. Nothing could be further from the truth. As Prechter wrote in 1999,

> [There has been] failure after failure of officials to control money, interest rates, commodity prices, retail prices, stock markets, and economic growth and contraction. [M]echanics and "tools" are of no assistance unless you are tinkering with a machine, and human society is not a machine. Harboring an illusion of being in control of the waves is a guarantee of getting caught up in them. This is yet another illusion that socionomics has the power to eliminate.[31]

Nearly all members of society participate in social mood. Therefore, by definition under socionomics, nearly everyone is going to be wrong about the social future at social mood extremes. No legislatures or social policy groups will anticipate a coming reversal; doing so is up to the individual who knowingly stands apart from the herd.

Conclusion

As we have repeatedly noted, socionomics is not a crystal ball. But sometimes understanding mood phases can help a socionomist identify which specific events are more or less likely to happen. Often, that insight can give individuals an extraordinary view of a future to which others are oblivious.

NOTES AND REFERENCES

[1] Hall, A. (2011, September). To Apply Socionomics Properly, Follow These Principles. *The Socionomist*.

[2] Daly, E. (2001, January 31). Council Leader Says Euro is Just a Start. *The New York Times*.

[3] Devitt, J. (2002, September 18). Nobel Laureate Robert Mundell Sees Bright Future for Euro. *Columbia News*.

[4] Bergsten, C. F. (2002, January 4). The Euro Versus the Dollar: Will There Be a Struggle for Dominance? Peterson Institute for International Economics.

[5] Bruni, F. (2003, April 17). 10 Countries Sign to Join European Union. *The New York Times*.

[6] Bowley, G. (2004, October 30). Heads of State Sign the European Union's First Constitution. *The New York Times*.

[7] Whitmer, B. (2010, March). The "Flawed Euro" Concept Takes a Giant Leap Forward. *The European Financial Forecast*.

[8] Kendall, P. (1998, May). Cultural Trends. *The Elliott Wave Theorist*.

[9] Prechter, R. (1999). *The Wave Principle of Human Social Behavior*, p. 266. Gainesville, GA: New Classics Library.

[10] Hochberg, S., & Kendall, P. (2005, May). Global Wrap. *The Elliott Wave Financial Forecast*.

[11] Kendall, P. (2006, December 18). New EU Entrants: The Straw That Breaks Its Back. *SocioTimes*.

[12] Kendall, P. (2007, October 10). Belgian Split Places Euro Union on Brink of a Big Break. *SocioTimes*.

[13] Whitmer, B. (2009, April). A Rearview Mirror or a Windshield? *The European Financial Forecast*.

[14] Whitmer, B. (2009, December). The Developing European Tinderbox: A Socionomic Study. *The Socionomist*.

[15] Kendall, P. (2010, March). Special Section: Where Credit is Due. *The Elliott Wave Financial Forecast*.

[16] Prechter, R. (2011, July). Twilight of the Financial Engineers. *The Elliott Wave Theorist*.

[17] Ames, P. (2011, December 9). EU Leaders' Latest Agreement Still Leaves Unfinished Work. *USA Today*.

[18] Ball, D., Cohan, S., & Bouras, S. (2011, December 19). Beyond Borders: Europeans Stash Money Elsewhere. *The Wall Street Journal*.

[19] Almand, M., & Prechter, R. (2010, June). An Interview With Robert Prechter, Jr.: Where I Believe Socionomics is Heading. *The Socionomist*.

[20] Whitmer, B. (2011, November). Cultural Trends. *The European Financial Forecast.*

[21] *The Wave Principle of Human Social Behavior* (p. 231).

[22] *The Wave Principle of Human Social Behavior* (p. 336).

[23] *The Wave Principle of Human Social Behavior* (p. 230).

[24] Kendall, P. (2011, November). The Next Big Craze: The Euro-Haircut. *The Elliott Wave Financial Forecast.*

[25] Whitmer, B. (2009, April). A Rearview Mirror or a Windshield? *The European Financial Forecast.*

[26] Hochberg, S., & Kendall, P. (2010, March). Special Section: Where Credit is Due. *The Elliott Wave Financial Forecast.*

[27] Decker, B.M. (2011, October 21). Europe's Savior: A New Deutsche Mark. Viable Economies Need to Break Away from Collapsing Euro Currency. *The Washington Times.*

[28] Froymovich, R., & Stevis, M. (2011, November 14). Europe's Rescue Funds Get Little Traction. *The Wall Street Journal.*

[29] Toyer, J., & Breidthardt, A. (2011, November 9). French, Germans Explore Idea of Smaller Eurozone. Reuters.

[30] Erlanger, S. (2011, October 19). Euro, Meant to Unite Europe, Seems to Rend it. *The New York Times.*

[31] Prechter, R. (1999). *The Wave Principle of Human Social Behavior* (pp. 365-370).

Chapter 45

Negative Social Mood and Political Developments in Greece Bear a Striking Resemblance to Those in Germany Before World War II

February 1, 2013 / May 27, 2016 (TS)

Nazi salutes, praise for Adolf Hitler, swastika-like banners: All were hallmarks of Germany's Third Reich. A rising political party known as Golden Dawn is resurrecting such practices in modern-day Greece.

A 1989 *Elliott Wave Theorist* Special Report noted that periods of negative social mood are fertile ground for political shifts away from individual liberty:

> In the formalization of the negative mood within a bear market, one or more of the new parties is likely to represent ideals inimical to individual liberty (such as socialist, racist, fascist or fundamentalist). In some cases, such as Russia in the 1910s, Germany in the 1930s, China in the late 1940s, Cambodia in the 1970s, and Iran in the late 1970s, such parties have achieved power.

Likewise, Golden Dawn is riding a wave of extremely negative social mood, as reflected in Greece's tremendous, five-year stock market decline. The party's tactics are reminiscent of those employed by Adolf Hitler and his National Socialist German Workers Party.

Golden Dawn capitalizes on fear and anger and promotes xenophobia. Like Hitler's Nazi Party, it targets—and seems to appeal to—the young.

Golden Dawn Exploits Emotions Deriving from Negative Mood

At first, the Nazi Party of Germany had only limited success. It won just 3% of the vote in December 1924, when mood was waxing positive and the German stock market was rising. But from 1927 to 1932, Germany suffered a bout of negative social mood, which prompted a disastrous stock market decline of 73% over five years (see Figure 1). At the bottom, six million people were unemployed, and the Weimar government was weak. Germany also suffered outside financial pressure in the form of reparations required by the Versailles Treaty and other consequences of its involvement in World War I.[1]

Hitler argued that the German government had betrayed its people when it signed the Versailles Treaty.[2] He promised that if he were elected, the nation would stop paying the reparations.[3]

In November 1932, in the midst of the Great Depression, the Nazi Party suddenly captured 33% of the vote—more than any other party.[12] That year, a Hamburg schoolteacher named Louis Solmitz wrote about Hitler, "How many look to him with touching faith as their helper, their savior, their deliverer from unbearable distress."[13]

Modern-day Greece has experienced an even larger descent into negative mood than Weimar Germany did. Its stock market has fallen 88% in five years, and the country has suffered a debt crisis. As a condition of bailouts aimed at helping Greece recover, the European Union has imposed tough austerity measures, which the Greek government has implemented. Meanwhile, the deepening polarization within Greece has fueled protests against the measures.

Greece is in an economic depression like that experienced by Germany in the 1930s.[4] More than 90% of Greek households have experienced income reductions, with the average drop being 38%. Unemployment in Greece now

Source: CBS News/Associated Press

Forget the Payments: Nikolaos Michaloliakos, head of the Golden Dawn party, has called for Greece to renege on its debt and disregard its bailout commitments.

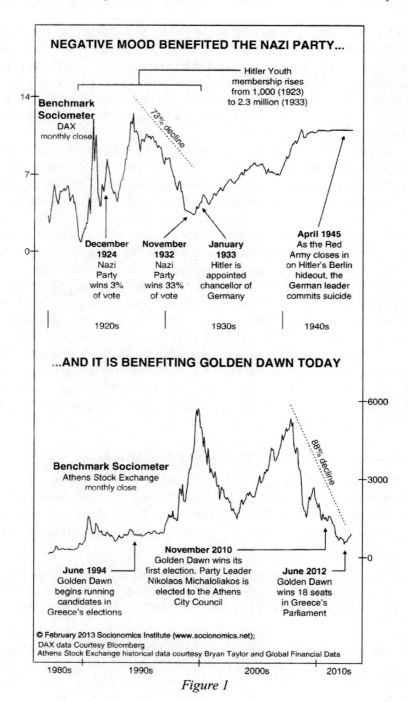

Figure 1

stands at a record 26.8% overall and at nearly 60% among young adults. In November, the Greek Parliament imposed tax hikes and spending cuts demanded by creditors. Supermarket sales in the country declined by 500 million euros ($669 million) last year,[5] and people are burning wood because the price of electricity has risen and taxes on heating oil have increased.[6] Journalist Nikos Zydakis says the nation is "cracking. When that happens, all the barriers to extremism fall."[7]

Similarly to the Nazis a century ago, Golden Dawn began running candidates in June 1994, long before the nation's mood turned negative. Also as with the Nazis, Golden Dawn achieved success only after the nation's stock market crashed. In November 2010, party leader Michaloliakos was elected to the Athens City Council. In 2012, with social mood still in a negative trend, Golden Dawn won 6.9% of the national vote and 18 seats in the Greek Parliament.[20] EurActiv.com says the party has "manipulated a weak Greek state and disastrous austerity management by European bureaucrats to become, according to recent polls, the third most popular political party in the country."[9] As the Nazi Party did, Golden Dawn is pushing for Greece to cease its foreign payments—in this case, to renege on its debt and its bailout commitments. Golden Dawn's leader, Nikolaos Michaloliakos, has said his party will "fight to free Greece from the global loan sharks." He has condemned the Greek "traitors" whom he says are responsible for his nation's financial woes.[8] The party has also promised to cancel household debt for unemployed and low-wage earners. Such positions have worked in Golden Dawn's favor.

Xenophobia Is a Key to Golden Dawn's Propaganda

Germany's Nazi Party used fear of outsiders to its advantage. Its core philosophies included racism, anti-Semitism and anti-Bolshevism, all of which were espoused in Hitler's book, *Mein Kampf*. Hitler's Nazi party promoted a "national community" to Germans. But not everyone was welcome in this new society:

> Exploiting pre-existing images and stereotypes, Nazi propagandists portrayed Jews as an "alien race" that fed off the host nation, poisoned its culture, seized its economy, and enslaved its workers and farmers.[11]

After Hitler became Germany's chancellor, he began a series of legal actions that stripped Jews of their rights. By 1938, Jews in Germany could no longer vote or own guns, and they had to carry identification cards.[14]

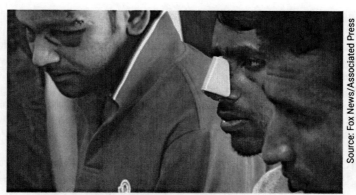

Source: Fox News/Associated Press

War on Immigrants: These men were photographed during a June 2012 press conference organized by the United Against Racism and Fascist Violence Movement. They said their wounds were the result of an attack by members of Golden Dawn.

That same year, German Storm Troopers and Hitler Youth instigated the "Night of Broken Glass," in which synagogues and Jewish-owned homes and businesses were plundered and destroyed. Thirty thousand Jews were arrested and sent to concentration camps, and in the next seven years, millions more would suffer the same fate.[15]

Sentiment within the Golden Dawn party has a similar ring to it. Last year, Artemis Matthaiopoulos was among the first-ever Golden Dawn party members to join the nation's parliament. Matthaiopoulos is the former bass player for the punk band Pogrom, whose songs include "Auschwitz." The tune was named for the former prison camp where the Nazis killed an estimated one million Jews. The band's most popular song is "Speak Greek or Die," an anti-immigrant diatribe that goes,

> You come to our country, you don't have any work;
> You're starving, you bums, and you eat children;
> You speak Russian, you speak Albanian, but now you will speak Greek.
> Speak Greek or die, speak Greek or die.[16]

Greece has become the host country for a huge number of illegal aliens. The Center for Migration Studies says that Golden Dawn blames unauthorized immigrants for stealing jobs from Greek citizens. Intensely negative social mood has resulted in escalating suspicion, fear, hatred and violence toward immigrants:

Golden Dawn "citizen groups," created to engage "pure" Greeks in the protection of Greek citizens from crimes committed by immigrants, have been accused of chasing, stabbing, and seriously injuring immigrants and anyone who looks foreign or non-Greek.... Golden Dawn members have also been accused of breaking the windows of houses or shops owned by immigrants, and beating them.... In the summer of 2012, Golden Dawn members, dressed in black T-shirts and holding Greek flags, reportedly visited an open-air market and smashed every stall belonging to persons they believed to be foreigners....[17]

Frontex, an agency that monitors the EU's external borders, says more than 55,000 illegal immigrants were detected in Greece's Evros border region in 2011—a 17% increase compared to 2010.[18] Golden Dawn has "proposed the construction of minefields between Turkey and Greece to prevent further unauthorized migration into the country."[19] Such views are unquestionably extreme. Yet they are gaining traction in Greece because of the nation's extremely negative mood.

Golden Dawn Is Making Strides Among the Young

One of Hitler's key objectives was to indoctrinate the nation's youth in Nazi philosophies. In 1920, he authorized the formation of a Nazi Party youth league.[22] The U.S. Holocaust Memorial Museum says the Nazi Party considered youth a "special audience" for its propaganda messages:

These messages emphasized that the Party was a movement of youth: dynamic, resilient, forward-looking and hopeful. Millions of German young people were won over to Nazism in the classroom and through extracurricular activities.[23]

In its infancy, the Hitler Youth's reach was limited to Munich, and in 1923 it had just over 1,000 members. In 1925, membership totaled 5,000, and five years later it was 25,000. But by the end of 1932, a few weeks before Hitler came to power, the organization had more than 107,000 members. Membership soared afterward, reaching 2.3 million by the end of 1933.[24]

Golden Dawn likewise goes to great lengths to appeal to youth. On February 2, the British newspaper *The Independent* reported that Golden Dawn was using social media, the Internet and youth clubs to reach "patriotic youths as they watch their country's sovereignty being eroded by foreign creditors." The paper interviewed a number of young Golden Dawn supporters, including a 16-year-old boy who said that he and others like him fear they won't be able to find jobs "because of all those illegal immigrants." A 16-year-old girl related that an African immigrant had robbed her cousin. The paper said she was attracted to Golden Dawn because of its "Zorro-style savior tactics," referring to the masked hero who defends fellow citizens against villains and oppressive public officials.[28]

According to *The Independent*, Golden Dawn's efforts to reach the young are paying off:

Source: Business Insider/AFP

Grassroots mobilization is its main recruitment technique, and the party is ac-

Winning the Hearts of Youth: Golden Dawn has mounted a tireless and successful campaign to reach young people like this supporter, who is attending a pre-election rally in Athens.

tively involved in neighborhood initiatives, especially in areas that saw a rise of crime and strong influx of migrants.... Graffiti of Greek flags, nationalist slogans, and signs that bear a resemblance to swastikas have started appearing around schools.... The widespread anger that Greeks have experienced since the beginning of the economic crisis has been channeled to children and is shaping their psyche, experts say. Child psychologist Amalia Louizou explains that in such an environment, children are the easiest recipients of extremist messages.[30]

Might Authoritarians Capture Greece?

The Center for Migration Studies expresses surprise that Greece is now embracing a party such as Golden Dawn. The Center points out that Greece fought against Germany and Italy in World War II, suffered its own fascist military junta (during the bear market of 1967-74) and has a long history of emigration to Germany, the Americas and Australia.[32] Furthermore, in the year 2000 Greece joined the 26-nation Schengen Area, where there are common rules on asylum and where internal borders are abolished, allowing for passport-free movement. Such a set of circumstances would not seem to favor the party's rise, the Center points out. But socionomists recognize that these events are utterly irrelevant. They were products of old social-mood conditions, not today's.

The success of Golden Dawn's effort to persuade a growing number of Greeks to adopt its extreme philosophies will depend upon the continuation or reversal of Greece's negative mood. Social mood will also determine whether the Greek government can carry out its plan to solve the nation's debt crisis, maintain order and avoid losing its power to parties at the fringes of the political spectrum. If it fails, Golden Dawn, like Hitler's Nazi party, could succeed in institutionalizing policies that express the negative social mood that has brought it to prominence.

2016 Update: Golden Dawn Hasn't Gone Away

In September 2013, seven months after our previous article was published, a Golden Dawn thug killed left-wing rapper Pavlos Fyssas, Greece's foremost hip-hop artist. Hours later, police raided several Golden Dawn offices in Athens.[26] They arrested party leader Nikolaos Michaloliakos, four Golden Dawn members of parliament and 15 other party members.[27]

After a rally, Greece's stock market index (ASE) turned down again in March 2014. Two months later, Golden Dawn won three seats in the European Parliament. The party continued to hold 18 seats in the Hellenic Parliament following the elections in 2015.

This year, a high-profile trial of 68 Golden Dawn members charged with running a criminal organization has stalled out. The list of charges tops 30,000 pages, but only 16 of 132 witnesses in the trial have given evidence.[28] A number of Golden Dawn members who were jailed in conjunction with the trial were released after 18 months— the maximum time allowed for pre-trial imprisonment. The trial resumed on May 25 before an empty courtroom because only six of the 68 defendants showed up.[29] Greece's social mood remains in Golden Dawn's favor, as the ASE has fallen back to 88% below its 2007 high.

Rally: Golden Dawn members carry the party's red and black flag at a March 2015 event in Athens, Greece.

In the meantime, Golden Dawn is staging public anti-immigrant protests and causing scenes in Greece's government. Two of its politicians were escorted out of parliament after unleashing what broadcaster Deutsche Well called "an obscene torrent of abuse" aimed at Greece's defense minister and armed forces leaders.[30]

Golden Dawn's leaders owe their party's successes to extremely negative social mood, which paves the way for political extremists. The success of Golden Dawn's efforts to enlist a growing number of Greeks continues to depend on the progression of social mood in Greece.

NOTES AND REFERENCES

[1] Hitler Comes to Power. United States Holocaust Memorial Museum.

[2] Beer Hall Putsch (Munich Putsch). United States Holocaust Memorial Museum.

[3] Reparations: Nazi Germany. Spartacus Educational.

[4] Hitler Comes to Power. United States Holocaust Memorial Museum.

[5] Making a Leader. United States Holocaust Memorial Museum.

[6] Henley, J., & Davies, L. (2012, June 18). Greece's Far-right Golden Dawn Party Maintains Share of Vote. *The Guardian*.

[7] Dabilis, A. (2013, February 7). Austerity Cuts Greek Household Income 38%. *Greek Reporter*.

[8] Greece: Pictures of Greeks Scrambling for Food Sparks Fresh Anger Over Austerity Measures (2013, February 6). *The Huffington Post.*

[9] Henley, J., & Davies, L. (2012, June 18). Greece's Far-right Golden Dawn Party Maintains Share of Vote. *The Guardian.*

[10] Qena, N. (2012, May 6). Extreme Right Leader Lashes Greece's 'Traitors'. *U.S. News & World Report.*

[11] Greece's 'Golden Dawn' and the Anti-immigrant Platform (2013, February 4). Center for Migration Studies.

[12] Mokhtar, H. (2013, February 5). Rise of Golden Dawn: A Presage of Doom? EurActiv.

[13] Defining the Enemy. United States Holocaust Memorial Museum.

[14] Kristallnacht: Background and Overview. Jewish Virtual Library.

[15] Kristallnacht: A Nationwide Pogrom, November 9-10, 1938. United States Holocaust Memorial Museum.

[16] Greece Welcomes Newest MP: A 'Nazi Punk' Musician (2012, July 26). Ynet News.

[17] Greece's 'Golden Dawn' and the Anti-immigrant Platform (2013, February 4). Center for Migration Studies.

[18] Q&A: Schengen Agreement (2012, March 12). BBC News.

[19] Q&A: Schengen Agreement (2012, March 12). BBC News.

[20] The Hitler Youth. Holocaust Education and Archive Research Team.

[21] Indoctrinating Youth. United States Holocaust Memorial Museum.

[22] The Hitler Youth. Holocaust Education and Archive Research Team.

[23] Savaricas, N. (2013, February 1). Greece's Neo-fascists Are On the Rise...And Now They're Going Into Schools: How Golden Dawn is Nurturing the Next Generation. *The Independent.*

[24] Savaricas, N. (2013, February 2). Greece's Neo-fascists Are On the Rise...And Now They're Going Into Schools: How Golden Dawn is Nurturing the Next Generation. *The Independent.*

[25] Greece's 'Golden Dawn' and the Anti-immigrant Platform (2013, February 4). Center for Migration Studies.

[26] Smith, H. (2013, September 18). Greek Golden Dawn Member Arrested Over Murder of Leftwing Hip-hop Artist. *The Guardian.*

[27] Greece Crackdown: Golden Dawn Leader Michaloliakos Charged. *BBC World.*

[28] Gill, O. (2016, April 20). Greece's Golden Dawn Trial Going Nowhere Fast. *Deutsche Welle.*

[29] Golden Dawn Trial Restarts, Though Most Defendants Absent. (2016, May 25). *Kathimerini.*

[30] Zafiropoulos, P. (2016, February 19). Golden Dawn Seeks to Exploit Greek Refugee Crisis. *Deutsche Welle.*

Chapter 46

Trends in Mood Are Affecting
the European Union

Brian Whitmer

April 30, 2015 (TS)

The Euro Stoxx 50 Index, which consists of stocks of big-name companies such as BMW, Bayer and Siemens, is the Dow Jones Industrial Average of Europe. It is a reliable proxy for overall social mood on the continent. For fifteen years, this index has been weaker than U.S. stock indexes, which have been making all-time highs. The Euro Stoxx 50 reached its all-time high back in 2000, and recoveries since then have managed only partial retracements, as shown in Figure 1.

We can break this period into distinct eras. The first is the "Enactment Era," when the dream of a united Europe came to fruition. That's when the European Central Bank was established and the euro was launched. The Treaty of Nice, signed on February 26, 2001, cleared the way for the EU to expand into the Eastern Bloc, but a wave of negative social mood had begun a year earlier, so the EU did not expand eastward immediately but waited for the next trend toward positive mood. The positive mood behind the rally of 2003-2007 fueled the "Expansion Era," which ran from 2004 to 2007. Although it was the largest EU expansion in terms of people and land mass, it occurred during the smallest expansion in terms of GDP, a condition compatible with the lower peak in the Euro Stoxx 50.

The 2007 peak in our sociometer is a critical marker, because thereafter the substantial amount of progress that Europe had made over the previous decades started to come undone as the new negative mood progressed. The "Bailout Era," in which officials toiled to save the union, accompanied the next phase of positive mood. It began in May 2010 with Greece. Bailouts followed for Ireland, Portugal, Greece again in 2012 and Cyprus in 2013. Here in 2015, Greece is negotiating its third financial rescue.

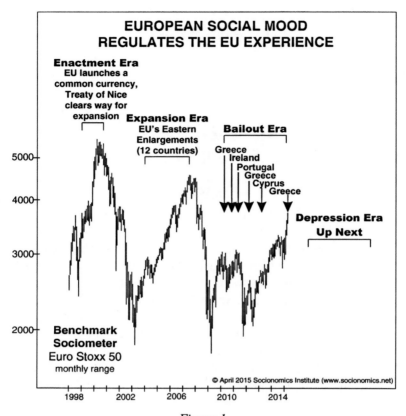

Figure 1

The bailout trend involves changes in how the rescues have been funded. The European Commission, European Central Bank and International Monetary Fund created an international aid package totaling 110 billion euros ($118 billion) in order to bail out Greece in 2010. Euro area members funded 80 billion euros of the total package. At the time, economists declared that authorities had safeguarded Europe's financial stability and restored confidence in the EU. They believed that Europe's central bank could simply offer credit to make Europe's economic problems go away.

Socionomists see it differently. We understand that trends in social mood govern what is politically possible. Negative mood limits the actions of central bankers and politicians, and it limits the extent to which Europe will be willing to provide open-ended, taxpayer-funded bailouts.

When Greece was bailed out the second time, something important changed. The government strong-armed private holders of Greek bonds to take a 53% loss, shifting the burden more appropriately from ordinary taxpayers to the creditors who took the risk in the first place.

In the 2013 Cyprus bailout, the burden shifted again, this time onto ordinary bank depositors. The government raided bank accounts, shut down the Bank of Cyprus, controlled money transfers and confiscated funds. It referred to these actions as a "tax," but it was un-voted-upon confiscation from depositors, who rarely understand their role as creditors.

Mario Draghi, president of the European Central Bank, recently decided to employ "helicopters" by launching a quantitative easing program of up to 1.1 trillion euros ($1.3 trillion) that will run over the course of the next year. The press calls Draghi "Super Mario," but the reputation of central bankers will be far from super by the time the long term negative social mood trend in Europe comes to an end.

Greece's current, third bailout process has become even more contentious. There's an old video that just resurfaced showing the Greek finance minister gesturing to the German government. We'll spare you the details, but you can do an online search for "fingergate" to see all you want. The socionomic takeaway here is simple: Europe is running out of goodwill. Consequently, it is running out of the political will to keep the union together.

The Mood in Individual Countries

Our conclusions about social mood on the continent are based primarily on the trend in the Euro Stoxx 50. When we look at stock indexes of European countries with the weakest economies, we can see manifestations of negative mood even more clearly. The December 2009 issue of *The Socionomist* featured a chart of stock indexes for Portugal, Italy, Greece and Spain. We contended that the rally from 2009 was countertrend, meaning that stocks would see new lows for the bear market. The socionomic implication was that southern Europe was about to destabilize in a big way, not only economically but also financially and politically.

Figure 2 updates our chart. We can see why so many things fell apart in southern Europe and especially in Greece: Negative social mood drove all four markets below their 2009 lows. The Athens Stock Exchange General Index had the biggest overall selloff and remains down 86% today. The three other markets have rallied but remain significantly below their highs.

It is not an oversimplification to say that the only thing that a Greek bondholder and a Cypriot bank depositor needed to understand in order to avoid losing money was the social-mood implication of a chart of the ASE. A discreet transfer of funds would have protected all of that person's

Figure 2

wealth. Anyone who is socionomically aware has a huge advantage over everyone else.

Let's briefly return to another illustration of how dramatically things changed after the reversal in European social mood in 2007. As you can see in Figure 3, unemployment rates in southern Europe (aside from Portugal) were drifting lower until 2007. But once stocks peaked, the unemployment rate skyrocketed.

Economists typically cite Germany's 30% unemployment rate of 1932 as an illustration of Europe's grim economic landscape during the Great Depression. In some European countries today, unemployment figures are approaching that level, and the youth unemployment rate (for workers aged 18-25) exceeds double the overall percentages shown in Figure 3 for all four countries. As the December 2009 issue of *The Socionomist* contended, the essence of this chaos was foreseeable just by keeping an eye on stocks as a meter of social mood.

Figure 3

Deflation

As a market forecaster, I use socionomics to get an edge over everyone else. It helps me to see around corners. One of the blind corners for nearly all conventional analysts has been Europe's trend toward deflation. The subtitle to Robert Prechter's *Conquer the Crash* is "You Can Survive and Prosper in a Deflationary Depression." The book came out in 2002, so deflation has been on the minds of socionomists for quite some time. Back in 2002, deflationists were exceptionally rare. Now, even though deflation has arrived in Europe, conventional analysts remain slow to grasp its implications.

In 2009, as several European Consumer Price Indexes went negative, I noted that deflation is here, and we'd better get used to it. Yet until this year, only a tiny minority of Europe's economic forecasters have recognized the deflation trend. Consider these quotes that appeared in the press last year:

> "With the average euro area inflation rate standing at 0.8 percent, we are clearly not in deflation."
> —European Central Bank president, 2/27/14

> "European Commission sees 'very low' deflation risk."
> —Morningstar.co.uk, 5/5/14

> "[T]he probability of outright deflation...remains very low."
> —European Commission, 5/5/14

> "We think there is a 25 percent probability that we see deflation in the Eurozone by the end of 2015."
> —IMF Chief Economist, 5/14/14

> "[The German Finance Minister] sees no deflation risk, says German pickup broadbased."
> —Reuters, 5/15/14

> "European Central Bank executive board member...says there is no risk of deflation in the Eurozone...."
> —CNBC, 7/9/14

There were hundreds of such articles. Yet total money and credit in Europe began contracting years ago. That's deflation. Now its effect is showing up in consumer prices.

Here in 2015, inflation in Greece is negative for the first time in more than four decades. In Spain, it is negative for the second time in nearly five decades. The story is similar all over Europe, and it is merely the beginning of a long term trend. Even in countries such as Britain and Germany, where stock markets have been strong, consumer prices are slipping.

In European countries where social mood is trending positively, the opinion among economists has gone from "deflation is impossible" to "deflation is a good thing." The United Kingdom's Chancellor of the Exchequer tweeted as much last month, saying that zero inflation is "good news for family budgets." But nobody is making the case that deflation is good news for families in Greece. As Wayne Gorman showed [see Chapter 27 of *The Socionomic Theory of Finance*], trends in social mood provide the key to understanding most people's perception of monetary conditions. When Britain's FTSE 100 index or Germany's DAX index begin to look like Greece's stock index, you will not see monetary authorities tweeting that deflation is a good thing.

Once the current partial recovery ends, the next European Union era will be the "Depression Era." Debt levels across the continent are at record highs, and deflation will make those burdens too onerous to bear, leading to widespread bankruptcies.

Given the extent of the negative mood trend under way in Europe, the European Union should ultimately come apart. Europe and the Eurozone will likely look a lot different five to ten years from now. Most economists won't recognize it until well after it is too late to prepare.

Political Changes

I sometimes use the metaphor of a centrifuge to describe the effect of negative social mood on elections. Negative mood flings votes from the political center—from centrist politicians and the status quo—to fringe candidates, especially populists far to the right and left. Alan Hall's treatise on the Socionomic Nolan Chart [Chapter 36] depicts this idea visually. In Europe, negative mood has pulled votes from so-called Europhiles, who support the European Union, and flung support to so-called Eurosceptics, who distrust the euro and do not support a large, multi-national bureaucracy.

We saw the first substantial manifestation of this trend in elections for the European Parliament after the 2009 low in European stocks [see Chapter 8]. As socionomists would expect, Eurosceptics pulled out big wins. An article in *The Economist* (6/8/09) noted, "In many countries, large protest votes went to populist, fringe and hard-right politicians vowing to close borders, repatriate immigrants or even dismantle the European Union in its current form." There has not been much good news for Europhiles since then. *The Financial Times* called last year's European Parliament election a "populist earthquake," as nationalist parties dealt a heavy blow to the European project. Figures 4 through 7 give us an idea of how Europe's political landscape has changed since 2000, when the mood trend in Europe shifted from positive to negative on a long term basis.

Figure 4 shows a representation of the incoming Parliament of 1999, which was constituted just prior to the all-time high in the Euro Stoxx 50 Index. Each dot represents one of the 626 members of Parliament (MEPs). MEPs form coalitions based on ideology, and the large unboxed areas toward the sides represent the status quo. You could compare them to Republicans and Democrats in the U.S. The narrow unboxed areas near the top represent far-left-leaning MEPs, who could be compared to the Green Party in the U.S. The two slivers within the box are where the Eurosceptics hang out—the EDD (Europe of Democracies and Diversities) and UEN (Union for Europe of the Nations). There were relatively few Eurosceptics in 1999. Just 47 MEPs—7.5% of Parliament—were against the idea of the EU.

What about today? Figure 5 shows the political orientation of the 751 MEPs of 2014's incoming European Parliament. Today's Eurosceptic parties are the EFDD (Europe of Freedom and Direct Democracy) and the ECR (European Conservatives and Reformists), whose representation is outlined in the now much larger box. These parties now compromise 118 MEPs—nearly 16% of Parliament. Eurosceptic party numbers in Parliament today are 2.5 times what they were in 1999.

These are not the only brands of politicians to have increased their numbers since 1999. In a 1989 Special Report, Prechter wrote that negative mood ushers in parties representing "ideals inimical to individual liberty (such as socialist, racist, fascist or fundamentalist)." Indeed there is a sliver in the Parliament where these types of politicians tend to reside. They're called Non-Inscrits, or non-affiliated members. Their views are so outside the mainstream that no other party in the Parliament will form a coalition with them. As Figure 6 shows, there were eight of them in 1999. In 2014, their numbers increased to 52—6.5 times as many as there were fifteen years prior, as depicted in Figure 7. The Non-Inscrits include members of France's National Front, Hungary's Jobbik and Greece's neo-Nazi Golden Dawn.

The negative mood trend in Europe is still under way, and it is closer to the middle than the end. This environment represents a window of opportunity for parties formerly on the outskirts of political discourse to make inroads. For everyone else, it is a time to keep yourself, your family and your assets safe. The recent countertrend move toward less negative social mood in much of the continent represents an opportunity to seek shelter from the next wave of the storm.

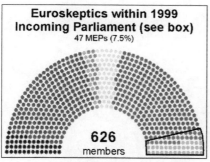

Europe of Democracies and Diversities
16 MEPs (2.5%)

Union for Europe of the Nations
31 MEPs (5%)

Figure 4

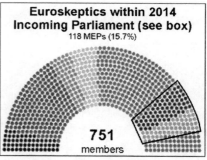

European Conservatives and Reformists
70 MEPs (9.3%)

Europe of Freedom and Direct Democracy
48 MEPs (6.4%)

Figure 5

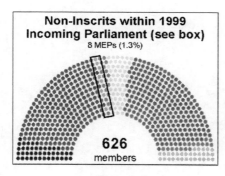

Figure 6

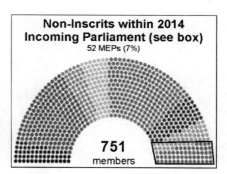

Figure 7

Chapter 47

Euroscepticism Succeeded with Brexit and Is On the Move in Italy and France

Chuck Thompson

November 29, 2016 (TS)

Seven years ago, in the December 26, 2012 issue of *The European Financial Forecast*, editor Brian Whitmer forecast, "Britain's ties to Europe, already severely strained, will probably dissolve completely."[1] This year, Britain voted to leave the European Union, and now anti-EU sentiment is spreading to Italy and France.

Italy Poses another Risk to the EU

Italy has had 64 governments since it became a republic in 1946.[2] Its current prime minister, Matteo Renzi, has proposed reforms to Italy's constitution to streamline the country's political system. But as a December 4 referendum on those reforms nears, the polls are not in Renzi's favor. Since early October, results of 32 polls have shown the "No" camp ahead by a growing margin.[3]

Italy's two houses of parliament currently share equal power, and the requirement that bills must be passed by both houses in identical form often results in political gridlock. Renzi wants to reduce the number of senators from 320 to 100, reduce the powers of the country's 20 regions and place more of the decision-making power in Rome. Critics of the reforms argue that they will give too much power to the prime minister.[4] They are using the Brexit vote and Donald Trump's victory in the U.S. as rallying cries to defeat the proposal. Italy's former prime minister, Silvio Berlusconi, says the "same spirit of rejection" that drove the U.S. election will induce Italians to vote against Renzi's reforms.[5]

Renzi promised to step down if the reforms do not pass. His resignation would open the door to Italy's three opposition parties, all of which hold

Eurosceptic views. The largest of these parties, known as the Five Star Movement, wants to hold a referendum on Italy abandoning the euro. The party's leader, Beppe Grillo, has used expletives to complain about unemployment, rail against the euro and call for better relations with Russia.[6]

Italy's FTSE MIB Index is down 61% from its 2007 high, and negative mood in the country is driving both Euroscepticism and anti-immigrant sentiments, not to mention Renzi's approval ratings, which have fallen from 70% to 40%.[7] [Keeping his promise, Renzi resigned on December 12, 2016.]

The Far Right Is a Contender in France's 2017 Presidential Election

In France, Marine Le Pen, head of the country's far-right National Front, is expected to occupy one of two spots in a May 2017 run-off for president. Le Pen wants to pull France out of the euro and hold a referendum on the country's membership in the European Union. Observers warn that while the EU can survive the loss of Britain, it cannot exist without France.[8]

A negative mood trend would favor Le Pen's platform. France's CAC 40 index is up but still 13% below its April 2015 high. The question is, how much negative mood would it take to drive the French toward a radical candidate? Political analyst Dominique Moïsi noted that the country is the closest yet to making such a choice: "The French system mitigates against a far-right victory; this remains unlikely, but for the

On Her Way Up: Marine Le Pen delivers a speech during her 2012 campaign.

first time I would not say it is impossible."[11] A win by Le Pen or independent candidate Emmanuel Macron in France's presidential election would mean that the country's top leader comes from neither of its traditional mainstream parties, the Socialists and the Republicans. [Macron won the election.]

Whatever the outcomes of these votes, it is clear that recurring waves of negative social mood are rattling the foundations that underpin the European experiment.

NOTES AND REFERENCES

[1] Whitmer, B. (2009, December). The Developing European Tinderbox. *The Socionomist.*

[2] Harris, C. (2016, October 17). Renzi, Reform and the Paradox of Italy's Referendum. *Euronews.*

[3] Jones, G. (2016, November 15). Italy Polls Get Worse for Renzi as Referendum Nears. Reuters.

[4] Massaro, C. (2016, October 26). Renzi's High Stake Gamble in Italian Constitutional Referendum. *Epoch Times.*

[5] Politi, J. (2016, November 13). Renzi Critics Scent Victory in Reform Battle After U.S. Vote. *Financial Times.*

[6] Migliaccio, A. (2016, November 23). To Understand Europe's Political Tremors, Take a Look at Italy. *Bloomberg Businessweek.*

[7] Dennison, J., & Draege, J.B. (2016, November 1). Unless the Yes Campaign Can Shift Tactics, Italy's Constitutional Referendum is Heading for a No Vote. The London School of Economics and Political Science.

[8] Europe's Biggest Populist Danger. (2016, November 19). *The Economist.*

[9] McKenzie, S., & Dewan, A. (2016, November 28). 'French Thatcher' Francois Fillon Wins France's Republican Primary. *CNN Europe.*

Chapter 48

First, They Told Us the Euro Was a Good Thing; Now They Say It's a Bad Thing

Alan Hall

September 28, 2016 (TS)

Socionomists were among the first eurosceptics, because we knew that the extreme optimism that propelled European unity in the late 1990s, near the end of a major trend toward positive social mood, would not last. From the beginning, socionomists have anticipated the breakup of the European Union and commented on the trend in real time [see quotes in Chapters 43, 44, 46 and 47].

Optimism was so pervasive when Europe achieved unity that a Nobel Prize winner in economics, Robert Mundell, opined that the introduction of the euro would have no negative effect on any country in the world.[1]

Now that a large-degree trend toward negative social mood is dividing Europe, another Nobel laureate, economist Joseph E. Stiglitz, is blaming the euro for the malaise. His new book, *The Euro: How a Common Currency Threatens the Future of Europe*, describes the euro as a "tragic mistake." In an interview with *The New York Times*, Stiglitz said, "The creation of the euro is the single most important explanation for the extraordinarily poor performance of the eurozone economies since the crisis of 2008."[2] The *Times* wrote,

> It was started in the name of forging a greater sense of union among the disparate nations of Europe. It was supposed to enhance commercial ties, erode borders and foster a spirit of collective interest, furthering the evolution of former wartime combatants into fellow nations of a united Europe. But the euro, in the 17 years since the common currency came into existence, has instead reinvigorated conflicts, yielding new crises, fresh grievances and a spirit of distrust.[3]

But why is the euro per se to blame? And why should it be more blameworthy than other aspects of the European Union?

Figure 1

All potential "culprits," including the euro, are not culprits at all. A large-degree trend toward negative social mood, as reflected in the long term setback in the Euro Stoxx 50 Index (see Figure 1) and declines in numerous individual European stock indexes, is the reason for Europe's economic slowdown as well as its social polarization, xenophobia, authoritarianism, nationalism, separatism—including Brexit—and the widespread feeling that the future of the EU is shaky. We can make this assessment with confidence because socionomic theory anticipated the character and trend of today's negative social expressions, long before they were evident.

NOTES AND REFERENCES

[1] Devitt, J. (2002, September 18). Nobel Laureate Robert Mundell Sees Bright Future for Euro. *Columbia News*.

[2] Whitmer, B. (2012, December 26). *The Socionomist*. p. 9.

[3] Goodman, P.S. (2016, July 27). How a Currency Intended to Unite Europe Wound Up Dividing It. *The New York Times*.

Part V:

RUSSIA

Chapter 49

A Socionomic Study of Russia

Alan Hall

November 14, 2007 (GMP)

Russian history is a tale of extremes. The country has gone from battleground to superpower to second-tier state, from totalitarianism to dysfunctional democracy, from Gulag to glasnost, and from communism to a mixed economy.

A stock market would certainly have reflected Russia's extreme social swings had the Kremlin allowed one, but no pre-1995 Russian stock market data exist. Fortunately for socionomists, events in Russia correlate well with the social mood of the U.S. (see Figure 1), which we have found to be an acceptable proxy for tracking global social mood.

1859-1892: Waves I, II and III of (III)

Negative social mood during wave (II), which fostered the worldwide bear market of 1835-1859, led to the Crimean War (1853-1856), which devastated Russia. With 256,000 dead, Grand Duke Konstantin Nikolayevich declared, "we are both weaker and poorer not only in material but also in mental resources, especially in matters of administration."[1]

Constructive events began occurring in Russia in 1861 as positive mood progressed in wave I of (III). Tsar Alexander II emancipated the serfs in an attempt to relieve revolutionary pressures and move Russia out of its feudal economy.

The wave II setback in social mood saw several uprisings in Russia. In one bright spot, in 1864 Alexander finally declared the end of the 50-year-long Caucasian War.

The positive social mood that supported wave III from 1865 to 1892 generated no major stresses for Russia and only one war, the brief Russo-Turkish War, from 1877 to 1878, which coincided with a pullback in the middle of wave III. Such a period of relative peace is normal for third waves.

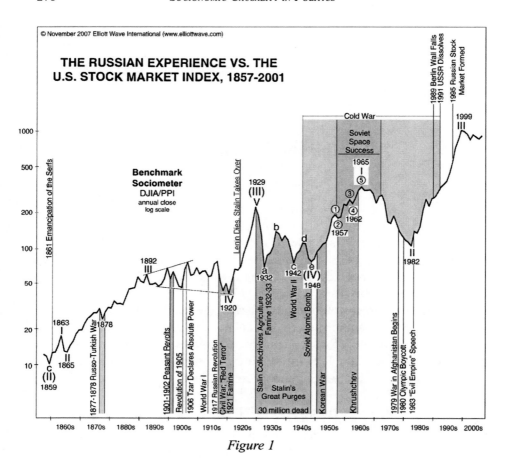

Figure 1

1892-1921: Wave IV of (III)

Wave IV from 1892 to 1920 saw increasingly negative social activity in Russia. The years 1901 through 1903 brought a steady increase in peasant revolts, in which mobs burned manor houses and mutilated animals. The Russo-Japanese War, initially popular with Russians in 1904, ended a year and a half later in crushing defeat. The Russian Revolution of 1905 brought nominal reforms by the Tsar, followed by a crackdown in 1906 in which the Tsar declared absolute executive power, disrupted revolutionary groups and imprisoned or exiled their leaders.

By 1913, deep into wave IV, the average Russian was earning 27% of an average Englishman's wages and paid 50% more in taxes. The global bear market and the decaying czarist autocracy exacted terrible social costs.

Russia had the highest mortality rate in Europe and a lower literacy rate than England had 163 years earlier in 1750.

Negative social mood worldwide led to the start of World War I in 1914. By its end, 3.3 million Russians had died, by far the largest death toll of any combatant nation. The massive social and political chaos at the end of wave IV decimated Russia's manufacturing, foreign trade, agricultural production and its already pitiful per capita income, which fell more than 70%.

Radicalism tends to emerge and become entrenched in periods of negative social mood. Near the end of wave IV, Marxism provided the intellectual basis for the Russian Revolution of 1917, which ended the reign of the Tsars and eventually led to a savage civil war.

Vladimir Lenin led the socialist revolution with the slogan, "Peace, Land and Bread," but his promises proved empty. In 1918, as the five-year civil war wore on and wave IV approached its nadir, Lenin narrowly survived an assassination attempt. Shortly afterward came the successful assassination of a secret-police chief, after which Lenin instituted a policy of "Red Terror." His handwritten "Hanging Order" of August 11, 1918 began the campaign. That edict illustrates how bear markets accommodate Russia's tendency toward social extremes, in this case with fear, recrimination and scapegoating. Here is its translated text[2]:

> 11 VIII 1918
> Send to Penza To Comrades Kuraev, Bosh, Minkin and other Penza communists
> Comrades! The revolt by the five kulak volosts must be suppressed without mercy. The interest of the entire revolution demands this, because we have now before us our final decisive battle "with the kulaks." We need to set an example.
> 1) You need to hang (hang without fail, so that the public sees) at least 100 notorious kulaks, the rich, and the bloodsuckers.
> 2) Publish their names.
> 3) Take away all of their grain.
> 4) Execute the hostages—in accordance with yesterday's telegram.
>
> This needs to be accomplished in such a way, that people for hundreds of miles around will see, tremble, know and scream out: let's choke and strangle those blood-sucking kulaks.
>
> Telegraph us acknowledging receipt and execution of this.
> Yours, Lenin
>
> P.S. Use your toughest people for this.

Translator's Comments: Lenin uses the derogative term *kulach'e* in reference to the class of prosperous peasants. A *volost'* was a territorial/administrative unit consisting of a few villages and surrounding land.

Scholars estimate that Lenin's Red Terror campaign caused the execution of up to 200,000 people between 1918 and 1921. The concurrent civil war took the lives of seven to eight million people, five million of whom died by famine.

Events during wave IV wreaked tremendous economic and social damage on Russia. From 1914 to 1921, Russia's population fell by more than 22%. Industrial output plunged 87% between 1913 and 1922, and gross crop yield fell by more than half. From these depths, a positive trend in social mood emerged, but due to the authoritarian form of government that took over in wave IV, Russia's recovery was much weaker than would have been the case in a freer society.

1921-1929: Wave V of (III)

In 1921, the year wave V began, Lenin abandoned attempts at communal agriculture and allowed individual farming. The following year, the U.S.S.R. was formed. By 1926, agricultural output had returned to at least the pre-revolution level of thirteen years previous, and industrial output did so two years later.

1929-1949: Wave (IV)

The following commentary, from *The Elliott Wave Theorist* of September 2001, describes how some points in the Elliott wave pattern enable unique social forecasting:

Forecasting Styles of Social Events

A section on "Nuances" in Chapter 15 of *The Wave Principle of Human Social Behavior* explains that negative social themes due to appear in any approaching bear market first express themselves in milder form in the preceding fourth wave of one lesser degree. ...In an earlier fourth wave from 1916 to 1921, collectivists took over Russia. In the larger fourth wave that followed, from 1929 to 1949, collectivists took over nearly half of the earth's population, in Germany, Italy, Eastern Europe and China.

So, the collectivism and social repression that emerged during wave IV foreshadowed what was to come in wave (IV).

Even at the peak of wave (III) in 1929, the Soviet economy was unable to support the combined growth of industry and the armed forces. Foreign investors were not interested in the country, and the middle class had been exterminated. Joseph Stalin, who took power after Lenin's death in 1924, had few sources of revenue. He decided to plunder the 78% of the population working in the agricultural sector. In 1929, at the onset of wave (IV), he began transferring control of farms, equipment and livestock to the government.

Farmers considered this policy a return to serfdom. They resisted and destroyed about half the U.S.S.R.'s livestock—some 55 million horses and cows—whereupon Stalin responded by sending about a million families into exile. This conflict, and a catastrophic decline in grain production, exacerbated the famine of 1932-1933 that killed between five and ten million people.

Stalin's move to bring farmers under state domination exemplified the classic bear market trait: a desire to exercise control over people. By most accounts, Stalin was rude, ruthless, unforgiving and without pity or empathy. As the wave (IV) bear market wore on, his malevolence expanded dramatically.

Stalin's purges and deportations were a huge magnification of Lenin's "Red Terror" campaign of the preceding fourth wave of one lesser degree. His social repression spanned all of wave (IV) from 1929 to 1949. His purges were initially aimed at the most prosperous peasants (or "kulaks") who resisted collectivization, but they expanded into genocide in which tens of millions of people were starved, exiled or killed. This wave also amplified another fixture of wave IV, the "katorga," the predecessor of the gulag.

The global negative social mood of wave (IV) ultimately gave rise to World War II. Nearly 24 million of the U.S.S.R.'s civilians and soldiers (13% of the population) died at the hands of the Axis.

The social environment today is so radically different from that of the 1940s that few people can imagine the destructive power of a major period of negative social mood. Photos of the kind that appeared in 1940s-era issues of *Life* magazine—of the dead, wounded and gangrenous—are not published in any mainstream media today.

Stalin executed millions of comrades and other Communist Party members, officers and even heroes in the Soviet Army—anyone who might have threatened his power. He used fear, anti-Semitism, racial polarization, starvations and secret police to consolidate his power so firmly that no political opposition was possible. He used scapegoats to cover his failures and re-wrote history to his advantage. His police state forced Russians into submission. His impetus to "cleanse" society escalated into mass hysteria, in which people denounced their neighbors, co-workers and even parents. The economic costs were immense, as the state killed the brightest people or hauled them off to the gulag. Fear played a dominant social role in stifling innovation, experimentation and constructive criticism.

Democracies typically oust leaders when anger reigns, but dictators turn their anger on the citizens. Stalin died a natural death in office in 1953 while apparently planning yet another purge of top men in his government.

1949-1966: Wave I of (V)

The return of positive social mood in wave I of wave (V) pulled Russia out of its worst depths. The communist state engineered a weapons and space program that gave it superpower status. With Stalin gone, the Communist Party resurged. In 1953, Nikita Khrushchev was confirmed as head of the Central Committee, and change was in the air.

Social mood can make or break political careers, and the politicians that thrive are either lucky or canny enough to ride the winds of change. Prior to Stalin's death in 1953, Khrushchev was a devoted Stalinist. In the 1940s, near the end of wave (IV), his participation in Stalin's purges earned him the nickname "The Butcher of the Ukraine." But Khrushchev would soon put this past behind him.

In 1956, near the middle of wave ① of wave I (see Figure 1), Khrushchev read a speech, "On the Personality Cult and its Consequences," denouncing Stalin and weakening the Stalinists in the government. This marked the beginning of the "Khrushchev Thaw," a period in which the Soviets partially reversed repression and censorship, improved relations with the West and released thousands of political prisoners from the gulags.

Figure 2 zooms in on a few notable Russia-related events within wave I. In late 1956, during a setback in mood, unrest in the U.S.S.R.'s satellite states erupted when a Hungarian protest march led to a Soviet invasion. Near the subsequent bottom in 1957, the Stalinists saw their chance to depose Khrushchev, but they failed. The larger trend toward positive mood prevailed, and key members of the Stalinist Anti-Party Group were ousted. In 1958, near the end of wave ③, Khrushchev became Premier of the Soviet Union. On October 12, 1960, near the end of a minor setback in mood, he famously interrupted a United Nations debate by banging his shoe on the table and told the U.S., "We will bury you." The 1962 Cuban Missile Crisis came at the low of wave ④, and Russia had to back down. In October 1964,

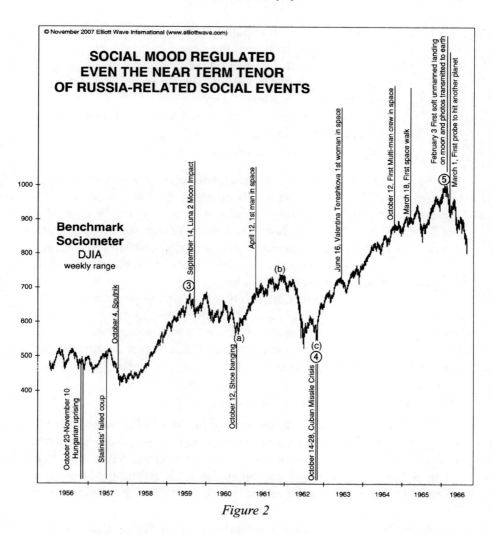

Figure 2

Khrushchev was voted out and replaced by Leonid Brezhnev, about a year before the top of wave ⑤.

Conciliation and cooperation characterize large-degree extremes in positive social mood, and the peak of wave I brought about a cluster of arms control treaties. The year 1964 also marked the first major U.S. sale of grain to Russia. The superpowers adopted an attitude of détente, a word meaning "relaxing" or "easing," and effected an uneasy truce.

During and just after wave I, the U.S.S.R. was first in a number of critical space successes:

- 1957: launched a satellite, Sputnik, into orbit
- 1959: crashed a spacecraft into the moon
- 1959: photographed the moon's far side
- 1961: launched a man, Yuri Gagarin, into space
- 1965: walked in space, Alexi Leonov
- 1966: landed on the moon with an unmanned craft and returned photographs from the moon's surface
- 1971: launched a space station, the Salyut 1

The U.S. and the U.S.S.R.'s achievements in space were an expression of positive social mood that has not been equaled by governments in the 35 years since. The list of positive aspects of social mood in Chapter 14 of *The Wave Principle of Human Social Behavior* includes the ones that made this achievement possible: adventurousness, clarity, confidence, constructiveness, daring, desiring power over nature, embrace of effort, optimism, practical thinking and sharpness of focus.

It is not coincidence that the U.S.S.R.'s moon landing came in 1965, the last full year of rise within wave I. Four years later, as the achievements deriving from a positive social mood reached a peak along with the Value Line Composite index in December 1968, the U.S. achieved the first manned lunar orbit, and seven months later it put men on the moon.

Wave II *(1966-1982)* (back to Figure 1)

The trend toward negative social mood of 1966-1982, labeled wave II, was characterized by indirect superpower competition, mainly expressed in proxy conflicts in the third world. The Soviets played a role in wars in Vietnam, Somalia, Angola, Mozambique, Laos, Cambodia and Nicaragua, while each time the U.S. government countered with materiel and support for the other side.

As the two superpowers' economies contracted, their fortunes waned. Both countries' space programs atrophied. The Soviet Union continued to suppress dissent. In 1968, it sent 500,000 troops into Czechoslovakia to crush the Prague Spring and negate reforms that had promised new freedoms of speech, travel, debate and association. In 1973, Alexandr Solzhenitsyn's *Gulag Archipelago* was smuggled out and published in the West, exposing the Soviet government's dependence on the gulag system.

U.S. foreign aid and the grain sales that continued throughout wave II propped up the U.S.S.R.'s failed agricultural program and postponed its collapse. In December 1979, the Soviets began their ill-fated war in Afghanistan.

In 1980, near the bottom of wave II, the U.S. boycotted the 1980 Moscow Summer Olympics. As tensions mounted, U.S. voters elected Ronald Reagan on a platform opposed to détente. In 1983, he gave his pivotal "Evil Empire" speech, describing the U.S.S.R. as "totalitarian" and attempting to take the moral high ground in the Cold War. This speech marked a new period of change within the U.S.S.R.

Wave III (1982-1997)

Soon after wave III's onset, the Russian Politburo unanimously chose Mikhail Gorbachev as General Secretary, and he began "perestroika," a process of restructuring that weakened the Communist Party's grip within Russia. He also applied a policy of "glasnost," meaning maximal transparency in the activities of the Soviet government. In August 1987, *The Elliott Wave Theorist* commented on this germinating, positive vibe:

> The most important popular cultural event is occurring not in the U.S., but in Russia. Glasnost may have bitten off more than it can chew. Allowing private taxis and tailors is one thing. But now that the Soviets have let rock 'n' roll get a foot in the door [allowing a concert of U.S. pop music in Moscow], there will be no easy turning back from the desire for greater knowledge of the tempting joys of the freedom-loving West.

On November 9, 1989, during the steepest ascent in wave III, glasnost and freedom came together, and the Berlin Wall fell in a global wave of euphoria. Prechter described the transition:

> What about the social consequences? Look around and witness how the results of this upswing in mood have become manifest. In only the past six years, in moves previously unimaginable, the forty-year-long Cold War has been pronounced officially over, and the USSR has freed Eastern Europe, creating what *The Wall Street Journal* called "a period of euphoria unequaled in the postwar era...".[3]

In 1991, during a recession at the end of wave ④ in U.S. stocks (not shown), the KGB failed in a coup attempt against Gorbachev, and the U.S.S.R. collapsed. Crisis followed. Russia experienced a shattered

economy, millions of citizens pushed into poverty, pervasive political corruption, an explosion of organized crime and the looting of state assets.
These developments were extreme given the small degree of the mood
change, but the decades of structural damage ultimately deriving from the
negative mood of 1917 had left little infrastructure or social organization
to cushion the setback.

As the positive mood trend resumed, the Gorbachev era gave way to
that of Boris Yeltsin, the first democratically elected president of Russia. The
country even initiated a stock market. The Russian Trading System Index
(RTSI) was formed in 1995 and immediately began an ascent to a peak in
late 1997. In the December 1996 issue of *The Elliott Wave Theorist*, Peter
Kendall depicted aspects of Russia's first bull market:

> The events in Russia will surely stand as one of the bull market's most
> impressive feats.... The investment scene in Moscow is as vibrant
> as in New York.... In its first international debt offering since the
> 1917 Bolshevik revolution, [the cash-strapped Russian government]
> was hoping to get $300 million. Despite continued contraction in the
> economy, routine Mafia hits on prominent businessmen, revelations
> that most Russian firms do not pay tax bills, entrenched communist
> politicians, a "backlash against foreign investment" and a long history
> of turning on capitalists, international investors so love Russia that
> they more than tripled the size of the offering to $1 billion.

In 1996, in the heart of that bull market, Yeltsin won reelection with help
from newly wealthy "oligarchs," or business magnates. The First Chechen
War was the only major Russian conflict of the period.

Russia's Financial Crisis of 1998

The Value Line Composite index reversed downward from a multi-year
peak in April 1998, and financial crisis hit Russia in August. It accompanied
a global recession and a bear market in commodity prices at a time when
Russia got 80% of its revenue from oil, gas, metals and timber. Despite an
IMF bailout, Russia had to devalue the ruble deeply to avoid default, and
investors fled the country. As the RTSI fell below its starting level, Yeltsin's
popularity plunged, making his previously tolerated buffoonery distaste-
ful. The next president, Vladimir Putin, took office on December 30, 1999.
Although a bear market was about to commence globally, Putin inherited a
young bull market locally along with a new positive trend in Russian social
mood that is still going strong.

Relative Strength in the Russian Stock Market

From 1998 to date, Russia's RTSI has increased 7,000%. The real-money comparison presented in Figure 3 is even more astounding. Valuing a stock market index in real money—gold—rips away the influence of fiat currencies to produce comparable sociometers. No other chart so well conveys the stark contrast in social mood between Russia and the U.S. Social attitudes bear out these diverging paths, as Russia possesses assertiveness, confidence and waxing machismo, while the U.S. acts tame and tentative in comparison.

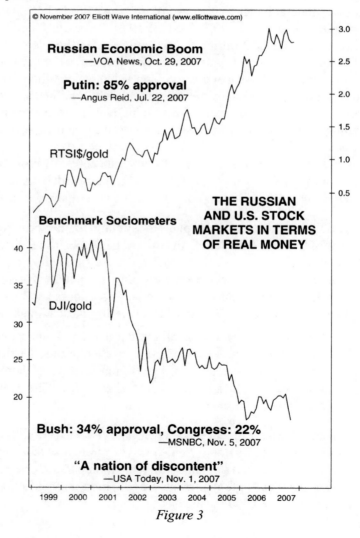

Figure 3

The Power of Today's Positive Mood in Russia

Russia is flexing its economic muscle. In 1992, the first year that Russia calculated its GDP, it weighed in at less than $90 billion. In 2006, it approached $1 trillion. From 1998 to 2006, Russia's economy grew 6.7% annually.[4] It maintained that rate in 2006, while growth in Germany was 2.7%, in the U.K. 2.8%, in France 2.2% and in the Netherlands 3%. Russia was finally, for the first time ever, outperforming its European neighbors in an economic expansion. In Eurasia, only the Chinese economy, with its 10.7% annual growth, was more impressive.[5]

Russia's federal budget has run surpluses since 2001 and ended 2006 with a surplus equal to 9% of GDP. Since 1999, Russia has increased its foreign reserves from $12 billion to $420 billion, the third largest in the world. According to Moody's Investors Service, the structured finance market is booming in Russia and could hit a value of $5 billion this year. As liquidity flows in, Russians are embracing debt, and household consumption and investment are rising. Loans to individuals rose 75% in 2006. Outstanding mortgage loans in Russia have risen more than 460% since the first quarter of 2006.

Positive social mood is a powerful human incentive. It brought on a market economy in Russia and transformed a feeble new democracy into a global player. The country's new confidence shows in many ways:

- Russia recently announced plans to lay claim to the North Pole and half of the Arctic, including the oil and gas deposits believed to be there. In the first week of August, an expedition led by renowned Russian polar scientist Artur Chilingarov planted the Russian flag four kilometers underwater on the polar seafloor. The U.S. questioned the claim, and Canada said it owns the pole. Chilingarov said,

    I don't give a damn what all these foreign politicians there are saying about this. If someone doesn't like this, let them go down themselves...and then try to put something there. Russia must win. Russia has what it takes to win. The Arctic has always been Russian.[6]

- Moscow burns with real estate fever. The city wants to sell most of Gorky Park (equivalent to New York's Central Park) to a "mysterious partner focused on managing recreation parks in the region." The hope is that "elite apartments are built there and sold at $10,000/ sq. meter to $20,000/sq. meter."

• The ruble has a shaky history, but on August 10 an article in Russia's online daily, Kommersant, extolled the strength of the ruble and suggested that the currency would appreciate during the current liquidity crisis and even gain safe-haven status.

• Also in August, Russian and European space agencies announced a cooperative effort to develop a spaceship for flights to the International Space Station, the moon and Mars. Russia also announced a simulated Mars mission that will confine the crew to an experimental research complex for almost two years. It's no surprise that the Russians now see themselves as spaceworthy. After the last U.S. Space Shuttle disaster, survival on the International Space Station depended completely on the Russian space program for over two and a half years. And Russia is the first and only country offering space charters. Russia has traveled a long road from the negative-mood pole of desire for power over people toward the positive-mood pole of desire for power over nature.

Putin as a Paragon

Presidential popularity tends to move in tandem with stock markets. Review this comment from the April 1991 issue of *The Elliott Wave Theorist* about George H.W. Bush:

> In July 1990, with the Dow at 3000, George Bush was winning praise and high approval ratings. He was "a man for the season," riding "a huge current of political popularity." Just four months later, with the Dow below 2400, he was being bombed with derisive headlines. "Bush May Have Lost 1992 Already," "From Sizzle to Fizzle," "a quagmire of indecision and ineptitude which could take him the rest of the Presidency to dig out" typified the press's reports. Here it is, exactly four months later once again, with the Dow back at 3000, and George Bush has a 91% approval rating, the highest in the history of the records, and the media love him again... The precision with which the level of presidential popularity has tracked the Dow and its rate of change is remarkable.

Extreme highs and lows in presidential popularity tend to mark extreme highs and lows in stock prices. To get a feel for the extremity of Russia's positive mood today, consider that Vladimir Putin's presidential approval rating is nearly 80%. "In contrast to his predecessor, Boris Yeltsin, notorious for drunken antics, Putin has established an image as serious, energetic, sober and sharp-witted."[7] Putin is comparing himself to Franklin Roosevelt, the four-term U.S. president whom the Kremlin, political consultants and state controlled news media currently admire. According to a *Washington Post* translation of a recent article in the Russian tabloid *Komsomolskaya Pravda*,

> Putin rescued an enfeebled Russia from the chaos of the 1990s, banished or imprisoned dangerous billionaires and regained respect for his newly enriched country on the world stage. And Roosevelt ran for a third and fourth term because his country needed him. Translation: Putin, too, should stay.[8]

The Russian presidential campaign is in movie theaters, and Russia's beloved "otets" (father) Putin is the patriarchal, behind-the-scenes star. A personal friend of Putin has produced a Kremlin-inspired film about an uprising in 1612 against foreign occupiers of Moscow. The revolt resulted in a special national congress choosing Mikhail Romanov as tsar. Current Kremlin ideology holds that Putin, like Romanov, patriotically rescued Russia from "national turmoil" and "treacherous foreign intervention."[9] The movie aims to cement this idea into popular culture, and a senior United Russia party member wants to use an archaic 17th-century legal mechanism to install Putin as a modern tsar and anoint him as the "father of the nation." The United Russia party's leader says, "Putin will remain Russia's leader."

President Putin's popularity is approaching cult status. The Russian media "can't get enough of him," and children wear photos of his face on T-shirts. His recent bare-chested photos while fishing in Siberia were promi-nently posted on the presidential Web site. "*Komsomolskaya Pravda* reported that women who visited its Web site posted comments on Putin's 'vigorous torso' and said they 'were screaming with delight and showering (him) with compliments.'"[10]

Russian radio plays a pop song called "A Man Like Putin." The vocalist sings of her desire to leave her drunken boyfriend and be with "Someone like Putin, full of strength/ Someone like Putin, who doesn't drink/ Someone like

A Russian tabloid published a step-by-step guide on how to build a body like Putin's last week.

Putin, who doesn't hurt me/ Someone like Putin, who won't run away."
One Muscovite said, "The lyrics are awful and the melody is even worse,
and it seems that Moscow women are singing the song everywhere you go,
especially to their boyfriends."[11] Muscovites can buy an ice cream called
"Sweet Little Vladimir," as well as Putin kebabs, portraits, watches, T-shirts
and dishtowels. The Putin label sells well. This extensive adoration is a sign
of a positive social mood extreme.

Putin has become so confident that he's even taken to forecasting the
stock market. As *The Elliott Wave Theorist* has noted, in the late stages of
a bull run, extrapolation of the old uptrend seems so intuitively right that
non-professionals—including teenagers, *Playboy* playmates, reporters and
politicians—begin to think they can forecast the stock market. Putin recently
offered his stock market analysis at a government meeting on August 22,
saying, "For us, it wasn't such a critical fall, but more like a correction with
regard to the previous unprecedented growth...." When the call for more
bull market comes easily and naturally to people, the market is usually near
a top, meaning that social mood is at a correspondingly positive extreme,
which in turn suggests an approaching reversal to the downside.

My next study will present a forecast for Russia, with an assessment
of the opportunities and dangers it presents to Russia and the world.

NOTES AND REFERENCES

[1] Tsygankov, Andrei P. (2014) *The Strong State in Russia: Development and Crisis*. New York: Oxford University Press, p. 48.

[2] Library of Congress.

[3] Prechter, R. *The Elliott Wave Theorist*, Special Report, February 1989.

[4] CIA World Factbook.

[5] World Bank.

[6] Eckel, Mike (AP) "Russia Defends North Pole Flag-Planting," *Washington Post*, August 8, 2007.

[7] Eckel, Mike (AP) "Photos of Bare-Chested Putin Create Stir," *Washington Post*, August 22, 2007.

[8] Finn, Peter, "Putin Finds Expedient Hero in Four-Term U.S. President," *Washington Post*, October 19, 2007.

[9] Osborn, Andrew and Alan Cullison, "Putin's Next Role: 'Father of Nation," *The Wall Street Journal*, November 8, 2007.

[10] Eckel, Mike (AP) "Photos of Bare-Chested Putin Create Stir," *Washington Post*, August 22, 2007.

[11] Delio, Michelle, "Russian Mania in Putin it Mildly," *Wired*, August 30, 2002.

Chapter 50

Sizing Up a Superpower:
Portents of Extreme Behavior
in the Next Russian Bear Market

Alan Hall

November 30, 2007 (GMP)

Russia today enjoys a powerfully positive social mood. Confidence radiates from the Russian economy, politics, international relations and the military. Russians are embracing debt as never before. As for its stock market, the past decade has seen a *sixty-fold increase* in the Russian Trading System Index. All of these events [as detailed at the end of Chapter 49] indicate that Russian social mood has reached a historically unprecedented, positive extreme. Corroborating this observation, our long term Elliott wave labeling for the Russian stock market indicates that a major top is imminent. This conclusion has serious implications for Russia and its neighbors in Europe, Central Asia and the Far East.

Elliott Wave Forecast

Figure 1 is a chart of the Russian Trading System Index from its inception. Our Elliott wave labeling for the RTSI shows that a clear five-wave advance of at least Primary degree that began in 1999 is near completion.

This index should soon begin its biggest bear market since the five-wave pattern began. The minimum probable drop—a move into the area of the fourth wave of 2004—would more than halve the value of the index.

The trend toward negative social mood implied by such a decline should produce financial and social events of a character similar to those seen during comparable periods of negative social mood over the past two centuries, as detailed in the previous report. Viewed in the context of Russian history, this outlook has serious geostrategic implications.

Figure 1

Recent events seem to foreshadow the character of the coming contraction. They suggest that the onset of a bear market in Russia should be
taken very seriously.

Social Signs of Coming Political Danger

When social mood shifts from positive to negative at a large degree
of trend, people need to protect their assets and ensure their livelihood and
safety in advance. Doing so successfully requires anticipation of major
change, a task made difficult by humans' psychological tendency to envision the future by linearly extrapolating present trends. The Wave Principle
provides a basis for escaping this mental default and allows for some anticipation of trend change, as Prechter outlined in Chapter 20 of *The Wave
Principle of Human Social Behavior*:

> The Wave Principle guarantees reliable forecasting only of
> probabilities. It allows us to predict some aspects of the future and
> not others. For example, early in a new social mood trend, we can

forecast society's coming character changes but not necessarily specific events. We can forecast that a major rising impulse wave will bring an increase in goodwill and productivity. The specific decisions that each person makes and the specific social actions and events that result depend upon countless details and are therefore chaotic. *As the trend progresses, however, we can watch for signs to indicate such specifics and actually anticipate some of them quite well*, as demonstrated in Chapter 17.[1]

Positive social mood has kept international relations peaceful thus far, but shifts toward negative social mood turn cooperation into conflict. Russia seems more ready to confront the U.S. today than at any time since the Cuban Missile Crisis 45 years ago. Indeed, on October 26, Putin made a comparison to that dangerous confrontation, reversing the protagonists' roles, with the U.S. this time placing missiles at Russia's doorstep via the European missile defense shield. The steadily increasing potential for conflict between the two superpowers represents the potential for serious trouble. On November 20, Putin warned that Russia will respond to a NATO military buildup on its borders.

Social mood change at large-degree turns is not instantaneous. It can seem broad and slow as it develops. As times of reversal approach, social actions can signal which entities will act most strongly in accordance with the coming mood shift. Below are recent topics in the news that show how Russia is converting its newfound prosperity into a growing military threat.

Stalin Resurrected

Although positive social mood produced the ideas of *glasnost* and *perestroika* and moved Russia toward democracy and capitalism, socialism and autocracy are deep in Russia's bones. Reverence for Stalin is resurging, along with his penchant for rewriting history. Stalin watched Lenin inspire a cult of personality, and he encouraged it for himself. Stalin eventually accepted titles from fawning devotees, such as "Father of Nations," "Brilliant Genius of Humanity," "Great Architect of Communism" and, ironically, "Gardener of Human Happiness."

Recently, President Putin endorsed a new guide for history teachers, "A Modern History of Russia: 1945-2006." The book favorably compares Stalin to Otto von Bismarck and Peter the Great, and seeks to qualify and justify his crimes. It describes him as "one of the most successful leaders of the U.S.S.R.," who created "the best educational system in the world." Despite the devastation of the purges, one passage translates like this:

> The result of Stalin's purges was a new class of managers capable
> of solving the task of modernization in conditions of shortages of
> resources, loyal to the supreme power and immaculate from the point
> of view of executive discipline.[2]

Some observers have noticed the change:

> Just as the Nazis in the 1930s rewrote Germany's history, the Putin
> Kremlin is rewriting Russia's. It has rehabilitated Stalin, the greatest
> mass murderer of the 20th century. And it is demonizing Boris Yeltsin,
> Russia's first democratically elected president. That he destroyed
> totalitarianism is ignored. Instead, he is denounced for his "weak"
> pro-Western policies.[3]

Russia is sliding toward greater state control of the economy, media,
politics and society. Eastern Europe is watching this cultural repression
nervously as Russia increasingly "sees the collapse of communism not as
a time of liberation, but as an era of pitiable weakness."[4]

Nazi Parallels

Interesting parallels exist between Russia today and Germany in the
late 1920s. Both nations suffered a humiliating political setback, a loss of
territory and an episode of hyperinflation that led to poverty, social ills and
widespread dissatisfaction. Germany suffered defeat in 1917 and hyperinflation in 1923; Russia lost its conquered territories in 1991 and suffered
hyperinflation in 1993. Thereafter, Germany began a rearmament effort;
Russia appears to be on a similar path as it rebuilds its military capabilities.

A *Daily Mail* article titled "Sex for the motherland: Russian youths
encouraged to procreate at camp" describes a Kremlin-sponsored youth
movement called "Nashi." Critics call the 10,000 young campers "Putinju-
gend," or "Putin Youth," derived from "Hitlerjugend," German for "Hitler
Youth." "Behind the group's childlike promotional literature urging patrio-
tism, athleticism, hard work and family values, Nashi is a slick, well-funded
instrument of Mr. Putin's government."[5] Nashi members have harassed the
British ambassador for months, quashed opposition dissent at rallies and
enjoy support from police. Critics say they feed xenophobia, vigilantism
and intolerance. If these characteristics are present now, they will surely
expand in a negative social-mood environment.

Bombers Resume Flights

Russia recently resumed long-range bomber patrols. In a scene out of
"Top Gun Meets Dr. Strangelove," Russian bomber pilots exchanged smiles

with U.S. fighter pilots who met them above a U.S. naval base on Guam on August 8. Russia's 79 strategic bombers have begun regular forays along the U.S. East Coast and in the Pacific and Arctic. Smiles were not reported on September 6, when Britain's Air Force scrambled four warplanes to intercept eight Russian bombers over international waters. "Relations between London and Moscow are at their worst since the Cold War."[6]

Putin's recent appearance on television in a military flight suit is among the many events suggesting that the Russian government harbors hope of a return to the "good old days" of superpower status. Observers say Putin is trying to boost service morale, gain respect and make a political statement. Media sources from *Newsweek* to France's *Le Figaro* have argued that this is not a regression to the Cold War, because Putin only wants respect, not real confrontation. The Cold War was fought via dialogue, the arms race and proxy wars in the Third World. It never escalated into a hot war among the superpowers because social mood was positive throughout waves I and III as depicted in Figure 1 of our previous report. As Prechter put it, "Although it is not widely appreciated, the Cold War was over four decades of peace."[7]

Stock prices, because they reflect social mood, are the key indicator of whether today's bluster and posturing between Russia and other governments will come to blows. Our forecasts for the U.S. and Russian stock markets imply that confrontation could become hotter this time.

New Offensive Missiles

Similar to Germany's rapid military expansion during the 1930s, Russia's military budget has quadrupled under Putin. New weaponry includes modern nuclear submarines, intercontinental ballistic missiles with maneuverable warheads that Russia claims can evade U.S. anti-missile defenses, and plans for a second deployment of Topol-M mobile ICBMs that can be launched from forests. Russia says that this development is in response to the U.S.'s withdrawal from the Anti-Ballistic Missile Treaty and plans for a European-based missile shield. "Russia's military chief recently told the Czech Republic it was making a 'big mistake' by hosting the shield."[8] On October 12, Putin threatened to pull out of a Cold-War-era missile treaty.

New Air Defense

On August 6, Russia deployed the new S-400 combination air and missile defense system that can destroy targets traveling up to three miles per second, such as aircraft and medium-range missiles. An S-500 mobile antimissile system is in the works. In a recent televised ceremony near Moscow, a Russian Orthodox priest blessed the new weapons.

Naval Activity

The Russian Navy recently announced plans to return to the Mediterranean Sea and began dredging and building docks in Syrian ports. Israel expressed alarm that Russian ships in Syrian bases will allow electronic surveillance of the entire Middle East and an air defense umbrella over much of Syria. Russia downplays the deployment as only a symbolic presence.

Georgia Missile Crisis

Georgia's claim that a Russian warplane dropped a missile on its territory reveals increasing international tension. This ex-Soviet republic is of strategic interest to both Moscow and Washington because it has energy pipelines that skirt Russia. Georgia seeks to join NATO and distance itself from Russia. The U.S. supports Georgia's desire to bring its pro-Russian separatist regions under control, but Russia has military plans to stop any move by Georgia to secure those regions.

Serbia/Kosovo Tension

Russia opposes pro-Western Kosovo's independence from Russian ally Serbia. In a speech on September 2, Russian Foreign Minister Lavrov drew a "red line in the sand" opposing U.S. missile defense plans and Western proposals for Kosovo's independence from Serbia: "There we cannot fail to react and we must stick to our positions to the end."[9]

Alleged Assassinations

In the same speech, Lavrov dismissed Britain's attempts to extradite a KGB veteran suspected of the radiation poisoning of Putin critic Alexander Litvinenko in London. Lavrov called it "a noisy propaganda show" and quoted from Shakespeare's *Hamlet* to accuse the British government of plotting against Russia. When Russia denied the extradition request, Britain expelled four Russian diplomats from London, and Moscow replied in kind. Vladimir Putin accused Britain of "thinking colonially" and expressed relief that Russia had never been a colony of Britain. The accused KGB veteran, Andrei Lugovoi, announced his candidacy for the Kremlin on September 17. In London in July, Scotland Yard stopped a second alleged Russian plot to kill billionaire Russian exile Boris Beresovsky, another opponent of Putin.

Censorship and Propaganda

In 2003 President Putin shut down Russia's last large independent TV station, and his pressure on the media has not relented since. Putin signed a new law in July 2006 that granted authorities virtually unchecked power against critics. Recent murders and unexplained deaths of journalists have intimidated the media, as has the Kremlin's campaign against "Russian radio stations that rebroadcast [U.S. government-funded] Radio Liberty programs—subjecting them to debilitating harassment."[10] The state has also forced the BBC's Russian language broadcasts off the air. Russian television has reverted to the Soviet-era practice of presenting the news as, "Here is the news, and this is what you should think about it," as most Russians now get their news from three state-controlled television channels. The Kremlin's last media obstacle may be the Internet. It has yet to curb the free debate on Internet forums, but it already controls many "plain-clothes" websites used to dilute opposition.

Human Rights Constraints

The U.S. State Department's most recent human rights report on Russia observed "continuing centralization of power in the Kremlin, a compliant legislature, political pressure on the judiciary, intolerance of ethnic minorities, corruption and selectivity in enforcement of the law, and media restrictions and self-censorship."[11]

Siege Mentality

In 1999, Putin told the Russian Federal Security Service (FSB), "A few years ago, we succumbed to the illusion that we don't have enemies, and we have paid dearly for that." Hinting at an approaching turn toward negative mood, siege mentality is playing well with the Russian public. A recent TV news story showing the launch of a new Navy ship pointed out a "spy ship" on the horizon and a "spy plane" in the sky, and mentioned how foreigners always watch Russia. This form of propaganda leverages the historical Russian feeling of being encircled and besieged. One spokesman complained, "In Gorbachev's time, Russia was liked by the West and what did we get for it? We have surrendered everything: Eastern Europe, Ukraine, Georgia. NATO has moved to our borders."[12] *The Economist* responded,

> The creation of enemies may smooth over clan disagreements and fuel nationalism, but it does not make the country more secure or prosperous. While the FSB reports on the ever-rising numbers of foreign spies, accuses scientists of treason and hails its "brotherhood," Russia remains one of the most criminalised, corrupt and bureaucratic countries in the world.[13]

Retreat from Private Ownership

In the vacuum that followed the collapse of the U.S.S.R. in 1991, well-connected citizens and criminal bosses bought state-owned assets dirt cheap. This action provoked resentment among former Soviet managers as well as the "siloviki," former members of the KGB. The Kremlin's takeover of Yukos, Russia's first privately owned oil company, was the first and most obvious example of property seizure from the new capitalist oligarchs and redistribution to the "siloviki":

> Most of Yukos has ended up with state-controlled Rosneft, now Russia's largest oil company, run from a low-rise office within shouting distance of the Kremlin.... In a few weeks a clerk will cross out Yukos's name from an official register and Russia's first-ever private oil company will cease to exist as a legal entity.[14]

Protectionism

The Russian government has made life difficult for Western oil interests, specifically Shell, BP and ExxonMobil. ExxonMobil developed Russia's Sakhalin 1 gas fields, but Russia's powerful Gazprom recently told ExxonMobil not to honor its contract to sell gas to China, because Russia needs the gas at home at a cheaper price. On September 11, Putin derided U.S. legislation to control foreign investment in the U.S. and threatened new restrictions on foreign investment in Russia.

Eastern Europe, the Middle East and Oil: A Volatile Mix

Russia is now the world's largest producer of natural gas and the second-largest producer of oil. The country's substantial energy production has fueled its political and strategic return to power. On October 10, [2007,] Azerbaijan, Georgia, Lithuania, Poland and Ukraine created a consortium to build an alternate energy pipeline for Eastern Europe, aiming to lessen Russia's ability to use energy as a political tool. Such actions by former Soviet states are increasing tensions, as Moscow strongly opposes U.S.-supported efforts to bypass Russia with energy pipelines to the West.

Russia and the U.S. both seek a strategic position in the Middle East. Putin expanded Russia's influence there with a September trip to "widen ties with the Arab community." In the United Arab Emirates, he discussed energy deals, proposed to create a natural gas equivalent of OPEC and negotiated to pay Russia's UAE debt of $500 million with Russian weapons.

On October 16, Putin braved report of an assassination plot and made a high-profile visit to Tehran, where he gave a non-specific warning (obviously aimed at the U.S.) against any outside interference in the Caspian Sea area, including the use—or even the mention—of military force against Iran. He delivered his statement to the presidents of five Caspian Sea states, who had convened to divide the oil and gas resources of the area, estimated to be the world's third-largest reserves. Warnings may become more specific soon, as Russia is increasing its arms sales to U.S. adversaries, Syria, Iran and Venezuela. Russia has now blocked and/or circumvented three sets of nuclear sanctions by the United Nations against Iran.

Belligerent Rhetoric

President Putin has unleashed a barrage of insults toward the West. In May, he compared the policies of President Bush to those of Nazi Germany. A few days later, after he attended Bush's "lobster summit" in Kennebunkport, Maine, he pulled Russia out of a key NATO arms control treaty.

On October 12, Putin mocked the U.S. plan to build a European missile defense system and warned that U.S.-Russia relations could suffer if the U.S. goes forward with it. On October 13, U.S. Secretary of State Condoleezza Rice met with Russian rights activists and reported that Putin's concentration of power is "stifling his country's transition to democracy."[15] The chairwoman of a Russian human rights organization responded that the United States had "lost the high moral ground." She told Rice, "The American voice alone doesn't work anymore," and Rice bristled at the criticism, replying sharply, "We never lost the high moral ground."[16] This exchange is a near inversion of U.S. President Ronald Reagan's 1983 "Evil Empire" speech.

During the Cold War, U.S. criticism of the Soviet state was met with the flat admonition, "Don't interfere in internal affairs of the Soviet Union." We are seeing a return to this kind of language.

Moves Toward Dictatorship

The stage is set for a return to autocracy in Russia. Russia's FSB succeeded the KGB, and today it is reputed to be a more pervasive, powerful and nepotistic organization than the KGB ever was. FSB officials control tremendous financial resources and exert influence in all areas of Russian life. New recruits are literally the children and grandchildren of the "siloviki." They attend the same schools and are encouraged to intermarry. "All the strategic decisions, according to Ms. Kryshtanovskaya [a sociologist at the Russian Academy of Sciences], were and still are made by the small group of people who have formed Mr. Putin's informal politburo."[17] "Putin '...has more power today than the pharaoh of Egypt, the tsar and the Soviet Union's general secretary combined,' says Communist leader Gennady Zyuganov."[18]

This situation indicates the re-emergence of a ruling class and perhaps new dictatorship in Russia. Putin's power now is nearly absolute, and he probably won't relinquish it. On October 1, he signaled his intent to remain in power when he agreed to head the pro-Kremlin, United Russia Party's candidate list.

As popularity and power surround Putin, secrecy has returned to Russia's election process. On October 31, Russia announced that it would restrict both the number of election observers from the Organization for Security and Cooperation in Europe and how long they could stay. On November 19, the OSCE cancelled plans to observe the upcoming election. On November 21, Putin accused the West of "dirty tricks" and "meddling in Russian politics."[19] On November 24, chess grandmaster and Putin critic Garry Kasparov was jailed for leading a protest rally in Moscow. His assistant said he was forced to the ground and beaten. "The Kremlin has mounted a major campaign to orchestrate a crushing victory for Putin's United Russia party...."[20]

Putin could end up as a powerful prime minister directing a weak president, or, if the United Russia Party retains a two-thirds majority in the State Duma, it can change the constitution to allow him to return to the presidency. Public opinion surveys show that most Russians want Putin to remain in power. He stated on September 14 that he has no intention to "tinker with democracy," but he seems to be getting in position to do just that. If he succeeds, the world may see an even darker side of Putin. As our previous report detailed, history offers many examples of how Russian leaders behave in bear markets. It is not a heartening record.

Social Implications

The stock market is our best sociometer. A stock market forecast is more importantly a social-mood forecast, which implies a commensurate change in the character of social actions. In the U.S. stock market, wave IV from 1892 to 1920, shown in Figure 1 of [Chapter 49], retraced about 30% of the wave III that began in 1865. Wave (IV) from 1929 to 1948 retraced about 40% of the previous wave (III) that began in 1859. Those declines may have understated contemporaneous mood shifts in Russia, which were accompanied by the extremely violent Russian social history described in our previous report. They brought intense social repression, redirection of capital from infrastructure to weaponry, and war and death on a massive scale. Although the coming bear market will start from a much higher level, realization of our forecast for a large-degree decline in the RTSI implies a coming shift toward negative social mood in Russia that will have major negative effects on Russia, her neighbors and perhaps the rest of the world.

A Summary of Conditions

Here is a short list of Russia's social characteristics: extreme confidence, increasing authoritarianism, siege mentality, waxing belligerence and a history so full of extremes that most Russians have rarely experienced what most other people around the world consider to be normalcy. The list of recent events includes suppression of the media, nationalistic youth movements, resurging cultural repression, nostalgia for Stalin, new Middle East alliances, renewed weapons development and deployment, the "father of all bombs," nationalization of private assets, the resurgence of a secretive ruling class, a steady retreat from democracy, renewed opposition to the West and eerie similarities to Nazi Germany. The increasing frequency and strength of these events amplifies their significance.

U.S.-U.S.S.R. Parallels

Russia is the subject of this report, but that doesn't mean that a negative social mood trend in Russia is the only threat on the horizon. The U.S. has been threatening, sanctioning and pressuring a growing list of countries. In 2006 and 2007 alone, U.S. sanctions punished the Balkans, Belarus, Burma, Cote d'Ivoire, Cuba, the Democratic Republic of the Congo, Iran, Iraq, Liberia, North Korea, Sudan, Syria and Zimbabwe.[21] This type of punitive behavior has escalated markedly since global social mood reached a positive extreme in 2000, as indicated by all-time highs in the Euro Stoxx 50 [see Figure 1 in Chapter 46], the inflation-adjusted World Stock Index [see Figure 1 in Chapter 77] and the Dow/gold ratio [see Figure 1 in Chapter 77]. The U.S. government's behavior may have the unintended consequence of directing the growing global feelings of stress, frustration and anger toward the U.S. Russia may soon accuse the U.S. of being an "Evil Empire."

The U.S. also faces problems similar to those the U.S.S.R. experienced prior to its collapse: unsustainable deficits and foreign debt, declining oil production [since alleviated], massive military budgets, involvement in protracted guerrilla wars, oversized, inefficient government and costly missions to spread ideology.

The U.S. has also undergone radical changes that make it increasingly similar to Russia: a huge wealth disparity; a strong trend toward political dynasty (in both major parties) [since rejected, for now]; loss of confidence in the election process; extreme tactics against national security threats; massive detention centers; secret prosecutions, trials and torture; and spy programs against citizens. The U.S. House recently passed HR 1955, "The Violent Radicalization and Homegrown Terrorism Prevention Act of 2007," which defines "violent radicalization" as "the process of adopting or promoting an extremist belief system for the purpose of facilitating ideologically based violence to advance political, religious, or social change."[22] If the bill becomes law, critics say it will give the government the Orwellian right to define and prosecute "thought crime." In 2002, the U.S. led the world, just ahead of Russia, in the percentage of its population in prison.[23]

Implications

A long term trend toward positive social mood leads to peace and political cooperation, and long term trend toward negative social mood leads to turmoil. A situation in which the trends of social mood in the U.S. and Russia are simultaneously negative would be quite different from the Cold War and the period of cooperation, respectively, that occurred during the previously shared bull markets of 1949-1966 and 1982-1997.

Russia's long history of border wars and its desire to reclaim the resources of satellite states lost upon the collapse of the U.S.S.R. make future border conflicts likely. NATO, Muslim and Asian countries border Russia on the west and south. The ethnic diversity within these states represents conflicts-in-waiting for the xenophobia that attends times of negative social mood.

A large slide in the RTSI Index accompanied by declines in Western stock markets would signal that Russia's opposition to the UK and the U.S. would likely increase, along with the chances of nuclear war. Recent articles about U.S. plans to use tactical nukes against Iran have not gone unnoticed in Russia, which is siding with Iran. Each time the U.S. makes a threat, calls for sanctions or takes military action against weaker countries, Putin opposes it. Each time, the U.S. hands another measure of the moral high ground, power and influence to Putin, who may be playing his game as well as his political opponent Garry Kasparov plays chess.

These observations are not intended to judge or lament the behavior of Russia or the U.S. The point is to explain what these actions mean in the context of social mood trends in both countries. Just as plunges in the

Real Dow [see Figure 3 in Chapter 49] correlate with U.S. attacks on other countries, a decline in the Real RTSI will indicate a trend toward negative mood that would likely provoke Russia to similar attacks.

Russia's extreme social history defines the parameters by which Russian people judge what is normal. While many Europeans would strongly resist dictatorship, social repression, censorship and extreme collectivism, Russians are already accepting moves in that direction, even after a ten-year trend toward more positive social mood. Whereas Americans would regard an invasion of Canada or Mexico as a completely new idea, many Russians would see an invasion of neighboring countries as simply reclaiming lost territory, somewhat as Germans viewed the Nazis' opening military moves just before and after the start of World War II. The U.S., in contrast, has historically shown fewer qualms about invading countries outside North America, including Nicaragua, Korea, Vietnam, Serbia, Grenada and Iraq. So, a war with Russia is hardly out of the question.

Britain's contentiousness with Russia contrasts sharply with the Bush administration's silent response to Putin's insults. In the prelude to World War II, Britain saw the threat of Nazi Germany clearly while the U.S. dismissed it. Today has some similarities. Given the outlook for a strong shift toward negative social mood in both the U.S. and Russia, we believe it is a mistake to underestimate the significance of recent events in Russia and to dismiss the importance of its military buildup or its slide back into the social danger zone. Socionomically, sociologically, and from an Elliott wave perspective, Russia is a growing military threat and has the potential to become once again one of the world's dangerous powers. Its willingness to insult and engage the U.S. indicates a return to a geostrategic scene of polarized superpowers, bringing increased potential for conflict.

Much as investors descend a "slope of hope" in a bear market, we can expect the popular media to continue to underestimate the seriousness of Russia's having resurged to become the world's second-largest military power. You should remain alert to the patterns unfolding in our benchmark sociometers and to social and political events in Russia. We will continue to follow this developing story.

NOTES AND REFERENCES

[1] Prechter, Robert R. (1999). *The Wave Principle of Human Social Behavior.* New Classics Library, p. 404.

[2] Kramer, Andrew E. "Yes, a Lot of People Died, But...", *International Herald Tribune,* August 12, 2007.

[3] Lucas, Edward, "Sex for the Motherland: Russian Youths Encouraged to Procreate at Camp," *UK Daily Mail,* July 30, 2007.

[4] *Ibid.*

[5] Armstrong, Jane, "The Nashi," *Globe and Mail,* October 13, 2007.

[6] Walker, Sophie, "British Jets Intercept Eight Russian Bombers," Reuters, September 6, 2007.

[7] Prechter, Robert R., *The Elliott Wave Theorist,* October 1, 1994.

[8] Baldwin, Chris, "Czechs Make 'Big Mistake' on U.S. Radar: Russia," Reuters, August 21, 2007.

[9] Mitchell, Paul, "US Steps Up Push for Kosovo Independence," World Socialist Web Site, September 13, 2007.

[10] Walker, Christopher and Robert Orttung, "Democracy's Facade," *Moscow Times,* cited by Freedom House, October 5, 2007.

[11] Lee, Matthew, "Rice Worried by Putin's Broad Powers," *The Washington Post,* October 14, 2007.

[12] "The Making of a Neo-KGB State," *The Economist,* August 23, 2007.

[13] *Ibid.*

[14] "After Yukos: The Far-Reaching Legacy of the Yukos Affair," *The Economist,* May 10, 2007.

[15] "Rice Criticizes Putin's Concentration of Power," *The Wall Street Journal,* October 13, 2007.

[16] Myers, Steven Lee, "U.S. Frustrated by Putin's Grip on Power," *The New York Times,* October 15, 2007.

[17] "The Making of a Neo-KGB State," *The Economist,* August 23, 2007.

[18] Zhdannikov, Dmitry, "Russian Communists Say Putin More Powerful than Tsar," Reuters, September 22, 2007.

[19] Harding, Luke, "Putin Decries Western Meddling," *The Guardian,* November 21, 2007.

[20] Mirovalev, Mansur, "Kasparov Jailed After Anti-Putin Protest," The Associated Press, November 24, 2007.

[21] U.S. Department of the Treasury.

[22] H.R. 1955

[23] International Center for Prison Studies, Kings College, London.

Chapter 51

A Forecast Fulfilled:
Russia Invades a Neighbor

Alan Hall

August 29, 2008 (EFF)

Nine months ago, we published special reports for the November and December 2007 issues of *Global Market Perspective*. The second report, "Sizing Up a Superpower," used wave patterns in its benchmark sociometer to predict a more bellicose Russia. Here are the two key statements from near the beginning and the end of that report:

- Our long term Elliott wave labeling for the Russian stock market indicates that a major top is imminent. This conclusion has serious implications for Russia and its neighbors in Europe, Central Asia and the Far East.

- Just as plunges in the Real Dow correlate with U.S. attacks on other countries, a decline in the Real RTSI will indicate a trend toward negative social mood that would likely provoke Russia to similar attacks.

As global social mood trended toward the negative in the past year, the major European and U.S. stock indexes fell about 25%. Russia lagged somewhat, but once its mood shift began, the Russian Trading System Index lost more than a third of its value in nominal and real terms in less than three and eight months, respectively. The change in mood led directly to social conflict.

This month, Russia invaded Georgia. Russia's neighbors are rushing to reevaluate a newly belligerent Russia as well as their recent alliance with a hesitant and overextended West. They also see unsettling new cracks in the foundation of global capitalism. In some former satellite states, the post-Soviet embrace of democracy is sliding toward ambivalence. In the August 24 issue of *The New York Times*, the director of New York University in

Prague said, "Today...almost two decades after communism, an increasing number of Czechs and Slovaks are critical of their existing democracies, which are marked by corruption, cynicism of political parties, populism and the capitalist pressure to turn citizens into consumers." The winds of change are in the air, and after Russia's invasion of Georgia, more people feel it.

Yet the important socionomic point—that stock market declines *precede and predict conflict*—has been overlooked by every media report we have seen. The conventional view that events move markets is so entrenched that one interviewer inadvertently reversed the title he gave my August 12 television appearance. The actual title read, "Russian Stock Market Signaled Coming Conflict," an accurate and interesting statement of causality. He changed it to "Analyst Hall Says Conflict Adds Risk to Russia's Stocks" so as to make it conform to the ubiquitous, and erroneous, mechanical view of social causality.

Our report also said that Russia's "willingness to insult and engage the U.S. indicates a return to a geostrategic scene of polarized superpowers, bringing increased potential for conflict." This scenario, too, is playing out. On August 14, Poland signed the controversial U.S. missile shield agreement. The next day, Russia threatened Poland with nuclear attack. On August 20, U.S. Secretary of State Condoleezza Rice ridiculed the threats, saying that they "border on the bizarre, frankly." Expect more such underestimation. Russia warned months ago that it had military plans to stop moves by Georgia to secure its pro-Russian separatist regions.

When Russian social mood shifted to join the negative trends in Europe, the U.S. and Asia, the sea change in social vision in all these areas was sudden and astonishing. References to the new Cold War now permeate the media. On August 12, a *Financial Times* article began like this: "In 1989, the Berlin Wall fell, democracy was on the march and we declared the End of History. Nearly two decades later, a neo-imperialist Russia is at war with Georgia, Communist China is proudly hosting the Olympics, and we find that, instead, we have entered the Age of Authoritarianism. It is worth recalling how different we thought the future would be in the immediate, happy aftermath of the end of the cold war." On August 16, *The New York Times* described the West as struggling with the "question of how to deal with these reinvigorated autocracies."

The U.S. is struggling with its own drift toward authoritarianism. The August 21 issue of *The New York Times* described the latest move in that direction: a U.S. Justice Department plan to give the F.B.I. the power to "open a national security or criminal investigation against someone *without any clear basis for suspicion."* (emphasis added) The debate about this idea is framed as privacy versus security, but the real argument is about liberty versus state control.

From a socionomic perspective, it is not surprising that the beginning of wave (C) downward in the DJIA finds the world's leading democracy flirting with bankruptcy, embroiled in two wars while considering another, embarrassed and unprepared when an ally is invaded, yet still willing to engage in threats, ultimatums and foreign entanglements. Neither is it a surprise that the world's leading autocracy, still strong after its roaring bull market of the past several years, is confident, solvent and willing to fight. On August 26 Russian President Medvedev said, "We're not afraid of anything [including] the prospect of a Cold War." A power shift from democracy to autocracy in Russia would reflect a turning point of significant degree, just as the long term wave pattern suggests.

The acid test is approaching. In the past, when Russia blockaded Berlin, crushed the Hungarian Revolution, put nuclear missiles in Cuba, suppressed the Prague Spring, invaded Afghanistan, quashed Solidarity in Poland, and shot down an airliner carrying U.S. citizens and a congress-man, U.S. presidents refrained from conflict. As far as we know, the times when the U.S. and Russia came closest to a shooting war were during the Cuban missile crisis in 1962 and in the environment of nuclear paranoia in 1983. The former event occurred near the end of wave (C) of wave ④ in the DJIA. The U.S. is again in wave (C) of wave ④, implying risk of conflict, but Russia is only in wave A. Warring between the U.S. and Russia will become more likely when both markets are in C-wave declines [see Chapter 26], implying joint negative mood trends that would bring about a radically different and dangerous new era.

The trend toward negative social mood in Russia is still progressing, so we can expect more conflict between Russia and its neighbors. Likely flashpoints are Ukraine, Poland and other westward-leaning border states with pro-Russian enclaves. Expect increasing opposition to the West, already visible in Russia's threats to place strategic bombers and surveillance sites in Cuba, its recent naval activity in the Black Sea, and its military alliances with Venezuela, Algeria and Syria. Stock markets should continue to be a leading indicator of social conflict and its remission.

Russia and the U.S. have, so far, heeded the timeless advice of Sun Tzu in *The Art of War*: "To overcome other's armies without fighting is the best of skills." The anger that characterizes major trends toward negative social mood, however, often trumps restraint.

Chapter 52

Russia: From Buff to Rebuffed

Alan Hall

December 5, 2008 (EFF)

Russia has seen a change of fortune since we showed Putin's bare-chested photo and described his adoration by Russian women in our special report of November 2007, "A Socionomic Study of Russia." Figure 1 is updated from our follow-up report, "Sizing Up a Superpower." The classic Elliott-wave target of the previous fourth wave has proven itself once again. Russia's commodity-based financial boom set up the country for a tremendous economic loss in this year's joint declines in stock and commodity prices.

Russia behaved much as we predicted, with increasing bluster, renewed bellicosity, and open opposition to the United States. Russia has talked and acted tough lately, both before and after its August 2008 war with Georgia, which erupted as the Russian Trading System index was in the middle of its deepest plunge in a decade.

As Russian President Medvedev toured Latin America this month to seek energy and arms deals, boost political ties and challenge the United States in its own backyard, Russian warships arrived in Venezuela in the "most significant appearance of Russian military assets in the hemisphere since the 1962 Cuban missile crisis." (*LA Times*, November 27, 2008) In a tit-for-tat response to the United States' having sent warships through the Bosphorus Strait into the Black Sea to deliver aid to Georgia, a Russian warship will sail through the Panama Canal this week for the first time since World War II. Russia has recently sold Venezuela $4.4 billion in arms and fighter planes, and has promised money for energy exploration and nuclear technology.

But, according to a November 26 article in *The Telegraph*, "instead of causing alarm, the exercises are prompting little more than irritation and even mirth in Washington. A spokesman for the U.S. State Department said,

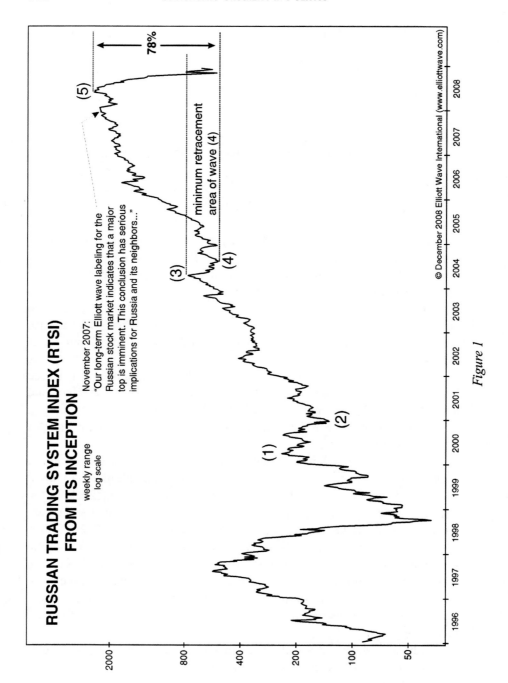

RUSSIAN TRADING SYSTEM INDEX (RTSI) FROM ITS INCEPTION

weekly range
log scale

November 2007:
"Our long-term Elliott wave labeling for the
Russian stock market indicates that a major
top is imminent. This conclusion has serious
implications for Russia and its neighbors..."

78%

(5)

(1)

(2)

(3)

(4)

minimum retracement
area of wave (4)

© December 2008 Elliott Wave International (www.elliottwave.com)

Figure 1

'Are they accompanied by tugboats this time?'…Mr. Medvedev's trip is increasingly looking like an embarrassment." A *Washington Post* headline called the trip "Russia's Caribbean Farce."

Medvedev was rebuffed in Brazil, which declined to buy Russian arms and whose strategic affairs minister said that Brazil has no interest in "containing the United States." Cuba, too, was reluctant to rekindle its relationship with Russia amid hopes that President-elect Obama will end its 46-year Cuban trade embargo. Russia's best relations are with Bolivia, Nicaragua and Venezuela, but as a Bush administration official said, "The Russians have picked the most erratic and unreliable partners in the region." (*The New York Times,* November 21, 2008)

These news items express, for now, a dismissive doubt in the U.S. about Russia's superpower status and little fear of its combative bluster. On December 4, Putin eased Russia/U.S. tensions when he retracted an earlier stance saying, "Today there is no need to build permanent bases" in Cuba and Venezuela.

Russia's international rebuff accompanies economic problems at home: a $3.6 billion loss in international reserves, the ruble near a 3-year low against the dollar and manufacturing indexes at record lows. Politically, the Kremlin has supported renewed reverence for Stalin, but Ukraine visibly commemorated this month's 75th anniversary of the Holodomor, the Stalinist genocide by starvation of at least 10 million Ukrainians in 1932-1933. The famine occurred during a bumper crop of Ukrainian wheat that Stalin confiscated because he "was desperate for grain that he could trade on the open markets, since most banks would not recognize the ruble." (projo. com, November 9, 2008) The Soviet Union long denied that the Holomodor happened, and Medvedev declined to attend the memorial, increasing the already-palpable Russia/Ukraine tension.

Overall, Russia still tends toward its historical feeling of being encircled and besieged. On November 28, Russia tested, and said it had started, "mass production" of the Bulava, the first of a new generation of ICBMs that Putin said can penetrate anti-missile shields. (Reuters, December 1, 2008)

Much as positive social mood slowly put in place conditions for later financial destruction, negative social mood appears to be putting in place conditions for later physical destruction. We will keep a close eye on Russia and on key equity markets, our leading indicators of societies' propensities for war.

Chapter 53

Russian Bear Set to Reappear

Brian Whitmer
December 31, 2010 (EFF)

Back in November 2007, Alan Hall published a two-issue Special Report detailing the case for a peak in Russian stocks that would be followed by a "minimum probable drop" of more than 50% in the Russian Trading System Index, with the ideal range being 62%-75%. As the RTSI held up into early 2008, *Time* magazine honored President Putin as its Person of the Year. The good times didn't last long. The RTSI topped in May 2008 and subsequently plunged 80% by early 2009. From there, it joined the global countertrend rally that has been kind to many emerging markets.

After retracing 64% of its previous decline, Russia is being tapped as a star performer in 2011. "Russian stocks will offer investors over 20% gains in the coming year, more than double the growth in 2010," a Reuters poll showed. This ebullient sentiment, in conjunction with the wave pattern shown on the updated chart of the RTSI (see Figure 1), suggests something quite different: The 24-month countertrend rally is ending. Russian shares should soon fall back into a crushing decline that draws the index below the January 2009 low of 492.59.

Only positive social mood can account for Russia's recent financial recovery despite a dysfunctional government and economy. According to recently leaked cables from the United States Embassy in Moscow, "official malfeasance and corruption infect all elements of Russian public life." Despite his formidable will and intellect, Prime Minister Vladimir Putin is "beholden to intractable larger forces, including an inefficient and unmanageable bureaucracy that often ignores his edicts," says *The New York Times*. "In 2006, at the height of Putin's control in a booming economy," one of the leaked cables says, "it was rumored within the Presidential Administration that as many as 60% of his orders were not being followed."

One sign of an uptrend's vulnerability to reversal is the characterization of flaws as "investment opportunities." Everything from global warming, which "enables vast tracts of Siberian landscape to be developed," to a

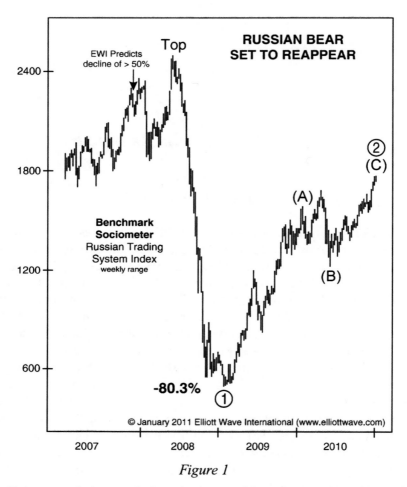

Figure 1

declining population are being cited as positives for Russia. After noting that Russia is a "perpetual totalitarian mafia state," an investment missive on "Why the Russian Stock Market Is Great for Investors" noted that Russia's population is down 10% in 20 years and that it is "targeting" a further drop of 15 million over the next 20 years. Nevertheless, it asserts, "On the bright side for investors, Russia at $16,000 per capita is starting from a low base" and can "therefore grow far more strongly than the West." As Voltaire put it satirically in *Candide*, "The more private misfortunes there are, the more everything is well."

The current widespread optimism toward Russia despite the persistent presence of these same problems throughout the Russian stock market's fall *and* rise testifies to the epic power of social mood to influence people's assessments. Once the chaos starts, all kinds of new reasons will appear to explain the jarring downside reversal.

Chapter 54

Late Autumn in U.S.-Russia Relations

Brian Whitmer

May 31, 2013 (EFF)

Back in January 2011, when a Reuters poll predicted that the Russian stock market would double its 20% growth of 2010, EWI's *European Financial Forecast* argued, "This ebullient sentiment, in conjunction with the wave pattern shown on [this] chart of the RTSI, suggests something quite different. The 24-month countertrend rally is ending." An updated RTSI chart (see Figure 1) shows the result: Russian shares peaked three months later, tracing out a succession of lower lows and lower highs that have pushed the index down 32% to date.

The inset on the chart is significant, too. It shows that the RTSI has declined in five waves and rallied in three waves, delineating the larger trend as down. After the RTSI breaks a shelf of support at 1200, the selloff should intensify. The larger degree ①–② wave labels on the chart imply that the RTSI will eventually penetrate 493, the January 2009 low.

The "recent unprecedented chill" in U.S.-Russia relations (Voice of Russia, 5/17) confirms that social mood in Russia has reversed at a high degree. The temperature began falling five months ago, when U.S. President Barack Obama signed a law prohibiting 18 senior Russian officials from entering the United States. The Magnitsky Act—which also prevents the same officials from using the U.S. banking system—stems from alleged human rights abuses in the death of Sergei Magnitsky, a Russian accountant. The new law "poisons our relationship [with the U.S.]," proclaimed Russian President Vladimir Putin, but it is actually one of the milder controversies that has recently erupted between the two countries. Take, for instance, the "U.S.-Russian Cold War over Adoptions" (*The Record*, 5/13), which blew up in December 2012 when Russia's State Duma voted 400 to 4 to ban adoptions of Russian children into the United States. Legislators refused to overturn the ban last month despite outrage from human rights groups, adoption agencies and the 700-plus American families who are currently involved in the process.

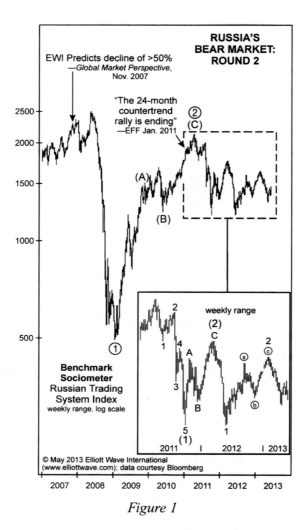

Figure 1

Then there is last month's arrest of U.S. diplomat Ryan Fogle in Moscow. Details remain elusive, but we do know that the Russian secret police arrested Fogle on May 14, alleging that he tried to recruit a Kremlin official to work for the U.S. Central Intelligence Agency, and that Russian officials expelled Fogle from the country on May 15.

The growing list of controversial incidents speak to social mood's influence over U.S.-Russian relations. The next time social mood trends negatively in both countries simultaneously, today's mixed relationship between the U.S. and Russia will devolve back into bilateral fear and suspicion.

Chapter 55

The "Darker Side of Putin"
Emerges as Predicted

Alan Hall

November 28, 2014 (TS)

Back in November 2007, when we wrote, "the world may see an even darker side of Putin," Russia was the darling of emerging-market investors. The Russian Trading System Index was up over 5000% from its 1998 low, and broader social expression was wildly positive. President Vladimir Putin was riding a wave of adoration and cultish popularity.

Most investors looked at the situation and saw nothing but blue skies ahead for the former Soviet republic and other emerging markets. *Forbes* magazine reported that Russia had 60 billionaires, making Moscow "home to more billionaires than any other city in the world. It is quite a change for a place that 15 years ago had no millionaires, let alone billionaires."[1] In July 2007, *Fortune* magazine reported, "These days more and more CEOs are livin' la vida BRIC" [Brazil, Russia, India and China]. At that time, U.S. Treasury Secretary Hank Paulson declared, "This is far and away the strongest global economy I've seen in my business lifetime."[2]

We socionomists looked at the data and saw the opposite implications. The rise in the RTSI from the 1998 low was a classic five-wave pattern under the Elliott wave model, indicating that a major top was due. Figure 1 shows the chart we published in 2007, which applied the Elliott wave model to forecast a 62-75% decline in the Russian stock market and added,

> This index should soon begin its biggest bear market since the five-wave pattern began. The minimum probable drop—a move into the area of the fourth wave of 2004—would more than halve the value of the index. The trend toward negative mood implied by such a decline should produce financial and social events of a character comparable to those seen during comparable periods of negative

As published in November 2007

Figure 1

social mood over the past two centuries, as detailed in the previous report. Viewed in the context of Russian history, this outlook has serious geostrategic implications.

We simultaneously identified the ebullient social and political conditions in Russia that confirmed a state of extremely positive social mood compatible with a stock market top. We applied socionomic theory to forecast the country's resurgence as a military threat to its neighbors, specifically Georgia and Ukraine. We also said that Russia would become increasingly belligerent toward the West while ratcheting up state control of the economy, media, politics and the broader society. We wrote, "The stage is set for a return to autocracy in Russia. Russia's FSB succeeded the KGB, and today it is reputed to be a more pervasive, powerful and nepotistic organization than the KGB ever was."

We used Russia's socionomic history to observe that the social mood behind comparable declines in the past had produced peasant revolts, authoritarian crackdowns, the Russian Revolution of 1905, tremendous mortality rates, Russia's involvement in World War I, the Russian Revolution of 1917, Lenin's "Red Terror" campaign of fear, recrimination and scape-goating, civil war in 1918-1921, the exodus of foreign investors, Stalin's collectivization of farms, famines, purges, deportations, the gulag and the Soviet Union's entry into World War II.

Figure 2 shows what happened during the sixteen months after we published our report. The RTSI made one more new high—to which we have moved the label (5)—and then plunged to the bottom of our target zone in a textbook Elliott wave retracement of the preceding advance. About a third of the way down, Russian troops invaded the Republic of Georgia.

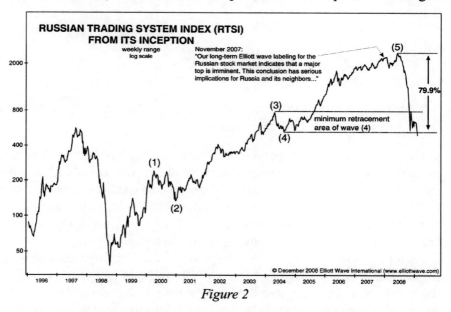

Figure 2

Negative mood in Russia has continued since the 2008 peak in the RTSI, as shown in Figure 3. Recent social manifestations reflecting that mood include increasing economic duress, tens of thousands of people protesting in Moscow,[3] military conflict with Ukraine, increasing opposition to the West, economic sanctions, trade restrictions and authoritarianism.

The darker side of Putin has come more sharply into focus. On September 29, *The New York Times* reported that Putin shifted state money into a private bank in a move that made his loyalists billionaires.[4] Putin's domestic and international surveillance machine is running at high capacity. In April 2014, the World Policy Institute reported, "Over the last two years, the Kremlin has transformed Russia into a surveillance state—at a level that would have made the Soviet KGB envious."[5] Czech intelligence reported that Russian spies are increasingly active across Europe. Russian agents kidnaped an Estonian official, took him to Moscow and paraded him on TV

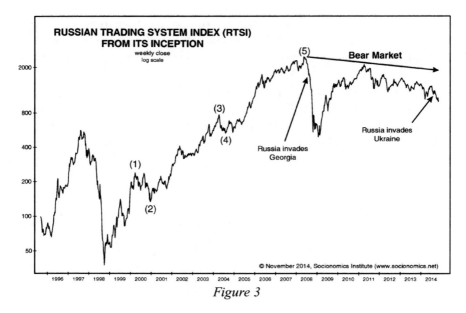

Figure 3

as a spy.[6] In Strasbourg, the seat of the European Court of Human Rights, suspected Russian agents abducted and tortured a 68-year old Chechen refugee who had accused Putin of "war crimes in a criminal complaint he had sent to the International Criminal Court (ICC) and to the Kremlin." *Time* magazine wrote, "Not since the Cold War have Russian operatives been accused of such violence and intimidation abroad."[7]

Putin is also ramping up cyberespionage. U.S. intelligence officials suspect that Russia is behind a breach of White House computer systems. Russian hackers have targeted NATO, Mexico and the governments and militaries of Georgia, Poland, Hungary and other Eastern European countries.[8] The Department of Homeland Security declared, "hackers believed to be sponsored by the Russian government" are responsible for a "destructive 'Trojan Horse' malware program [that] has penetrated the software that runs much of the [United States'] critical infrastructure and is poised to cause an economic catastrophe."[9]

On September 30, Russian chess champion Garry Kasparov warned, "Putin is the most dangerous man in the world and a bigger threat to the U.S. than the Islamic State."[10] In his October 24 Valdai conference speech, "one of the most hostile Putin has delivered against the West," the Russian president accused the U.S. of damaging world order and repeatedly emphasized that Russia only wants peace.[11] On November 12, U.S. Ambassador Samantha Power told the United Nations Security Council that Russia "talks of peace, but it keeps fueling war."[12]

Our 2007 report alerted readers to the high probability of a Russian military resurgence by observing, "Russia is converting its newfound prosperity into a growing military threat." That trend has continued and intensified. On March 29, 2013, "six Russian military planes—including four heavy bombers—carried out a simulated missile attack on Stockholm and southern Sweden."[13] In February 2014, Russia began sending "tanks, artillery and infantry" into Ukraine in a "stealth invasion" that continued until September.[14] The Russian Federation annexed Crimea in mid-March,[15] and on July 17 Malaysia Airlines Flight 17 was shot down over an area of Ukraine controlled by pro-Russia separatists.[16,17] In recent months, Russian warplanes have approached or intruded multiple times into the airspace of the U.S., the UK, Sweden, Portugal, Estonia, Finland, Guam and Japan. On October 28 and 29, NATO planes intercepted a total of 26 Russian jets over the Baltic Sea, the North Sea, the Atlantic Ocean and the Black Sea, indicating "an unusual level of air activity over European airspace."[18] "NATO has conducted more than 100 intercepts of Russian aircraft this year," far more than last year.[19] Also in October, Sweden launched ships to search for a Russian submarine suspected of trolling its waters.[20] In November, the European Leadership Network, a London-based think tank, produced "Dangerous Brinkmanship: Close Military Encounters between Russia and the West in 2014,"[21] which chronicles almost 40 such incidents since March. According to the European Leadership Network,

> These events…add up to a highly disturbing picture of violations of national airspace, emergency scrambles, narrowly avoided midair collisions, close encounters at sea, simulated attack runs and other dangerous actions happening on a regular basis over a very wide geographical area. [The] mix of more aggressive Russian posturing and the readiness of Western forces to show resolve increases the risk of unintended escalation and the danger of losing control over events…. Russian armed forces and security agencies seem to have been authorized and encouraged to act in a much more aggressive way towards NATO countries, Sweden and Finland.[22]

On November 9, a date that marked the 25th anniversary of the fall of the Berlin Wall, former Soviet President Mikhail Gorbachev said, "The world is on the brink of a new Cold War…. Some are even saying that it's already begun."[23] On November 12, Russia announced that its "long-range [nuclear] bombers will conduct regular patrol missions from the Arctic Ocean to the Caribbean and the Gulf of Mexico" in response to "tensions with the West over Ukraine."[24]

Escalating War Risk

In 2007, we wrote, "On November 20, Putin warned that Russia will respond to a NATO military buildup on its borders." The subsequent NATO buildup—as evidenced most recently by U.S. soldiers in Poland, Latvia and the Baltic states, and U.S. and French ships in the Black Sea[25]—has provided a renewed basis for what we described in 2007 as "the historical Russian feeling of being encircled and besieged." On November 18, NATO accused Russia of a "'serious military buildup' on the Russian side of the border with Ukraine."[26] Nobel Peace Prize nominee Dr. Helen Caldicott recently warned of the hazards associated with NATO's expansion to Russia's borders:

> We are in a very fallible, very dangerous situation operated by mere mortals.... The United States and Russia have...94 percent of all the 16,300 nuclear weapons in the world.... You don't provoke paranoid countries armed with nuclear weapons.... Ukraine is a lot bigger (and more important) than Cuba.[27]

Media references to the Cold War and its accompanying fear of nuclear war are resurging along with Putin and company's recent boasts about Russia's impressive warhead capability. Broader fears of a hot war may not be far behind. On March 16, Kremlin-backed journalist Dmitry Kiselyov said, "Russia is the only country in the world that is realistically capable of turning the United States into radioactive ash."[28] On August 14 at Yalta, Putin mentioned that Russia was capable of "surprising the West with our new developments in offensive nuclear weapons about which we do not talk yet."[29] On August 29, as Russian tanks and troops crossed the border into eastern Ukraine, Putin warned, "I want to remind you that Russia is one of the most powerful nuclear nations.... This is a reality, not just words. [Russia is] strengthening our nuclear deterrence forces."[30]

These statements may not be empty bluster. On November 13, U.S. Defense Secretary Chuck Hagel announced more money for maintenance of U.S. nuclear arsenals and admitted to the military's "neglect of the country's nuclear programs, rendering some infrastructure outdated and maintenance deteriorated."[32] When the Pentagon conducted a broad review of America's "systemic problems" across its "nuclear enterprise," it found:

> huge problems, including aging blast doors over 60-year-old silos that would not seal shut and, in one case, the discovery that the crews that maintain the nation's 450 intercontinental ballistic missiles had only a single wrench that could attach the nuclear warheads. "They

started FedExing the one tool" to three bases spread across the country...one of many maintenance problems that had "been around so long that no one reported them anymore."[32]

Such conditions are a symptom of complacency and heightened risk borne of a longstanding positive trend in social mood such as the U.S. has enjoyed for most of the time since 1982. Now, social mood in Russia is sounding a wake-up call, but with mood trending positively in the U.S., concern there remains muted.

In September, Putin "privately threatened to invade Poland, Romania and the Baltic states." He allegedly told Ukraine's President Poroshenko, "If I wanted, in two days I could have Russian troops not only in Kiev, but also in Riga, Vilnius, Tallinn, Warsaw and Bucharest."[33] Poland is moving thousands of troops toward its eastern border after its defense minister announced, "The geopolitical situation has changed. We have the biggest crisis of security since the Cold War."[34] *Newsweek* reported on November 19, "Tiny Baltic States Prepare to Hit Back at Mighty Russia."[35] Estonia has doubled the number of soldiers in its voluntary Defense League, fast-tracked military procurement and asked NATO to base troops and equipment there permanently. Lithuania has "launched a high-readiness combat response force comprising some 1,600 troops," and Latvia has requested NATO troops "on permanent rotation."[36]

We will keep an eye on our sociometers. If mood turns positive in Russia and continues along its positive path in the U.S., tensions between these two powers should ease. If Russian social mood continues to trend negatively, or upon its next negative trend, the social manifestations outlined in this article and detailed in our 2007 report should intensify, manifesting in startling new events. If social mood in the U.S. were to join the negative trend, it may spark actions that present Russia with an even larger external enemy than its Eastern European neighbors, further strengthening Putin's grip on power and providing a compelling rationalization for escalating Russia's mood-motivated military resurgence.

History gives examples of how Russian leaders behave in times of negatively trending social mood. It is not a heartening record. But Putin is just one actor on this stage. When broader social mood embarks on a strong negative trend, we are likely to see the darker sides of many leaders.

NOTES AND REFERENCES

[1] Wingfield-Hayes, R. (2007, April 21). Moscow's Suburb for Billionaires. *BBC News*.

[2] Kirkland, R. (2007, July 12). The Greatest Economic Boom Ever. *Fortune*.

[3] Vasilyeva, N. (2014, September 21). Thousands March in Moscow Against Ukraine Fighting. Associated Press.

[4] Myers, S.L., Becker, J., & Yardley, J. (2014, September 27). Private Bank Fuels Fortunes of Putin's Inner Circle. *The New York Times*.

[5] Soldatov, A., & Borogan, I. Russia's Surveillance State. World Policy Institute.

[6] Borger, J. (2014, September 7). Russians Open New Front After Estonian Official is Captured in "Cross-border Raid." *The Guardian*.

[7] Shuster, S. Putin's Secret Agents. *Time*.

[8] Sanger, D.E., & Perlroth, N. (2014, October 30). New Russian Boldness Revives a Cold War Tradition: Testing the Other Side. *The New York Times*.

[9] Cloherty, J., & Thomas, P. (2014, November 6). "Trojan Horse" Bug Lurking in Vital US Computers Since 2011. *ABC News*.

[10] Golodryge, B. (2014, September 30). Garry Kasparov: Putin is "The Most Dangerous Man" in the World and a Bigger Threat to the U.S. Than the Islamic State. *Yahoo! News*.

[11] Anishchuk, A. (2014, October 24). Putin Accuses United States of Damaging World Order. Reuters.

[12] Anna, C. (2014, November 12). For 26th Time, UN Has Emergency Meeting on Ukraine. Associated Press.

[13] Braw, E. (2014, October 21). The "Russian Submarine" in Swedish Waters Isn't the Only Unwelcome Visitor in the Baltic Sea. *Newsweek*.

[14] Kramer, A.E., & Gordon, M.R. (2014, August 27). Ukraine Reports Russian Invasion on a New Front. *The New York Times*.

[15] Morello, C., Constable, P., & Faiola, A. (2014, March 16). Crimeans Vote to Break Away From Ukraine, join Russia. *The Washington Post*.

[16] Knight, A. (2014, November 19). Flight MH17: Will Russia Get Away With It? *The New York Review of Books*.

[17] Tharoor, I. (2014, July 20). The Evidence That May Prove Pro-Russian Separatists Shot Down MH17. *The Washington Post*.

[18] NATO Tracks Large-scale Russian Air Activity in Europe. (2014, October 29). Allied Command Operations.

[19] See endnote 8.

[20] See endnote 13.

[21] Frear, T., Kulesa, L., & Kearns, I. (2014, November 10). Dangerous Brinkmanship: Close Military Encounters Between Russia and the West in 2014. European Leadership Network.

[22] *Ibid.*

[23] Cowell, A. (2014, November 10). Researchers Detail a Spike in NATO-Russia Close Calls. *The New York Times.*

[24] Isachenkov, V. (2014, November 12). Russia's Bombers to Conduct Regular Patrols, Ranging from the Arctic to the Gulf of Mexico. *Yahoo! News.*

[25] Russia Questions NATO Military Buildup Near Border. (2014, April 26). *RT.*

[26] Taylor, G. (2014, November 18). NATO: Russia Engaged in "Serious Military Buildup" Near Ukrainian Border. *The Washington Times.*

[27] Sieff, M. (2014, October 13). Nuclear War Could Be Near, According to a Nobel Laureate. *Global Research.*

[28] Kelly, L. (2014, March 16). Russia Can Turn U.S. to Radioactive Ash: Kremlin-backed Journalist. Reuters.

[29] Tayler, J. (2014, August 28). Vladimir Putin Goes Rogue: Ukraine, NATO, Nuclear Weapons—And a Very Dangerous New Reality. *Salon.*

[30] Scotti, E. (2014, August 31). Putin Threatens Nuclear War Over Ukraine. *The Daily Beast.*

[31] Yenko, A. (2014, November 15). Nuclear War: Russia Shocks US With Tactical Weapons, Pentagon Retaliates. *International Business Times.*

[32] Sanger, D.E., & Broad, W.J. (2014, November 13). Pentagon Studies Reveal Major Nuclear Problems. *The New York Times.*

[33] Huggler, J. (2014, September 18). Putin "Privately Threatened to Invade Poland, Romania and the Baltic States." *The Telegraph.*

[34] Scislowska, M. (2014, October 27). Poland to Move Thousands of Troops East, Defense Minister Says. *The Washington Times.*

[35] Braw, E. (2014, November 19). Tiny Baltic States Prepare to Hit Back at Mighty Russia. *Newsweek.*

[36] *Ibid.*

Chapter 56

Social Mood in Russia Continues
a Dangerous Trend

Alan Hall

June 30, 2015 (TS)

Russian social mood, as reflected in its benchmark Russian Trading System Index (RTSI), took another turn toward the negative on May 13. Other social expressions of negative mood rapidly followed. The rapidity may be due to the length of time Russia has endured its negative mood trend. The RTSI has yet to surpass its 2008 all-time high, and it remains about 63% below that level. Figure 1 plots Russia's trend toward negative mood as it enters its eighth year.

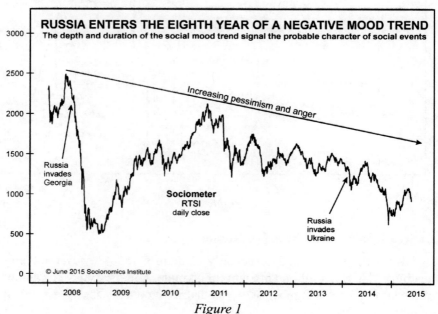

RUSSIA ENTERS THE EIGHTH YEAR OF A NEGATIVE MOOD TREND
The depth and duration of the social mood trend signal the probable character of social events

Increasing pessimism and anger

Russia invades Georgia

Sociometer
RTSI
daily close

Russia invades Ukraine

© June 2015 Socionomics Institute

Figure 1

Figure 2 plots daily data for the RTSI over the past eighteen months, since the start of the Ukraine crisis. Arrows mark socionomically significant events in the ongoing conflict, most of which are reported in a timeline from the Center for Strategic and International Studies.[1] The timing of the fluctuations in the character of these events suggests that social mood is regulating even the smaller waves of concord and discord within the overall crisis.

Figure 2

Expressions of Social Mood in Russia

Russia's pessimism is especially clear in a June 7 *Moscow Times* headline, "No Peaceful End in Sight for Ukraine, Analysts Say." The author of the article listed a number of events that we recognize as expressions of negative social mood:

the continuous failure of the diplomatic process...the revival of fighting...the frailty of the internationally brokered Minsk accords.... Kiev does not want to talk to the insurgents, whom the leaders regularly refer to as "terrorists."[2]

Other expressions that reveal the tenor of the trend are also coming to the fore.

Get Me Out of Here

People increasingly want to leave the country. According to a 2014 Russian Federal State Statistics Service report, 186,400 citizens left Russia in 2013, and 203,600 left in just the first eight months of 2014. And it's not your average Ivan who is hitting the road. On April 7, the Institute of Modern Russia reported,

a new wave of Russian emigration is different from the previous ones: it's the most secure social groups, people [who have] achieved success in Russia and who understand that they will not be able to live under the growing authoritarianism, that are leaving the country.[3]

A former BBC Moscow correspondent recently returned to Russia and interviewed an old friend who said,

I've sent my family to live abroad.... It's better that way. I've sold everything, and now I commute. The health service here is crumbling, and so are schools. Sanctions have started to bite, but it's not that—it's the political atmosphere. It's stifling, and it's getting worse.[4]

On June 9, AFP.com reported, "The eldest daughter of slain Kremlin critic Boris Nemtsov has left Russia, slamming the climate of hatred whipped up by pro-Kremlin propaganda in a letter published Tuesday." From relative safety in Europe, Zhanna Nemtsova wrote, "Putin's information machine—similar to those in Nazi Germany and Rwanda—is using criminal methods of propaganda, and sowing hatred which generates violence and terror."[5]

Lost in Space

"Russia's space program in crisis?" asked CNN on June 3, describing a recent "catalogue of embarrassing setbacks." In early May, an unmanned Russian spacecraft that was headed to resupply the International Space Station went out of control and "died a fiery death in Earth's atmosphere."[6] On May 16, a Russian rocket carrying a Mexican satellite burnt up over Siberia minutes after launch.[7] Russia's new $6 billion high-tech launch site, the Vostochny Cosmodrome, is "mired in scandal. There have been numerous government-led corruption probes into missing funds. And there has even been a hunger strike by unpaid workers."[8] $1.8 billion is missing, and even Russian officials say the industry is in "crisis caused by funding cuts, corruption and 'moral decay.'"[9] Another telling result of negative mood is this report: "Unlike the Soviet program, critics say Russia's space industry lacks ambition. There are no trips to Mars on the horizon, no exploration of deep space planned."[10] This outlook is in stark contrast to that of 2007.

Economic Malaise

On June 3, Bloomberg reported that former Russian Finance Minister Alexei Kudrin, a long-time ally of President Putin, broke with the party line and said Russia faces a longer recession than the government forecasted. "We are now in a full-fledged crisis.... The situation in the real sector is still very bad."[11]

A website sponsored by the Russian government's official newspaper reported, "More and more Russians [are] slipping below poverty line as recession bites." The article says the statistics are inexact, but what may be more important are perceptions:

> According to the Public Opinion Foundation, 47 percent of the population consider themselves "the working poor." "It's hard to give up what you used to have, so people feel they have become much poorer, even if this is not quite the case."[12]

Exclusionism Is On the Wax

Racism, xenophobia and intolerance have been increasing for years in Russia. A recent report chronicled racism on the soccer pitch, where there were "99 racist and far-right displays and 21 racially motivated attacks by Russian football fans during the 2012-13 and 2013-14 seasons."[13]

Russia's bid to host the 2018 World Cup is in jeopardy due to an ongoing bribery investigation.[14] If Russia does host the event and the mood trend remains negative, things could get ugly. "The likelihood of a racist incident is very high. It's not just that it might happen but that it happens very often," said Alexander Verkhovsky, the director of a Moscow-based think tank that studies racism and xenophobia.[15]

In a May 19 op-ed, "Putin's Disunited Nation," a history professor at Loyola University Chicago wrote, "The fragmentation of Russia, with its multiple ethnic, regional and religious identities, is seen by the Kremlin as a growing threat."[16] Putin seems worried about rising xenophobia. In early

March, he quietly inaugurated "a new federal agency that would work toward 'consolidating the unity of the multiethnic nation of the Russian Federation.'"[17] Positive social mood can lead to unity on inclusionist issues, but government efforts to do so in a negative mood environment are more apt to fail.

Russia Is Becoming Increasingly Isolated and Paranoid

A June 2 *Foreign Policy* article echoed many of our 2007 observations. James Stavridis, retired U.S. Navy admiral and dean of the Fletcher School of Law and Diplomacy at Tufts University, wrote,

> As Russia becomes increasingly isolated from Europe and the West over everything from the annexation of Crimea to the jailing of Pussy Riot and the treatment of gays and lesbians, their society will increasingly reject the "norms" of the West and become more "the other"—a place they have been before.[18]

The *Moscow Times* recently reported that more and more Russians—47% in 2007; 59% today—see America as a threat.[19] Russia's relations with Europe aren't much better. On June 2, the European Parliament "banned Russia's Brussels envoy from its sessions, retaliating against a Russian blacklist that bars 89 Europeans from visiting Russia—which was itself retaliation against European bans on key Russians."[20] *Der Spiegel* reported on June 4 that Russia is the "chief suspect" in an investigation of a recent hack of Germany's parliament, the Bundestag.[21]

For the second year in a row, Russia is being excluded[22] from the annual summit of representatives from major world economies, which were formerly known as the G-8 but we now called the G-7 because the other seven members ousted Russia in 2014.[23] Furthermore, Russia and NATO "aren't talking to each other." A former Russian defense ministry spokesman observed,

> I don't want to sound alarmist, but judging by the rapid pace of events and growing aggressiveness on all sides, we may be moving toward disaster. It's like we're all priming a bomb, but no one knows when or how it will explode. Gradually, we are moving from cold to hot war.[24]

Dr. William R. Polk,[25] a close advisor to President Kennedy during the Cuban Missile Crisis, agreed. In his February essay, "The Cuban Missile Crisis in Reverse," he described disturbing similarities between the buildups to the 1962 crisis and the current Ukraine conflict. Reminding readers that there "is no such thing as a 'limited' nuclear war if both sides are armed with nuclear weapons," he advises that first steps toward peace could be for the U.S. "not to push our military activities into their sphere," and "for the Ukraine to join the European Union."[26] But on June 20, U.S. Senator John McCain again called for the United States to arm Ukraine,[27] and, as the drama surrounding a potential Greek exit from the European Union shows, solidarity is waning within the EU.[28]

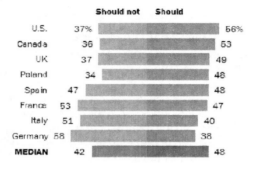

Many NATO Countries Reluctant to Use Force to Defend Allies

If Russia got into a serious military conflict with one of its neighboring countries that is our NATO ally, do you think our country should or should not use military force to defend that country?

	Should not	Should
U.S.	37%	56%
Canada	36	53
UK	37	49
Poland	34	48
Spain	47	48
France	53	47
Italy	51	40
Germany	58	38
MEDIAN	42	48

Source: Spring 2015 Global Attitudes survey Q52.
PEW RESEARCH CENTER

Solidarity is also fading within some NATO countries, where voters are losing the political will to defend their allies on Russia's border.[29] "[At] least half of Germans, French and Italians say their country should not use military force to defend a NATO ally attacked by Russia."[30]

Predicting vs. Reporting

Such observations from current commentators are seven years too late. They bear out our forecast but in themselves forecast nothing. A socionomic perspective allowed us to foresee the essence of all these changes back in 2007, when most news reports relating to Russia accented nothing but the positive. To us, that very situation was one of the warning signs.

What's next? If negative mood continues to incline Russia toward belligerence, and if the U.S. goes through with its plan[31] to "station tanks and heavy weapons in NATO states on Russia's border...the most aggressive U.S. act since the Cold War," a dangerous new crisis might become unavoidable.[32] Former U.S. diplomat Dr. William R. Polk wrote, "As President Kennedy and the rest of us understood in the 1962 crisis, even if leaders want to avoid conflict, at a certain point in their mutual threats, events replace policy and leaders become bystanders."[33]

Right now, however, the persistence of positive social mood in the U.S. has muted the potential for a worsening crisis. The return of a negative mood trend in the West would signal an elevated risk of conflict. Only if social mood trends positively in both Russia and the West is a return to an environment of less conflict, more accord and less potential danger likely.

NOTES AND REFERENCES

[1] The Ukraine Crisis Timeline. Center for Strategic & International Studies.

[2] Nechepurenko, I. (2015, June 7). No Peaceful End in Sight for Ukraine, Analysts Say. *The Moscow Times.*

[3] Semenova, K. (2015, April 7). A New Emigration: The Best are Leaving. Part 1. Institute of Modern Russia.

[4] Russians Looking for the Exit. (2015, June 3). *BBC News.*

[5] Russians Looking for the Exit. (2015, June 3). *BBC News.*

[6] David, L. (2015, May 8). Out-of-control Russian Cargo Spaceship Falls Back to Earth. Space.com.

[7] Solovyov, D. (2015, May 16). Russian Rocket with Mexican Satellite Destroyed Over Siberia. Reuters.

[8] Chance, M. (2015, June 3). Russia's Space Program in Crisis? CNN.

[9] $1.8 Billion Disappears in Russian Space Program. (2015, May 25). *CNN Money.*

[10] Chance, M. (2015, June 3). Russia's Space Program in Crisis? CNN.

[11] Andrianova, A. (2015, June 3). Russia in Full "Crisis" to Kudrin Forecasting Longer Recession. *Bloomberg Business.*

[12] Sinelschikova, Y. (2015, June 4). More and More Russians Slipping Below Poverty Line as Recession Bites. *Russia Beyond the Headlines.*

[13] Luhn, A. (2015, June 4). Racism in Russia Laid Bare: More Than 100 Incidents in Just Two Seasons. *The Guardian.*

[14] Morgenstein, M. (2015, June 8). FIFA Investigating If Bribes Influenced World Cup Bid Process. CNN.

15 Luhn, A. (2015, June 4). Racism in Russia Laid Bare: More Than 100 Incidents in Just Two Seasons. *The Guardian.*

[16] Khodarkovsky, Michael. (2015, May 19). Putin's Disunited Nation. *The New York Times.*

[17] Ibid.

[18] Stavridis, J. (2015, June 2). What Russian Literature Tells us About Vladimir Putin's World. *Foreign Policy.*

[19] Gladkova, Y. (2015, May 12). More and More Russians See America As a Threat, Poll Reveals. *The Moscow Times.*

[20] LeVine, S. (2015, June 3). After Today, Russia Can Forget About Europe Lifting Sanctions Any Time Soon. *Quartz.*

[21] Baker, J. (2015, June 4). Ruskies Behind German Govt Cyber Attack—Report. *The Register.*

[22] Hjelmgaard, K. (2015, June 7). Russia Left in Summit Cold for Second Year Running. *USA Today.*

[23] Smale, A., & Shear, M.D. (2014, March 24). Russia is Ousted From Group of 8 by US and Allies. *The New York Times.*

[24] Mulrine, A., & Weir, F. (2015, June 9). NATO and Russia Aren't Talking to Each Other. Cold War Lessons Forgotten? *The Christian Science Monitor.*

[25] Articles: William Roe Polk. WilliamPolk.com.

[26] Polk, W.R. (2015, February 24). The Cuban Missile Crisis in Reverse. WilliamPolk.com.

[27] US Senators Call for Arming Ukraine. (2015, June 20). *Radio Free Europe.*

[28] Fouquet, H., Connan, C., & Viscusi, G. (2015, June 23). Marine Le Pen: Just Call me Madame Frexit. *Bloomberg Business.*

[29] Fisher, M. (2015, June 11). This Chart Should Terrify Russia's Neighbors. *Vox World.*

[30] Many NATO Countries Reluctant to Use Force to Defend Allies. (2015, June 8). Pew Research Center.

[31] Lubold, G. (2015, June 23). US Sends Tanks, Military Equipment to Deter Russia Aggression. *The Wall Street Journal.*

[32] Baczynska, G., & Szary, W. (2015, June 15). Russia Says Will Retaliate if US Weapons Stationed on its Borders. *Yahoo! News.*

[33] Polk, William R. "Ukraine War: A Reverse Cuban Missile Crisis." Consortium News, February 2, 2015.

Chapter 57

Originally published in
*The Journal of Behavioral Finance and Economics, Vol. 5, Issues 1-2,
pp. 145-164, 2016.*

Behavioral Finance Beyond the Markets: A Real-Time Case Study of Russia's Military Resurgence

Matt Lampert[1], Alyssa Hayden[1,2] and Alan Hall[1]

*Socionomic theory proposes that social mood manifests across the
spectrum of social behavior, from the movements of stock market
indexes to the leaders we elect to the songs we choose to hear and
even to changes in the social propensity toward peace or war. This
case study tracks a real-time socionomic analysis of the Russian
Trading System Index and Russia's military resurgence from 2007
to 2016. It illustrates the utility of the theory for anticipating the
character of social actions that express swings in social mood.*

Introduction

Socionomic theory proposes that social mood manifests across the
spectrum of social behavior, from the movements of stock market indexes
to the leaders we elect to the songs we choose to hear and even to changes
in the social propensity toward peace or war. This case study tracks a real-
time analysis of the Russian Trading System Index (RTSI) conducted from
2007 to 2016. It illustrates the utility of socionomic theory for anticipating
the character of social actions that express swings in social mood.

[1] Socionomics Institute, P.O. Box 1618, Gainesville, GA 30503, USA:
mattl@socionomics.net, alyssah@socionomics.net, alanh@socionomics.net.
[2] Corresponding author.

Hardly a day passes without another reminder in the media that relations between the U.S. and Russia are at their most tense since the Cold War. Such was not the case just ten short years ago when Russia was a darling among Western investors. Its benchmark stock index, the RTSI, was up more than 5000% from its 1998 low. A pop song called "A Man Like Putin" rocketed up the Russian pop charts (PBS 2012). Moscow had more billionaires than any city in the world even though just 15 years prior it didn't even have one millionaire (Wingfield-Hayes 2007). Fortune magazine wrote, "These days more and more CEOs are livin' la vida BRIC [Brazil, Russia, India and China]" (Kirkland 2007). In the midst of ebullient optimism toward Russia, Hall (2007a, 2007b) reached a counterintuitive conclusion about the country's future. He used the Elliott wave model (Elliott 1938) to diagnose a high probability for a major top in the RTSI and employed Prechter's (1999, 2003) socionomic theory to surmise that the change in social mood that would impel a change in the RTSI's direction would also impel a change in the tenor and character of social actions in Russia. Despite relatively rosy relations among Russia, its neighbors and the West, Hall (2007b: 2) forecast that an upcoming change toward negative social mood would have "serious geostrategic implications." Specifically, he forecast that Russia would seek to reclaim its former USSR borders and identified Georgia, Ukraine and Syria among the likely locales for conflict. After the report was published, the RTSI plunged in just a few months to the bottom of Hall's target zone. About one-third of the way through the steep drop, Russia invaded Georgia.

The RTSI has continued its net downward trend from its 2008 high. In this paper, we detail the social and geopolitical developments that have transpired during the Russian stock market's decline and explicate how socionomists were able to contextualize and forecast many of them using the tools of socionomic theory. In the process, we introduce readers to socionomic research methods and suggest that the insights of socionomics— and behavioral finance more generally—contain a utility value far beyond crucially important insights into financial markets and decision-making.

Mood and Emotion in Behavioral Finance

Though neoclassical theorists have traditionally ignored the roles of mood and emotion in financial decision-making, behavioral finance scholars have begun to fill this gap. Kuhnen & Knutson (2011), for example, reported that positive emotions such as excitement compelled participants in their laboratory study to be more inclined to invest in stocks instead of assets with a guaranteed rate of return and to be more confident in their abilities to assess investment options, while negative emotions such as anxiety were associated with the opposite behaviors. Similarly, Hall (2010) found that participants in a study that were shown happy facial expressions were more likely to invest in stocks, whereas participants that were shown fearful and angry facial expressions were more likely to make safer, more conservative investment decisions. Au et al. (2003) found that participants in an experiment who were induced to experience positive emotional states were more confident and made less profitable trading decisions than participants induced to experience neutral or negative emotional states. Some authors, such as Bassi et al. (2013), linked changes in the weather to subsequent changes in mood or emotion which prompted changes in individuals' financial decisions.

Although many studies in behavioral finance examine how mood and emotion impact financial decision-making on the *individual* level, a small but growing number of scholars have expanded their unit of analysis to consider how mood and emotion in the aggregate influence stock market pricing. The roles of mood and emotion in the origins of financial bubbles and crashes has received particular attention. Smith et al. (1988) found that participants in a trading game consistently generated bubbles and crashes despite having knowledge of the fundamental value of the financial asset. Prechter (1999: 153) discussed a herding dynamic that may be the source of speculative bubbles in stock markets: "'Wall Street' certainly shares aspects of a crowd, and there is abundant evidence that herding behavior exists among stock market participants." Shiller (2000: 148) reached a similar conclusion: "if less-than-mechanistic or irrational thinking is in fact similar over large numbers of people, then such thinking can indeed be the source of stock market booms and busts." He proposed that the high valuations in the stock market at the turn of the century were the "combined effect of indifferent thinking by millions of people. ... who are motivated substantially by their own emotions" (203). Roszczynska-Kurasinska et al. (2012: 5) found a similar phenomenon at work in their study on the formation of bubbles and anti-bubbles. They concluded that spontaneous collective "moods" or "biases" governed participants' decisions in a trading game and led to the generation of speculative bubbles. In sum, this literature demonstrates that mood and emotion strongly influence the behaviors of financial market participants at the individual and aggregate levels.

One potential area for confusion in this line of research is that some authors use terms such as *affect*, *emotion* and *mood* interchangeably, whereas others assign a distinct meaning to each term. For our purposes, we adopt the following definitions: "Affect" is an umbrella term, encompassing both emotion and mood, meaning "the specific quality of goodness or badness (1) experienced as a feeling state (with or without consciousness) and (2) demarcating a positive or negative quality...." (Slovic et al. 2004: 312). Emotions are "feelings about a particular circumstance or event (someone or something) that arise from cognitive appraisals for circumstances" (Grable & Roszkowski 2008: 906). Moods are "more generalized non-specific states that are not directed at any particular target" (Grable & Roszkowski 2008: 906) and last longer than emotions (Grable & Roszkowski 2008: 907). In other words, emotions are intense, short-term, consciously experienced feelings that have a known stimulus or referent. Mood is a more diffuse, longer-term, unconsciously generated feeling that lacks a known stimulus or referent.

Socionomic Theory

Prechter's (1999, 2003, 2016) socionomic theory contributes to the literature by extending the behavioral analysis of collective psychology beyond financial markets into other areas of decision-making. Socionomists have argued that *social mood* is the most important affective motivator of social trends in financial and non-financial domains. According to the theory, social mood arises unconsciously as a result of social interaction. Trends in social mood motivate trends in feelings, perceptions and behaviors. This theory replaces the intuitive postulation that social actions (e.g., events) regulate the net aggregate tenor and character of social mood with the claim that social mood regulates the net aggregate tenor and character of social actions. In the socionomic formulation, social mood influences actors' behaviors, but actors' behaviors do not influence social mood.

Prechter (1999: 228-229, 2014: 3) presented a typology of traits that are more frequent and intense during positive social mood trends vs. traits that are more frequent and intense during negative social mood trends (Table I).

These traits manifest in various social actions, such as stock-market valuation (Prechter 1999, 2016), macroeconomic trends (Prechter 2016), propensities toward mass violence (Galasiewski 2011), political tendencies (Hall 2012; Prechter et al. 2012) and cultural trends (Prechter 1985, 1999, 2003; Kendall & Prechter 2009). For example, during positive social mood periods, speculation in the stock market, retention of incumbent leaders and frisky fashions tend to be more common, and during negative social mood periods, more conservative investing behavior, rejection of incumbent leaders and somber fashions tend to be more common (Prechter 1999: 230-231). There is always a mix of positive and negative social expressions, but the

POSITIVE MOOD	NEGATIVE MOOD
Acceptance	Rejection
Accommodation	Obstruction
Adventurousness	Protectionism
Agreeableness	Antagonism
Alignment	Opposition
Allowance	Restriction
Benevolence	Malevolence
Centrism	Radicalism
Certainty	Uncertainty
Clarity	Fuzziness
Concord	Discord
Confidence	Fear
Constructiveness	Destructiveness
Convergence	Polarization
Daring	Defensiveness
Desiring Power Over Nature	Desiring Power Over People
Ebullience	Depression
Embrace of Effort	Avoidance of Effort
Feelings of Safety	Feelings of Vulnerability
Forbearance	Anger
Friskiness	Somberness
Frivolity	Seriousness
Happiness	Unhappiness
Homogeneity	Heterogeneity
Hopefulness	Despair
Inclusion	Exclusion
Interest in Love	Interest in Sex
Optimism	Pessimism
Practical Thinking	Magical Thinking
Romanticism	Cynicism
Search for Joy	Search for Pleasure
Self-Assurance	Anxiety
Self-Providence	Self-Deprivation
Sharpness of Focus	Dullness of Focus
Supportiveness	Opposition
Sympathy	Meanness
Tendency to Excuse	Tendency to Accuse
Tendency to Praise	Tendency to Criticize
Togetherness	Separatism
Trust	Suspicion

Table I

Aspects of Social Polarity. A typology of traits that are more frequent and intense during positive social mood trends vs. traits that are more frequent and intense during negative social mood trends.

quantity and intensity of each wax and wane in concert with the direction and extremity of the social mood trend, as illustrated in Figure I (Prechter 2011, 2016).

Socionomists use stock indexes as indicators of social mood. Positive social mood trends motivate advances in the stock market, and negative social mood trends motivate declines in the stock market (Prechter 1985, 1999). Gilbert & Karahalios (2010) and Bollen et al. (2011) validated this methodology by independently showing that changes in social mood, as registered in changes in the aggregate sentiment expressed on online social media platforms, are positively associated with subsequent changes in national stock market indexes. Among other potential metrics of social mood, the stock market is especially valuable because investors can reprice stocks almost immediately in response to changes in social mood (Prechter 1999). Other mood-motivated actions, such as those that lead to fluctuations in business activity, election outcomes, climates of peace or war, and the tone of popular entertainment, take longer to execute than stock trades and therefore tend to lag the overall trends of stock market indexes (Prechter 1999). Finally, data on major stock markets are typically accurate, detailed, cheap to obtain and combine long data histories with instant, real-time updates. In summary, because stock market indexes quickly respond to changes in social mood

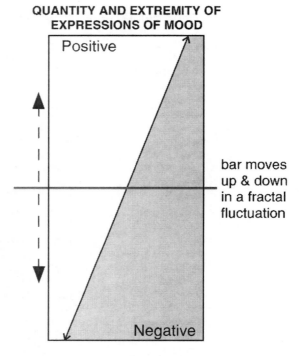

Figure I

Quantity and Intensity of Expressions of Mood, from Prechter (2016). The quantity and intensity of positive and negative social expressions wax and wane in concert with the direction and extremity of the social mood trend.

and provide inexpensive data suitable for historical, real-time and future-oriented analyses, socionomic studies have employed them as primary meters of social mood, or sociometers.

The task of historical socionomic studies is to identify qualitative and quantitative associations between a sociometer's trends and other social behaviors motivated by trends in social mood. Once identified, these historical associations can be used to forecast social behavior during subsequent positive and negative mood trends, as reflected by subsequent advances and declines in the stock market or other sociometers.

Readers interested in additional thorough treatments of socionomic theory, its methods, causal propositions and applications are invited to access Prechter (1999, 2003, 2016) and Prechter et al. (2012). For further illustrations of the theory's applicability to military conflict in other countries, see Prechter (1982: 1, 1999: 266-271), Wilson (2010), Lampert & Galasiewski (2012: 9-10), Hall (2014a, 2015b) and Thompson (2015), several of which are collected in Prechter (2017).

Hall's Forecast

Socionomic causality offers a useful basis for predicting the tenor and character of social actions. It is especially forward-looking when employed in conjunction with an accurate stock market forecast. Although myriad market forecasting approaches exist, in his study of Russia, Hall (2007b) used a fractal form of technical analysis called the Elliott wave model (Elliott 1938; Frost & Prechter 1978) to forecast the RTSI. The Market Technicians Association, an organization of approximately 4,500 investment professionals in 85 countries, defines technical analysis as:

> [T]he study of data generated by the action of markets and by the behavior and psychology of market participants and observers. Such study is usually applied to estimating the probabilities for the future course of prices for a market, investment or speculation by interpreting the data in the context of precedent. (Market Technicians Association, Inc. 2003: 1)

The RTSI is "based on prices of the 50 most liquid Russian stocks of the largest and dynamically developing issuers presented on the Moscow Exchange" (Bloomberg Business 2015). Hall's analysis indicated that an upward wave in the RTSI of nine years' duration appeared to be near the point of termination. He forecast a 62-75% decline in the RTSI, which would carry the index into the area of the preceding fourth wave, a normal retracement level according to the Elliott wave model. Figure II below, from Hall's 2007 study, published in November 2007, depicts that forecast.

Hall then used socionomic theory to predict that the same large-degree negative social mood trend that would soon impel the RTSI into a steep decline would also shift Russia's social system toward increased discord, destructiveness, exclusion, restriction, opposition and other traits listed in the right column of Table I. In applying these generalities to Russia, Hall (2007a) increased the specificity of his forecast by observing the historical behavior of Russia and the Soviet Union during past global bear markets and identifying patterns in their actions. He found that during negative social mood periods over the previous 150 years, Russia had tended to consolidate political power under an increasingly authoritarian executive, who attempted to expand the country's territory, bolster its military and play the role of outsider on the international stage while exhibiting feelings of opposition to its neighbors and the West that were drawn from an increased sense that the country was encircled and besieged. Based on these historical tendencies, Hall (2007b) predicted an acceleration in the country's military aggression

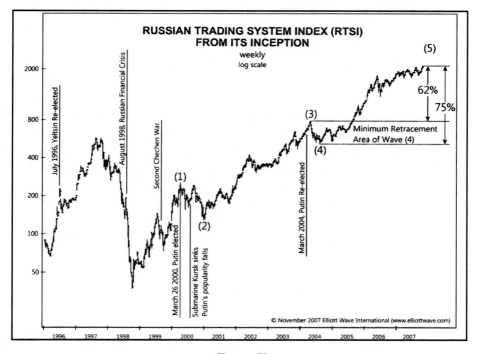

Figure II

Hall's Forecast for the Russian Trading System Index,
from Hall (2007b).

toward its neighbors and named Kosovo, Azerbaijan, Lithuania, Poland, Syria, Georgia and Ukraine as potential sites of conflict. Hall (2007b: 10) also surmised "Russia's opposition to the U.K. and the U.S. would likely increase...." He additionally forecast increased centralization of power under Vladimir Putin and greater state control of the media, politics, economy and society.

Results
Initial RTSI Decline and the Georgia Conflict

In November 2007, just before the RTSI began a final advance to its all-time high, Russia completed its withdrawal of troops that had been stationed in Georgia since 1991 (Associated Press 2007). This action reflected an elevated social mood.

In May 2008, six months after Hall (2007a, 2007b) published his report, the RTSI peaked and then plummeted 79.9% into January 2009 (see Figure III). During the initial stages of this decline, tensions reignited between Russia and Georgia. In late May 2008, Russia sent several hundred troops to Abkhazia (an internationally recognized though disputed territory of Georgia) reportedly to conduct railway repairs. Georgia suspected Russia

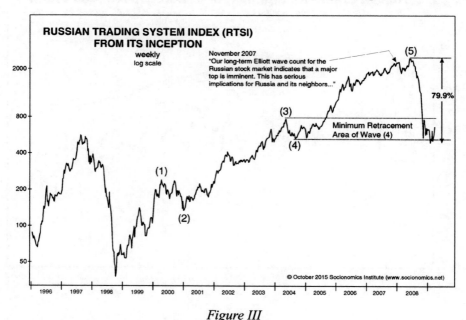

Figure III

May 2008 Peak and Subsequent Decline in the Russian Trading System Index, adapted from Hall (2014b).

was planning a military attack (The New York Times 2008). Just two months later, as the RTSI fell sharply, South Ossetian separatists began attacking Georgian peacekeepers. Georgian President Mikhail Saakashvili directed troops into South Ossetia (another disputed territory of Georgia), and Russia began air strikes there (CNN 2015). In mid-August, Georgian and Russian leaders signed a ceasefire agreement, yet Russia did not withdraw the bulk of its forces until later in the year (Blomfield 2008), near the conclusion of the initial decline in the RTSI.

The Ukraine Conflict

The RTSI made a low in late January 2009 and rallied into 2011 (see Figure IV). Consistent with socionomic theory, Russia did not engage in any armed conflicts with any external nations or territories during this period.

The downtrend in the RTSI resumed in April 2011, and the index plunged 45% through February 2014. The renewed decline signaled a continuation of the trend toward negative mood, which increased the probability for subsequent conflict. But where would Russia direct its aggression next?

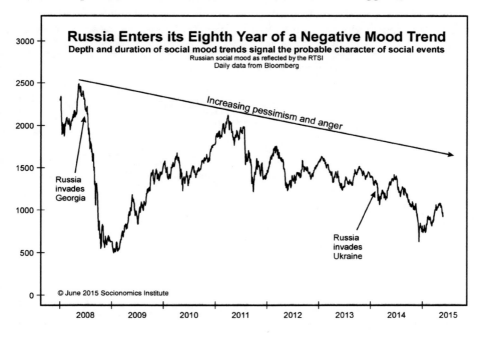

Figure IV

Russia's Negative Mood Trend from 2008 to 2015, from Hall (2015a).

Socionomists addressed this question in real time. Hall's colleague, Robert Folsom, noted that tension was increasing between Russia and Ukraine at a time when stock indexes in both countries were undergoing sizeable declines. On December 9, 2013, Folsom issued the following commentary on the potential for Russia-Ukraine conflict:

> Negative mood is now driving Ukraine's politics, foreign relations and financial system (its stock market is down some 75 percent). The country is wedged economically and geographically between West and East, and its neighbor to the east is particularly unlikely to tolerate much more instability before intervening. (Folsom 2013)

Russia did intervene in Ukraine. It began its occupation of the Crimean Peninsula less than three months after Folsom's forecast (see Figure IV) and then annexed Crimea three weeks later (see Figure V).

In Senate Armed Services Committee testimony in July 2015, U.S. Joint Chiefs of Staff Chairman Joseph Dunford stated that official U.S. military intelligence and defense strategy "did not fully anticipate growing Russian aggression" even as late as early 2014 (Garver 2015). Folsom not only anticipated growing Russian aggression but also recognized a serious implication of the conflict in Ukraine. His article titled "Ukraine: The Geographic Center of a New Cold War?" showed that he understood that any emerging conflict could serve as the focal point for a wider renewal of hostility and tension between Russia and the West, a condition that has indeed developed since.

Folsom's analysis is particularly illustrative of the utility of the socionomic perspective, as opposed to traditional forecasting methods. Consider that the degree of Russia's aggression evaded Pentagon planners with access to untold volumes of intelligence, yet Folsom was able to diagnose the elevated probability of Russian intervention in Ukraine with only three tools: socionomic theory, a couple of stock index charts and an awareness of the political landscape.

Prechter (1999: 234) explained that "the social mood is always in flux at *all degrees of trend... .*" The events of the Ukraine crisis illustrate how social mood can impel changes in the tenor and character of events not only at large degrees but at smaller degrees of scale as well. Figure V, from Hall (2016), shows the timing of the chief developments in the conflict relative to changes in the RTSI. Positive social mood trends, reflected by advances in the index, tend to be associated with respites in the violence and acts of concord, whereas negative social mood trends, reflected by declines in the index, tend to be associated with resumption of violence and acts of discord.

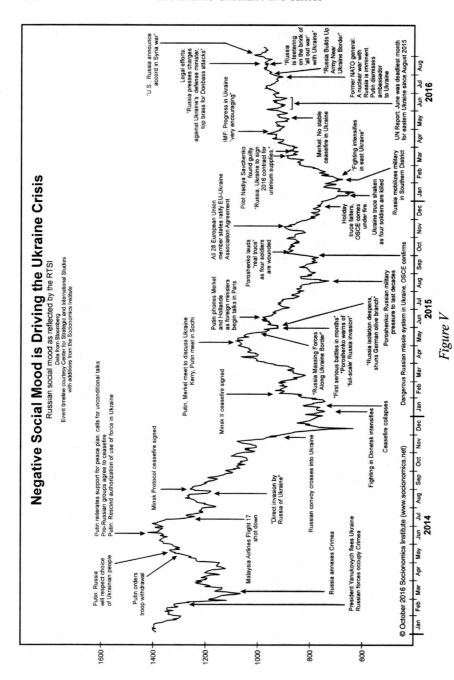

Figure V

The Major Events of the Ukraine Crisis Plotted Against the Russian Trading System Index, from Hall (2016).

Conflict with Other Nations

As Hall (2007b) anticipated, Russia's negative social mood trend has been associated with increased tensions with the West, including a hardened military posture. On March 29, 2013, Russian military planes performed a mock missile attack on targets in Stockholm and southern Sweden (Cenciotti 2013). Putin and other state officials have praised Russia's nuclear arsenal and suggested that it is superior to the West's. At a conference in Crimea on August 14, 2014, Putin declared that Russia was capable of "surprising the West with our new developments in offensive nuclear weapons about which we do not talk yet" (Tayler 2014). In an October 24, 2014, speech at the Valdai Discussion Club in Sochi, described as "one of the most hostile Putin has delivered against the West," Putin accused the U.S. of endangering global security (Anishchuk 2014). The U.S. and Russia have also been embroiled in cyber conflict, as U.S. intelligence agencies identified Russia as the source of leaked documents obtained through online hacks that aimed to sway the outcome of the 2016 U.S. presidential election (Entous & Nakashima 2016).

Russia's tensions with the West are also on display in the Middle East. Hall (2007b: 6) reported,

> The Russian Navy recently announced plans to return to the Mediterranean Sea and began dredging and building docks in Syrian ports. Israel expressed alarm that Russian ships in Syrian bases will allow electronic surveillance of the entire Middle East and an air defense umbrella over much of Syria. Russia downplays the deployment as only a symbolic presence.

On September 30, 2015, Russia launched air strikes in Syria against anti-Assad rebels trained by the CIA, "putting Moscow and Washington on opposing sides in a Middle East conflict for the first time since the Cold War" (Bassam & Osborn 2015). Moscow claimed to have targeted Islamic State camps, but the areas it struck largely appear to be held by U.S.-backed insurgents (Cooper et al. 2015). Secretary of State John Kerry stated that the U.S. had "grave concerns" about the Russian strikes in Syria (Schwartz 2015). Hall (2016) observed that a U.S.-and-Russia-backed ceasefire in the Syria conflict in September 2016 was short-lived and that the brief partnership between the countries, consummated at a rally peak in the RTSI, broke down as social mood resumed its negative trend in Russia, as indicated by the resumption of the negative trend in the RTSI. The West has begun to adopt a more adversarial posture toward Russia through military, political and economic means. Following the annexation of Crimea in March 2014, the U.S. and the EU have implemented multiple sanctions on Russia's state finances, energy and arms sectors (BBC News 2014). Since 2014, Russia has been excluded from the former-"G8" (now "G7") annual summit of major world economies (BBC News 2015a). In June 2015, the U.S. announced its plans to send 250 tanks, along with other weapons and artillery, to nations along the Russian border (Dearden 2015), prompting a Russian defense official to declare that as the plan unfolds, "[Russia's] hands are completely free to organize retaliatory steps to strengthen [its] Western frontiers" (Baczynska & Szary 2015). So far, the potential for these actions to boil over into a hotter conflict between the two nations, as Hall (2015a: 8) observed, "may be muted only by the persistence of positive mood in the U.S."

Many Eastern European countries, whose stock markets have also trended downward in recent years, have taken steps to prepare for conflict with Russia. In October 2014, Poland's defense minister announced it would move thousands of troops toward its eastern border because "the geopolitical situation has changed. We have the biggest crisis of security since the Cold War" (Scislowska 2014). Estonia doubled the number of soldiers in its voluntary Defense League, fast-tracked military procurement and requested that NATO permanently base troops and equipment there. Lithuania "launched a high-readiness combat response force comprising some 1,600 troops," and Latvia requested that NATO troops be "on permanent rotation" in the state (Braw 2014). In short, a negative social mood trend throughout Eastern Europe is prompting numerous governments to prepare for conflict, isolating Russia further.

A June 2, 2015, Foreign Policy article reported conditions that fulfilled Hall's (2007b) prediction of Russia's outsider status:

> As Russia becomes increasingly isolated from Europe and the West over everything from the annexation of Crimea to the jailing of Pussy Riot and the treatment of gays and lesbians, their society will increasingly reject the 'norms' of the West and become more 'the other' – a place they have been before. (Stavridis 2015)

Internal Authoritarian Measures

Hall (2007b: 4) also forecast that Russia would slide toward "greater state control of the economy, media, politics and society." Since then, Russia has implemented multiple economic sanctions and authoritarian social and political restraints. In August 2014, Russia banned imports of fruit, vegetables, meat, fish and dairy products from the 28 countries of the European Union, the U.S., Canada, Norway and Australia for one year (Birnbaum 2014). In August 2015, Russia added more foods (Kottasova 2015) and more countries (BBC News 2015b) to the ban and made a show of burning banned foods. Putin has increased surveillance measures within Russia. The World Policy Institute reported in 2007 that seven Russian investigative and security agencies had been given the right to intercept phone calls and emails within the nation (Soldatov & Borogan 2013). According to Russia's Supreme Court, the number of state-intercepted telephone conversations and email messages doubled from 2007 to 2012 (Soldatov & Borogan 2013).

Putin's attempts to consolidate power have intensified since Hall's (2007b) report. In 2008, term limits forced Putin to step down from the presidency, yet his hand-picked successor, Dmitry Medvedev, appointed him prime minister. Putin regained the presidency in 2012 and appointed seven members of his former cabinet to Kremlin posts (Gutterman 2012). Many of them are ex-KGB veterans and members of the "siloviki" faction in the Russian elite who promote a large state role in economic and political affairs (Gutterman 2012). On September 29, 2014, The New York Times reported that Putin shifted state money into a private bank in a move that made his loyalists into billionaires (Myers et al. 2014). A newly-amended constitution now enables Putin to serve a six-year term, and if he is re-elected in 2018, he could remain in power until 2024. Doing so would give him the longest tenure of any Russian leader since Stalin (Black 2012).

It may be tempting for psychologists to speculate about causality with reference to Putin's idiosyncratic mix of charm and ruthlessness in pursuit of his aims. While he may possess such personality traits, they carry little predictive value. In contrast, his actions have fit the behavioral patterns of Russian leaders during periods of negative social mood, just as Hall (2007b) anticipated.

Looking Ahead

At a private meeting at the Vatican on June 10, 2015, Pope Francis implored Putin to make a "sincere and great effort" to allow peace in Ukraine (Center for Strategic & International Studies 2015). Yet here at the end of 2016, the RTSI remains approximately 54% below its 2008 all-time high, indicating the continuatio—so far—of a negative social mood trend and therefore low prospects for a peaceful resolution to conflicts involving Russia. According to socionomic theory, the likelihood of a peaceful resolution will increase when Russia experiences a substantial trend toward positive social mood. That is when the corresponding traits of concord, constructiveness and togetherness are more apt to manifest in social interaction.

As long as the RTSI remains entrenched in a bear market, the potential for conflict between Russia and its neighbors will remain high. The additional probable locales for conflict that Hall (2007b) identified—Kosovo, Azerbaijan, Lithuania and Poland—may still experience clashes with Russia. It is worth noting that conflict did, in fact, threaten to erupt between Russia and Kosovo just three months after Hall published his report, when Kosovo declared independence from Serbia, one of Russia's allies. The United States and many European Union nations recognized Kosovo's independence, despite significant Russian opposition, and Putin threatened to retaliate (Sweeney & Lowe 2008). At the time, the RTSI was at an all-time high and was just months away from reaching the peak of a bull market. We conjecture that the extremely positive social mood in Russia ultimately disinclined the country to act militarily, despite substantial geopolitical motivation to do so. The Russia-Kosovo case illustrates that geopolitical factors alone do not propel countries' military actions; social mood ultimately regulates a society's propensity to go to war or to seek peace.

We further surmise that the persistence of positive social mood in the United States and many Western European countries since 2009 has helped prevent verbal threats and military shows of force between Russia and the West from escalating a cold war into a hot war. The return of a major negative social mood trend in Western countries would signal an elevated risk of hotter conflict, whereas a major positive mood trend in *both* Russia and the West would signal a return to an environment of less conflict, more accord and less potential danger (Hall 2015a).

Conclusion

One of the preeminent contributions of the field of behavioral finance is the realization and substantiation that mood and emotion influence the behavior of decision makers in financial markets. Hall's prescient study of Russia's social mood and its implications demonstrates the utility of socionomic theory for anticipating the degree to which social mood manifests not only in financial market indexes but also across the full spectrum of human social behavior. The results suggest that employing the insights of behavioral finance in general, and socionomic theory in particular, to examine the relationship between social mood and social events is a fruitful area of both research and application.

Acknowledgments

The authors are grateful to Robert Prechter of the Socionomics Institute for editing the manuscript. The authors also kindly thank participants at the 2015 Annual Meeting of the Academy of Behavioral Finance and Economics, especially discussant Deborah W. Gregory of Bentley University, for insightful comments and feedback on an early draft of the paper.

REFERENCES

Anishchuk, A., 2014, "Putin Accuses United States of Damaging World Order," *Reuters.*

Associated Press, 2007, "Russia Withdraws All Troops from Georgia," *NBC News.*

Au, K., Chan, F., Wang, D., and I. Vertinsky, 2003, "Mood in Foreign Exchange Trading: Cognitive Processes and Performance," *Organizational Behavior and Human Decision Processes,* 91:2, 322-338.

Baczynska, G., and W. Szary, 2015, "Russia Will Retaliate If U.S. Weapons Stationed on its Borders," *Reuters.*

Bassam, L., and A. Osborn, 2015, "Iran Troops to Join Syria War, Russia Bombs Group Trained by CIA," *Reuters.*

Bassi, A., Colacito, R., and P. Fulghieri, 2013, "O Sole Mio: An Experimental Analysis of Weather and Risk Attitudes in Financial Decisions," *Review of Financial Studies,* 26:7, 1824-1852.

BBC News, 2014, "How Far Do EU-US Sanctions on Russia Go?"

—————————2015a, "G7 Summit: Obama and Merkel Firm on Russia Sanctions."

—————————2015b, "Russia Adds Countries to Food Import Ban Over Sanctions."

Birnbaum, M., 2014, "Russia Bans Food Imports from U.S., E.U." *The Washington Post.*

Black, P., 2012, "Putin Returns as Russia's President Amid Protests," *CNN.*

Bloomberg Business, 2015, "Russian Trading System Cash Index."

Blomfield, A., 2008, "Russia Completes Troops Withdrawal From Georgia Buffer Zones," *The Telegraph.*

Bollen, J., Mao, H., and X. Zeng, 2011, "Twitter Mood Predicts the Stock Market," *Journal of Computational Science* 2:1, 1-8.

Braw, E., 2014, "Tiny Baltic States Prepare to Hit Back at Mighty Russia," *Newsweek.*

Cenciotti, D., 2013, "Russia Simulated a Large-Scale Aerial Night Attack on Sweden," *Business Insider.*

Center for Strategic & International Studies, 2015, "The Ukraine Crisis Timeline."

CNN, 2015, "2008 Georgia Russia Conflict Fast Facts."

Cooper, H., Gordon, M.R., and N. MacFarquhar, 2015, "Russians Strike Targets in Syria, but Not ISIS Areas" *The New York Times.*

Dearden, L., 2015, "US to Send 250 Tanks to Countries Along Russian Border to 'Respond to Russian Aggression'," *The Independent.*

Elliott, R. N., 1938, *The Wave Principle.* In R.R. Prechter, Ed., *R.N. Elliott's Masterworks—The Definitive Collection*, 1994, Gainesville, New Classics Library.

Entous, A., and E. Nakashima, "FBI in Agreement with CIA That Russia Aimed to Help Trump Win White House," *The Washington Post.*

Folsom, R., 2013, "Ukraine: The Geographic Center of a New Cold War?" *The Socionomics Institute.*

Frost, A.J., and R.R. Prechter, 1978, *Elliott Wave Principle: Key to Market Behavior*, Gainesville, New Classics Library.

Galasiewski, M., 2011, "Arabia's 'Days of Rage' Reflect Its Stock Markets," *The Socionomist*, 8-9.

Garver, R., 2015, "A New Warning About Putin's Russia From a Top U.S. General," *The Fiscal Times.*

Gilbert, E., and K. Karahalios, 2010, "Widespread Worry and the Stock Market," Fourth International AAAI Conference on Weblogs and Social Media.

Gladkova, Y., 2015, "More and More Russians See America as a Threat, Poll Reveals," *The Moscow Times.*

Grable, J., and M.J. Roszkowski, 2008, "The Influence of Mood on the Willingness to Take Financial Risks," *Journal of Risk Research* 11:7, 905-923.

Gutterman, S., 2012, "Putin Shifts Former Ministers to Kremlin," *Reuters.*

Hall, A., 2007a, "Sizing Up a Superpower: A Socionomic Study of Russia: Part I: Russian History and Global Social Mood," *Global Market Perspective*, 1-11.

————————2007b, "Sizing Up a Superpower: A Socionomic Study of Russia: Part II: Social Portents of Extreme Behavior in the Resurging Russian Bear," *Global Market Perspective*, 1-11.

————————2012, "Coming Up: A Historic Peak in the Amount of U.S. Government Entitlements," *The Socionomist*, 1-5.

————————2014a, "A Quarter Century of Waxing Authoritarianism: From the Third Reich to the Holocaust," *The Socionomist*, 1-3.

————————2014b, "The World May See an Even Darker Side of Putin," *The Socionomist*, 1-9.

————————2015a, "Social Mood in Russia Continues a Dangerous Trend," *The Socionomist*, 4-8.

————————2015b, "Syria: Epicenter of a Negative Mood Vortex," *The Socionomist*, 1-2.

————————2016, "Is Russia About to Attack...Everyone?" *The Socionomist*, 4-6.

Hall, J.L., 2010, "Affect, Risk-Taking, and Financial Decisions: Investigating the Psychological and Neural Mechanisms by which Conscious and Unconscious Affective Processes Influence Decisions," The University of Michigan, Doctoral Dissertation.

Kendall, P., and R.R. Prechter, 2009, *The Mania Chronicles: A Real-Time Account of the Great Financial Bubble (1995-2008)*, Gainesville, New Classics Library.

Kirkland, R., 2007, "The Greatest Economic Boom Ever," *Fortune*.

Kottasova, I., 2015, "Russia Bans More Foreign Foods," *CNNMoney*.

Kuhnen, C.M., and B. Knutson, 2011, "The Influence of Affect on Beliefs, Preferences, and Financial Decisions," *Journal of Financial and Quantitative Analysis* 46:3, 605-626.

Lampert, M., and M. Galasiewski, 2012, "The Global Financial Crisis and Outbreaks of Violence in Asia and the Middle East," *Market Technician* 72, 9-11.

Market Technicians Association, Inc., 2003, "Constitution of the Market Technicians Association (Revised 2003)."

Myers, S., Becker, J., and J. Yardley, 2014, "Private Bank Fuels Fortunes of Putin's Inner Circle," *The New York Times*.

The New York Times, "Russia Sends 300 Troops to Abkhazia." June 1, 2008.

PBS, 2012, "A Man Like Putin."

Prechter, R.R., 1982, "Wave V Confirmed—Super Bull Market Underway," *The Elliott Wave Theorist*, October Interim Report, 1-2.

————————1985, "Popular Culture and the Stock Market," *The Elliott Wave Theorist*, 1-20.

————————1999, *The Wave Principle of Human Social Behavior and the New Science of Socionomics*, Gainesville, New Classics Library.

————————2003, *Pioneering Studies in Socionomics*, Gainesville, New Classics Library.

————————2011, "Predicting Social Change," Presentation at the 2011 Socionomics Summit.

————————2014, "Turning Point Toward a Different World," *The Elliott Wave Theorist*, 1-8.

————————2016, *The Socionomic Theory of Finance*, Gainesville, Socionomics Institute Press.

————————(Ed.), 2017, *Socionomic Causality in Politics*, Gainesville, Socionomics Institute Press. Forthcoming.

Prechter, R.R., Goel, D., Parker, W.D., and M. Lampert, 2012, "Social Mood, Stock Market Performance and U.S. Presidential Elections: A Socionomic Perspective on Voting Results," *SAGE Open*, doi: 10.1177/2158244012459194.

Roszczynska-Kurasinska, M., Nowak, A., Kamieniarz, D., Solomon, S., and J.V. Andersen, 2012, "Short and Long Term Investor Synchronization Caused by Decoupling," *PLoS ONE* 7:12, doi: 10.1371/journal.pone.0050700.

Schwartz, F., 2015, "John Kerry Says U.S. Has 'Grave Concerns' About Russian Airstrikes in Syria," *The Wall Street Journal*.

Scislowska, M., 2014, "Poland to Move Thousands of Troops East, Defense Minister Says," *The Washington Times*.

Shiller, R.J., 2000, *Irrational Exuberance*, Princeton, Princeton University Press.

Slovic, P., Finucane, M.L., Peters, E., and D.G. MacGregor, 2004, "Risk as Analysis and Risk as Feelings: Some Thoughts about Affect, Reason, Risk, and Rationality," *Risk Analysis* 24:2, 311-322.

Smith, V.L., Suchanek, G.L., and A.W. Williams, 1988, "Bubbles, Crashes, and Endogenous Expectations in Experimental Spot Asset Markets," *Econometrica* 56:5, 1119-1151.

Soldatov, A., and I. Borogan, 2013, "Russia's Surveillance State," *World Policy Institute*.

Stavridis, J., 2015, "What Russian Literature Tells Us about Vladimir Putin's World," *Foreign Policy*.

Sweeney, C., and C. Lowe, 2008, "Russia's Options Limited for Kosovo Retaliation," *Reuters*.

Tayler, J., 2014, "Would Russia's President Really Be Willing to Start World War III?" *Foreign Policy*.

Thompson, C., 2015, "Conflict or Cooperation: In North Korea, It's a Matter of Social Mood," *The Socionomist*, 1-7.

Wilson, E., 2010, "Parting of Peaceful Ways: A Socionomic Review of Civil War," *The Socionomist*, 1-7.

Wingfield-Hayes, R., 2007, "Moscow's Suburb for Billionaires," *BBC News*.

Part VI:

MIDDLE EAST AND AFRICA

Chapter 58

Mood in the Middle East:
A Historical Perspective

Mark Galasiewski

December 1, 2010 (TS)

Astute observers can see that the stock market leads the economy. After stock prices rise for some time, economic conditions usually improve, and after they decline, conditions usually get worse. But deeper analysis reveals that the stock market is also a kind of meter of social mood and therefore a leading indicator of a whole range of social actions. Inclusionist social actions, for example, tend to follow periods of rising stock prices, and exclusionist social actions tend to erupt after prices have declined significantly. This article illustrates that relationship using contemporary and historical examples from the Middle East.

Figure 1 shows major social events in the Middle East in conjunction with three benchmark sociometers: the S&P 500, the Tel Aviv 100 and the Amman General stock price indexes, which reflect the social mood in the United States, Israel and the Arab world, respectively. The Jordanian stock market is a useful indicator of pan-Arabian mood, because it is the oldest continually traded Arabian market, and the others tend to trend with it. On the chart, inclusionist actions are displayed above the price lines, exclusionist actions below them. As you can see, these events generally express the previously positive or negative trends in mood for each society.

Notice the timing of the start of the Gaza War, which erupted in late 2008 after declines of more than 50% in both the Israeli and the Jordanian stock indexes. This chronology makes sense socionomically: When social mood trends toward the negative, it shows up immediately in falling stock prices. As fear and anger strain weak relationships, conflicts erupt. The opposite dynamic is at work when social mood is trending positively. Three

MARKET TRENDS PRECEDE COMPATIBLE SOCIAL EVENTS
American, Israeli, and Arab relations have ebbed and flowed with the social mood underlying their stock markets.

S&P 500 (United States)

UN authorizes war on Iraq

U.S. declares war on Iraq

Israel withdraws from Gaza

Israel completes withdrawal from Lebanon

Gaza flotilla raid

Gaza War

Oslo Accords

Tel Aviv 100 (Israel)

Syria ends 30-year occupation of Lebanon

Hamas seizes Gaza

Benchmark Sociometers
monthly close
log scale

Israel-Jordan peace treaty

2006 Lebanon War

Egyptian-Israeli peace treaty

Amman S.E. General Index (Jordan)

Sep 11, 2001 attacks on U.S.

Second intifada begins

Iraq invades Kuwait

First intifada begins

Iraq invades Iran

© May 2008, Dec. 2010
Socionomics Institute
(www.socionomics.net)
Data courtesy CQG, Bloomberg and Global Financial Data

1980   1984   1988   1992   1996   2000   2004   2008

Figure 1

years prior to the Gaza War, in the middle of the 2003-2007 rally in the Tel Aviv 100, Israel's goodwill toward the Palestinians rose to such a high level that the government voluntarily decided to dismantle Jewish settlements in Gaza and to withdraw its forces from the territory.

When sociometers indicate that mood is positive in one society and negative in another, social results generally remain compatible with the socionomic hypothesis. For example, a lengthy trend toward positive mood in both Israeli and Arab societies paved the way for the Oslo Accords of 1993. In July 2000, one month from the end of a 5½-year advance in the Tel Aviv 100, the leaders of Israel and Palestine held a similar summit at Camp David in the United States. But at that time the Arab stock index was near the end of a two-year bear market on the low side of an eight-year trading range, and the two sides walked away without shaking hands.

Two months later—and four trading days from the end of the Amman index's setback—the violent events that would later be labeled the start of the Second Intifada erupted. One year afterward, on September 11, 2001, with social mood as reflected by the Amman Index still very negative, Arab militants executed suicide attacks on targets in the United States.

Figure 2 offers a more detailed view of Israel's actions in relation to its Arab neighbors from 1948 to the present. As with Figure 1, it displays inclusionist actions above the price line and exclusionist actions below it. Events that support the socionomic hypothesis are in bold type, and those that do not are in regular type. The chart displays thirteen major historical events from the period that would be prominent in the minds of Israelis. Of the thirteen events, eleven reflect socionomic causality; only two seem to counter it. One possible explanation for the exceptions is that in the early 1980s most of the world—in particular the United States, Israel's main ally—was nearing the end of the largest trend toward negative mood since the Great Depression, and its effects may have influenced Israel's decisions.

Figure 3 shows how strongly social mood and compatible actions can align even in the short term. It shows all the violent events since 2005 listed on Wikipedia's "Arab-Israeli Conflict" page, charted against our Israeli and Arab sociometers. All of these events occurred after declines in the stock market, a correlation that is neatly compatible with the socionomic hypothesis.

The negative mood implied by the bear market in the Amman index also explains many other incidents of violence that originated in the region. An attack by a Jordanian suicide bomber killed seven CIA officers in Afghanistan in December 2009. Increasing activities by al Qaeda on the Arabian Peninsula (AQAP) since early 2009 include the following actions:

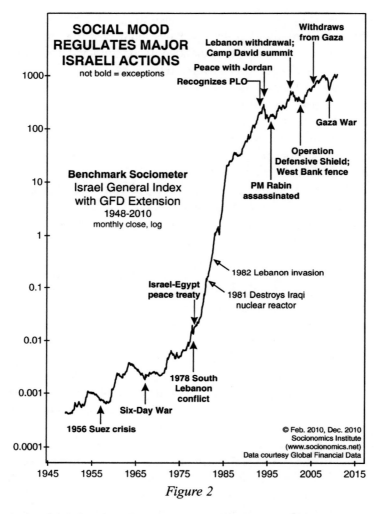

Figure 2

- the drive-by shooting at a U.S. military recruiting office in Little Rock, Arkansas in June 2009;

- the suicide bombing attempts on tourists in Yemen in March and a Saudi royal in August, 2009;

- the attempted bombing of Northwest Airlines flight 253 on Christmas day, 2009 by a Nigerian man who had plastic explosives sewn into his underwear;

- suicide bombing and rocket attacks on British targets in Yemen in April and October 2010; and

- the October 2010 cargo plane bomb plot.

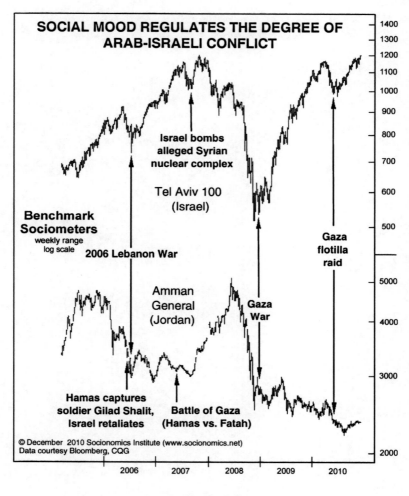

Figure 3

In November, the AQAP publicly outlined its strategy—called Operation Hemorrhage—which calls for inexpensive, small-scale attacks against U.S. interests designed to "bleed the enemy to death."

The important message from these charts is the temporal relationship between the sociometers' trends and compatible social events. It supports the case that changes in social mood—as reflected in the stock market—determine the nature of ensuing social events.

Chapter 59

Waves of War and Peace in the Middle East, 2008-2016

Mark Galasiewski

September 26, 2008 / September 25, 2009 / September 30, 2016 (APFF)

Contrarian investors have long known, "the time to buy is when blood is running in the streets." That statement, famously made by 19th-century London financier Nathan Rothschild, makes sense when viewed from the socionomic perspective.

Socionomics is the study of human mood-sharing and the collective behavior that follows from it. It holds that society's mood regulates overall optimism and pessimism, which in turn determine aggregate stock market trends, which are patterned according to the Wave Principle. A positive trend in social mood simultaneously supports rising stock prices and constructive social behavior. A negative trend in social mood fosters falling stock prices and destructive social behavior.

For a closer look at the negative side of social mood, we have collected data from Asia's three active warfronts to see whether they support the socionomic hypothesis. We examine past and current violence in Afghanistan and Iraq as well as Al Qaeda's war on the United States.

Afghanistan

Our investigation begins with a chart of Pakistan's main stock index, the Karachi Stock Exchange 100 (KSE 100), because we have determined that it is an acceptable proxy for the social mood in Islamic Central Asia. (For background, see the August and September 2008 issues of *The Asian Financial Forecast*.) Fluctuations in Pakistan's stock market have great significance for the conflict in neighboring Afghanistan, as the two societies overlap culturally in many ways. We would prefer to use data from Afghanistan's stock exchange, but we know of no index for that market. First, let's analyze the KSE 100 in terms of the Wave Principle.

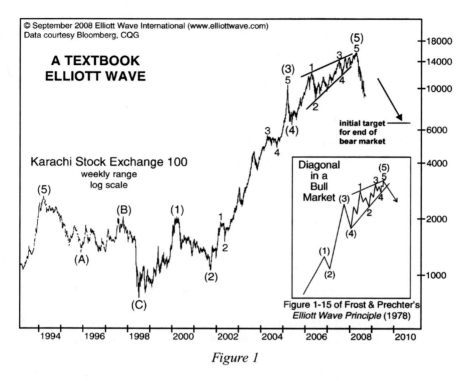

Figure 1

Figure 1 shows that at the April 2008 high, the KSE 100 completed a ten-year, five-wave bull market with an ending diagonal in the fifth-wave position. It is currently heading down from that peak. Our minimum target for the end of the correction is 6500. That level sits near the end of the previous fourth wave of one lesser degree, wave (4), and marks a 61.8% retracement of the previous advance of 1998-2008, areas that frequently mark the end of corrections. Depending on the position of the 1998-2008 advance within Pakistan's unknown multi-decade wave structure, the ultimate end to the bear market could be much lower.

Within Figure 1 is an illustration originally published in 1978 in *Elliott Wave Principle*. A.J. Frost and Robert Prechter wrote that book as a guide to the financial-market price patterns that Ralph Nelson Elliott discovered in the 1930s. The inset shows an idealized impulse wave with an ending diagonal in the fifth-wave position. Its resemblance to the advance in the KSE 100 since 1998 is no mere coincidence. Such patterns occur often in stock markets around the world at smaller degrees of magnitude. This one is of at least Primary degree and has implications reaching far beyond the borders of Pakistan.

Afghan resistance fighters tend to become more active when regional social mood—as reflected by the Pakistani stock market—is trending negatively. Foreign military fatalities in Afghanistan have generally surged during declines in the KSE 100, as shown by the grey circles in Figure 2. Those waves have tended to peak at the same time as or (more commonly) soon after major bottoms in stocks, whereas fatalities have generally subsided during rallies. The gradual decrease in fatalities from 2002 to early 2005 (as marked by the downward-sloping arrow) reflects the increasingly positive mood behind wave (3). Third waves (per Chapter 2 of *Elliott Wave Principle*) are generally strong and broad. In Afghanistan, you can see the power of the positive mood of wave (3) in guerrillas' lesser use of arms during that period.

The escalation in fatalities during 2005 reflects the severity of wave (4), which was the largest percentage decline in our sociometer since the end of wave (2) in 2001. The spikes in fatalities during 2005, 2006 and 2007 graphically illustrate another socionomic observation: that

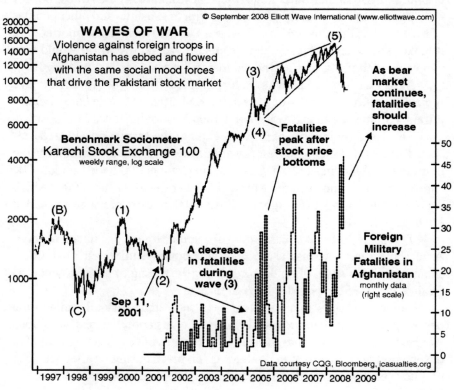

Figure 2

events characterizing an approaching period of negative mood are often foreshadowed during the preceding wave four of one lesser degree and can even show up during setbacks within wave five.

With the new negative mood trend now well under way, its consequences in social action are becoming widely manifest in areas other than the stock market. In August, foreign forces suffered their largest monthly losses ever in Afghanistan. With our minimum target for the end of the bear market in the KSE 100 still well below current levels, we believe those losses are likely to continue to escalate, while countertrend stock market rallies should coincide with lulls in insurgent activity.

Al Qaeda

Pakistan's stock market also appears to be a meter of the mood within Al Qaeda, the Sunni Islamic movement dedicated to ending foreign influence in Muslim countries and to the creation of an Islamic caliphate (state). Osama bin Laden and other key Al Qaeda leaders may be Arabs, but for most of the past 30 years, they have lived with the Pashtun and other peoples of the former Afghan *Mujahideen*, whom Pakistan has long supported. So, it makes some sense that Al Qaeda's attacks around the world would wax and wane with the KSE 100. Indeed that is the case, as shown in Figure 3.

Al Qaeda-inspired attacks on targets perceived to be American have typically occurred near major lows in the KSE 100. Al Qaeda has generally refrained from such attacks when social mood is moving toward the positive.

The same sociometer appears to explain the timing of Al Qaeda-inspired attacks that aren't necessarily aimed at American targets, such as the bombing of nightclubs in Bali, Indonesia in October 2002; the London, UK subway in 2005; and even the Mumbai, India railway in July 2006 (which was conducted by another Afghan-Pakistani Islamic extremist group, called Lashkar-e-Toiba).

The KSE 100 does not account for some timing of attacks on non-American targets, such as the Madrid train bombings in March 2004. Local sociometers, however, often do account for the timing of such violence, as Spain's IBEX 35 stock index does in this case.

Our studies show that the intensity of such attacks usually reflects the degree of the negative trend in social mood. For instance, the most ambitious Al Qaeda attacks—whether measured by the size of the structures targeted or the number of people killed—have taken place during or after setbacks of Intermediate degree in our sociometer. The most severe of those, the 1998 U.S. Embassy bombings and the 9/11 attacks on the U.S. in 2001,

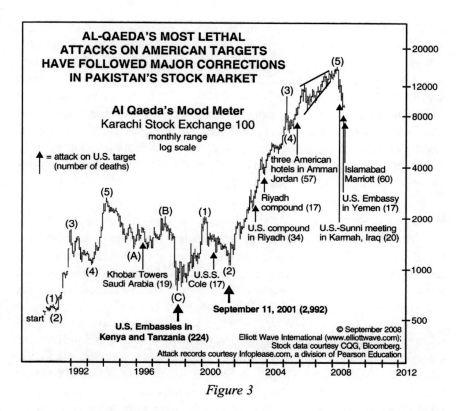

Figure 3

reflect negative mood extremes at large degree. The 1998 low marked the end of the Primary-degree correction from the 1994 high, and 9/11 took place near the end of the second-wave retracement toward that year's low. As we have often noted, actions that express social mood tend to reach an extreme either at the end of C waves or at the end of ensuing second waves. In *Elliott Wave Principle*, Frost and Prechter wrote that second waves typically coincide with "fundamental conditions often as bad as or worse than those at the previous bottom." The most violent event on the list, the attack on U.S. soil on September 11, 2001 fits that profile.

Both the Taliban's attacks against foreign forces in Afghanistan and the severity of Al Qaeda's attacks on American targets waned during wave (3) up in the KSE 100. During most of wave (5), Al Qaeda gave up attacking Americans completely. The organization may have diverted its attention to the Sunni-Shiite civil war in Iraq during that time (see next section). Regardless, the escalation of attacks in recent months suggests that the lull was only temporary. The attacks in September [2008] on the U.S. Embassy

in Yemen and the Marriott hotel in Islamabad, Pakistan were the most ambitious since those on three American hotels in Amman, Jordan in 2005,
which took place following an Intermediate-degree setback in the KSE 100.

The bull market that ended at the April 2008 high was of at least Primary
degree, so the current decline is also at least of Primary degree. As long as
Al Qaeda remains a viable organization, we should expect to see it escalate
attacks against targets associated with the United States as Pakistan's trend
toward negative mood grinds on. Attacks are most likely to occur near the
ends of major price declines in the KSE 100, and the most lethal ones are
likely to take place near or shortly after the end of the bear market.

Iraq

Turning to Iraq, we can see yet another link between social mood and
social violence. Fatality data from Iraq support the idea that social mood
determines the timing and intensity of violence. Figure 4 shows that Iraqi
fatalities in the civil war between Sunnis and Shiites surged during the
decline in Iraq's sociometer, the ISX, from 2005 to 2007.

We know of no prewar Iraqi stock index, but if one exists it likely resembles indexes in nations dominated by Sunni Arabs, such as Saudi Arabia,
Kuwait, Jordan and Lebanon. The Jordanian and Lebanese indexes (see June
2008 issue of APFF) began major declines in the winter of 2005-2006, a year

after Iraq's ISX turned
down. They also reached
their lows along with
the Iraqi index between
the summer of 2006 and
the summer of 2007.
According to socionom-
ics, it is no coincidence
that monthly Iraqi fa-
talities in the civil war
double-topped during
that period, specifically
in September 2006 and
February 2007.

In January 2007,
the U.S. government an-
nounced a large increase
in the number of U.S.

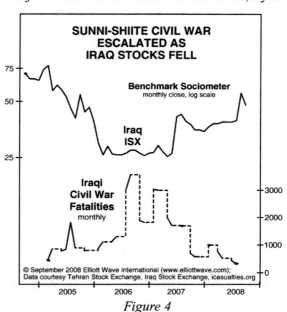

Figure 4

occupation forces—a "troop surge"—near the low of the decline in Iraq's
stock market. It finally deployed those troops in major counter-insurgency
efforts five months later. EWI's studies have long demonstrated that government tends to take actions that express social mood after the trend has
reached or passed an extreme, and the battlefield is no exception. Watch
for that principle to apply to the foreign military's behavior in Afghanistan
or Pakistan sometime in the future. Don't be surprised if the United States
withdraws or reduces troops in Iraq near the end of the current bull market
in Iraqi stocks.

2009 Update: More Waves of War in Afghanistan

One year ago, we showed how foreign military fatalities in Afghanistan
have ebbed and flowed with the waves in Pakistan's KSE 100 index, which
we used as a measure of social mood in the region. We forecast a continued
decline in the index as well as a surge in fatalities.

Fast forward to the present, and we can see that's exactly what happened. Figure 5 shows that prices hit our initial target and eventually reversed
in the usual area, near the end of a previous fourth wave of one lesser degree,
in this case wave 4 of (3). Since then, fatalities have spiked to their highest

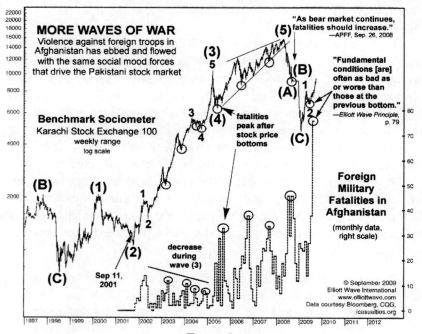

Figure 5

monthly level since the start of the U.S. occupation of Afghanistan. Fitting socionomic theory, the largest trend toward negative social mood of the past decade in the Afghan-Pakistani region has also generated the largest incidence of violence.

As noted last year, *Elliott Wave Principle* states that second waves typically coincide with "fundamental conditions often as bad as or worse than those at the previous bottom." The spike in violence in July and August (76 fatalities each), following the end of a small second wave pullback in June, fits this description.

We can use waves of social mood to predict violence, and we can use them to predict peace. As mood in Central Asia continues to trend toward the positive, violence in the region should subside. Fatalities may continue to rise for a while, especially if the United States decides to intervene heavily in the region. But if it does, it will have only proved yet again the socionomic hypothesis that government tends to express mood trends after they have already passed their extremes.

2016 Update: Positive Mood Leads to Peace in Afghanistan

With Pakistan's stock market well into a fifth wave of the advance from the 2009 low, now is a good time to review our analysis of the war in Afghanistan.

Eight years ago, our September 2008 article posited that Pakistan's Karachi Stock Exchange 100 Index provides a good proxy for the social mood in Islamic Central Asia. Based on that assumption, we showed that fluctuations in the KSE 100 held great significance for the conflict in neighboring Afghanistan. At that time, the KSE 100 had begun a decline from its 2008 high, which led us to forecast that foreign military fatalities in Afghanistan would continue to increase (see Figure 6). The index ultimately fell by 70%, and foreign military fatalities in the nation subsequently surged.

A year later, our September 2009 article identified a newly emerging advance in the KSE 100, but knowledge of the timing of earlier wars—including the U.S. Civil War and the Iraq War, each of which began *after* the trend toward more negative mood ended—prompted us to issue these words of caution:

> Fatalities may continue to rise for a while, especially if the United States decides to intervene heavily in the region. But if it does, it will have only proved yet again the socionomic hypothesis that government tends to express mood trends after they have already passed their extremes. (APFF, Sep. 25, 2009)

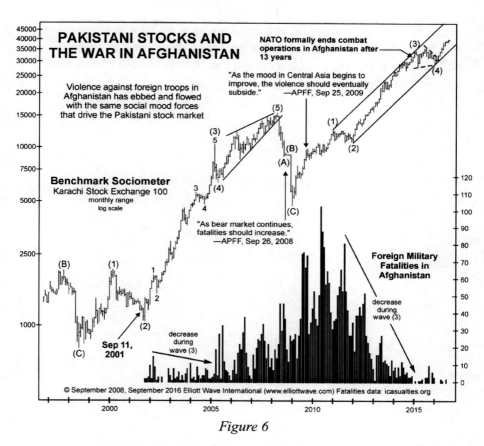

Figure 6

Two months later, in late November 2009, U.S. President Barack Obama announced a troop surge that quickly doubled the number of U.S. soldiers stationed in Afghanistan. Foreign military fatalities in the region peaked seven months later, in June 2010. There was another, lesser, surge in fatalities in 2011, the year the Dow/gold ratio bottomed, signaling a second extremity of negative mood in the U.S.

As wave (3) up from 2012 lows in both the DJIA and the KSE 100 gathered steam, foreign military fatalities in Afghanistan began to decrease. This change repeated a pattern seen during the previous rising wave (3) in the index from 2001 to 2005. In the final days of 2014, about a month before the peak of wave (3), NATO formally ended its 13-year combat operations in Afghanistan.

Conventional observers might believe that the increased presence of foreign troops in Afghanistan brought stability to the region, allowing stock prices to rise. But the socionomic interpretation is that a positive trend in social mood both in the region and in the occupiers' home countries spurred bull markets in both sets of places and ultimately influenced foreign leaders to withdraw their troops.

Chapter 60

More Results of Positive Mood:
Including the Exclusionists

Mark Galasiewski

January 4, 2013 (APFF)

Pioneering Studies in Socionomics (2003) observed that negative mood breeds "anger, fear, intolerance, disagreement and exclusion," while positive mood fosters "benevolence, confidence, tolerance, agreement and inclusion." Afghanistan's relations with its religious extremists over the past two decades demonstrate that point very well on the long term chart of the KSE 100, our proxy for Afghan social mood [see Chapter 59].

In the early 1990s, parts of Afghan society welcomed the growing Islamic movement called the Taliban as an alternative to the chaos that had followed the end of Soviet occupation of the nation in 1989. In early 1994, as the KSE 100 began a large-degree bear market that would bring Pakistani stocks down 72% over the next 4½ years, this organization of disciplined, young, male, religious students became a military force. By November 1994, the Taliban had captured their city of origin, Kandahar. Within two years they had seized the capital, Kabul, and founded a caliphate (Islamic state), the Islamic Emirate of Afghanistan, a month before the KSE 100's 1996 low.

In its mode of governing, the Taliban expressed the negative social mood very severely. It imposed strict codes for appearance and behavior for both men and women, cut off the hands of thieves, and publicly beat or executed those who violated the Islamic moral codes known as sharia law. In March 2001, during the wave (2) setback in the KSE 100, the Taliban detonated and destroyed the Buddhas of Bamiyan, two monumental statues that dated from the 6th century. U.S. and NATO forces invaded Afghanistan during the very month of the 2001 low in the KSE 100. They ended the Taliban's reign within weeks, turning them again into rebels.

Figure 1

Now, eleven years into the ensuing bull market, we can see a more cooperative spirit within Afghan society. In November, we saw how the waxing positive mood in emerging markets in 2012 had prompted ceasefires and peace agreements between government and rebel groups in Myanmar, the Philippines and Colombia. Prospects for peace have now risen in Afghanistan as well, as the United States and the Afghan government met with Taliban leaders in Paris last month to discuss possible peace talks. "I think one consensus was that everybody acknowledged that nobody will win by military [means]," said one Afghan government representative at the meeting. "Everybody acknowledged that we have to enter into a meaningful negotiation." (Reuters, December 31, 2012)

Neighboring Pakistan, which has long suffered violence at the hands of the Pakistani Taliban, also appears to be aiding the reconciliation process. This week, Bloomberg reported that in November and December, Pakistan released 26 Afghan Taliban prisoners, including former regional governors and ministers, "as it bids to help create conditions for substantial negotiations with insurgents." Afghanistan and Pakistan are both pushing to have Taliban members removed from the United Nations' terrorist list to enable them to join negotiations and hold Afghan government posts, including even the presidency. Reuters reports that the most experienced guerrilla rebels, those of the Haqqani network, would join the peace process if the Taliban were to start formal talks.

Governments are adopting a strategy of including the Taliban rebels partly because they are unable to defeat them completely. But from a socionomic perspective, they are also giving in because the social mood in the region makes all groups more open to cooperation and agreement now than at any time in the past two decades. If, as we expect, Asia's emerging boom continues, Afghans may once again accept Taliban representatives in leadership positions, this time after voting them into office.

Chapter 61

Bin Laden Exits in a Climate of
Positive Social Mood

Mark Galasiewski

June 6, 2011 (TS)

The assassination of al-Qaeda head Osama bin Laden on May 1, 2011 was a result of the cooperation and success accommodated by the positive social mood trend underlying the global stock market advance since 2009. Bin Laden had been fighting two inverse trends: the increasing commitment of the intelligence analysts pursuing him and the decreasing commitment of

Figure 1

his own followers. The increasingly positive social mood behind the stock market advance encouraged those trying to find bin Laden, while the waning negative mood deprived him of many of his traditional sources of support, thereby undermining his security.

As explained in Chapter 21 of *The Socionomic Theory of Finance*, the conventional, linear approach to social forecasting is the opposite of the socionomic, fractal approach. In March 2009, the very month of the low in the DJIA, *Newsweek* magazine penned this cover title in Arabic script on an Islamic green background: "Radical Islam is a Fact of Life: How to Live with It." The magazine was linearly extrapolating the trend that was in force at that time. But in the April 3, 2009 issue of *The Asian-Pacific Financial Forecast*, we viewed that cover as a capitulation to the negative mood trend expressed both in stock prices and extremists' behavior and forecast a reversal in both:

Markets Down: March 2009

> [The] extremists probably do have one or two big tricks up their sleeve yet, [because] the mood in the early stages of a bull market tends to stay negative for some time. ...But from a pure pattern perspective, these provocateurs will now have to wage their battle uphill [as] societies tend to lose their tolerance for antisocial behavior during bull markets.

Events since then have unfolded in accordance with our contrary forecast. As the stock market advance pressed higher, evidence of waning support for extremists began to mount. In February 2010, *Newsweek* finally aligned with the new trend by reversing its stance with a cover titled, "How Bin Laden Lost the Clash of Civilizations: The Untold Story of the Triumph of Muslim Moderation." In September last year, the magazine *Foreign Policy* asked, "Is Bin Laden Still Relevant?" In early April 2011, three weeks before bin Laden was killed, a BBC news headline asked that same question.

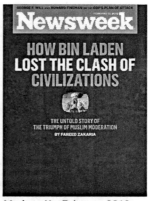

Markets Up: February 2010

Even the Afghan Taliban have adapted to the new social climate. The Taliban were bin Laden's longtime hosts, and their reign of terror from 1996 to 2001 paralleled al-Qaeda's heyday during emerging Asia's long period of negative mood from the late 1990s to the early 2000s, as depicted in Figure 1. In a widely syndicated article titled, "Taliban Try Soft Power," the Institute for War & Peace reported in April, "Experts in Afghanistan say a softer line the Taliban are taking on issues like education and reconstruction projects is a tactical ploy to win broader popular support." It quotes a high school educator saying, "*We don't know why* the Taliban have become so flexible.... I left my home because I was a teacher and I was scared. But now the Taliban are encouraging us to go into school and teach." The trend toward positive social mood in the region—implied by years of rising stock prices—explains the underlying reason for this change.

Some analysts suspect that Pakistan sheltered bin Laden. True or not, Pakistan's army is an ally of the Afghan Taliban. If the Afghan Taliban have moved mainstream, Pakistan's military might have become less interested in protecting the head of an organization that had bombed targets in Pakistan. In the end, it was an errant phone call made by bin Laden's personal courier in the middle of 2010 that enabled the Americans to uncover bin Laden's location in Pakistan.

The more positive social mood globally has brightened social conditions considerably since the dark days of late 2008 and early 2009. Once mood turns negative again, we expect the return of the kind of environment that supports extremist attitudes and violent behavior.

Chapter 62

As Mood Goes, So Goes
Arab Spring and the Middle East

Matt Lampert and Mark Galasiewski

December 26, 2012 (TS)

An earlier version of this article appeared in the May 2012 issue of
Market Technician, *the journal of the Society of Technical Analysts (UK).*

In recent years, *The Asian-Pacific Financial Forecast* (APFF) has detailed the periods of tumult and relative peace in the Middle East and Asia, either as they happened or in advance. APFF's commentary shows how a socionomist can anticipate the changing character of social events by monitoring social mood.

Troubling Signs

By October 2008, many Asian markets had fallen by more than 50% in the space of a year. Volatility was at an all-time high. In the face of global financial panic, APFF observed that stock markets in the region had reached a crucial juncture:

> Corrections of such large degree open the door to opportunity. This month, we will discuss how indicators of momentum, volatility and sentiment hit extremes during October's selloff that have not been seen since the middle of the region's last Primary degree correction in 2000-2003. For about half the region's stock markets, the 2001 low was only temporary. But for others…it marked the low for the bear market. As our wave counts show, the current juncture may mark a similar point of divergence for the region.[1]

The region immediately underwent a remarkable divergence: Many emerging countries' stock markets registered price lows in October 2008 and began to rally. But markets in most developed nations continued to fall to new lows in 2009. Some markets, especially in Arabia and southern Europe, continued lower even beyond 2009. APFF further pointed out that the October 2008 juncture had implications not only for stocks but also for non-financial social events:

> If this analogy and forecast are correct, investors should be even more alert to the possibility of what comes along with...major declines within bear markets—outbreaks of violence. The Al Qaeda inspired attacks on American targets in Yemen and Pakistan—the group's most ambitious since 9/11, measured by the number of people killed—may turn out to be the most spectacular products of the negative mood of the past year. But sometimes the ugliest manifestations of a decline in social mood show up weeks or months after absolute stock market lows.... The most spectacular violence of 2001 in the Asian-Pacific region—the U.S. invasion of Afghanistan and the terrorist attacks on India's Parliament—took place weeks and months, respectively, after the September lows in the region's stock markets. The recent escalation of grassroots violence in Afghanistan, Pakistan and India shows the potential for a sequel to those violent events.[2]

Growing Hostilities

Social actions soon began to fall in line with APFF's forecast. Just weeks after the November 2008 issue was published, terrorists killed 164

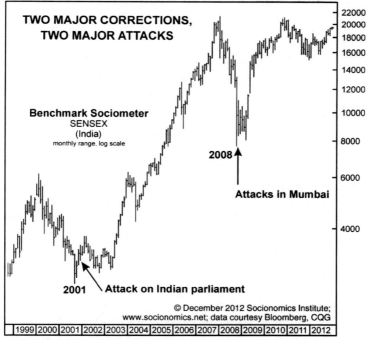

Figure 1

people during a series of attacks on downtown Mumbai. It was an act commensurate with the 2001 attack on the Indian parliament, and it occurred at a similar extreme in negative social mood, as you can see in Figure 1.

Elsewhere, a six-month, Egypt-brokered truce between Israeli and Palestinian forces came to a halt in December. Hamas leaders declared an end to the ceasefire, and in response to rocket fire into Israel from Palestinian militants, Israel launched air strikes in cities across Gaza. Both sides ratcheted up the violence, and Israel continued its military assault with a ground invasion in Gaza in early January. Six days after the ground invasion began, APFF put the conflict's escalation into socionomic perspective:

> Socionomics allows us to find some order in the chaos. The negative trend in social mood that is responsible for stock market declines also manifests in other social activities, such as politics. The severity of the Israelis' behavior mirrors the severity of the decline in Israel's stock market leading up to the recent conflict—a 60% decline, its largest in at least 17 years. The negative trend in social mood appears to have motivated calls for extreme violence on the Palestinian side as well.[3]

Figure 2 marks the timing of the key events on charts of Israeli and Jordanian stock prices. Jordan has the oldest continually traded stock market

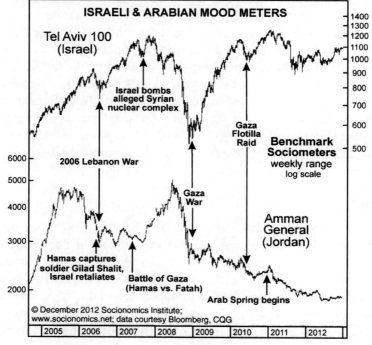

Figure 2

in the Arab world, and APFF had established it as a proxy for Arabian mood several months earlier. Charts of Arabian markets often look very different from other global markets, but the socionomic relationships remain the same: Dramatic expressions of violence tend to accompany major negative trends in mood.

The Gaza War ultimately resulted in 1,100 Palestinian and 13 Israeli deaths before a ceasefire took place on January 18, 2009. Mood throughout much of Arabia continued to trend negatively, as illustrated by a further net decline in the Jordanian stock market. Meanwhile, mood in Israel grew more positive, as indicated by the net rally in the Israeli market. But when it resumed its negative trend, the violence re-emerged.

Flotilla Attacked During Gaza Blockade

In May 2010, following sharp declines in the Tel Aviv 100, Israeli forces raided a flotilla that had attempted to break through an Israeli-Egyptian Gaza Strip blockade. The flotilla, reportedly carrying humanitarian supplies, had been organized by a Turkish human rights group. Nine activists were killed in the confrontation. Later in the year, direct negotiations between Israeli and Palestinian Authority leaders over a possible two-state solution to the Israeli-Palestinian conflict broke down. The talks were marred from the beginning, as a Hamas-led coalition of 13 Palestinian factions was coordinating deadly attacks on Israeli civilians. Palestinians also escalated rocket fire into Israel in an attempt to derail the negotiations.

Socionomists propose that both the violence and the failure to reach an agreement were manifestations of the negative trend in social mood. The peace talks had little chance of success from the start. Negotiators from the two sides literally were not in the mood for peace. Peace in the region and bipartisan solutions will be far more probable after strong, persistent trends of increasingly positive mood as evidenced by commensurate advances in the region's benchmark sociometers.

Middle East Uprisings

The Arab Spring of late 2010-early 2011 broke out as the large-degree trend toward negative mood in Arabia continued to unfold. Popular accounts of the Arabian revolutions tend to emphasize the sequence of events: A Tunisian street vendor set himself on fire on December 17, 2010 in a region that was home to decades of political oppression and a large, dissatisfied youth population. Sympathy protests followed. They, in turn, inspired mass demonstrations. The civil unrest grew and culminated in violent uprisings and eventual regime changes throughout much of the Arab world.

The standard, mechanistic, event-oriented approach of most futurists fails to take social mood into account. But social mood in the area had become extremely negative before the uprisings began, as evidenced by a multi-year decline in the regional stock index. That negative mood provided a fitting environment for revolutionary fervor to increase. The uprisings in the region were manifestations of the negative mood, and their severity reflected the extremity of the mood trend. The sequence of events per se is incidental to understanding the chief cause of the Arab Spring.

Uprising in Iran

During the summer of 2009, the most intense violence since the Iranian Revolution of 1979 swept through the streets of Tehran following the Iranian presidential election. Tens of thousands of people protested, and dozens died.

Many observers feared that violence in Iran would worsen. But socionomic analysis brought news of impending peace. The arrow in Figure 3 shows the timing of the outbreak of violence on a chart of Iran's TEPIX stock index. Prices had fallen for four and a half years and then started to advance. The Elliott wave structure indicated that the correction had reached a turning point, and the ensuing advance signified that a trend toward positive social mood was beginning to take hold. With the country already in the

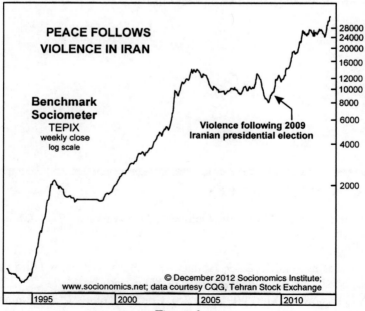

Figure 3

throes of violence and protests—which were lagging manifestations of the four-year negative-mood trend—APFF stated, "At such a juncture, Iran holds the potential for even greater violence. But with a wave up likely already under way, a wave of acceptance should eventually replace the current anger."[4]

In subsequent months, APFF's forecasts of an end to the violence—and subsequent increases in both price and peace—came to pass. As social mood in Iran continued to trend more positively, its stock market continued to rally, and the controversy surrounding the election subsided.

Conclusion

Social events are never all positive or all negative, even on the day of a major top or bottom in the stock market. There is always a mix of social expression. But the frequencies and intensities of positive and negative events shift over time in accordance with fluctuations in social mood. Socionomics offers a guide for assessing and sometimes predicting both the timing and the magnitude of such shifts.

This article has interpreted recent instances of unrest and conflict in the Middle East and Asia from a socionomic perspective. The same template can be used to understand the emergence of major social breakdowns anywhere in the world and throughout history.

NOTES AND REFERENCES

[1] Galasiewski, M. (2008, October 31). Overview. *The Asian-Pacific Financial Forecast.*

[2] *Ibid.*

[3] Galasiewski, M. (2009, January 9). Cultural Trends: A Third Palestinian Intifada? *The Asian-Pacific Financial Forecast.*

[4] Galasiewski, M. (2009, June 26). Cultural Trends: 2009 Iranian Presidential Election. *The Asian-Pacific Financial Forecast.*

Chapter 63

Social Mood Has Continued to Regulate the Degree of Conflict in Iraq

Mark Galasiewski

July 3, 2014 (APFF)

The pattern of peace vs. violence in Iraq over the past decade well displays socionomic causality at work. Stock markets throughout the Arab world, including Iraq's, began large-degree declines in 2005 and 2006. As the Iraq Stock Index (ISX) fell by two thirds between 2005 and 2007, fighting between Sunni and Shia Islamic groups in the nation intensified, and thousands of civilians each month died at their hands. The United States in January 2007 augmented the conflict by announcing a large increase in the number of U.S. occupation forces—the so-called "troop surge"—right at the bottom of the decline in the ISX.

As it turned out, the extreme bloodshed at that time marked a major buy signal for Iraqi stocks. From a low in May 2007, the ISX rocketed more than eleven fold in just under two years. The following year, in the early stages of that advance, *The Asian-Pacific Financial Forecast* published "The Waves of War" [Chapter 59], which identified the socionomic significance of the troop surge, which occurred at the low in Iraqi stocks, and forecasted the pivotal event that would likely mark the eventual end of the of the new bull market then under way: "Don't be surprised if the United States withdraws or reduces troops in Iraq near the end of the current bull market in Iraqi stocks."

About a year after that, our June 26, 2009 update said that the near-vertical advance in Iraqi stocks occurring then was a third wave in a developing five-wave advance. Following the socionomic pattern of increasing social harmony in positive-mood periods, the violence subsided as the advance continued into 2011. During wave 5 up, monthly deaths fell to their lowest level since the start of the Iraq war in 2003. Two months after the top in the ISX in 2011, the United States withdrew the last of its occupation forces, right in line with our forecast.

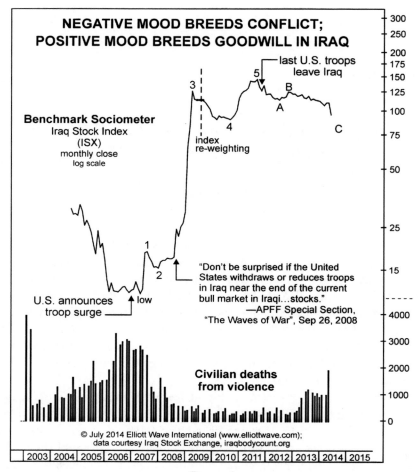

Figure 1

Since then, the ISX has fallen, indicating a new trend toward negative social mood. After an almost three-year decline in the Iraqi stock market to date, sectarian violence in Iraq erupted in June [2014]. "Iraq preps for a civil war rematch," predicts the Daily Beast website (6/22/14). From our perspective, the violence is simply expressing current-time negative mood in the nation and has no forecasting value in and of itself. The direction of social mood will determine whether or not a civil war erupts.

Chapter 64

Socionomic Timing of the Coup Attempt in Turkey

Mark Galasiewski

August 6, 2016 (APFF)

What message can we take from the failed coup d'état in Turkey by a faction in that country's military? The answer once again is: Negative social mood precipitates polarization and conflict.

At the time of the coup attempt on July 15, Turkey's ISE 100 Index was tracing out the final stages of a contracting triangle pattern that began at its 2013 high. Wave ⓓ of the pattern equaled about 61.8% of wave ⓑ, which *Elliott Wave Principle* identified as a common relationship within

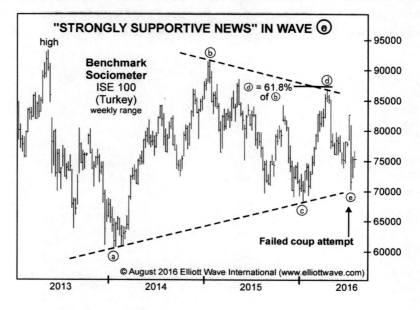

"STRONGLY SUPPORTIVE NEWS" IN WAVE ⓔ

© August 2016 Elliott Wave International (www.elliottwave.com)

triangles. Wave ⓔ so far appears to have ended near the triangle's ⓐ-ⓒ line, another common occurrence. *Elliott Wave Principle* further describes how such formations resolve in terms of social action: "E waves in triangles appear to most market observers to be the dramatic kickoff of a new down-trend after a top has been built. *[They] almost always are accompanied by strongly supportive [negative] news.*" In line with that description, the timing of the coup attempt signaled the end of the corrective pattern.

In response to the attempted overthrow, President Recep Tayyip Erdogan declared a three-month national state of emergency. Since then, he has ordered and presided over the killing of more than 250 people, the closing of more than 130 media organizations and the suspension or removal of more than 60,000 people from their jobs in the military, the government and academia.

All that upheaval notwithstanding, the authoritarian crackdown actually supports a bullish forecast for Turkish stocks. Not only do these social events match expectations for the style of news expected at the end of a triangle (as quoted above), but stock markets also have a long history of booming after strongmen tighten their grip on power. Let's be sure to understand the cause-and-effect relationship properly: It's not that authoritarian leaders inspire bull markets. Rather, it's that the fear attending the late stages of a negative mood period helps authoritarian leaders expand their power and influence. Their machinations often continue for a while even after the negative social mood subsides from its deepest extreme.

Chapter 65

Social Mood Has Influenced an
African Politician's Fortunes

Mark Galasiewski

January/August 2012 / December 2016 (APFF)

If conditions are right, the negative mood that fuels large-degree bear markets can also bring dictators to power. Some instances that come quickly to mind are Germany's Hitler in 1933, China's Mao in 1949, Uganda's Amin in 1971, Zimbabwe's Mugabe in 1980, and Venezuela's Chavez in 1998. With unemployment currently running at about 50% for black South African youth between the ages of 15 and 24, South Africa strikes us as a likely country to produce a dictator. As it happens, there is a strong contender for that role.

Julius Malema: Bear Market Icon

The fortunes of individual public figures often ebb and flow with the waves of social mood. One such figure has benefitted from the political climate in South Africa during times of negative social mood. In *The Wave Principle of Human Social Behavior*, Robert Prechter described the political effect of mood trends:

> In bull markets, politics tends to be middle-of-the-road; in bear markets, radical positions gain acceptance, and the electorate becomes polarized. Free trade is encouraged in bull markets; protectionism is demanded in bear markets. Racial harmony is promoted in bull markets, racial separation in bear markets. (p.230-231)

Julius Malema is a charismatic politician who rose from a life of poverty in one of South

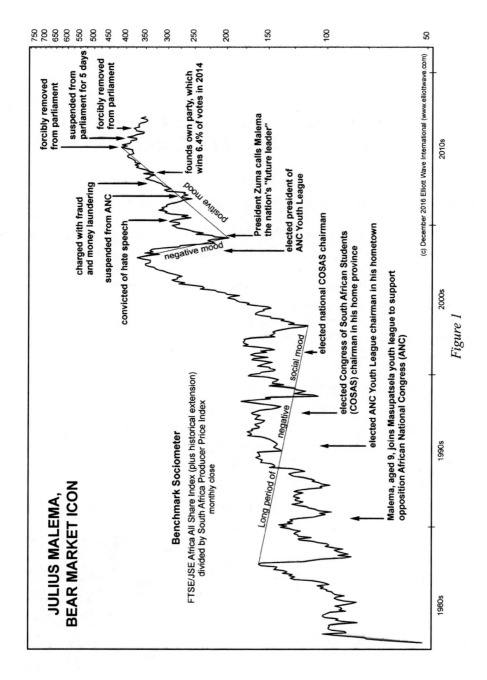

Figure 1

Africa's poorest provinces. He has become the nation's most vocal proponent of nationalization—an idea that still tantalizes many citizens 18 years after South Africa dismantled apartheid. Malema wants to distribute more of the nation's wealth to its poor black population by nationalizing the mines and other properties traditionally owned by whites. At the young age of 30, he has time to wait for waves of negative mood to support his brand of politics.

Riding Waves of Negative Mood

Malema began his career during a long period of negative social mood that held sway from 1987 to 2003, as indicated by our benchmark sociometer for South Africa (see Figure 1). At age nine in 1990, Malema joined the Masupatsela ("Trailblazers"), an organization for young people under the umbrella of the African National Congress (ANC). He busied himself tearing down posters supporting the National Party, which then governed the nation under the apartheid it had established in 1948, at the end of a global, 20-year period of negative social mood. In 1995, Malema was elected chairman of the ANC's Youth League at town and provincial levels. In 1997, he was elected chairman of the Congress of South African Students (Cosas) at the regional level, and in 2001 he became chairman of that organization nationally.

Malema first became widely known in 2002, the final full year of the negative mood period. That is when he led mobs of Cosas members on a chaotic march through the streets of Johannesburg, in which students trashed hawker stalls and stole from shops. He reached national prominence during the period of negatively trending mood that produced the bear market of 2008. That's when he was elected president of the ANC's Youth League at its national conference, which—in negative-mood fashion—was marked by drunkenness, nudity and violence.

Malema used his new position to campaign for the election of a controversial candidate, Jacob Zuma, as South Africa's president. Zuma was elected president in April 2009 in a climate of deeply negative social mood as indicated by the global bottom in stock prices of March 2009. Zuma rewarded Malema by calling him the "future leader" of the nation.

That same year, Malema launched a campaign to nationalize the country's mines and to expropriate land owned by whites, without compensation. In the process, he leveraged his massive following among the nation's youth to change policy within the ANC.

Social mood became more positive thereafter but then turned negative again during "wave two" of the new bull market, the correction of 2011. At that time, Malema raised his rhetoric to another level. Shortly following that year's low in the FTSE/JSE Africa All Share Index, Malema declared "economic war" on the "white minority," claiming that "there will be casualties." (News24) He also took the bold and dangerous step of calling for Zuma's deputy to replace Zuma as leader of the ANC.

Retreat During a Wave of Reconciliation

Thereafter, social mood began to trend positively in earnest, propelling South African stocks strongly upward for four years. During this time, Malema's broad support crumbled. In November 2011, the ANC leadership suspended him from the party for five years. According to one poll, 70% of South Africans agreed that the suspension was appropriate. In September 2012, things got worse for Malema, as he was charged with fraud and money laundering. In February 2013, a court ordered his properties sold to cover unpaid taxes, making him destitute.

In June 2013, Malema formed his own party, the Economic Freedom Fighters, which subsequently won a modest 6.4% of the vote in the May 2014 general election. The election placed Malema in South Africa's parliament, providing him a national political platform. As social mood in the nation reached a positive extreme, however, that governing body showed little tolerance for his disruptive behavior. In February 2015, the month of the high in South Africa's benchmark sociometer, guards forcibly removed Malema from the chamber. In September 2015, the month of a secondary high for stocks, Malema was ejected again and suspended from parliament for five days. In May 2016, the month of the stock market's high that year, he was forcibly removed a third time.

Malema's Political Future

Malema's bad fortune will likely prove temporary. When people are under the sway of positive social mood, they tend to disrespect public figures who represent negative mood. Such figures must await a change in mood to make their moves. For example, Adolph Hitler participated in a failed coup attempt in 1923 during a positive mood period and went to jail. He spent the late 1920s gaining respectability for his National Socialist Party until the powerfully negative mood of the Great Depression served to broaden his appeal. Osama Bin Laden expanded his influence during Asia's bear market of the 1990s and early 2000s. As social mood thereafter trended positively, he failed to form an Islamic state, gradually lost popular support, and eventually met his end in May 2011, near a peak in positive social mood as indicated by trends in Pakistan's stock market [see Chapter 61].

Julius Malema is still a young man. The negative social mood that placed him on the national stage will return to fuel the next sizeable bear market in South African stocks. For now, he need only bide his time. Many black South Africans feel that apartheid was dismantled in name only in 1994 and that the ANC has yet to achieve its goal of providing economic opportunity for all Africans. They are also frustrated by corruption within the ruling party. In April 2016, just before the year's high in South Africa's benchmark sociometer, Malema told Al-Jazeera that if the government were to use violence to suppress peaceful protest, his party would "remove this government through the barrel of a gun." Malema at present may merely be an extremist thorn in the ANC's side, but in the next major trend toward negative social mood, support for him and his policies could broaden faster than anyone now expects.

Part VII:

FAR EAST

Chapter 66

Social Mood Has Influenced
a Malaysian Politician's Fortunes

Mark Galasiewski

February 6, 2012 / February 27, 2015 (APFF) (updated through 2015)

The career of Malaysian politician Anwar Ibrahim has been shaped largely by social mood trends as depicted by trends in Malaysia's benchmark sociometer, the FTSE Bursa Malaysia KLCI. Let's look at Anwar's fortunes through the lens of socionomics.

Anwar first felt the power of negative social mood during the bear market year of 1974. As the founder and leader of an Islamic youth organization, he was arrested during student protests against rural poverty and hunger. He was imprisoned under the Internal Security Act, which allows for detention without trial, and spent 20 months in jail.

Positive social mood heals wounds, however, and in 1982, following a six-fold advance in the KLCI over four years, the ambitious Anwar shocked his supporters by accepting an invitation from Prime Minister Mahathir Mohamad to join the ruling United Malays National Organization (UMNO). The UMNO has dominated Malaysian politics since independence from the British in 1957.

After a three-year decline in stock prices, Anwar began to advance under Mahathir during the trend toward positive social mood that lasted from the mid-1980s to the early 1990s, consecutively heading several ministries, including Agriculture, Education and Finance. A few weeks ahead of the 1994 stock market high, he became Deputy Prime Minister. Soon after the 1997 high, Mahathir even appointed Anwar to be Acting Prime Minister while he took a two-month holiday.

The negative mood that brought on the Asian Financial Crisis of 1997-1998 tested the relationship between the two men. As Finance Minister, Anwar backed the free-market policies advocated by the International

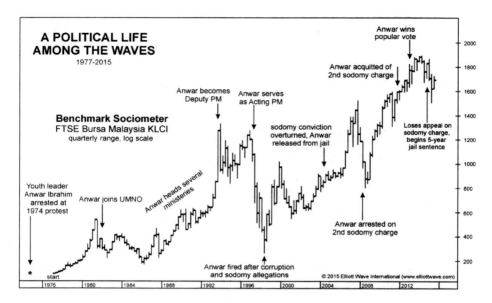

Figure 1

Monetary Fund. He implemented an austerity package that cut government spending by 18%, cut ministerial salaries, and curtailed many of the "mega projects" that Mahathir had championed. He rejected bailouts and encouraged foreign investment and trade liberalization, while Mahathir advocated currency controls and tighter regulation of foreign investment.

In mid-1998, negative mood finally led to a reversal of Anwar's fortunes. At the UMNO General Assembly, his enemies circulated copies of a book called "50 Reasons Why Anwar Cannot Become Prime Minister," which accused him of corruption and sodomy, which is illegal in Malaysia. Exactly one day after the 1998 bottom in the KLCI, Mahathir fired his former protégé. Anwar defended himself against the allegations, which he claimed were baseless and politically motivated, but he was convicted on both charges and sentenced to 15 years in prison.

The erstwhile insider was now once again an opposition leader. His supporters began circulating posters featuring a photo of Anwar with a black eye and one hand raised as an anti-establishment symbol. Anwar's wife won his former seat in parliament in 1999 as a member of an opposition party.

In 2004, as the KLCI surged higher during the 2002-2008 bull market, the Federal Court overturned Anwar's sodomy conviction. With time off for good behavior, he had already completed his sentence for corruption in 2003. But, under Malaysian law, former prisoners are banned from running for political office for five years after the end of their sentence. So any comeback would have to wait until 2008. He bided his time by developing relationships abroad and supporting opposition candidates.

The delay may have worked in Anwar's favor. Opposition candidates tend to fare best during periods of negative social mood, and in early 2008 the KLCI dropped 16% before the general election took place. Voters returned the ruling coalition to government but also handed it some of its largest losses ever. For instance, the coalition lost the two-thirds supermajority required to pass constitutional amendments. The opposition also won five of thirteen state legislatures, up from only one in the 2004 election. In August 2008, Anwar regained his old seat in parliament after defeating the ruling coalition candidate by a landslide.

His enemies did not sit by quietly. About a month earlier, an aide had filed a police report claiming that Anwar had sodomized him. The case dragged on so long—three and a half years—that when the High Court acquitted Anwar in January 2012, it caught observers off guard. Media worldwide described the decision as "unexpected" and "surprising," and they described those hearing the news as "disbelieving" and "perplexed." Even Anwar himself said, "To be honest, I am a little surprised." (BBC) His enemies had been so determined to silence him that most people thought he was certain to be convicted.

One reason for the leniency is that positive social mood had been waxing for more than three years as evidenced by a bull market in the KLCI. Other effects of positive social mood were evident: Prime Minister Najib Razak had rolled back some affirmative action programs that favored Malays, eliminated barriers to investment in certain industrial sectors, and outlined plans to reduce the influence of the government's investment funds. In September 2011, he announced that the government would abolish the Internal Security Act. He also said that newspapers and broadcasters would no longer be required to renew their licenses each year but could operate indefinitely, unless the licenses were expressly revoked.

In December 2011, we noted that the Malaysian government's introduction of a bill that would guarantee citizens freedom of assembly was a sign of positive mood in the nation. That same social mood prompted investors to bid Malaysia's stock market higher, nudged its society toward more freedom, and led to Anwar's acquittal.

Positive social mood continued to work in Anwar's favor. As the KLCI continued to rise, Anwar's party won the popular vote in the national election of 2013. This vote would have made Anwar the Prime Minister of Malaysia, except that a malapportionment of seats served to deny him power, leaving the ruling party in office by the skin of its teeth.

This technical quirk robbed Anwar of his socionomic reward. Nearly losing power for the first time in its history was a frightening experience for the ruling party, and so it determined to bury Anwar for good. A lower court overturned his sodomy acquittal in March 2014, two weeks before an election that would have made him the chief minister of the state that is the main economic hub around Kuala Lumpur. Anwar was allowed almost a year for appeal, but in that time social mood turned against him. In February 2015, in the midst of a 20% decline in the KLCI that year, Malaysia's top court upheld the lower court's decision to convict and sentence Anwar to five years in jail. He will also face a five-year ban from politics upon his release. Because Anwar is now 67 years old, the ten-year span effectively ends his political career—that is, unless positive social mood can manage once again to come to his aid.

Chapter 67

Mass Demonstrations in Hong Kong
Repeatedly Signal Stock Market Lows

Mark Galasiewski

October 31, 2014 (APFF)

Figure 1 is a graph of Hang Seng Index marked with all the major riots and demonstrations in Hong Kong compiled by Bloomberg in "Hong Kong's Cultural Revolution to Democracy Protests 1967-2014," which was published on October 1. Notice that after each incident, the index rallied persistently for at least two years.

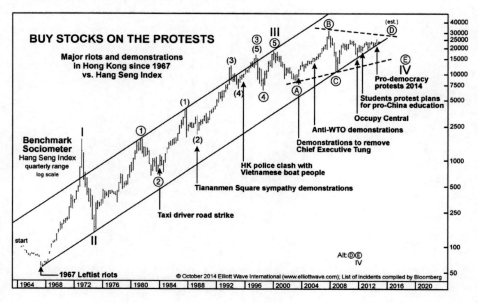

Figure 1

Only the first three incidents preceded significant further retrenchment in stock prices: (1) After the initial leftist riots in 1967, the index fell about 20% over several months before beginning a powerful bull market to the 1973 high. (2) Following the 1984 taxi-driver strike, the index initially rallied but then gave back those gains plus about 20% before beginning a strong bull market that carried to the 1987 high. (3) During the 1989 Tiananmen Square sympathy demonstrations, the index fell 27% before beginning a strong advance to the 1994 high. Still, in the context of what followed in each case, the preceding bouts of weakness were negligible.

The next five incidents marked negative mood extremes and led to stock market rallies almost immediately, each time after final slippage in index prices of less than 5%. Rises on the chart from the dates of the protests to the next labeled peaks range between 47% and 2200%.

The Bloomberg list names the pro-democracy march of July 1, 2014—the sixth incident noted on the chart—as the start of the latest rash of demonstrations. That signal is bullish but so far unproven.

Chapter 68

Conflict or Cooperation—
In North Korea, It's a Matter of Social Mood

Chuck Thompson

May 28, 2015 (TS)

To agree or not to agree? That is the continual question at the center of North Korea's foreign relations. Since the end of World War II, the so-called Hermit Kingdom has displayed sharply differing degrees of cooperation on the international stage. It has struck deals and reneged. It has shifted from conciliation to aggression and back again.

Might these actions be manifestations of social mood? In the November 2006 and June 2013 issues of *The Elliott Wave Financial Forecast*, Peter Kendall found that tension between the U.S. and North Korea has tended to escalate near negative extremes in U.S. social mood and to recede near positive extremes.[1,2]

Anticipating the tone of North Korea's engagement with other countries is important because, as Kendall pointed out, "Tension is basically a fixture of North Korea's foreign relations."[3] The country is authoritarian, insular, isolated and armed with nuclear weapons. It is noted for conducting "routine missile tests,"[4] detaining Westerners,[5] "making dramatic yet empty threats"[6] and clashing with its neighbor, South Korea.

In this article, we focus on the history of North Korea's diplomatic relations. We find that during periods of positive social mood, the country is considerably more willing to engage in dialogues with other countries and to reach international agreements. During periods of negative social mood, it is considerably more inclined to break off dialogues with other countries and to withdraw from international agreements.

In Search of a Sociometer

Socionomic analysis of North Korea is difficult due to the absence of a national stock market. The country's opaqueness has resulted in scant availability of sociometers of any kind. In his studies of tension between the U.S. and North Korea, Kendall looked at the history with respect to social mood on the U.S. side of the relationship, using the Dow Jones Industrial Average as his sociometer. Mark Galasiewski, writing in *The Asian-Pacific Financial Forecast,* sought to understand the mood on the North Korean side by employing South Korea's benchmark sociometer, the KOSPI, as a proxy for mood on the Korean Peninsula. We follow these conventions in this article, using the Dow Jones Industrial Average to contextualize America's posture toward North Korea and the KOSPI to contextualize North Korea's posture toward the rest of the world.

Sociometers measure actions taken in response to changes in social mood; we cannot measure social mood itself. The result is that, "unlike a thermometer, they are not perfect gauges of what they attempt to measure, which is the underlying social mood."[7] This imperfection becomes more pronounced as we move from measuring the actions of people in a country to measuring the actions of people in other countries as a proxy for those of the people in the country of interest. Nevertheless, since diplomatic engagement is necessarily a multilateral process, available sociometers should be sufficient to account for the tone of North Korea's foreign relations.

Early History

The socionomic roots of North Korea's history reach all the way back to the nation's founding. Following World War II and the end of the Japanese occupation of Korea, Soviet troops occupied the northern half of the country while U.S. troops occupied the south. In May 1948, South Korea elected a national assembly, which adopted a constitution that established a representative government. On August 15, 1948, the Republic of Korea (South Korea) was formed. On September 8, the communist Democratic People's Republic of Korea (North Korea) was established under Premier Kim Il Sung, who claimed authority over the entire Korean Peninsula. In June 1950, Kim's forces invaded South Korea, launching the Korean War.[8] As Kendall observed,[9] this conflict, which involved South Korea, the U.S., the U.K. and a U.N. alliance on one side and North Korea, China and the Soviet Union on the other, occurred near the end of a 20-year bear market pattern in the PPI-adjusted Dow, a reasonable proxy for global social mood absent other measures.

Since the war, and in response to U.S. threats to use nuclear weapons against it, North Korea has pushed to build its own nuclear arsenal. In 1952, North Korea created an institute and an academy to facilitate nuclear research. Four years later, it began sending scientists and technicians to the

Soviet Union for training in nuclear engineering.[10] The effort culminated in the Yongbyon Nuclear Scientific Research Center, North Korea's major nuclear research facility.[11]

Social Mood Has Regulated North Korea's Stance Toward Nuclear Weapons

In 1980, the KOSPI entered a sideways trend that would last five years. At the beginning of this negative mood period, North Korea secretly purchased Soviet R-17 (SCUD-B) missiles in Egypt. It reverse-engineered the missiles and began to produce simplified copies. It attempted to use the technology to build long-range missiles that could carry nuclear warheads, a step that would establish it as a major nuclear threat.[12]

The KOSPI began rising in 1985, and North Korea swiftly changed its stance. It joined the international Treaty on the Non-Proliferation of Nuclear Weapons (NPT), which required the country to halt nuclear weapons development and pursue only peaceful uses of nuclear technology. North Korea abided by the NPT throughout the remainder of the positive mood period that supported the 1980s bull market.

In the early 1990s, mood turned negative both in the U.S. and on the Korean Peninsula. Relations grew tense as U.S. concerns over North Korea's nuclear program escalated. On March 12, 1993, North Korea announced that it would withdraw from the NPT. The announcement came within ten days of an intermediate low in the KOSPI, as shown in Figure 1.

Three rounds of intense bilateral negotiations with the U.S. ensued during a time of new all-time highs in the Dow and a three-month rally in the KOSPI. With the mood trend inclining both sides toward a settlement, North Korea reversed its decision to withdraw from the NPT on June 11. That date was within five days of the peak of the KOSPI's rally and a day before the withdrawal would have taken effect.[13]

The "Agreed Framework" Caps a Positive Mood Trend

On February 15, 1994, North Korea formalized an agreement with the International Atomic Energy Agency (IAEA) to allow inspections of all seven of its declared nuclear facilities. If you guessed that the agreement came near a high in the KOSPI, you are correct (see Figure 1). But a few months later, North Korea got cold feet and threatened to withdraw from the IAEA. Both the pullback in the KOSPI and the accompanying threat were short-lived, and North Korea agreed to freeze its nuclear weapons program.[14] After the KOSPI blasted upward in a continuation of a powerful bull market, the U.S. and North Korea came back to the negotiating table on July 8, 1994

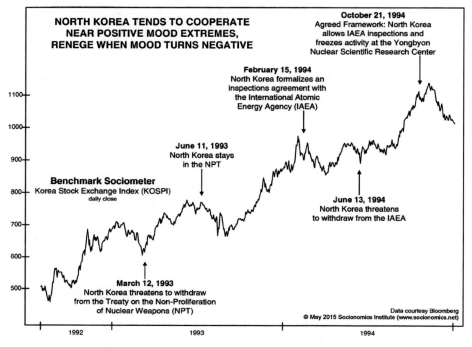

Figure 1

to begin talks on what would come to be known as the Agreed Framework. North Korea finally pledged to freeze all activity at Yongbyon and allow IAEA inspections at the site. In return, the U.S. promised to provide North Korea with two light-water reactors and 500,000 tons of heavy fuel oil per year.[15] A positive mood motivated both parties; the document was signed on October 21, with the Dow hovering near all-time highs and the KOSPI undergoing the final thrust of its bull market.

In the November 1994 issue of *The Elliott Wave Theorist*, Robert Prechter noted, "the idea of a pact between the U.S. and North Korea has been unthinkable for 40 years, until now."[16] Three months later, the first shipload of U.S. oil arrived, marking the first time since 1949 that a U.S. merchant ship had entered one of North Korea's ports.[17] Regarding the Agreed Framework, Galasiewski wrote, "The Clinton Administration took credit for the achievement. But followers of the Wave Principle also recognized the deal as a sign of a major peak in social mood."[18]

Following the Agreed Framework, the U.S. seemed to have every reason to be politically ambitious in the pursuit of further concessions from North

Korea. After all, the countries had hammered out a major deal that just two years prior would have been unimaginable. By the mid-1990s, social mood in the U.S. was in the middle of a positive trend that ushered in the dot-com boom and the decade's most intense years of financial mania. In this environment of soaring confidence and optimism, U.S. negotiators invited North Korean leaders back to the table in 1996 in an effort to control the latter country's production and sale of ballistic missile systems, components and technology.

There was, however, a problem. The KOSPI was mired in a downtrend that would eventually erase 75% of the index's value, indicating that mood on the Korean Peninsula had turned negative. As a result, the two sides were unable to reach an agreement when they met in Berlin in April 1996. Six more rounds of U.S.-North Korea missile talks took place between June 1997 and November 2000, and all but two of the meetings were held during declines in the KOSPI. None of the talks produced an agreement.[19] In 2000, the U.S. stock market joined the KOSPI in the downward trend. The condition of negative mood in both countries prompted both sides to abandon further attempts to reach a deal.

The trend toward negative social mood on the Korean Peninsula—and indeed around the globe—persisted into early 2003. In the midst of this environment, in July 2002, reports surfaced of a barter deal under which Pakistan would deliver technology to North Korea that it could use to enrich uranium (see Figure 2).[20] In mid-October, North Korea admitted to having a plan to enrich uranium for nuclear weapons.

In December, as negative mood on the Korean Peninsula drove the KOSPI toward its low for the bear market, North Korea ordered IAEA nuclear inspectors to leave the country[21] and lifted the freeze on its nuclear facilities that had been in effect since 1994.[22] The next month, North Korea announced that it would withdraw from the non-proliferation treaty. The withdrawal officially went into effect in April 2003, just one month after major bottoms in the KOSPI and the World Stock Index [see Figure 1 in Chapter 77], making North Korea the first country to leave the NPT in the treaty's three-decade history.[23]

At that time, efforts to monitor and control North Korea's nuclear program seemed to be in jeopardy. But social mood turned positive, sending the KOSPI on its longest upward run since the 1990s as the index more than quadrupled from 2003 to 2007. During this time, from August 27, 2003 to February 13, 2007, North Korea participated in five rounds of talks with China, Japan, Russia, South Korea and the U.S. on the topic of ending North Korea's nuclear program. Unlike the unproductive U.S.-North Korea missile talks in the late 1990s, these Six-Party Talks were held during rises

Figure 2

in nearly all of the participants' benchmark sociometers. (China's Shanghai Composite Index was in decline when the talks began, but it eventually had a net rise more than 99% over the course of the negotiations.)

The political outcome is a testament to the difference that a positive trend in social mood makes in fostering agreement. On September 19, 2005, the six parties adopted a "Statement of Principles" defining steps toward the denuclearization of the Korean Peninsula. North Korea committed to abandoning all nuclear weapons, returning to the NPT and allowing IAEA inspections. The other nations acknowledged North Korea's right to peaceful uses of nuclear energy. In addition, they agreed to discuss providing a light water reactor to North Korea "at an appropriate time."[24]

The productive talks took a detour in early October 2006, when North Korea detonated a nuclear device in a weapons test. Reports surfaced that the country's leader, Kim Jong-il, had apologized for the test later in the month, though officials at the U.S. State Department remained dubious that an apology was ever issued.[25] Because the trend in mood for both countries was still positive, not even a betrayal of this magnitude could stop them from meeting for a fifth round of talks in mid-December. In follow-up meetings held in February 2007, North Korea agreed to cease operations at Yongbyon in return for an initial shipment of 50,000 tons of heavy fuel oil.[26] On June 27, 2008, North Korea demolished the cooling tower at Yongbyon.[27]

The demolition occurred shortly after the peak of a strong rebound in the KOSPI. But, like many stock indexes around the globe, the KOSPI was already on its way down in expressing what would prove to be one of the severest negative mood trends in decades.

In December 2008, the KOSPI registered its low for the bear market. An attempted sixth round of Six-Party Talks collapsed amidst negative mood in all six countries. North Korea announced that it would participate in no further talks and would increase its nuclear efforts, including uranium enrichment.[28]

In March 2009 (see Figure 3), the very month of a major low in many stock indexes around the world and a smaller-degree low in the KOSPI, North Korea—much as it had done near the stock market bottom of 2003—expelled IAEA and U.S. nuclear inspectors and started rebuilding its Yongbyon reactor.[29] It also detained a South Korean technician[30] and two American journalists.[31] Two months later, North Korea announced that it had detonated another nuclear device in a weapons test.[32]

By August, the KOSPI had rallied substantially, and North Korea expressed its more positive mood by welcoming former president Bill Clinton to the country and releasing the detained technician and American journalists. Galasiewski wrote in the September 2009 issue of *The Asian-Pacific Financial Forecast*, "As we see it, thanks to a positive trend in social mood, North Korea's leader Kim Jong-il was willing to let [the detainees] go in exchange for Clinton's visit."[33]

The advance from the December 2008 low in the KOSPI reached its peak in May 2011. Since then, the index has gone sideways. Reflecting the mixed mood behind this trend, the tone of North Korea's foreign relations has been primarily tense and combative, though a handful of positive manifestations have materialized, as noted in Figure 3.

As this review demonstrates, North Korea's greatest periods of cooperation with other nations have tended to occur when the best available benchmark sociometer, the KOSPI, is moving upward, indicating that social mood is trending positively. Conversely, North Korea tends to be more prone toward resistance and conflict when the KOSPI is moving sideways or downward, indicating that social mood is trending negatively.

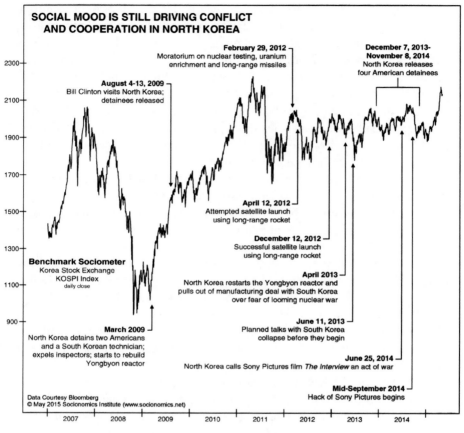

Figure 3

Outlook

What can these insights tell us about the future? To answer that question, let's first consider North Korea's present strategic position. The country's nuclear capabilities continue to increase, making it a growing threat to its enemies. In a closed-door meeting with U.S. nuclear specialists, Chinese officials estimated that North Korea may already have 20 nuclear warheads and the capability to double its nuclear arsenal by 2016.[34] North Korea has 1,000 ballistic missiles,[35] and a March 29 article noted that it may secretly be storing nuclear weapons for Iran.[36] A North Korean official recently said the country has the missile capability to strike the U.S. and would do so if U.S. officials "forced their hand."[37]

Furthermore, Russia has been strengthening its relationship with North Korea. Russian President Vladimir Putin canceled $10 billion in North Korean debt, and the two nations are planning military exercises for the first time in decades.[38] The Russian Foreign Ministry has designated 2015 as a "Year of Friendship" with North Korea,[39] and the two countries have signed an agreement to build a new connecting road.[40]

On the other hand, North Korea "faces chronic economic problems." Its industrial capital stock is "nearly beyond repair." Its massive military spending has devoured resources needed for investment and civilian consumption.[41] On more than one occasion, the U.S. has been able to use North Korea's economic needs as a bargaining chip, although Russia could alleviate some of those needs.

The bottom line is that with North Korea's growing weapons capability, its deepening partnership with Russia, and the worsening relations between Russia and the West, the groundwork is set for North Korea to be a more serious threat should social mood turn strongly negative both in the West and on the Korean Peninsula.

On the other hand, if social mood on the peninsula turns positive and the KOSPI turns upward from its four-year sideways trend while the Dow continues to trend higher, the socionomic window of opportunity for productive official dialogue between the two countries would probably re-open, at least until a downtrend resumed in either sociometer. If both countries' sociometers were to fall, tensions would surely escalate into belligerent actions.

Historically, however, the notion of "productive dialogue" with regard to North Korea is transient at best and an oxymoron at worst. Promises forged in the euphoria of positive social mood have melted away in the blink of an eye when mood has turned negative. As we've seen from our review, it is much easier to forecast the character of political actions using a sociometer than for such actions actually to achieve anything of lasting value.

[On a hopeful note, the trend toward positive social mood globally over the past 30 years has led to the softening, if not the dismantling, of most of the world's communist regimes, including those of China, Russia, Eastern Europe, Vietnam and Cuba. It is possible that the trend toward positive social mood of Grand Supercycle degree still evident in U.S. sociometers will have just enough influence to bring some liberalization, or perhaps even an end, to the last bastion of hardline communism, North Korea. If it fails to do so, armed conflict will become highly likely near the next major extreme in negative social mood.—Ed.]

NOTES AND REFERENCES

[1] Hochberg, S., & Kendall, P. (2006, November 3). Cultural Trends. *The Elliott Wave Financial Forecast*.

[2] Hochberg, S., & Kendall, P. (2013, May 31). Cultural Trends. *The Elliott Wave Financial Forecast*.

[3] Hochberg, S., & Kendall, P. (2006, November 3). Cultural Trends. *The Elliott Wave Financial Forecast*.

[4] North Korea Tested Two Missiles, Says S Korean Ministry. (2007, June 8). *Taipei Times*.

[5] Jones, L. (2015, March 6). Canadian Pastor Detained in North Korea. *World*.

[6] Saccone, L. Joke's Over: North Korea Preparing to Launch Missiles. *Daily Lounge*.

[7] Prechter, R. (2004, September 17). Data Inexactness and Relativity. *The Elliott Wave Theorist*.

[8] South Korea Under United States Occupation, 1945-48. U.S. Library of Congress.

[9] Hochberg, S., & Kendall, P. (2006, November 3). Cultural Trends. *The Elliott Wave Financial Forecast*.

[10] North Korea. (2014, November). The Nuclear Threat Initiative.

[11] Tanner, A. (1994, June 22). Russia: Korea Could Build Bomb. *The Moscow Times*.

[12] Lankov, A. (2015, March 26). North Korea and Nukes: It's Not All Bluff. *Al Jazeera*.

[13] North Korea. (2014, November). The Nuclear Threat Initiative.

[14] Chronology of U.S.-North Korean Nuclear and Missile Diplomacy. (2015, February). Arms Control Association.

[15] Agreed Framework: United States and North Korea. (2014, September 7). *Encyclopedia Britannica*.

[16] Prechter, R. (1994, November 1). Cultural Trends: More Political Inclusion. *The Elliott Wave Theorist*.

[17] Prechter, R. (1995, February 1). Fruits of the Long Bull Market. *The Elliott Wave Theorist*.

[18] Galasiewski, M. (2009, August 28). Cultural Trends: Playing Hide and Seek With North Korea. *The Asian-Pacific Financial Forecast*.

[19] Chronology of U.S.-North Korean Nuclear and Missile Diplomacy. (2015, February). Arms Control Association.

[20] Pinkston, D.A. (2002). Collapse of the Agreed Framework? Center for Nonproliferation Studies.

[21] Chronology of U.S.-North Korean Nuclear and Missile Diplomacy. (2015, February). Arms Control Association.

[22] North Korea. (2014, November). The Nuclear Threat Initiative.

[23] Du Preez, J., & Potter, W. (2003, April 10). North Korea's Withdrawal From the NPT: A Reality Check. CNS. James Martin Center for Nonproliferation Studies.

[24] The Six-Party Talks at a Glance. (2012, May). Arms Control Association.

[25] Report: Kim "Sorry" About N. Korea Nuclear Test. (2006, October 20). *NBC News.*

[26] Chronology of U.S.-North Korean Nuclear and Missile Diplomacy. (2015, February). Arms Control Association.

[27] Associated Press. (2008, June 27). North Korea Destroys Nuclear Reactor's Cooling Tower. *Fox News.*

[28] Timeline on North Korea's Nuclear Program. (2014, November 20). *The New York Times.*

[29] North Korea. (2014, November). The Nuclear Threat Initiative.

[30] N. Korea Releases South Employee After Hyundai Chief Visit. (2009, August 13). *International Business Times.*

[31] Kessler, G. (2009, August 5). During Visit by Bill Clinton, North Korea Releases American Journalists. *The Washington Post.*

[32] North Korea Conducts Nuclear Test. (2009, May 25). *BBC News.*

[33] Galasiewski, M. (2009, August 28). Cultural Trends: Playing Hide and Seek with North Korea. *The Asian-Pacific Financial Forecast.*

[34] Page, J., & Solomon, J. (2015, April 22). China Warns North Korean Nuclear Threat is Rising. *The Wall Street Journal.*

[35] North Korea's Nuclear Expansion. (2015, February 27). *The New York Times.*

[36] Chang, G.G. (2015, March 29). Does Iran Have Secret Nukes in North Korea? *The Daily Beast.*

[37] Ripley, W., & Schwarz, T. (2015, May 7). Exclusive: North Korea Would Use Nukes If "Forced," Official Says. CNN.

[38] Jackson, V. (2015, February 22). Putin and the Hermit Kingdom. *Foreign Affairs.*

[39] Herszenhorn, D.M. (2015, March 11). Western Relations Frosty, Russia Warms to North Korea. *The New York Times.*

[40] Rivituso, C. (2015, April 16). North Korea, Russia Sign Road Connection Deal. NK News.org.

[41] North Korea. The World Factbook. CIA.

[42] Fifield, A. (2015, February 2). U.S. and North Korea Have Been Secretly Discussing Having "Talks About Talks." *The Washington Post.*

[43] Toosi, N. (2015, May 6). Barack Obama's True Nuclear Test: North Korea. *Politico.* Retrieved from http://www.politico.com/story/2015/05/barack-obamas-true-nuclear-test-north-korea-117651.html

Chapter 69

Tension Growing in South China Sea

Chuck Thompson

Aptil 29, 2016 (TS)

The South China Sea is one of the world's most contested regions. This body of water is subject to competing territorial claims by China, Vietnam, the Philippines, Brunei, Malaysia, Taiwan and, most recently, Indonesia. Though social mood is trending positively in many of these nations, a trend toward negative mood in China, which claims more than 80% of the Sea's territory, is fueling conflict.

China's benchmark sociometer—the Shanghai Composite index—reflects the country's trend toward negative mood. The index is 41% below its June 2015 high and 50% below its 2007 all-time high. China's negative mood is also evident in its flagging economy and escalating authoritarianism.

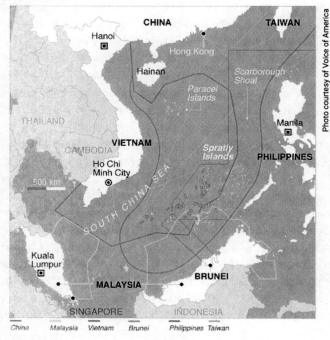

It's Mine: Claims of various countries on the South China Sea

In recent years, China has seized many areas of the South China Sea that had been claimed by other nations. In 2012, it took the uninhabited Scarborough Shoal from the Philippines. In 2014, China towed an oil rig to the mouth of the Gulf of Tonkin, off the eastern coast of Vietnam.[1]

China has also used dredging to build up 3,000 acres of artificial islands within disputed waters, where it has constructed runways for military aircraft and deep harbors for naval ships. In February, China placed a missile system on Woody Island, the largest of the Paracel Islands.[2] James R. Clapper, President Obama's director of national intelligence, said in February that by early next year, China will "have significant capacity to quickly project substantial military power to the region."[3]

Many of the countries involved in the territorial disputes over the South China Sea are boosting their defenses in response to China's expansion efforts. Fearing that China could take over its entire western coast, leaders of the Philippines are thinking about acquiring their first-ever submarine fleet. In addition, they have ordered two anti-submarine helicopters.[4]

In March, the Philippines opened the door for the U.S. military to set up bases on its territory for the first time since 1991. A total of five bases are planned.[5] In early April, 5,000 U.S. troops took part in a military exercise with troops from the Philippines.[6] At the same time, a Japanese submarine made its first port call to the Philippines in 15 years—a sign of increased military cooperation between the two countries.[7] Japan is involved in its own dispute with China over the Senkaku Islands in the East China Sea, where ships from the two countries regularly tail each other.[8]

On March 31, China's defense ministry criticized the U.S.-Philippines partnership and suggested that U.S. ships in the area "be careful."[9] China's President, Xi Jinping, told President Obama that he would not accept American actions in the South China Sea under the "disguise of freedom of navigation."[10]

China has built up Subi Reef, where it has begun work on a combat-capable air facility. Now it is using the United States' involvement in the South China Sea as justification for a plan to start reclamation work at Scarborough Shoal before the end of this year. A spokesperson for China's navy told the *South China Morning Post* that his country needs to "regain the initiative." He accused Washington of "trying to contain Beijing by establishing a permanent military presence in the region."

This month, foreign ministers from the Group of Seven leading economies (G-7) criticized Beijing's actions in the South China Sea. Malcolm Davis, a senior analyst at the Australian Strategic Policy Institute, said, "The G-7 is going through the motions of making it clear to China that if they do something more there will be a cost to bear."[11]

The Philippines has asked the Permanent Court of Arbitration in The Hague to declare China's sea claims illegal. The court is likely to issue a ruling within the next three months. China is expected to lose some elements of the case, but time will tell if it accepts the ruling or bucks the international legal system.[12] If China's social mood becomes more negative, the country could escalate its assertive territorial claims and expansion efforts.

At the moment, social mood is positive in the U.S. and in most of the countries involved in the disputes with China over the South China Sea. As shown in Figure 1, the stock market indexes of four of these countries (Malaysia, Indonesia, the Philippines and the U.S.) reached all-time closing highs in the past two years.

Tensions in the area are high, but the potential for conflict is moderated by the "agreeableness and forbearance" that comes from positive social mood in the majority of the region's countries and in the U.S. If social mood turns negative in these countries, antagonism and anger will replace agreeableness and forbearance. As a result, mere verbal conflict could morph into physical clashes.

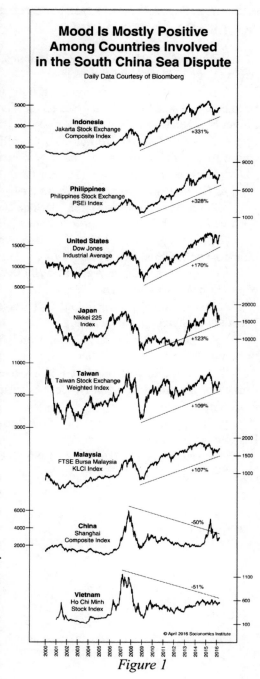

Mood Is Mostly Positive Among Countries Involved in the South China Sea Dispute

Daily Data Courtesy of Bloomberg

Indonesia
Jakarta Stock Exchange
Composite Index
+331%

Philippines
Philippines Stock Exchange
PSEi Index
+328%

United States
Dow Jones
Industrial Average
+170%

Japan
Nikkei 225
Index
+123%

Taiwan
Taiwan Stock Exchange
Weighted Index
+109%

Malaysia
FTSE Bursa Malaysia
KLCI Index
+107%

China
Shanghai
Composite Index
-50%

Vietnam
Ho Chi Minh
Stock Index
-51%

© April 2016 Socionomics Institute

Figure 1

NOTES AND REFERENCES

[1] Panda, A. (2014, August 27). Indonesia Keeps an Eye on the Natuna Archipelago. *The Diplomat*.

[2] Tomlinson, L., & Frilling, Y. (2016, April 12). Chinese Fighter Jets Seen on Contested South China Sea Island, Evidence of Beijing's Latest Bold Move. Fox News.

[3] Cooper, H. (2016, March 30). Patrolling Disputed Waters, U.S. and China Jockey for Dominance. *The New York Times*.

[4] Agence France-Presse. (2016, March 31). Philippines Mulls Submarines as China Row Simmers. *Defense News*.

[5] Tilghman, A. (2016, March 21). The US Military is Moving into These 5 Bases in the Philippines. *Military Times*.

[6] Johnson, K., & De Luce, D. (2016, April 7). Fishing Disputes Could Spark a South China Sea Crisis. *Foreign Policy*.

[7] Coughlin, C. (2016, April 8). Why the South China Sea Could Be the Next Global Flashpoint. *The Telegraph*.

[8] Sharp, A. (2016, April 11). G-7 Raises South China Sea Territorial Disputes in Statement. Bloomberg.

[9] Agence France-Presse. (2016, March 31). China to US: "Be Careful" in South China Sea. *Yahoo! News*.

[10] Tomkiw, L. (2016, March 31). Obama-Xi Meeting Update: South China Sea Tension Looms at Nuclear Security Summit. *International Business Times*.

[11] Sharp, A. (2016, April 11). G-7 Raises South China Sea Territorial Disputes in Statement. Bloomberg.

[12] Rosenfeld, E. (2016, April 6). South China Sea: Is Beijing Making a New "Strategic Strait"? CNBC.

Part VIII:

*POT, POTTERY, PUNISHMENT
AND 'POLOGIES*

Chapter 70

The Coming Collapse of Modern Prohibition

Euan Wilson

July 5, 2009 (TS)

History shows that social mood governs society's tolerance for recreational drugs. A trend toward positive mood prompts the prohibition of substances such as alcohol and marijuana; a trend toward negative mood prompts tolerance and relaxed regulation.

In the U.S., alcohol prohibition lasted from 1920 until 1933, ending in an environment of extremely negative social mood. We predict a similar fate for the prohibition of marijuana if not the entire War on Drugs. The March 1995 *Elliott Wave Theorist* first forecasted the Drug War's repeal at the end of the next major bear market, and in October 2003 EWT stated, "The drug war will turn more violent. Eventually, possession and sale of recreational drugs will be decriminalized."

Social mood influences people's actions and their moral judgments. As proposed in "Popular Culture and the Stock Market" (1985) (reprinted in *Pioneering Studies in Socionomics,* 2003), people prefer black-and-white moral stances during positive mood periods, and they have the resources to enforce their moral views. Recreational drug use is a favorite target.

During times of negative mood, society's priorities change. People have other, bigger worries and begin to view recreational drugs as less dangerous, if not innocuous.

Over the past century, governmental actions have reflected those changing attitudes. During periods of positive mood, policymakers have stepped up regulation of cannabis. During periods of negative mood, they have eased restrictions.

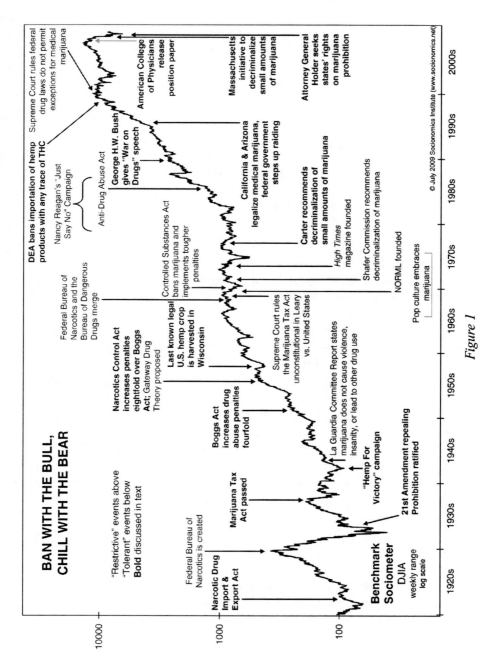

Figure 1

Positive Social Mood Prompts Restrictions on Marijuana Use

As shown in Figure 1, each attempt to restrict marijuana use by law followed three or more years of positive social mood as indicated by a rising stock market. In 1937, at a peak of positive mood after the Dow Jones Industrial Average had quintupled from its 1932 low, Congress passed the Marijuana Tax Act. The law banned casual consumption of the drug and limited its use to specific medical and industrial purposes. The real crackdown, however, came over a decade later during the extended wave of positive mood from 1942 to 1966. The Boggs Act of 1952, which increased drug-use penalties fourfold, and the Narcotic Control Act of 1956, which increased penalties another eightfold, both came during the strongest portion of the trend toward positive mood. In 1958, after two more years of positive mood, Wisconsin farmers harvested the last legal crop of U.S.-grown hemp. In 1989, President George H.W. Bush's famous "War on Drugs" speech came on the heels of seven years of net rise in the stock market. In 1999, the year of the all-time high in the Dow/gold ratio, the DEA banned the importation of hemp products that contained even a trace of tetrahydrocannabinol (THC), marijuana's psychoactive ingredient.

Negative Social Mood Fosters Tolerance for Marijuana Use

During negative mood periods, pot users have enjoyed liberal social tolerance. Figure 1 illustrates that during bear markets in stocks the government has tended to allow—and in some cases to encourage—the growing of marijuana. In the final year of the negative mood period of 1937-1942, Congress launched its "Hemp for Victory" campaign to encourage farmers to grow the crop for industrial purposes related to the war effort. According to *The Wall Street Journal*, farmers planted over 50,000 acres of hemp in 1942 and 240,000 acres in 1943. In 1977, eleven years into a sixteen-year trend toward negative mood as indicated by a bear market in the Dow/PPI, President Carter recommended that Congress legalize possession of small quantities of marijuana.

An exception occurred in 1996, when, during a historic bull market, California and Arizona voted to allow the use of marijuana for medical purposes. But the federal government remained consistent with positive social mood by stepping up its raids on marijuana facilities in the states where it was legalized. As *The New York Times* reported, federal lawyers wrenched convictions from juries who were denied the information that the drug dispensaries were legal in those states.

In 2008, as U.S. sociometers plunged more than at any time since the 1930s, Massachusetts' voters passed an initiative that decriminalized the possession of small amounts of marijuana, and Michigan's voters passed a law permitting the use of medical marijuana. On June 29, 2009, [the month of the Great Recession's end,] Oregon's House of Representatives passed a bill in favor of licensing hemp farming. Barring a veto, Oregon will be the sixth state this year to pass pro-hemp legislation. So far, in keeping with the negative mood, the feds have chosen not to interfere in these initiatives.

In February 2009, just a month before the recent stock market low, U.S. Attorney General Eric Holder announced his view that states should make their own rules on medical marijuana use and that federal raids on pot dispensaries should cease. In June, Congressman Barney Frank introduced two pieces of marijuana-related legislation, the first allowing states to pass medical cannabis laws without interference from the federal government and the second eliminating federal penalties for possessing 100 grams of pot or less (but adding a fine of $100 for public consumption). Frank had filed a similar bill last year that failed. We expect the current legislation to fail, too, as the period of negative mood has been too brief to inspire Congress to take such measures. But bills similar to Frank's will gain traction when social mood resumes its negative trend.

Private-sector groups are already proposing tolerance. In 2008, the prestigious American College of Physicians, the largest medical specialty organization and the second-largest physician group in the U.S., released a position paper urging the government to remove marijuana from its Schedule 1 classification, which the drug has held for 38 years. S1 is a classification reserved for drugs that the government considers to have no medical uses and to possess a "very high potential for abuse." The recent cry for reclassification from such a recognized body is a prime example of how changes in social mood modify attitudes toward recreational drugs.

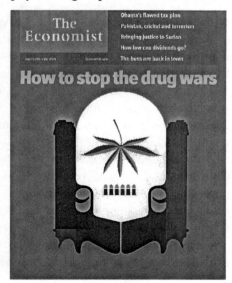

A number of critics of the War on Drugs have emerged in the media. CNN's Jack Cafferty posted an article in late March 2009 titled,

"War on Drugs is Insane." The same month, *The Economist* declared, "Prohibition has failed; legalization is the least bad solution." And in June, CNN aired Anderson Cooper's special report, "America's High: The Case For and Against Pot." Whenever social mood becomes even more negative and bloodshed increases, specials such as CNN's will drop the "and Against" from their titles.

Prohibition as a Model for the Drug War

As the saying goes, "History doesn't repeat, but it does rhyme." The Wave Principle explains why.

Alcohol prohibition began in 1920 and was maintained throughout the time the stock market was rising. Then came the 1929-1932 stock market collapse and the resulting economic depression, which bottomed in 1933. Three years of negatively trending social mood prompted the repeal of Prohibition one year after the 1932 low and the very year the Great Depression reached its nadir. Similarly, marijuana prohibition intensified in the 1980s and 1990s as stocks rose, and it persists nine years after the stock market top of 2000. This persistence speaks to the smaller size of the setback to date. Governments typically respond to social mood trends very late. So, our ideal socionomic scenario is for the Drug War's ultimate end to occur just after an upcoming major low, as approximated in Figure 2.

The Players and the Game

Today, in the deserts and border towns of Mexico, the west-based Sinaloa cartel and the east-based Gulf cartel are fighting modern versions of the 1920s North Side–South Side Chicago gang wars. The Sinaloa cartel's leader, Joaquin "El Chapo" Guzman, is practically the reincarnation of his Chicago mob boss predecessor, Al Capone. Guzman exhibits many of Capone's brazen, violent and charismatic traits. Both men are famed for their "hands on" management style and lionized for their sense of communal responsibility. Capone is rumored to have insisted on top-dollar medical treatment for a mother and son injured in the crossfire of a gangland firefight. Guzman purchases meals for fellow diners when he eats in restaurants. Both men became extraordinarily wealthy. At his peak, Capone earned $100 million a year, controlled all 10,000 speakeasies in Chicago and ran bootlegging operations from Illinois to Florida. In March 2009, *Forbes* named Guzman the 701st wealthiest man in the world, with assets over $1 billion, and noted that he practically runs the Mexican states of Sinaloa and Chihuahua. Guzman has echoed and surpassed Capone's propensity

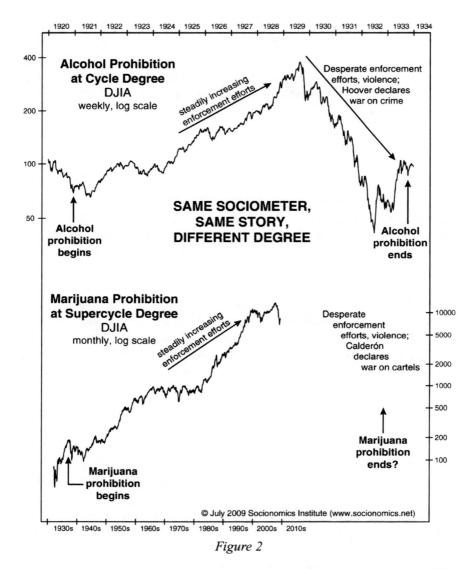

Figure 2

for violence. Hundreds of gangsters died nationwide during Capone's reign in Chicago, while hundreds die every *month* in Guzman's conflicts. The difference is another reflection of the larger degree of prohibition's modern incarnation.

Much as in Chicago in the 1930s, most of today's clashes among drug lords in Mexico are fights to control territory, product availability and distribution. Chicago's gangsters fought over docks to receive shipments from Canada and to keep their speakeasies safe. Mexico's cartels have developed advanced tunnel systems and mobile landing strips and have even attempted smuggling via submarine. Vast distribution networks crisscross the U.S., from Atlanta to Los Angeles to Seattle to New York. According to a March 2009 *USA Today* article,

> Rival drug cartels, the same violent groups warring in Mexico for control of routes to lucrative U.S. markets, have established Atlanta as the principal distribution center for the entire eastern U.S., according to the Justice Department's National Drug Intelligence Center. The same folks who are rolling heads in the streets of Ciudad Juárez… are operating in Atlanta. Here, they are just better behaved.

Drug runners' behavior, however, will probably worsen when negative mood deepens. Drug-related hostility is already beginning to plague Phoenix, where kidnaping and murder are on the rise. So far, most of the attackers have targeted Mexican immigrants, but their focus is likely to broaden.

Organized crime uses many tools to stay active, and corrupting government officials is one of their favorites. Capone bribed city officials and threatened witnesses in order to evade trial. Pablo Escobar described the options he offers as "Silver or Lead." It is alleged that Guzman corrupted the officials of his prison so completely that even the warden was aware of his plans to escape in 2001 and did nothing to interfere. Interpol arrested its own chief agent in Mexico in late 2008 on suspicions of ties to the drug cartels, while the Mexican government arrested its anti-organized-crime chief as well as Mexico City's police commissioner. In the waning days of Prohibition, corruption within the Chicago police force was so ubiquitous that the FBI formed The Untouchables to fight both the gangsters and the corrupt cops. The Untouchables were an elite squad of eleven men who, for the two-plus years of the squad's existence, refused to be bought or intimidated. We doubt the current war will bring a new version of the squad, but if it does, its existence will likely be as brief and ineffective as that of its predecessor.

Corruption is but one half of Escobar's "Silver or Lead" option for dealing with authorities. Murder works, too. The Center for International Policy reports that the two largest Mexican drug cartels boast a combined 100,000 foot soldiers. Deaths from the fighting on both sides of the border reached 6,800 last year. This year, more than 1,000 people are already dead from drug violence in the city of Juárez alone.

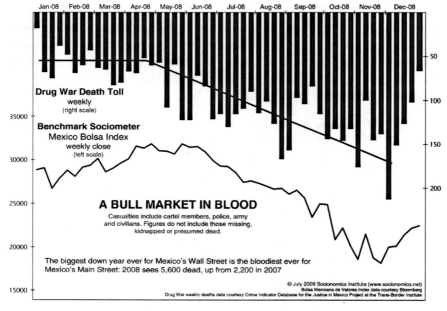

Figure 3

Figure 3 shows weekly Drug War deaths in 2008 and social mood as reflected by our benchmark sociometer for Mexico, the Bolsa Index. As mood trended negatively over the year, the number of drug-related murders increased. Reuters reported that January 2009 was the bloodiest month since December 2006, the month in which Mexican president Felipe Calderón mimicked FBI Director J. Edgar Hoover's 1931 declaration of war on crime by declaring war on the cartels.

Killing law enforcement officials is rampant today among cartel members in Mexico. In December 2008, Sinaloa members kidnapped, tortured and decapitated eight off-duty police officers, including a commander. Two months later, cartel members led a prison riot that left twenty people dead. In April 2009, allies of the Gulf cartel killed eight police officers in an attack on a prison convoy carrying Gulf leaders. Cartels became increasingly violent as social mood became more negative.

Since the Mexican stock market's low in March, the violence has ebbed somewhat, reflecting the positive mood behind the rebound. Whenever mood and the market resume their negative trends, violence will re-escalate. We expect drug runners to target non-corrupt American police officers, commanders, judges and public officials for kidnaping and outright murder.

Negative Mood Sponsors Violence Beyond the Drug Trade

As negative mood reached an extreme in the early 1930s, the wave of violence in America jumped beyond the alcohol trade. Bands of gangsters and bank robbers roamed across the country in the Public Enemy Era. Police were killed pursuing gangsters even as the gangsters killed each other. In the Kansas City Massacre of 1933, gangsters killed four FBI agents suspected of interfering with the mob's business. The same year, gangsters killed a jailor in a successful attempt to spring bank robber John Dillinger from the slammer. Bonnie and Clyde's gang killed nine police officers from 1932 to 1934. Other public enemies of the era include Pretty Boy Floyd, Baby Face Nelson and Ma Barker.

In coming negative-mood years, the scope of violence will likely expand. We could very well see modern-day Dillingers and Clydes embarking on their own voyage of illegal enrichment and violence.

How It All Might End

The story of Prohibition after the 1929 stock market peak is a model for how the current crisis in Mexico and the U.S. is likely to play out. In the late 1920s and early 1930s, as violence and corruption escalated, the majority of the public simply grew fed up with the mayhem. After the severest negative mood trend in U.S. history, the public demanded change and Prohibition was repealed.

It appears inevitable, then, that Drug-War-related carnage—and public disgust with it—will spread during the next major trend toward negative social mood. Southern regions of California, Arizona, New Mexico and Texas will likely see the same type of violence that is now plaguing Mexican states. During times of positively trending mood, some will argue to step up the Drug War and start mass incarcerations if not executions. But eventually the public will become open to decriminalization. The dialogue will cease to center on morality and will shift to focusing on stopping the chaos. Cash-strapped states will argue that they desperately need tax revenues from pot and that they can save money by releasing non-violent drug offenders from prison. Finally, the government will end its Drug War.

The history of Prohibition provides perspective on what society will look like after marijuana is decriminalized. Following the repeal of the 18th Amendment, organized crime and the violence that came with it almost completely disappeared as black market vendors lost the one condition that enabled them to maintain their monopoly and get unimaginably rich: illegality.

Chapter 71

Negative Social Mood Prompts New
Drug Program in Uruguay

Euan Wilson

November 30, 2012 (TS)

Different countries traverse different social mood phases at different times. The present in some countries sometimes depicts the future for others. Currently, Uruguay is providing a model for how the U.S. and other countries' marijuana policies may look in coming years.

Marijuana cultivation and possession for personal use were legalized in Uruguay in 1974, the year of major lows in stock markets around the world. Since 2008, Uruguay's primary stock market index, the BVMI, has fallen

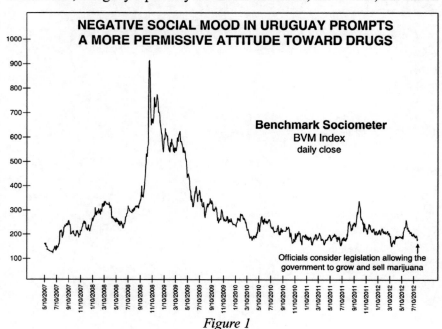

Figure 1

deeply and is languishing near its five-year low, a socionomically fitting time for another liberalization effort. Accordingly, newly proposed legislation would allow the government to produce and sell marijuana to its citizens in order to fund the rehabilitation of drug addicts. Officials would track all purchases, and government health officials would enroll heavy users in the rehab program. The legislation has the support of Uruguay's president and defense minister. Uruguay's Congress will vote on the proposal next year.

Post-production update: The proposal was signed into law in December 2013 and implemented over the next four years. By July 2017, the rollout was largely complete, as marijuana became legally available in 16 of the nation's pharmacies. In September 2017, the country even changed its policies to allow cash-only dispensaries to open after some banks refused to do business with pharmacies linked to marijuana, due to international financing standards that prohibit banks from receiving money tied to the drug trade.

Chapter 72

As Mood Shifts, Decades of Marijuana Prohibition Go Up in Smoke

Gary Grimes and Euan Wilson

November 8, 2013 (TS)

White Widow, Sour Diesel, Maui Wowie. When the smoke clears in the medical and recreational marijuana industries, pot strains such as these may be as commonly recognized as Miller and Budweiser.

Like it or not, the longtime prohibition of marijuana and hemp in America is coming to an end. It's not just stoners who are high on the idea. Industries from pharmaceuticals to fabric and fuel to foodstuffs have laid the groundwork for participating in a legal U.S. marijuana market.

History shows that social mood strongly influences society's tolerance for recreational drugs. As Robert Prechter noted in the March 1995 issue of *The Elliott Wave Theorist*,

> Prohibition was enacted in 1920, one year before Cycle wave V of Supercycle wave (III) blasted off, and repealed in 1933, the year of the bottom in the Great Depression. Today's Drug War began in 1982, the year Cycle wave V of Supercycle wave (V) blasted off, and will undoubtedly be abandoned at the bottom of the next depression. When drug prohibition is repealed, take it as a sign of an exhausted will, and therefore a bottom in social mood, and therefore a bullish signal for investments and businesses.

Prechter's assertion that drug legalization and the stock market are connected by way of a hidden influence was bold and radical. It came at a time when making pot legal wasn't even on the mainstream media's radar. The public was still strongly against the idea, too, as you can see by the statistics in Figure 1.

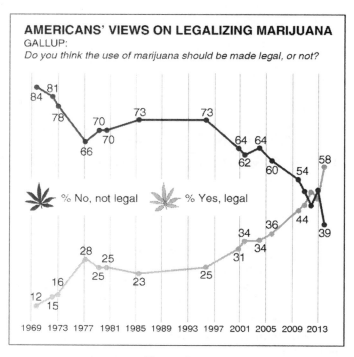

Figure 1

The Socionomic Connection

Positively trending social mood kindles desires to prohibit the use of substances such as alcohol and marijuana. Negatively trending mood prompts tolerance and relaxed regulation.

Tolerance increased during the negative mood period of the 1970s, then decreased during the ensuing positive mood period through at least 1996, when Gallup showed that roughly three quarters of Americans supported marijuana prohibition. The numbers began to decline sharply sometime between the positive-mood year of 1996 and the negative-mood year of 2001, the imprecision being due to a five-year gap in Gallup's data. From a socionomic viewpoint, this trend reversal pairs nicely with the timing of the all-time high in the Dow/gold ratio in 1999. Americans' growing support for marijuana legalization, now at 58%,[1] is compatible with EWI's conclusion that a subtle, prolonged period of negatively trending mood began at that time.

The July 2009 issue of *The Socionomist* updated subscribers to the approaching end of marijuana prohibition in a widely covered report by Euan Wilson, "The Coming Collapse of Modern Prohibition" [see Chapter 70]. *Time* and *Mother Jones* reprinted one of Wilson's charts [Figure 1 of that chapter], and Yahoo Finance, *New Scientist* and other major news outlets reported on his thesis.

Evidence for tolerance is mounting. The U.S. attorney general has assured states of their right to regulate marijuana. Mexican officials are considering

Changing Perception: Marijuana has gone from illegal drug to legitimate business opportunity.

legalization measures. Respected doctors are taking stands for the drug's medicinal use. Public polls are swinging in pot's favor. Even Republican Senator John McCain recently mused, "maybe we should legalize."

NORML, an organization "working to reform marijuana laws" for more than three decades and a reliable source of news on the topic, seemed surprised by a recent poll from the Bible Belt state of Louisiana:

> It is often said that the South will be the last region in the United States to take up marijuana legalization, but, as support grows nationwide, it is becoming evident the southern states likely won't be left behind. Polling data released today by the ACLU of Louisiana revealed that 53% of Louisiana voters supported regulating marijuana in a manner similar to the models approved last November in Colorado and Washington. Only 37% were opposed and 10% were not sure.[2]

There was also a recent surprise in Arkansas, when a 2012 ballot measure to legalize medical marijuana failed "but came surprisingly close, winning 48.5% of the vote, and encouraging Arkansas activists to try again (in 2014)."[3] Now, 20 states and Washington, D.C. have legalized medical marijuana, and two—Colorado and Washington—have legalized its recreational use.

The once-lopsided public debate has morphed into a balanced one. Commentators such as Dr. Sanjay Gupta have undergone striking changes of opinion. Long an opponent of legalization, Gupta had written a "Vote No" article for *Time* magazine as recently as 2009. He changed his opinion over the past year, while doing his research for a documentary. In an op-ed published on August 8, Gupta wrote,

I mistakenly believed the Drug Enforcement Agency.... Surely, they must have quality reasoning as to why marijuana is in the category of the most dangerous drugs that have "no accepted medicinal use and a high potential for abuse."...I now know that when it comes to marijuana neither of those things are true.... We have been terribly and systematically misled for nearly 70 years in the United States, and I apologize for my own role in that. I apologize because I didn't look hard enough, until now.[4]

U.S. News & World Report described Gupta's findings:

Gupta spent a year investigating by traveling to pot farms in Colorado and hospitals in Israel, where he studied the medicinal benefits for cancer patients. The program emphasized the underresearched healing effects of marijuana and had viewers glued to their TVs as they watched 5-year-old Charlotte Figi, now age 6, consume the drug to treat her seizures. While marijuana is classified as a schedule 1 substance—which the Drug Enforcement Agency defines as "drugs with no currently accepted medical use and a high potential for abuse"—it's the only one that has reduced Charlotte's seizures from 300 a month to two or three. As Gupta notes in his CNN editorial, Roger Egeberg, the Department of Health's assistant secretary of health and scientific affairs in 1970, recommended at that time for marijuana to be classified as a Schedule 1 substance "until the completion of certain studies now underway to resolve the issue." Forty-five years later, the majority of those studies were never completed, Gupta says, and the status hasn't changed. He points out that only 6 percent of marijuana studies in the United States have investigated the healing qualities of the drug, while the rest have focused on the harmful impact.[5]

Law Enforcement Addicted to Illegal Pot

Ironically, illegal drug cartels have long been aided by the positive social mood that drove both the stock market advance and the strict moral sentiment behind society's urge to keep their merchandise illegal. Just as ironically, law enforcement benefits from prohibition, too. Police confiscate assets connected—no matter how incidentally—to drug use, and they keep them. In 2009, marijuana arrests accounted for 52% of all drug arrests in the United States. By 2011, pot arrests had dropped to 43% of the overall tally, on par with the rate in the 1990s but still many multiples of pre-Drug-War figures.

With the U.S. prison system dependent on drug arrests—particularly those related to marijuana—any continued movement toward legalization will have a negative impact on the industries of confiscation and incarceration. Decreased drug arrests will negatively impact police budgets dependent on cash and property seized from suspected drug dealers,[6] and prisons will end up with fewer inmates and lower budgets. Profits for private prisons contracted by the government will fall when, as we described in 2009, states begin to argue that they can save money by releasing non-violent drug offenders from prison. The fortunes of lawyers involved in drug-related prosecutions and defense will also reverse.

The Future of Legislation

Although local, state and federal positions on marijuana are becoming increasingly relaxed, the U.S. Congress may not change its drug and hemp laws while the stock market is still holding up. The governments of both Mexico and the U.S. are at least a few years and probably a lot more violence away from ending marijuana prohibition and their ongoing War on Drugs. The biggest governmental bodies will likely be the last to act.

When negative social mood finally does bring the Drug War to an end, marijuana will play an increasing role as a tax-generating industry in the United States and elsewhere. As legal farm products, marijuana and hemp—which are different varieties of the same species of plant—have the potential to become two of the biggest cash crops. As an investment, pot stocks may soon be categorized alongside Big Pharma stocks and so-called "vice" industries such as gambling, alcohol and tobacco.

Post-production update: In March 2017, U.S. Attorney General Jeff Sessions called for reinvigorating the Drug War by having federal prosecutors demand the harshest allowable punishment, including mandatory minimum sentences, for violating drug laws. Some observers are aghast, but this harder-line stance neatly fits the currently positive state of social mood, as indicated by new all-time highs in the DJIA. Whether the government follows through on Sessions' initiative will be dependent upon the extent and duration of the trend toward positive mood.

NOTES AND REFERENCES

[1] Swift, A. (2013, October 22). For First Time, Americans Favor Legalizing Marijuana. Gallup.

[2] Altieri, E. (2013, September 5). Support for Marijuana Legalization Blooming in the South. NORML.

[3] Smith, P. (2013, August 9). Arkansas Medical Marijuana Initiatives Aim at 2014. StoptheDrugWar.org.

[4] Gupta, S. (2013, August 8). Why I Changed My Mind on Weed. *CNN Health*.

[5] Steinberg, S. (2013, August 16). CNN's Sanjay Gupta Reacts to Robust 'Weed' Documentary Response. *US News and World Report*.

[6] Drug Money Helps Police: Seized Assets Help Some Agencies Make Ends Meet. (2012, April 22). *Morning Sentinel*.

Chapter 73

Social Mood Influences the
Disciplinary Actions of Congress

Ben Hall

October 1, 2009 (TS)

Congressman Joe Wilson's outburst during President Obama's speech before a joint session of Congress on September 9 and his subsequent reprimand on September 15 reflect the tense environment that the negative trend in social mood of 2007-2009 has created. A reprimand is less severe than a censure or an expulsion, but it is still rare. *The New York Times* reported, "The vote came after a congressional clash over civility that showcased the deep partisan divisions in the House." The phrase "deep partisan divisions" is consistent with the social polarization typical of negative mood periods.

Figure 1 plots the two-century history of the DJIA along with the timing of Congressional disciplinary actions. As you can see, most such actions cluster during and shortly after declines in our benchmark sociometer, when social mood is negative. Expulsion is the strongest show of Congressional dissatisfaction, and the chart shows that most expulsions came near major lows in the stock market. Some members of Congress who were under indictment resigned before expulsion, but their departures are still a good indicator of an extreme in negative mood and therefore a stock market bottom.

A 24-year bear market took place from 1835 to 1859. The negative mood behind it polarized the nation. The period and its immediate aftermath saw 17 expulsions and 16 censures in Congress, not to mention the bloodiest war in U.S. history. It also included one senator's near-fatal beating of another on May 29, 1856 on the floor of the Senate.

The Great Depression saw only one censure, but the timing is significant; it came right the October 1929 crash.

There were no disciplinary actions from 1930 to 1932, which is contrary to our expectation. Nevertheless, in 1934 two Louisiana senators were

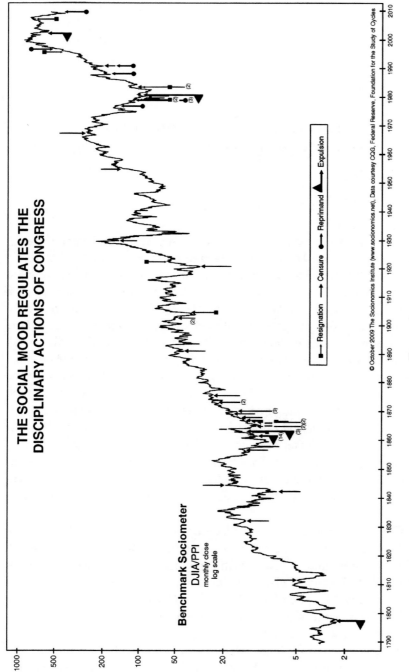

THE SOCIAL MOOD REGULATES THE
DISCIPLINARY ACTIONS OF CONGRESS

Benchmark Sociometer
DJIA/PPI
monthly close
log scale

■— Resignation —→ Censure ●— Reprimand ▼— Expulsion

© October 2009 The Socionomics Institute (www.socionomics.net). Data courtesy CGG, Federal Reserve, Foundation for the Study of Cycles

Figure 1

belatedly accused of having committed election fraud back in the bottom year of 1932 and became candidates for expulsion. After two years of deliberation during a period of positively trending social mood, Congress dropped the cases in 1936.

The U.S. entered World War II during the negative mood trend of 1937-1942, but unlike the Civil War period there were no disciplinary actions in Congress. This may be because Congressmen were all at one end of polarized opinion, united in outrage toward an outside enemy, a condition that would neuter this particular indicator of social mood while otherwise manifesting it in war against a common foe. [See further discussion of this point in Chapter 27.]

The negative mood behind the 1970s bear market produced four reprimands, three censures and one expulsion. The expulsion occurred in 1980, the very year of the low in the Dow/gold ratio.

The positive mood period of the 1980s was comparatively quiet except for two socionomically well-timed events: a couple of sexual misconduct charges in 1983—the year after a multi-decade low in the Dow/PPI—and a reprimand in December 1987, the exact month that the NYSE Composite Index bottomed following the 1987 crash. The year 1990 produced one censure and a reprimand as at least one sociometer—the Value Line Industrial index—fell back below its 1987 low. Heading into the stock market low of 2002, Congress expelled James Traficant. The latest event, the reprimand of September 2009, occurred just three months after the Great Recession of 2007-2009 ended, fitting right into the socionomic mold.

We expect the relationship between social mood and Congressional disciplinary actions to maintain into the future. Except in times of major war against an outside enemy, we expect Congress to vote more often for harsh disciplinary actions against its members during periods of negative social mood than during periods of positive social mood, as indicated by trends in our benchmark sociometers.

Chapter 74

Mudslinging in Seagrove: Social Mood First Divided and Then Reunited a Historically Cooperative Community

Alan Hall

November 30, 2015 (TS)

The September 11, 2001 issue of *The Elliott Wave Theorist* painted this picture:

> The coming trend of negative social psychology will be character-ized primarily by polarization between and among various perceived groups, whether political, ideological, religious, geographical, racial or economic. The result will be a net trend toward anger, fear, intol-erance, disagreement and exclusion, as opposed to the bull market years, whose net trend has been toward benevolence, confidence, tolerance, agreement and inclusion. Such a sentiment change typi-cally brings conflict in many forms, and evidence of it will be visible in all types of social organizations.

Social mood is unconscious and non-rational, so negative mood can impel conflict even when it hurts the people who participate in it. That is exactly what happened in the quiet little North Carolina town of Seagrove in the tumult of a powerful trend toward nega-tive social mood in 2008.

Seagrove is famous for its pottery tradition, which began before the Ameri-can Revolution due to local deposits of high quality clay and an early roadway.

In 1998, Seagrove established the North Carolina Pottery Center. More than 100 potters live and work there. The town claims to be "the pottery capital of the United States," and tourism is its dominant industry.[1]

You might remember 2008 as the year of a financial crisis, the year a U.S. president suffered the lowest approval ratings in 60 years or perhaps a year of anti-government protests, labor strikes or general riots that erupted in more than two dozen countries around the world.[2] But residents of Seagrove remember 2008 as the year of the great pottery feud.

Figure 1 shows the socionomic timing of the saga. Negative mood polarized Seagrove, and compatible actions among its residents achieved national notoriety due to a December 2008 article in *USA Today*. The article described "endless allegations of thievery, financial subterfuge and conspiracy" and offered the following details:

> The dispute has resulted in two pottery festivals in Seagrove scheduled for the same November weekend. One is new this year, the other has been held for the last 26.

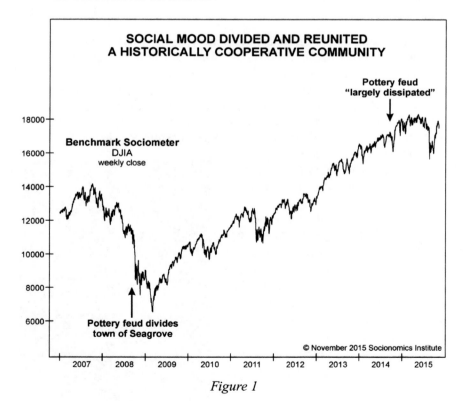

Figure 1

The divide, and all the confusing reasons for a fight over pottery, can appear ridiculous to outsiders. But it's venomous for those involved, resulting in ugly propaganda, reports of a gunshot fired at one shop and allegations of assault. Attempts to settle it have gotten nowhere.

"It's crazy. It's doing huge damage, and they should get over it," said Charlotte Brown, author of the 2006 book, *The Remarkable Potters of Seagrove* and director of the Gregg Museum of Art & Design at North Carolina State University in Raleigh. "It's not over anything that matters. It's personal. Everybody stands to lose."[3]

Clearly among the last things a tourism-dependent town would want to do is to plague its cottage industry with scandals, public disputes and violence. Yet as the June 2009 issue of *The Socionomist* explained, "A negative trend in social mood governs the character of interaction across groups of all sizes, from nations to political parties, to communities, churches and one-on-one settings."[4]

From Seagrove's darkest time in 2008, a remarkable transformation occurred over the six years leading up to a follow-up article dated September 2014:

NC Pottery Center rebounds after lean years
The Seagrove-based NC Pottery Center has hired a new director, secured a $130,000 grant and restarted its artist-in-residence program....

Six years ago, North Carolina's pottery community was at war. Potters known for throwing clay were openly slinging mud at one another. Some broke away to start their own pottery festival to compete against the long established event in Seagrove. And the N.C. Pottery Center was so strapped for cash that it had to jettison its full-time director.

Today, the feud has largely dissipated. The two pottery festivals co-exist peacefully on the same weekend before Thanksgiving.... "The turmoil has subsided," said Mark Hewitt, an internationally known potter.... Hewitt sees a brighter future for North Carolina potters and the pottery center....[5]

Six years and a 52% gain in the DJIA separate these stories about the feud and its resolution. Simply put, the substantial shift toward positive social mood motivated the combatants to make peace.

We hope this sad chapter in the history of Seagrove is closed and that Mark Hewitt gets his brighter future. But societies that undergo deeply negative mood can experience lasting fallout. The month after the September 2014 story published, a Seagrove potter was murdered.

As the town's potters continue to make pots, it is worth pondering that in many ways, society is as plastic as a potter's clay. Unconscious social mood continually shapes and reshapes it, producing the same emotions but never producing exactly the same events.

NOTES AND REFERENCES

[1] Retrieved from ncpotterycenter.org.

[2] Marshall, A.G. (2010, April 6). The Global Economic Crisis: Riots, Rebellion and Revolution. *Global Research*.

[3] Waggoner, M. (2008, September 4). Pottery Feud Divides NC Town of Seagrove. *USA Today*.

[4] Hall, A. (2009, June). A Soconomic View of Epidemic Disease. Part II: Stress, Physiology, Threats and Strategies. *The Socionomist*.

[5] Weigl, A. (2014, September 13). NC Pottery Center Rebounds After Lean Years. *The News & Observer*.

Chapter 75

Formerly Feuding Famous Families Cooperate to Distill Legal Moonshine in West Virginia

Chuck Thompson

February 27, 2015 (TS)

Chapter 16 of *The Wave Principle of Human Social Behavior* (1999) proposed that major positive trends in social mood "invariably produce overtures of reconciliation and treaty."[1] That dynamic was manifest again this month, as the legendary feuding families, the Hatfields and the Mc-Coys, are now working together to produce legal moonshine in southern West Virginia.

The feud originally involved the families of William Anderson Hatfield and Randolph McCoy. It began heating up in 1865, four years after the end of the long negative mood trend of 1835-1861, when Randolph's brother was killed by a local militia group with ties to the Hatfield family. Relations between the two families worsened in 1878 over an incident involving a stolen hog.[2] Within ten years, at least twelve people were killed as a result of the feud.

The fighting ended by 1900, and the two families signed a truce in 2003. Now, with U.S. stock prices at historically high valuations, indicating an extremely elevated social mood, the Hatfields and McCoys have teamed up to produce moonshine in a converted garage located six miles from William Anderson Hatfield's gravesite. The distillery sells as many as 3,000 bottles per month at $32.99 per bottle and currently ships its products to six states.[3]

NOTES AND REFERENCES

[1] Prechter, R. (1999) *The Wave Principle of Human Social Behavior* (p. 265). Gainesville, GA: New Classics Library.

[2] The Hatfield and McCoy Feud. *The History Channel.*

[3] Raby, J. (2015, January 31). Hatfields, McCoys Make Moonshine Legally in Southern W.Va. *Yahoo! News.*

Chapter 76

Still Sorry, for Now:
Historic Apologies Are Driven by Social Mood
Alan Hall

December 2, 2010 (TS)

Chapter 16 of *The Wave Principle of Human Social Behavior* (1999) explained, "Major advances in mood invariably produce overtures of reconciliation." As early as the August 1995 issue of *The Elliott Wave Theorist,* Peter Kendall reported that as the ebullient mood of the 1990s drove stock prices to historic highs, it also created bull markets in both regret and forgiveness:

> In bear markets, anger, fear and the urge to destroy overcome the social conscience. Remorse, on the other hand, is a bull market trait born of the larger trend toward inclusionist impulses…. The peaking social mood has brought apologies for a host of transgressions that are decades, generations, and even centuries old. After years of bickering, the Japanese government reached a "compromise" apology for its part in World War II. At a recent press conference, President Clinton resisted considerable public pressure to ask forgiveness for bombs dropped on Japan eight administrations ago. A group of ethicists and historians has decided that financial compensation and a formal government apology is due victims of secret human radiation experiments conducted in the U.S. during the Cold War. The United Church of Canada has apologized to a host of native tribes for sins of the past. Southern Baptists, the nation's largest Protestant denomination, have asked forgiveness for defending slavery in the 1800s. (The sect was founded in 1845 in a show of support for slavery.) The Catholic Church apologized to "every woman" in the world for centuries of relegation to "the margins of society"; then it apologized to the Czech Republic for the Catholic church's role in the 16th century wars that followed the Protestant Reformation; then

it agreed to join Protestants in ceremonies repenting the Crusades against Muslims and Jews 900 years ago! According to a Vatican spokesman, the Pope is "pushing hard toward unity." Though not exactly apologizing, the U.S. has just normalized relations with Vietnam, its bitterest enemy, and one of its longest standing, since World War II.[1]

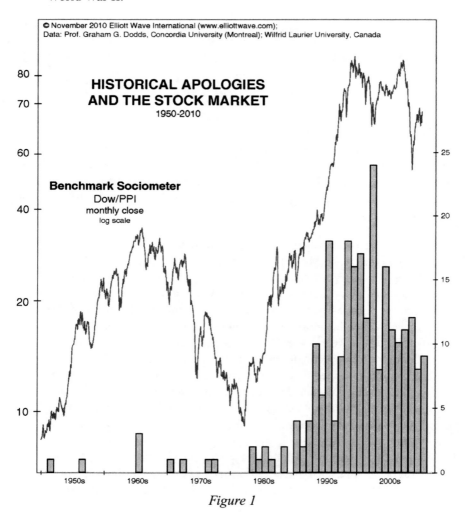

Figure 1

In the November 2007 issue of *The Elliott Wave Theorist,* socionomist Mark Galasiewski produced an early version of Figure 1 by charting historical apologies vs. a key sociometer. He commented,

Historical apologies have increased dramatically in the past fifteen years, along with the stock market. The coincidence is not random; both are driven by the wave of positive social mood that took off in 1982. Apologies made the greatest three-year total within the topping years of 1998, 1999 and 2000. There was a record one-year spike in 2002, during the first half of which other measures of sentiment, such as the number of S&P 500 futures contracts held by small traders, also made their all-time peaks (see January 2007 EWT). Since then, annual apologies have not kept pace with price, suggesting that the wave of reconciliation that took off in the early 1990s is almost exhausted. Once the bear market resumes, expect the public's willingness to acknowledge past wrongs to become itself a thing of the past. In its place will be an impetus to act in ways that will require apologies later.[2]

Socionomic Observations on the Tuskeegee and Guatemala Experiments

Dr. John Cutler, a government researcher, was involved in the infamous U.S. Public Health Service (PHS) study[3] in Tuskegee, Alabama, in which he helped chronicle the progression of late-stage syphilis in 399 black men while withholding treatment.

The Tuskegee experiment followed a socionomic script. The project began at the 1932 extreme in negative social mood, drew scrutiny at the 1966 peak in positive mood following a whistle-blower letter by a PHS investigator, and ended in July 1972, just before another major positive mood peak.[4] U.S. President Bill Clinton apologized for it in 1997, as social mood approached yet another positive extreme.[5]

A Wellesley College historian recently unearthed from Cutler's archives descriptions of a similar campaign in Guatemala in the 1940s. That episode followed a socionomic script as well. From 1946 to 1948—during a nadir in social mood as indicated by a 22% slide in the DJIA at the end of a 20-year bear market in the Dow/PPI—Cutler deliberately helped infect 696 Guatemalan men and women with syphilis and gonorrhea via injections and prostitutes, all paid for by U.S. taxpayers. The project occurred even as the U.S. conducted the "Nazi Doctors' Trial" in Nuremberg, Germany, in which it "tried, convicted and sentenced a score of Nazi doctors for performing macabre experiments on thousands of Jews during World War II."[6] Two months ago, after hearing about the barbaric medical experiments in Guatemala, President Obama and the Secretaries of State and Health promptly apologized for them.

The latest mea culpa is not the first time the U.S. has apologized to Guatemala for injuring its citizens during a time of negative social mood. In November 1965, just prior to that era's peak in positive social mood, the U.S. sent military advisors into Guatemala. As the subsequent turn toward negative mood progressed, death tolls mounted and the war accelerated to its "defining event," the burning of the Spanish Embassy in January 1980, the very month of the low in the Dow/gold ratio. Figure 2 shows data from a report titled "Institutional Violence in Guatemala, 1960-1996: a Quantitative Reflection"[7] along with a benchmark sociometer, the Dow/PPI. These graphs show that the level of state terror in Guatemala peaked in 1982, coinciding precisely with the end of the 16-year bear market. That's when the nation's army "killed thousands of civilians in the west of the country and decimated hundreds of indigenous communities."

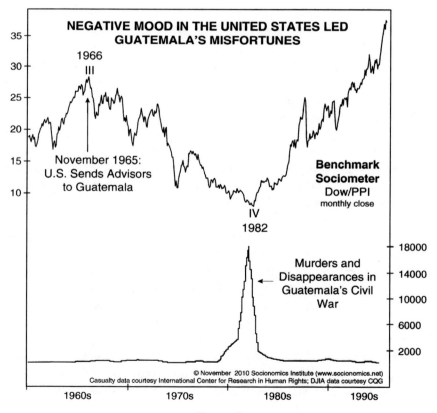

Figure 2

Seventeen years later, in March 1999, only four months before a major extreme in positive social mood as recorded by a peak in the Dow/gold ratio that stands to this day, President Bill Clinton, speaking in Guatemala City, admitted that the U.S. "was responsible for most of the human rights abuses committed" during the 36-year Guatemalan Civil War in which 200,000 people died.[8]

When social mood resumes its negative trend, the era of the historic apologies will fade. We recommend that you rush any requests.

NOTES AND REFERENCES

[1] Kendall, P. "Evidence of a Peak in Social Mood." *The Elliott Wave Theorist,* July 28, 1995, p. 9.

[2] Galasiewski, M. (2007, November 16). *The Elliott Wave Theorist.*

[3] Reverby, S. (2010). "Normal Exposure" and Inoculation Syphilis: A PHS "Tuskegee" Doctor in Guatemala, 1946-48. *Journal of Policy History.*

[4] *Research Ethics: The Tuskegee Syphilis Study.* (n.d.).

[5] Gault, C. (1997, May 16). *An Apology 65 Years Late.*

[6] Valladares, D. (2010, October 12). Guatemala to Investigate Human Experimentation by U.S. Doctors. *Inside Costa Rica.*

[7] Ball, P., Kobrak, P., & Spirer, H. (1999, March 12). Institutional Violence in Guatemala, 1960-1996: A Quantitative Reflection. *American Association for the Advancement of Science (AAAS) Science and Human Rights Program; International Center for Human Rights Research.*

[8] Kettle, M. (1999, March 12). Clinton Apology to Guatemala. *Guardian.*

Chapter 77

The Apology Wave Is Subsiding

Alan Hall

December 23, 2016 (TS)

In a June 2014 article for *Playboy* magazine, actor Gilbert Gottfried complained about the public pressure to apologize. For a decade, he had been the voice of the duck on Aflac's insurance commercials. But when he tweeted jokes about the tsunami that hit Japan in March 2011, it attracted global animosity and he was promptly fired. He wrote,

> For the next three days, every crazy person on the internet came out to punish me.... If you want to survive as a public figure in 2014, you have to treat the entire world as if it's your wife or girlfriend.... Imagine if the most brilliant comedians in history were working today. They'd never stop apologizing. Charlie Chaplin would have to apologize to all the homeless people he belittled with his Little Tramp character. W.C. Fields and Dean Martin would both have to apologize to alcoholics. The Marx brothers would have to apologize to Italians, mutes and uptight British ladies.[1]

Comedians working some years from now are likely to feel considerably less heat.

Positive Social Mood Has Driven a Desire for Reconciliation

Over 20 years ago, in August 1995, socionomists proposed that a large-degree trend toward positive social mood beginning in the early 1980s had produced a historic wave of publicly declared political, religious and social apologies.[2] In November 2007[3] and November 2010,[4] socionomists further chronicled the trend toward atonement. Recent data show that the apology tsunami has been subsiding as global social mood becomes less positive.

Figure 1 plots three global sociometers: the U.S. Home Price Index, the inflation-adjusted MSCI World Stock Index and the Dow Jones Industrial Average denominated in real money (gold)—along with two datasets of major political apologies. The black columns depict apologies data from Graham G. Dodds of Concordia University, and the grey columns depict apologies data from Rhoda E. Howard-Hassmann of Wilfrid Laurier University. Dodds created a chronological list of over 600 apologies, selected for significance as follows:

> The selection criteria for compiling the list are somewhat loose, but the intent is to include any and all apologies that involve states, nations, or major political groups and actors, generally for significant public wrongs. Thus, apologies by individual politicians for more narrow matters (e.g., alleged personal or criminal failings) are generally excluded.[5]

We included Dodds' data only on *actual* apologies, not on *refusals* to apologize or on *demands* for apologies.

Howard-Hassmann's criteria are a bit different:

> Our focus is on political apologies and reparations. We define political apologies broadly as apologies by a political or social entity (governments, religious organizations, or other bodies) for events that have harmed identifiable groups. We define reparations as financial reparations, return of property such as art works, symbolic reparations such as creations of museums and monuments, and acknowledgements of atrocities such as opening up of mass graves.[6]

We included apologies and reparations only for wrongs that occurred more than ten years prior.

Tallies of political apologies registered small peaks in 1955, as the bull market of 1949-1966 reached peak acceleration, and in 1965, the last full year of its rise. They zoomed far higher when our sociometer turned upward in the 1980s. Political apologies increased throughout the 1990s as global social mood trended even more strongly toward the positive. Apologies in the two datasets peaked in 2003 and in 2005, respectively. These years lagged the tops in the MSCI and the Dow/gold ratio, but the final full year of price gains in the global real estate boom was 2005, the exact year of the peak in apologies before both data series plunged along with other benchmark sociometers. As a colleague recently joked, "If Erich Segal had written *Love Story* [1970] 30 years later, the tagline would have been, 'Love

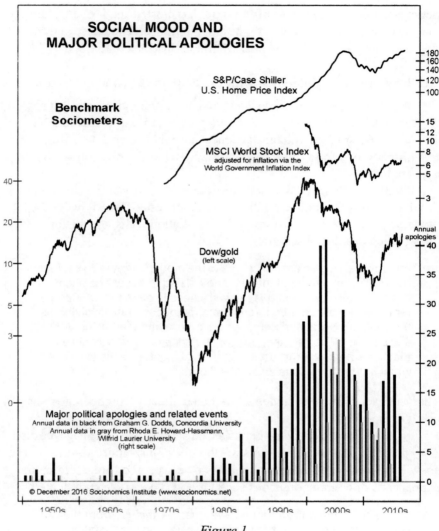

Figure 1

means *always* having to say you're sorry.'"[7] Apologies briefly increased again as the same measures advanced from their 2011-2012 lows, but they have waned somewhat recently.

In sum, the apology mania accompanied the final wave of a global trend toward positive social mood as measured by three sociometers, whose combined value remains below its highs of 2000 and 2006. So, history's perhaps unprecedented wave of apologies has crested and is ebbing, largely in sync with global social mood. The era of remorse, repentance and contrition is waning along with the positive mood that fueled it.

Academic Interest Coincided with the Peak in the Apology Mania

Academics finally became interested in the apology mania as it neared its extreme. The University of Pennsylvania commissioned Dodds' list in 1999, and Howard-Hassmann launched her website in 2003. Below are five observations from other academic writers, in the order in which they appeared:

In 2001, Robert R. Weyeneth, professor of history at the University of South Carolina–Columbia, published an article titled "The Power of Apology and the Process of Historical Reconciliation." His conclusion "Why Now?" includes this observation:

> Although apologies are not unique to the modern era, we do seem to be witnessing a flurry of intense apologizing today. ... The phenomenon is world-wide, and this pervasiveness is quite recent. Regular remorse has become an international preoccupation, involving nations in both North and South America, Asia and the Pacific, Africa, and Europe.... The new sense of connectedness on "spaceship earth" that has emerged in the last half century...heightens sensitivity to the wrongs done to nations and to neighbors.[8]

That "new sense of connectedness" stemmed directly from societies' shared positive mood.

In 2006, *The Independent* published an article titled "The Big Question: Are apologies for historical events worthwhile or just empty gestures?" The answer is: both. They are most certainly owed, yet they are but temporary expressions of contemporaneous social mood. The article commented,

> John Paul II apologized for no fewer than 94 things—from the Crusades, to the Inquisition, to the church's scientific obscurantism over Galileo, its oppression of women and the Holocaust. He did it throughout the 1980s and 1990s as a preparation for the new millennium....[9]

The article added, "everyone caught the bug," and it described a flood of apologies that poured forth from world leaders: F.W. de Klerk apologized for apartheid, Jacques Chirac apologized for France helping the Nazis, Shinzo Abe apologized for Japan's role in World War II and Boris Yeltsin apologized for the Bolshevik Revolution.

In 2007, Michael Marrus, professor emeritus of Holocaust Studies at the University of Toronto, published an article titled "Official Apologies and the Quest for Historical Justice." He wrote,

Sorry About That: Pope John Paul II apologized for more than 90 transgressions, including the Crusades and the Inquisition.

> We are, I contend here, awash in apologies, both trivial and highly consequential. [A]pologies have become a familiar part of our relational landscape....
>
> Apologies are a "political enthusiasm," writes the novelist and critic Marina Warner. "The theme of 'apology' is in the air: Governments are saying it to former colonial subjects, or to political prisoners in post-dictatorships; former terrorists to their targets; banks and businesses to looted or polluted clients; churches and cults to victims of abuse," she notes....
>
> Following the victory of George W. Bush in the American presidential elections of November 2004, a website suddenly appeared, sorryeverybody.com, which permitted Americans "to offer apologies to the rest of the world." Within hours of its being announced on CNN, the site was swamped, presumably both by visitors and what one report cited as a "torrent of apologies."
>
> Another sign of success: There is now a satirical novel on apologies ... British writer Jay Rayner's *The Apologist* (published in the United States as *Eating Crow*).... In this amusing fantasy, the tone is set by the UN Secretary General, who proclaims the "dawn of the empathetic era," in which "the world can get back in touch with its emotions." Unsurprisingly, there is an academic behind it all—Professor Thomas Schenke, "the founding father of a new and exciting strand of international relations theory known in diplomatic circles as 'Penitential Engagement.'"...
>
> University of San Diego law professor Roy Brooks, in a 500-page book entitled *When Sorry Isn't Enough*, refers to our "Age of Apology"; Janna Thompson, an Australian philosopher...identifies an "epidemic of apology"; historian Elazar Barkan refers to an "avalanche of apologies";

and ethicist Lee Taft...speaks about an "apology mania." "Apology has barged into the realm of international politics," say Mark Gibney and Niklaus Steiner, making the point that apologies are not only a real-life phenomenon, but a booming academic subject as well. Recent years have seen a wave in official apologies, or near apologies, for wrongs committed in the distant past—and sometimes the far distant past.[10]

In 2009, Joseph R. Blaney and Joseph A. Zompetti, associate professors of communication at Illinois State University, published a book titled *The Rhetoric of Pope John Paul II*. They wrote,

In the 1990s, there was an explosion of apologetic gestures by rhetors for crimes committed years, decades, sometimes hundreds of years earlier. These apologies became so prolific that one reporter stated the 1990s "turned out to be the decade of the group apology."...

The group apology became more prolific in the 1990s <u>because of the increasing interdependence and integration of the world</u> from the end of the Cold War. As relations between nation-states, organizations, institutions, and populations become more integrated past wrong-doings serve as an impediment to these communities to creating, restoring, strengthening, and deepening communal bonds in a global community.... This form of mea culpa is about respect for another community and the care of that relationship.[11]

But "the increasing interdependence and integration of the world" is not the *reason* for the apologies; both of these developments are *consequences* of the long trend toward more positive social mood.

In a 2015 book titled *A Guilted Age*, "Ashraf Rushdy argues that the proliferation of apologies by politicians, nations, and churches for past events—such as American slavery or the Holocaust—can be understood as a historical phenomenon."[12] He wrote, "apology had become a routine, expected form. That development is a novel thing, and one, I argue, that defines the guilted age."[13] But he doesn't say *why* it happened. Figure 1 shows that positive social mood drove asset prices and apologies to nearly coincident peaks.

Socionomists' observations along these lines predated academics' studies by four to twenty years. Better yet, we understand the underlying cause. Even better still, our theory allowed us to recognize and also to forecast a positive relationship between stock trends and apology trends, and it has maintained ever since.

Apologies Occurred at All Degrees of Scale

We suspect that the tendency to apologize has been expressed at all scales throughout society, from major social representatives apologizing for significant wrongs to family members apologizing for personal offenses. Though most of the apologies in Dodds' and Howard-Hassmann's lists were monumental in scope, Dodds' list contained a few accounts of individuals caught in the public spotlight trying to amend smaller-scale wrongs. Consider the following examples:

> February 3, 1999: Reverend Jerry Falwell apologized for having said that the Antichrist is (or will be) Jewish.
>
> June 14, 2003: Members of the Hatfield and McCoy families signed a truce to officially end the deadly feud that dated to the 19th century.
>
> September 22, 2004: Former televangelist Jimmy Swaggart apologized for threatening to kill any man who looks at him romantically.
>
> August 23, 2005: Pat Robertson apologized for suggesting that Venezuelan President Hugo Chavez be assassinated.

Reverend Jerry Falwell: In 1999, the renowned minister apologized for having said that the Antichrist is (or will be) Jewish.

March 23, 2015: Former Bob Jones University President Bob Jones III apologized for saying gays should be stoned.[14]

As Mood Becomes Less Positive, People Are Becoming Less Eager to Make Amends

Though the number of major apologies is still relatively high today in historical terms, in recent years we have observed a generally diminishing urge to forgive and make amends. For example, President Obama pledged in December 2014 to restore full relations between the U.S. and Cuba,[15] yet President-elect Trump threatened last month to roll back those efforts.[16] In September, the Colombian government signed a historic peace deal to end a half century of conflict with FARC rebels, only to have voters reject it.[17]

Defiant *non*-apologies appear to be increasing as apologies subside. A harbinger of this trend occurred in 2003, when Dixie Chicks vocalist Natalie Maines criticized President George W. Bush for pushing to invade Iraq. Controversy erupted, and the band members received death threats, yet they refused to apologize to agitated fans.[18] In 2006, the year the flood of political apologies began abating, the Dixie Chicks released their single, "Not Ready to Make Nice." The song won three Grammys in 2007 and remains the band's biggest hit to date.[19] The lyrics are decidedly non-apologetic:

I'm not ready to make nice
I'm not ready to back down
I'm still mad as hell, and I don't have time
To go 'round and 'round and 'round
It's too late to make it right
I probably wouldn't if I could
'Cause I'm mad as hell
Can't bring myself to do what it is
You think I should[20]

In June 2016, *The Huffington Post* reported, "The Dixie Chicks still aren't ready make to make nice, and they aren't ready to back down. Especially when it comes to Donald Trump."[21] During their summer European tour, the group "stuck it to the Republican presidential hopeful by unfurling a giant photo of him defaced with a devilish mustache, goatee and horns."[22]

For his part, Donald Trump, when campaigning for president, relied significantly on a staunch stance of non-apology. He made many insulting statements and innuendos and apologized for none of them. People found his stance refreshing, and many voted for him as a result.

As the total number of public apologies recedes, some of the apologies that do occur seem insincere. Consider, for example, CNN's October 8 headline: "Trump issues defiant apology for lewd remarks—then goes on the attack."[23] A "defiant" apology laced with an "attack" is not much of an apology.

A 2015 paper titled "Apologies Demanded Yet Devalued: Normative Dilution in the Age of Apology" suggested that major apologies have become increasingly ineffective, as recipients view them as disingenuous:

The apology norm (a) increased victim group members' desire for an apology, but (b) decreased their willingness to forgive upon its receipt, mediated by perceived apology sincerity. Results show evidence of a "normative dilution" effect, where the norms surrounding a behavior devalue its symbolic worth.[24]

Wikipedia lists nine major calls for reparations for slavery of African descendants that span the years 1999 to 2013.[25] Two additional demands for reparations have occurred since then. In September 2015, Jamaica called on Britain to pay billions of pounds in reparations for slavery.[26] In September 2016, a United Nations-affiliated panel concluded that the U.S. owes African Americans reparations for "the legacy of colonial history, enslavement, racial subordination and segregation, racial terrorism and racial inequality in the United States.... Contemporary police killings and the trauma that they create are reminiscent of the past racial terror of lynching."[27] Yet to date the only slavery reparations the U.S. has ever paid were to slave *owners*, who received up to $300 per slave for their losses upon emancipation.[28] That payment occurred in 1862, following a 26-year period of negative social mood that also impelled the Civil War. Another source claims that six European countries paid reparations to slave owners.[29] We were unable, however, to find any record of a country paying reparations to former slaves or their descendants.

The UN's exhortation may have arrived too late. Much as the last depositors to join a bank run leave empty-handed, late demands for major apologies are likely to find that the well of atonement has run dry.

The waning of the apology wave is yet another signal that an important era of inclusion and benevolence is drawing to a close. New highs in one or more sociometers may coincide with a few more grand apologies, but we doubt they will exceed the pace of 2003-2005.

The next monolithic trend toward negative social mood will bring the apology fad to a halt. Societies undergoing trends toward negative mood often come to believe that previous *manifestations* of positive mood, such as inclusiveness, political correctness or immigrant accommodation, helped cause their current problems. Such attitudes do not accommodate an atmosphere conducive to inclusion and apology but to exclusion and aggression.

In short, natural, patterned fluctuations in unconscious social mood regulate humans' aggregate desires either to apologize or to engage in behavior for which someone in the future will feel the urge to apologize.

Post-Production Note: As U.S. stock indexes ploughed to new all-time highs in Q2 2017, apologies from U.S. entities ballooned. On April 18, 2017, the Jesuit order that founded Georgetown University stated, "we are profoundly sorry [for having] greatly sinned" in selling 272 slaves in 1838 to pay off debts. On May 30, 2017, humorist Kathy Griffin pleaded, "I beg your forgiveness," for posting a picture of herself holding a likeness of Trump's severed head. On June 3, comedian Bill Maher apologized for using the "n-word" in a joke, calling it "completely inexcusable and tasteless." On June 22, 2017, Wesleyan College apologized for adopting Klan-tinged images as far back as 1908 and for using them in hazing rituals in the mid-1950s. "Wesleyan President Ruth Knox acknowledged that the college should have taken action sooner;"[30] but it didn't, because social mood was not positive enough until now. A whistle-blower denounced the tradition using one of our socionomic terms, saying, "It's exclusionary."[31] When social mood someday becomes commensurately negative, offensive images and what is currently deemed "politically incorrect" speech will become everyday occurrences.—Ed.

NOTES AND REFERENCES

[1] Gottfried, G. (2014, June 28). The Apology Epidemic. *Playboy.*

[2] Blaney, J.R., & Zompetti, J.P., Eds. (2009). *The Rhetoric of Pope John Paul II* (p. 84). Lanham, Maryland: Lexington Books.

[3] Galasiewski, M. (2007, November 16). Socionomic Snapshots. *The Elliott Wave Theorist.*

[4] Hall, A. (2010, December 4). Still Sorry for Now: Historic Apologies Are Driven by Social Mood—An Update. *The Socionomist.*

[5] Dodds, G. (2016, July 13). Chronological List of Political Apologies. *Textlab.*

[6] Howard-Hassmann, R.E. Political Apologies and Reparations. Wilfrid Laurier University.

[7] Love Means Never Having to Say You're Sorry. *Wikipedia.*

[8] Weyeneth, R.R. (2001, July 1). The Power of Apology and the Process of Historical Reconciliation. *Selected Works.*

[9] Vallely, P. (2006, November 27). The Big Question: Are Apologies for Historical Events Worthwhile or Just Empty Gestures? *The Independent.*

[10] Marrus, M.R. (2007). Official Apologies and the Quest for Historical Justice. *Journal of Human Rights*, 6(1), 75-105.

[11] Blaney, J.R., & Zompetti, J.P., Eds. (2009). *The Rhetoric of Pope John Paul II* (p. 84). Lanham, Maryland: Lexington Books.

[12] Rushdy, A.H.A. A Guilted Age. Temple University. Retrieved from http://www.temple.edu/tempress/titles/2389_reg.html

[13] *Ibid.*

[14] See Endnote 5.

[15] Baker, P. (2014, December 17). U.S. to Restore Full Relations With Cuba, Erasing a Last Trace of Cold War Hostility. *The New York Times.*

[16] Wright, D. (2016, November 28). Trump Threatens to Roll Back U.S.-Cuba relations. *CNN Politics.*

[17] Mailbag. (2016, October 26). *The Socionomist.*

[18] Silverman, S.M. (2006, May 12). Dixie Chicks Recall 'Scary' Death Threat. *People.*

[19] Not Ready to Make Nice. *Wikipedia.*

[20] Not Ready to Make Nice. *A-Z Lyrics,* azlyrics.com

[21] Brucculieri, J. (2016, June 6). Dixie Chicks Take Aim at Donald Trump With Defaced Poster at Concert. *The Huffington Post.*

[22] *Ibid.*

[23] Diamond, J. (2016, October 8). Trump Issues Defiant Apology for Lewd Remarks—Then Goes On the Attack. *CNN Politics.*

[24] Okimoto, T.G, Wenzel, M., & Hornsey, M.J. (2015). Apologies Demanded Yet Devalued: Normative Dilution in the Age of Apology. *Journal of Experimental Social Psychology*, 60, 133-136.

[25] Reparations for Slavery. *Wikipedia*. Retrieved from https://en.wikipedia.org/wiki/Reparations_for_slavery

[26] Mason, R. (2015, September 28). Jamaica Calls for Britain to Pay Billions of Pounds in Reparations for Slavery. *The Guardian*.

[27] Tharoor, I. (2016, September 27). U.S. Owes Black People Reparations for a History of 'Racial Terrorism,' Says U.N. Panel. *The Washington Post*.

[28] The District of Columbia Emancipation Act. The U.S. National Archives and Records Administration. Retrieved from https://www.archives.gov/exhibits/featured-documents/dc-emancipation-act

[29] Moore, A. (2014, June 9). 6 European Countries that Paid Millions in Reparations to Slave Owners When Enslaved Black People Were Freed. *Atlanta Black Star*.

[30] Schrade, Brad. (June 22, 2017). Ga. College Linked to Klan Rituals Apologizes for 'Pain' of Its History. *The Atlanta Journal-Constitution*.

[31] Schrade, Brad. (June 22, 2017). Macon Women's College Seeks to Atone for Ku Klux Klan's Legacy. *The Atlanta Journal-Constitution*.

Chapter 78

U.S. to Cuba:
You Guys Aren't So Bad After All

Chuck Thompson

June 30, 2015 (TS)

On May 29, 2015, the Obama Administration removed Cuba from a list of state sponsors of terrorism. The list now includes only Iran, Sudan and Syria. *The New York Times* called the move "an important step in Mr. Obama's effort to move past the Cold War-era hostility that has characterized the United States-Cuba relationship."[1]

Figure 1

The move is yet another manifestation of positive social mood, which exerts powerful influence and is making strange bedfellows. As we pointed out in the December 2014 issue, a rare coalition of conservatives and progressives supports the renewal of U.S.-Cuba relations. Figure 1 shows that the U.S. declared Cuba a sponsor of terrorism in 1982, the very year of the bottom in a 16-year bear market in the Dow/PPI. Now, 33 years later, the Dow/PPI is making all-time highs, indicating a historically positive social mood. In light of socionomic theory, it is not surprising that polarization is waning and former opponents are moving toward unity.

NOTES AND REFERENCES

[1] Hirschfield Davis, J. (2015, May 29). U.S. Removes Cuba From State-sponsored Terrorism List. *The New York Times*.

Chapter 79

The Fleeting Nature of Political Realities

Robert Prechter

2014

The fleeting nature of political realities is succinctly displayed in Figure 1. Toward the bottom left is an image of a young girl burning with napalm to the sounds of a bombing raid in an area just outside Ho Chi Minh City on June 8, 1972. Toward the upper right is an image of a young woman enjoying a McDonald's hamburger to the sounds of techno pop music in Ho Chi Minh City on February 8, 2014. As Figure 1 shows, negative social mood fostered conditions that led to the first image, and positive social mood fostered conditions that led to the second.

The United States lost the Vietnam war, but its loss did not create a permanent condition. The Viet Cong won the war, but its victory did not create a permanent condition, either; capitalistic free trade has since returned to the region. The U.S. and North Vietnam were enemies during the bear market of 1966-1974; now they are friends. Socionomics elucidates the primary cause of such changes: shifts in social mood.

Commentators typically describe all kinds of social actions, trends and conditions as implying more of the same to come. But social circumstances are weather vanes in the wind, turning with the breezes and gales of social mood, first one way and then the other, now benign, now deadly, back and forth.

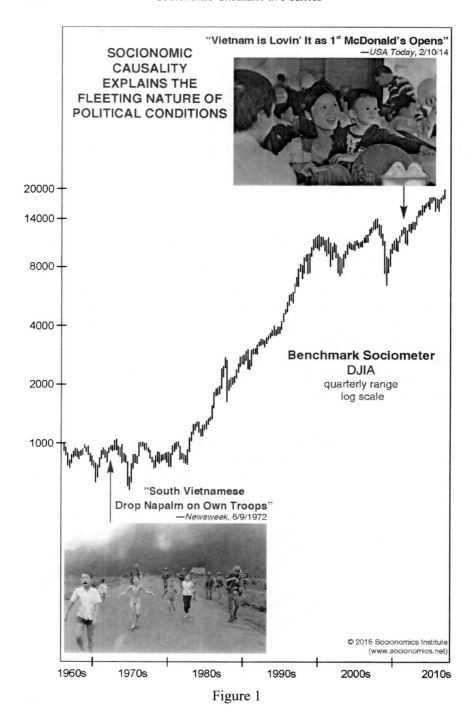

Figure 1

Chapter 80

Living Socionomics:
From Zimbabwe to Wall Street

Alastair J. Macdonald

April 9, 2016 (Socionomics Summit)

Alastair J. Macdonald is a fourth-generation Zimbabwean. His family lived in the country for about 120 years. In the late 1990s,

he moved to the United States and became an invest-ment consultant and writer. At the 2016 Social Mood Confer-ence, Macdonald gave a fascinating account of his life, which included his startling dis-covery of how much social mood had steered and shaped his experi-ences.

Alastair Macdonald shares his life experience at the 2016 Social Mood Conference

My entire youth was one of land mines, of random gunshots at night, of international sanctions, and of weekends at the shooting range where my Mom honed her skills while my Dad was out fighting in the war. I was born in the midst of a civil war that marked the transition between the dying colonial rule in Africa and the rise of black majority rule in what was then Rhodesia and was becoming Zimbabwe. I was five years old when

I looked at the front page of our newspaper and saw pictures of children my age whose lips and noses and ears had been severed off by a group of armed terrorists. I was six years old when my uncle died, and I was seven years old when I learned that a group of young women that had taken refuge at the Sacred Heart Catholic mission just eight miles from my home had been bayonetted to death in their pregnant bellies by unknown assailants.

We drove fast on rural roads. We kids knew the dangerous areas because we had to lie down in the back seat. We knew the ambush spots, and my mom used to flat-foot it through those areas. Every farm vehicle had bullet holes in it, and if it didn't, it was a new vehicle. But there weren't any new vehicles, because international sanctions had crippled the economy. Smuggling and the black market eventually took over; it was the only way to get ahead. And I can tell you...that a car oil filter fits perfectly inside an eight-year-old boy's underwear, if you're trying to get one of these across the border. This was the way that my family fed us. We literally had to smuggle goods in and out of the country to keep their business going.

In 1980, the war ended. Fear of retribution saw a mass exodus of white Zimbabweans out of the country. The white population collapsed from 180,000 to 40,000 almost overnight. It was strange for me; I recall the weeks of coming to school and seeing fewer and fewer students in my class. Strangely, at the time, the Zimbabwe dollar was on par with the U.S. dollar. Eventually, with the end of the war, things began to improve. Robert Mugabe, who had previously been the freedom fighter that had brought us through this civil war, was now our patron saint of hope, and hope was suddenly in a bull market. We wanted to believe in a bright future. Before we knew it, the economy had turned up. We saw the population start to rise; we saw crop production reach record levels; we saw Zimbabwe becoming a net exporter of capital and commodities for the first time in a generation. It was a remarkable time. Peace suddenly reigned. We used to leave our cars open when we were parked outside the grocery store. We would leave our homes unlocked at night and our windows open. It was a pretty good time.

The striking part is that we were the same people—the same people that had butchered each other in our sleep just ten years before. It wasn't as if enough time had passed for an entire generation to come through and change the old ways.

The boom manifested itself in the safari industry, and this was the business I moved into at age 18. The timing couldn't have been better. My life took off like a rocket—a rocket fueled with adventure and excitement and intrigue and money. I faced charging lions; I walked amongst elephants; I slept under the African stars 200 nights a year; I was struck by lightning; I survived three hippopotamus attacks. My life was amazing. The irony of course is that I thought I had earned all of this. I thought it was something remarkable about *me*. So I was emboldened, and I came to the United States, where I decided I would try my hand. At the same time, a huge influx of those same white Zimbabweans that had left were on their way back. I literally passed them at the airport.

Well, no sooner had I left than Zimbabwe's social implosion began. It started by way of a gentleman named Morgan Tsvangirai, who was a union worker. He had been toiling in obscurity for 20 years and didn't have much of an audience, but that changed quickly. He had been motivating people with talks of cronyism and corruption, all the way from the president on down. As if that was news!

President Mugabe is the same gentleman that had been our patron saint of hope, our freedom fighter. In Africa, we have the same leader for a generation. For a socionomist, it's perfect, because you have the same character that goes through periods of expansion and contraction. They are loved, and then they are hated.

Mugabe, for the first time ever, was threatened, and he responded by motivating a bunch of young thugs. He paid off cronies, and he started printing money and fixing votes. The economy began a freefall. Interest rates spiked. People were angry, and they needed an enemy. They found it in the white Zimbabweans—specifically, the white farm owners who accounted for 2.5% of the population but were suddenly responsible for 100% of its woes. The local dollar went from one-to-one versus the U.S. dollar eventually to trillions of dollars to one. To give you an idea: When you went out for dinner at night, you had to pay for your food when you ordered it, because when it had arrived, the price had changed. Fear of attacks turned foreigners away; the tourism industry collapsed.

Soon, this danger moved into the cities, and very quickly my own family was at risk. It was very soon thereafter that my parents were run off their personal property and surrounded by 50 employees smashing their windows and barricading them up in their offices. These were employees, over 50 or 60 of them, that had been working for my parents for over 25 years. My parents left with nothing but the shirts on their backs and some photographs of their grandchildren. They slipped across the border and bumped around looking for a new home.

When I came to America, I had unwittingly moved from one bubble to another. I walked out of the bubble of Zimbabwe—it imploded right behind me—and I stepped into the United States and the Internet and the investing mania here. I dove headlong into it. I went to work as a stockbroker on Wall Street. It was a very interesting time to be in the United States. We had a contested presidential election decided by Supreme Court decree. We had Red and Blue states. We started seeing this fractious [atmosphere], and it was strange for me, because this wasn't the America I had expected to find when I came here. Pretty soon after that, we had terrorist attacks, a global hunt for enemies, and retribution. A nation that just 18 months prior was divided to the extent that the Supreme Court had to choose [a president] was now unified behind one president looking for an enemy. When that happened, I began to sense a repeating pattern. Many of my experiences from Zimbabwe started to appear in the U.S., but I couldn't bring myself to believe that the backwater third-world nation that I'm so proud to be from would have anything in common with the most powerful and industrious nation on Earth.

In 2004, I learned of the Wave Principle, and that changed *everything*. Socionomics for me was an intellectual Cambrian explosion. I was immediately struck by two things. The first was that none of my successes were my own. And the second was that all of my mistakes *were* my own. I felt as if I had been a child sitting in the back seat of his mother's minivan with one of those fake steering wheels and a blue horn thinking that I was the one actually steering this two-ton box of steel down the highway. It turns out, that's not even Mom driving. It's seven billion marginally evolved primates all fighting for the same steering wheel.

So I was struck, and I didn't really know what to make of it. I felt like a leaf floating down a creek. I didn't know what to do. Then I came across a quote by Johann Wolfgang von Goethe: "All thought that does not lead to action is a disease." I had the disease, and it was born of inaction. So I set about correcting that right away. I jumped headlong into [socionomics] and began sharing my insights with my clients and readers.

The results were immediate for me. I was able to start talking about the concerns I had about real estate being in a bubble. As I researched the history of social mood and reread and reread the *Human Social Behavior* book and *Pioneering Studies*, the greater the housing bubble grew, until possibility became probability. It was a tremendous opportunity for me, avoiding that [debacle]. I was able to divest myself from the three properties I had. I chose to rent a four-bedroom home with a private beach and views of the ocean from every room in the house—all for less than the property taxes. It worked out well for me, but it's not about me. It's about the application of socionomics.

Real-Time Commentary from
Macdonald's *Parallax Letter*, 2004-2005

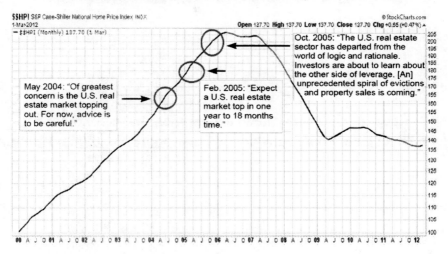

My parents built a business from nothing during the war. They lived, survived, built an industry, travelled the world, came back, fought for justice and supported their community. That community turned on them and threw them out, and they found themselves at 65 years of age packing milk at a milk factory at 3AM in a Portland, Maine winter.

Last week I said to my dad, "Knowing what you know and what you experienced in Zimbabwe, looking back, what do you wish you had known or done?" He said, "You know, my boy, I wish there was some way to anticipate the really big changes. I wish there was a way that I could have imagined how much and how fast things would change." My friends, I am here to advocate for that belief, which is that socionomics can give you that ability. It is up to us to choose to do the work and apply it. Socionomics had given me permission to trust my own experience, and I hope that it becomes true for you, too.

Keep up with every new development in socionomics.
Become an SI member now at www.socionomics.net/membership.

PRESS

Socionomics Institute

CPSIA information can be obtained
at www.ICGtesting.com
Printed in the USA
LVOW10*0418171017

552657LV00001B/1/P